Crisis of Care

Crisis of Care

Religion and Empire in the American West Since 1848

Edited by

BRANDI DENISON AND BRETT HENDRICKSON

The University of North Carolina Press
Chapel Hill

Published in association with the William P. Clements Center for Southwest Studies and Southern Methodist University by the University of North Carolina Press, Chapel Hill.

Set in Minion Pro by Westchester Publishing Services

Library of Congress Cataloging-in-Publication Data
Names: Denison, Brandi, editor. | Hendrickson, Brett, editor.
Title: Crisis of care : religion and empire in the American West since 1848 / edited by Brandi Denison, Brett Hendrickson.
Other titles: Crisis of care (Denison and Hendrickson)
Description: Chapel Hill : The University of North Carolina Press, [2026] | Includes bibliographical references and index.
Identifiers: LCCN 2026018179 | ISBN 9781469697710 (cloth) | ISBN 9781469697727 (paperback) | ISBN 9781469695754 (epub) | ISBN 9781469697734 (pdf)
Subjects: LCSH: Imperialism—Religious aspects. | Imperialism—History—19th century. | Imperialism—History—20th century. | West (U.S.)—Religion—19th century. | West (U.S.)—Religion—20th century. | West (U.S.)—History. | United States—Territorial expansion. | BISAC: RELIGION / History | HISTORY / United States / State & Local / West (AK, CA, CO, HI, ID, MT, NV, UT, WY)
Classification: LCC BL2527.W47 C+
LC record available at https://lccn.loc.gov/2026018179

Cover art: *The Dry Ditch*, 1964, by Kenneth Miller Adams. Eiteljorg Museum. Gift of Harrison Eiteljorg.

This book will be made open access within three years of publication thanks to Path to Open, a program developed in partnership between JSTOR, the American Council of Learned Societies (ACLS), the University of Michigan Press, and the University of North Carolina Press to bring about equitable access and impact for the entire scholarly community, including authors, researchers, libraries, and university presses around the world. Learn more at https://about.jstor.org/path-to-open/.

For product safety concerns under the European Union's General Product Safety Regulation (EU GPSR), please contact gpsr@mare-nostrum.co.uk or write to the University of North Carolina Press and Mare Nostrum Group B.V., Doelen 72, 4831 GR Breda, The Netherlands.

Contents

Crisis of Care

Introduction

Empire and Care in the American West

BRANDI DENISON AND BRETT HENDRICKSON

In the fall of 2022, this book's authors traveled from coast to coast, and to points in between, to Taos, New Mexico, the first location where we would come together as a symposium to workshop the chapters in this volume. Southern Methodist University (SMU) has a satellite campus in Taos, and SMU's Clements Center for Southwest Studies, one of the symposium's two hosts and sponsors, had invited us to this beautiful, verdant place, tucked between two streams south of Taos proper, in the Sangre de Cristo Mountains. The campus itself occupies the site of Fort Burgwin, a military encampment and stronghold established by US forces in 1852; its purpose was to gain control of the region after the US–Mexican War, the 1847 Taos Revolt, and subsequent Indian challenges to the US takeover.[1] Thus, the fort played an important role in establishing US sovereignty in the newly captured territory (and later state) of New Mexico. More than a century later, SMU acquired the fort and surrounding land, including a thirteenth-century Pueblo archaeological site. It is now an extension of the Dallas campus, dedicated to exploring the historical and natural context of northern New Mexico.[2]

We worked at the SMU facility but ate and wandered in the town of Taos, today a haven for tourists, artists, movie stars, skiers, and New Age seekers. An old town by US standards, Spanish settlers encamped in the area in 1615, on the very northern limits of New Spain, and permanently established the village of Taos in 1795. Taos Pueblo is nearby. As the area's original settlement, it is one of the oldest continuously inhabited sites in the United States and is recognized as a UNESCO World Heritage Site. On the first morning of our symposium gathering, we attended the San Geronimo Day festivities at Taos Pueblo, a day of dancing, foot races, and a harvest celebration open to the public but under strictly controlled terms. We were required to leave all cameras and phones in our vehicles to maintain the privacy and integrity of what the Pueblo's website describes as "religious ceremonies."[3] Non-Pueblos were invited to witness the ceremonies, but none of the events were interpreted for outsiders. Across the creek from the location of the ceremonies was a market featuring American Indian vendors selling food, crafts, and art. We watched the foot races and walked through the Pueblo's church, and many purchased jewelry and pottery. We were both present for and excluded from ceremonial knowledge, which many of us noted as exemplifying an act of communal care by the Pueblo.

Near the end of our fall meeting, we visited the Ranchos de Taos Catholic Church, a monumental adobe structure made famous by Georgia O'Keeffe's painting of it. In her depiction, the church's immense adobe buttresses seem to emerge like natural formations from the surrounding earth. Completed in 1815, the church is a relatively late example of dozens of adobe churches in northern New Spain originally built as Franciscan missions.[4] Today, it is surrounded by art galleries and touristy shops, similar to Taos's plaza. However, we could not enter the church on the evening of our visit since the local Hispano parish community had gathered for Mass. Like Taos Pueblo, the church drew outside visitors but retained boundaries around the care of its community and its ritual life. With the town's legacy of colonial violence amid communities that have guarded their agency, Taos is representative of the importance of religion in the American West and highlights one way communities in the region care for each other—by keeping at least some religious time and space reserved for community insiders.

The symposium's spring meeting in April 2023 likewise featured dynamic visions of the American West, its peoples, history, and religion. We met at the stunning Eiteljorg Museum of American Indians and Western Art in Indianapolis, Indiana. Our participation with the Eiteljorg formed part of a larger program at the museum, funded by the Lilly Endowment Inc., to explore religion in the American West in art and culture, a venture also connected to a collaboration between the New York Historical Society Library and Museum and the Eiteljorg Museum's exhibit *Acts of Faith: Religion and the American West*. While there, we learned that the Eiteljorg Museum has been dedicated to nurturing and funding Native artists since its founding in 1989. The museum boasts an extensive, world-class collection of American Indian art, much of it contemporary.[5] Messages around the building remind visitors that the museum occupies land that is and will always be Native land, and significant gallery and educational spaces are set aside to illustrate and uphold the history of American Indians in the Indiana area and beyond. Attention is focused on housing and caring for items in the collection that require special treatment, including some items that Native partners ritually and regularly care for. And even before the Native American Graves Protection and Repatriation Act (NAGPRA) was passed in 1990, the Eiteljorg had already begun the collaborative work of returning items that tribal groups identified for repatriation. The Eiteljorg is a beautiful space open to all, but always within the context of its intentional mission to maintain responsive and critical relationships of care with American Indian partners.

These essential and affirmative characteristics of the Eiteljorg exist alongside other facts. For instance, some of the older Western art in the collection depicts American Indians in ways that could be considered stereotypical or romanticizing. However, the museum's placards and educational materials call attention to the bias of these pieces. Additionally, in the broadest of terms, the museum's location in Indianapolis, not a place typically considered part of the American West, can create moments of dissonance for the Midwestern visitor; the Western art on display depicts a part of the nation that feels like a foreign country from central Indiana. To posit that Western and Indian art is American art that belongs in Indiana is a discursive move that sits in the tension between careful inclusion and the United States' imperial westward expansion.

The symposium's two meeting locations, Taos and Indianapolis, highlighted the physical and historical juxtapositions of empires, nations, and religions in the American West as a place both geographical and imagined. These juxtapositions, evident in the meeting sites where this volume took shape, are likewise evident in the following chapters. Similarly, the acts of care we witnessed from religious communities and institutions existed alongside the stories of conquest, dispossession, and struggles for self-determination that underlie so much of Western history. Religious actors in the American West, broadly conceived, have grappled with shifting imperial regimes and responded with various expressions of care.

Taken together, the chapters of this book reveal that the story of religion in the West is redolent with the experiences of making, sustaining, and resisting empire, as well as the myriad ways that religious people, in the context of empire, take part in care. To get at these overarching themes of empire and care, this book's essays focus their inquiries using a broad range of analytical frames, including racialization, aesthetics, assimilation, land stewardship, gender and sexuality, and secularization. In short, the chapters in this volume work together to contend that the nineteenth- and twentieth-century American West (conceived as a region, an overt settler imperial process, and a romanticized myth) is an urgent setting wherein religious people are discursive partners in creating, sustaining, and challenging imperial forces. Likewise, they creatively cared for those who found themselves in the region even as they sometimes functioned as stewards of imperial processes of dispossession and settlement. After all, the notion of "manifest destiny," a divine mandate for US dominance of the continent, was coined in 1845 shortly before open hostilities broke out in the US–Mexican War (1846–48).[6] The post-1848 US empire created a context in which religions in the American West took various shapes: in support of the US government, on its periphery, or in opposition to it. The way that empire gave shape to religious belief, practice, and institutions is not unique to the region. However, focusing on the American

West since 1848 allows us to see how people and groups in the West have shaped their notions of religion in complicated and diverse ways depending on their position in the US empire.

The essays in this book, read together, suggest that "care," broadly conceived, is a through line in these religious responses and negotiations with empire. The juxtaposition of "empire" and "care" in this volume presents a powerful interpretive framework for the study of religion in the North American West and Pacific, a framework we hope will be useful to the ongoing study of religion in the region—and potentially in other regions marked by rapid expansion, displacement, migration, and settlement. A look at terms will help define the utility of this approach.

Religion

In a book on "religion" in the "American West," it is useful to have working understandings, if not precise definitions, of these principal terms. The academic study of religion is humanistic in its orientation, typically eschewing confessional or normative statements about God, gods, or the supernatural. Instead, it focuses variously on the role of religion in historical, political, economic, and social contexts. Easy definitions of "religion" have proved elusive for religious studies scholars; in lieu of precise definitions, common characteristics of what we refer to as "religion" often orient religious studies scholarship. For instance, religions often have a metaphysical frame of reference. In many cases, this involves relationships with gods, spirits, or some other kind of force or personage that can pervade or transcend natural, sensible reality. Second, religions typically involve ritual practices such as prayer, worship, dietary restrictions, meditation, sacrifice, and rites of passage. Third, many people find ethical guidance in their religious traditions, which range from moral imperatives for behavior to elaborate judicial systems. Finally, religious people gather in communities to practice their traditions and identify themselves socially—and even ethnically—to create and maintain support networks.[7]

The chapters in this volume often find that their subjects' religious lives are less tidy than what can be captured in a definitional listing of religion's features. As Robert Orsi contends, religious people experience the "real presence" of their gods, and in so doing, they escape the legibility and order that modern academic analysis often tries to impose. The gods, says Orsi, therefore hold a "subversive potentiality" for religion.[8] As the chapters in the book demonstrate, this subversive quality of religious experience often makes it possible for people in the West to make homes where they are not always welcome and to find care, comfort, and joy in the face of both quotidian human suffering and the systemic and intersectional ordeals created by a racialized, capitalist empire.

The chapters in this volume also show that "religion" has a variable discursive function in the American West. In the time period that these essays cover, from the middle of the nineteenth century to the present, the American West served as a test case for what religious freedom means—sometimes urgently so. For example, constitutional freedoms allowing the "free exercise" of religion created an urgency to define how these freedoms would play out in practice. Which religions and religious practices would be protected, and which would not? The legal front was not the only place where definitional boundaries were created and tested. On the ground, as migrants and dispossessed peoples found themselves far from home, they created new religious, cultural, and legal frameworks to make sense of their place in the American West and to understand the people surrounding them. In a context where multiple "religions" from west, east, and south cross and dwell in an ostensibly secular state, the category of religion is necessarily multivalent, contested, and sometimes hegemonic.[9]

For readers approaching this book who may be unfamiliar with the academic study of religion, it is worth noting that the vibrant subfield of "American religions" has existed since at least the mid-nineteenth century.[10] The regional study of religion in the United States emerged early in this subfield, primarily in efforts to differentiate religious experience in the British colonies and the early Republic.[11] More recent scholarship focused on religion and region has attended to historical context, cultural geography, and "lived religions" (as opposed to religious institutional history); it also engages critically with questions of race, ethnicity, and settler colonialism.[12] A significant contention of such research is that attention to the region not only adds to our knowledge of religion in the United States but also illuminates unspoken assumptions that undergird familiar narratives of "American religion" that have privileged the eastern half of the country.[13] This volume adds to this literature, deepening our understanding of "American religions" and the "American West."

The American West

The American West can be considered as (a) process, (b) place, and (c) myth. These categories are not mutually exclusive. The overlapping and sometimes conflicting categories of the West as process, place, and myth have generated long arguments about the boundaries of the West.[14] However, getting mired in the debates about where (or when) the West is can be unproductive, as volume contributor Quincy Newell has noted elsewhere. Her solution, as is ours, is to be clear about how we are defining the region—and each of our contributors has done that in their individual essays.[15] Scholars of religion will be familiar with this discursive move, as Jonathan Z. Smith implored us to consider religion as a category created by scholars to establish a disciplinary horizon. As Smith noted, when doing religious things, religious people rarely label themselves as doing "religion." Rather, "religion" becomes useful as an analytical and comparative category for outsiders.[16] Similarly, the "American West" emerges as a discursive category useful to scholars to document the sometimes contested and contingent historical and religious trajectories of the Euro-American colonization of Indigenous lands and as a heuristic lens to document the intersection among land, identity, and political and religious institutions.

The West, as a process, anchors the American West in time. In doing so, this lens suggests that there are many Wests, and scholarship that uses this lens effectively shows that the history of European settlement in North America was contingent and contested. Furthermore, the centering of process over place pulls American Indian empires and nations into the history of the colonization of the American West. It highlights that what European settlers called the "West" was also "home" for many American Indian nations. "Process" suggests "frontier"—which harkens back to Fredrick Jackson Turner's "frontier thesis," itself rightly critiqued for its myopic history and racist framing of contact between Euro-American settlers and Native peoples. Nevertheless, as historian Stephen Aron argued, the framing of "frontier" and "borderlands" can highlight the variety of territories in US history "where political control was undetermined and boundaries—cultural and geographic—were uncertain."[17] Frontiers and borderlands are made through movement, and while the landscape can help to create the conditions of a frontier or borderland, ultimately, as Richard White has noted, these are politically contested spaces.[18]

Religious studies scholars have used the underlying ideas of the American West as process to understand religious formation in the American West.[19] A notable example is David Walker's argument that the West is defined by "shared concerns of federal territorialization, industrial development, and water acquisition." Thus, for Walker, the nineteenth-century colonization of the West means that "land, sociographical concerns, and religion have comaterialized in the West." Walker shifts the focus of religions in the American West away from studies that focus on the narratives of religious characters toward a focus on "diverse mundane concerns," such as land and infrastructure development, which have given rise to "the articulation and adjudication of 'western religiosity,' 'authentic religion,' and 'the sacred.'"[20] Similarly, Brennan Keegan, Sarah Dees, and Brandi Denison have focused on the intersection of mundane concerns and the production of "authentic religions" in the context of nation-building in the American West.[21]

The American West, as a place, moves beyond the story of conquest to center the diversity of human and natural life. Anchored in Yi-Fu Tuan's theorization regarding the creation of place, this cultural geography analysis focuses attention on the peoples that became swept up in the colonial aspirations of the United States and the many other non-US empires that attempted to carve up land and resources for their own.[22] The historians of the New West, such as Patricia Limerick, Charles Rankin, Richard White, Peggy Pascoe, and Elliot West, advocated for a place-centered approach as they pushed against the West as frontier and Fredrick Jackson Turner's legacy of centering white men in the story of the American West. Instead, these scholars documented the many peoples in the region and incorporated environmental history in understanding the making of the American West. Elliot West's environmental-focused studies on the Central Plains demonstrate how the geography and climate of the region intertwined with Indigenous and settler history.[23]

Religious studies scholars such as Laurie Maffly-Kipp, Tisa Wenger, Joshua Paddison, Quincy Newell, Brett Hendrickson, and Jennifer Graber aim to locate religious people within place, and in doing so, tell the religious and cultural experiences of non-white peoples, such as Chinese Californians, American Indians, and New Mexican Hispanos, among others.[24] This scholarship has also investigated multiple migration patterns—not just westward but also migrations to the east, north, and south. A place-focused history includes tribal histories, where a narrative frame of westward migrations does not make sense to people who are already home.

Daniel Richter's reframing of American West history through the lens of American Indians "facing east," as well as the scholarship of Inéz Talamantez, Gabriel Estrada, and Philip Deloria, among others, has brought into focus the religious lives of American Indians in light of Euro-American colonization.[25] Place is also a central theme for a 2022 edited volume on spirituality and secularism in the Pacific Northwest, as the volume includes the Cascadian Mountains as a key character in the spiritual lives of residents.[26]

The West as myth centers the stories people tell themselves about where they are from, which in turn become both identities and cultural memories.[27] Henry Nash Smith declared that the idea of the West gave shape to US identity.[28] David Wrobel and Robert Athearn discuss the role of boosterism, whose syntax is the language of myth, in drawing Euro-Americans westward. As Athearn wrote, settlers moved "because of highly inflated stories of continuing success," creating the idea of a "sagebrush Shangri-La where everyone was prosperous, happy, and young."[29] Similarly, Joy Kasson's work on Buffalo Bill's Wild West shows "became a passion play for the American frontier."[30]

Myths are anchored in stories and places, which provide an orientation to the world. These stories and places are created through power. Jonathan Z. Smith argued that "what we study when we study religion is the variety of attempts to map, construct, and inhabit such positions of power through the use of myths, rituals, and experiences of transformation."[31] As religious studies scholar Judith Weisenfeld noted, narratives can be "spiritual maps that orient . . . [people] toward the past and the future in new ways that, in turn, shapes . . . daily lives and interactions with others."[32] The mythmaking of the American West has national implications and is imbricated by power. As a case in point, Sarah Koenig argued that the legend of Marcus Whitman's failed mission to the Cayuse Indians and the related historical work transformed the American historical profession. Similarly, Thomas Bremer has documented the centrality of storytelling in tourism to the American Southwest, and Robert Lint Sagarena documented the use of Aztec imagery in fashioning a Southern California rooted in both the imagined Spanish missionary and Aztec pasts.[33] Defining the West as myth takes the narratives that emerge from the place and history into global discourse so that we might consider the exportation of the American West myth to other countries or how the idea of the frontier frames science fiction.[34] Within the framing of the American West as myth, the centrality of storytelling, cultural memory, and identity comes into focus, as does the multiplicity of Wests and the powerful tropes of the American West that seep into popular imaginaries of the Western frontier.[35]

This volume's contributors hail from several disciplines, including religious studies, history, ethnic studies, and sociology. They likewise employ various research methods—particularly historical analysis and ethnography. The multidisciplinary nature of the following chapters makes this book a needed exercise in academic bridge-building, especially between the "worlds" of Western history and the study of US religions. We stand to gain a great deal from this new scholarship both in our understanding of the history of the US West and our analysis of religion in its unique historical, environmental, demographic, and imperial contexts.

Empire

As should now be clear, "empire" is one of the key analytical categories in this book, and with good reason. Religion in the United States has been inextricably knitted into an imperial project from the very first moments of European colonial settlement.[36] Religious justifications for the taking of Native lands, missions, and other evangelistic movements, religious and racial classification of subjugated and enslaved people, and both real and de facto establishments are just some of the ways that religion has operated in US history to create and maintain white and Christian (primarily Protestant) settler dominance. The Catholic Church's 1493 Doctrine of Discovery influenced and codified how Catholic nations conceptualized other peoples. Spanish and French imperial settlement and control likewise shaped the histories of territories that would eventually come to comprise parts of the United States, even as Indigenous empires rose and fell.[37] Religious studies scholars Tisa Wenger and Sylvester Johnson, in their edited volume *Religion and US Empire*, contend that studying religion and empire together is important for at least three reasons. First, "religious institutions have been integral to structuring colonial power." Another reason is that religious groups of diverse types have been engaged at various points in "contesting or, at times, subverting colonial power." Finally, religions can set the "alliances and boundaries of imperial identities"; in this way, religions help define and police proper imperial subjects.[38]

To be sure, the seeds of empire have been part of the US experience from the earliest colonial period, but the westward expansion of the United States was definitional for the US imperial project. Spain's imperial claims over much of what is now considered the American West were made as early as the first half of the sixteenth century. More permanent Spanish settlement and evangelization of the area would occur later and in regional waves, with New Mexico's settlement coming first, followed by incursions and settlement in what are now Texas, Arizona, and California. By the time of Mexican independence from Spain in 1821, Spanish settlements and missions stretched from northern California to the Gulf of Mexico. To the north and east of Spanish territories lay an enormous section of North America claimed by the French but populated primarily by American Indians. The Louisiana Purchase in 1803 of these Native lands, which ostensibly belonged to France, guaranteed continued US westward settlement.

Indeed, the wars of Indian removal throughout the 1800s are textbook examples of imperial expansion for settlement and subjugation. The Anglo-led battles for Texas's independence from Mexico (1836) and eventual inclusion as a state (1845) set the stage for the US–Mexican War (1846–48). The Treaty of Guadalupe–Hidalgo, which ended the war, transferred the northern half of Mexico's territory into the southwestern and western United States with the stroke of a pen.[39] During this conflict, the phrase "manifest destiny" was coined to express a commonly held belief among white Protestants at the time: God had ordained that the United States was divinely fated to occupy the entirety of North America.[40] The Spanish–American War (1898) expanded the growing US empire into the Pacific by acquiring the Philippines and other Spanish territories. The US added other Pacific lands to its growing empire after World War II. Most of these diplomatic and military land acquisitions had a Western vector, associating the "West" indelibly with imperial expansion, settler colonialism, and overt and covert assimilation campaigns. Religion in the US West played complex and essential roles in a region that can be fairly characterized as the clearest expression of the US empire.

The intersection of race and religion, particularly how religion contributes to and is influenced by racial identity construction, often operates to justify and structure imperial power. The literature about religion, race, and empire is copious, and many of the essays in this volume directly address how religious and racial identities functioned in specific ways in the North American and Pacific West.[41] Groups on the periphery of the Anglo-Saxon Protestant imperial center were often considered racially and religiously inferior, needing strong and continuous oversight. A few of the chapters (for example, those by Brendan Keegan, Joshua Paddison, and Quincy Newell) explicitly tackle the role "whiteness" played in defining and classifying where certain religious groups sat in the racial and religious power structure.

Care

When the authors in this volume evoke care in the American West, we situate it within the context of imperial discourse and endeavors.[42] The juxtaposition of empire and care is purposefully jarring. Taken together, the analytics of care and empire expose the complexities of religious, ethnic, and racial identity formation within the constantly shifting relations of power and difference in the West. After all, as historians Ann Stoler and Anne F. Hyde have clearly demonstrated, empires are sustained, made, and resisted through the intimacies of families.[43] Empires, though, also act as political entities that seek to expand power and access to resources, sometimes through acts of imperial violence undertaken under the rhetoric of care—either as protective care for the nation or, more insidiously, as care that provides just enough succor to the afflicted to make them productive and docile subjects. Communities burdened with imperial violence are left to care for each other for survival, frequently through religious groups, and often to conform to the ideals of those in power. The essays in this volume take a critical approach to care, demonstrating the need to examine its many valences.

Care is frequently associated with mothering, and maternal care often evokes feelings of comfort, safety, and kindness, particularly in the face of vulnerability. Indeed, feminist ethicists have given us language to consider care as an organizing principle for an ethical theory that stands against theories that privilege rights and individuals. The ethics of care centers on context, responsibility, interdependency, and embodied experiences in ethical decisions.[44]

This scholarship describes good care in which reciprocity and mutuality sustain these interdependent relationships, and it aims to move ethical thinking toward considering these complexities rather than adhering to universalized principles. Care, however, can also be an analytical category for considering how societies shape institutions and relationships in ways that can support or hinder interdependency. As such, cultural geographers have recently considered care as it happens in place and how care can be sustained or impeded by geopolitics.[45] Care, then, defined through place, is "a complex set of emotionally felt experiences, bodily practices and social politics that connect people, space, place, and things."[46]

Care does not always engender equality, comfort, or acceptance, especially when coupled with empire. As philosopher Uma Narayan noted, care discourses have sustained imperial endeavors. For example, care for the enslaved and colonized "justif[ied] relationships of power and domination between groups of people, such as colonizers and colonized."[47] Narayan argued that colonized care discourses target other colonizers to justify the oppression of other people to render benign horrific, unethical acts, as if they were done out of care, either to protect the colonizer or in the best interests of the colonized. Such calls can often be distilled down to the message that we, as imperial actors, are right because they, the Other, need help. Moreover, rhetorics of care can discipline bodies according to normative standards, giving justification to imperial actors to take extreme actions under the aegis of concern and protection for the other.

Attending to the discourse of care in the context of empire brings focus to the inherent instability of power structures. Centering care shows that the seemingly stable identities of colonized and colonizer are, in fact, the result of ongoing social projects done amid a persistently shifting landscape of power and difference.[48] In the case studies presented here, we found that these rhetorics of care appear in situations of ethical ambivalence or shifting relations of power. Calls to care for the other demonstrate the vulnerability of those in power, and requests to care for the other by those in power tend to fortify unstable, porous identities. This "dark side of care" is described by disability studies, in which "caring for another can amount to an exercise of power,"[49] which in turn helps to sustain normative standards of ability. The dark side of care, then, becomes a mechanism for disciplining individuals and creating idealized standards, reflecting Foucault's governmentality, as Winnifred Sullivan has argued in relation to the American government's acceptance of chaplaincy as a practice of care.[50] The discourse of care, as Sullivan described, creates governable subjects in support of the State.

"Care" and "empire" taken together show that the formation of the American West created a crisis of care for settlers and Natives and generated ongoing care discourses to sustain imperial endeavors. The fragility of power created urgency among residents of the American West to survive through new care networks. This crisis of care is readily apparent in American Indian communities, where nations fought to protect their relationships with each other and the natural world. Settlers, including European, Euro-American, and Asian immigrants as well as nineteenth- and twentieth-century migrants from the eastern United States, also experienced kinship crises as they left behind extended family networks, even as these crises caused and exacerbated the trauma of American Indian communities. Considering the settlers as participants in their communities of care does not relieve them of responsibility for the acts of violence done by them or in their name; rather, it highlights the complexities of care discourse, which can harden and soften relational identities as well as be a vehicle for survival and destruction.

Considering the embodied experiences of those living in the West—Indigenous and settler alike—highlights the shared sense of urgency: to survive, to create community, to define boundaries both metaphorical and physical. Throughout the volume, readers will find religious communities intentionally providing care, which most readers will read as "good care"—care communicated through food, health care, and kindness. The essays also include critiques of care, particularly through historical actors who used a discourse of care to justify horrific acts, such as forced removal, the bombing of islands, or the paternalistic care of adults. It might be difficult for readers to identify these discourses and actions as care in these cases. However, as the essays show, the historical actors justified their responses through a language of care. Even as care ethicists or modern-day readers would not see these actions as caring, it would be historically inaccurate to overlook how historical actors thought of their actions as benevolent, good, and caring. Ultimately, one of the contributions this book makes is to show how fruitful it can be to think about the patterns and limitations of religious care in the wake of empire. Attending to this discourse of care in a colonial setting is a form of critique, which, in the words of volume contributor Thomas Bremer, is also a form of hope.

The volume is also a product of its time, which shaped the book's themes. The lived experience of COVID, the politically charged environment of public health, the increase in climate change–driven weather catastrophes, and the burden of care placed on women and Black, Indigenous, and people of color (BIPOC) communities were at the forefront of our minds when we gathered in Taos and Indianapolis. Conversely, the ability to be physically present with one another as we discussed our work was a tremendous gift, felt by everyone with deep gratitude. We were painfully aware of how quickly the gift of presence could be whisked away. Furthermore, the hospitality extended to us by the Clements Center and the Eiteljorg Museum helped to cultivate a sense of trust and care within the group.

Thus, as this book centers care as an analytical category, it also came about because of a community of care. This atmosphere was a combination of serendipity and intention. Six months before we convened in person, we met over Zoom to introduce the contributors to one another. We (Brett and Brandi) encouraged the formation of writing groups to support writing, and many participants did. When submitting the essays, we asked authors to reflect on what feedback would be most helpful and what work they knew they needed to do. During the workshop, Brett and Brandi asked participants to take notes and reflect on broader themes, and rather than squeezing every second out of discussion time, we set aside time to reflect, freewrite, and draw connections between their essays and other projects. Similarly, we drew on the vast knowledge of the scholars we had gathered in the room to help shape the volume's overarching themes. We provided the structure, but the authors sustained it. The participants did as much as the editors to help create the group's caring ethos.

Care is never neutral. Nevertheless, this volume emerges from years of mentorship, kindness, and support from this group of scholars and the network of mentors who have guided each of us. Academia does not need to be a cruel place, and we are all so grateful to be able to work and write among friends. We hope the readers of this volume can create similar spaces.

Moving Through the Book

During the symposia that shaped this book, the chapter authors decided to group the chapters into four sections to address the book's principal themes from particular angles. Yet within each section, considerable diversity of subject matter and analytical approach remains, and other groupings of the chapters are certainly possible. For example, readers interested in the diversity of immigrant experiences in the American West should focus on "Dutch Calvinist Imperials: Community Building and Global Engagement in the 19th-Century Trans-Mississippi West," by Andrew Klumpp; "The Working West: Religion, Labor, and the Making of Western Spaces," by Brennan Keegan; "To Always Be Better Neighbors: How the Japanese Episcopal Mission Leveraged Assimilation in Exclusion-Era California," by Chrissy Yee Lau; "Religion Among the Cannibals: Chinese–Paiute Rites of Care and Feeding," by Jennifer Graber; and "Jewish Pioneer Cemeteries: Caring for Implicated Sacred Spaces in the Arizona–Sonora Borderlands," by Max Greenberg.

Similarly, readers interested in how Westerners actively construct or theorize "religion" within their respective communities, or in response to other communities, should be directed to "California Cultbusters: The West Coast Origins of the Modern Anti-Cult Movement," by James B. Bennett; "Somewhat Secular Saints: Enacting and Resisting Modernity in the Church of Jesus Christ of Latter-day Saints During the 1918 Influenza Epidemic," by Quincy D. Newell; "Religious Labor at the Edge: AIDS, Religion, and Spirituality in San Francisco's Ward 5B," by Lynne Gerber; and "Jewish Pioneer Cemeteries: Caring for Implicated Sacred Spaces in the Arizona–Sonora Borderlands," by Max Greenberg.

The essays are organized thematically rather than chronologically because we found the variants of care and empire cut across the centuries. Likewise, these themes hold together across the region and within religious groups. Our hope is that readers will find other connections among the essays, pointing toward future scholarship. The sections we have selected intend to provoke reflection on how the study of religion in the American West deepens our understanding of the dynamics of empire, caregiving, and caretaking in this region and beyond.

The chapters in the first section, "The Religious Making and Maintaining of American Empire," examine various cases where religious care, in conjunction with racial categorization, was called upon to give structure to spaces and communities in the West. The essays show that religion served as a faithful partner in defining the bounds of freedom in the expanding United States, often under the guise of paternalistic care. The second section, "Caretaking and Imperial Enclaves," looks at the intertwining of empire and care in three unique settings. The chapters suggest that religious and ethnic enclaves in the US West fruitfully illustrate common dynamics throughout the region, as insular communities sought to care for their own. "Religious Responses to Insecurity," the third section, shows how religion functioned in the lives of those beleaguered by social and economic challenges in the West. With topics ranging from mines to circuses to immigrant neighborhoods, the chapters in this section reveal the complexities of religious care in times of tumult. Finally, the last section, "Caring for Bodies on Imperial Margins," seeks out the edges of Western American life where religious care can often feel desperate and costly. The cases profiled in this section suggest that care in the context of empire, while necessary, carries something of tragedy about it.

As *Crisis of Care* demonstrates, religions and religious people in the West have played essential roles in the creation, cultivation, and contestation of the US empire during the height of its continental and global expansion. Therefore, a clear understanding of religion in the region is necessary for the critical study of the US empire and its effects. And, as the chapters show, religion's imperial role is not merely in support of white Christian dominance but also plays out in complex modes of caretaking and caregiving that embody diverse processes such as racialization, health-seeking, boundary marking, and spiritual protection. Of course, an edited volume cannot claim to be comprehensive, and this one does not pretend to be. Our approach, as we hope is clear, was not an encyclopedic coverage of every religion in the region. Rather, we offer these essays, authored by provocative, critical, and generous conversation partners, to be just that: incitements to continue to think together about religion and the American West while remaining attentive to power in its many forms.

Notes

The authors of this introduction are indebted to the feedback from the contributors to this volume. Each of you has provided essential insights, labor, and collegiality to this project, and it has been our pleasure to work with you.

1. Ronald K. Wetherington, "Cantonment Burgwin: The Archaeological and Documentary Record," *New Mexico Historical Review* 81, no. 4 (2006): 392–93. Also see Garcia in this volume for more on the 1847 Taos Revolt.

2. "SMU Taos," *Southern Methodist University*, accessed May 17, 2023, www.smu.edu/taos.

3. "San Geronimo Eve Vespers & San Geronimo Day," *Taos Pueblo Central Management System*, accessed May 17, 2023, https://taospueblo.org/san-geronimo-eve-vespers-san-geronimo-day/.

4. Frank Graziano, *Historic Churches of New Mexico Today* (Oxford University Press, 2019), 66–69.

5. "Eiteljorg Contemporary Art Fellowship," *Eiteljorg Museum*, accessed May 17, 2023, https://contemporaryartfellowship.eiteljorg.org/.

6. Donald M. Scott, "The Religious Origins of Manifest Destiny," *Divining America: Religion in American History*, National Humanities Center, accessed June 10, 2025, https://nationalhumanitiescenter.org/tserve/nineteen/nkeyinfo/mandestiny.htm.

7. Catherine Albanese cleverly collates these common characteristics of religion as the "four Cs" (creed, cultus, code, and community) in her *America, Religions, and Religion*, 4th ed. (Thomson/Wadsworth, 2007), 7.

8. Robert A. Orsi, *History and Presence* (The Belknap Press of Harvard University Press, 2016), 5.

9. Two theories of religion that have influenced our thinking here are Thomas A. Tweed, *Crossing and Dwelling: A Theory of Religion* (Harvard University Press, 2006); and Bruce Lincoln, *Holy Terrors: Thinking about Religion after September 11* (University of Chicago Press, 2003).

10. For examples, see Robert Baird, *Religion in America* (Harper & Brothers, 1844); and Daniel Dorchester, *Christianity in the United States from the First Settlement down to the Present Time* (Hunt & Easton, 1888).

11. This influential article examines key narratives in American religious history by colonial region: David W. Wills, "The Central Themes of American Religious History:

Pluralism, Puritanism, and the Encounter of Black and White," *Religion and Intellectual Life* 5, no. 1 (1987): 30–41.

12. For examples, see Fay Botham and Sara M. Patterson, *Race, Religion, Region: Landscapes of Encounter in the American West* (University of Arizona Press, 2006); Jan Shipps and Mark Silk, eds., *Religion and Public Life in the Mountain West: Sacred Landscapes in Transition* (AltaMira Press, 2004); and Wade Clark Roof and Mark Silk, eds., *Religion and Public Life in the Pacific Region: Fluid Identities* (AltaMira Press, 2005).

13. Laurie F. Maffly-Kipp, "Eastward Ho! American Religion from the Perspective of the Pacific Rim," in *Retelling US Religious History*, ed. Thomas A. Tweed (University of California Press, 1997), 127–48.

14. For a discussion of these debates, see Stephan Aron, "Lessons in Conquest: Towards a Greater Western History," *Pacific Historical Review* 63, no. 2 (1994): 128–33.

15. Quincy D. Newell, "Religion and the American West," *Religion Compass* 6, no. 11 (November 2012), 8.

16. Jonathan Z. Smith, "Religion, Religions, Religious," in *Critical Terms for Religious Studies*, ed. Mark C. Taylor (University of Chicago Press, 1998), 281.

17. Stephen Aron, "The Making of the First American West and the Unmaking of Other Realms," in *Companion to the American West*, ed. William Deverell (Wiley-Blackwell, 2004), 6.

18. Richard White, *"It's Your Misfortune and None of My Own": A New History of the American West* (University of Oklahoma Press, 1993), 4.

19. One early foundational study that provides a broad overview of the West's multitude of religious leaders is Ferenc Morton Szasz, *Religion in the Modern American West* (University of Arizona Press, 2000).

20. David Walker, *Railroading Religion: Mormons, Tourists, and the Corporate Spirit of the West* (University of North Carolina Press, 2019), 57–58.

21. Brennan Keegan, "Gospel of Gold: Unearthing Religious Spaces in the Nineteenth-Century American West," *Religion and American Culture* 31, no. 1 (2021): 106–35; Brandi Denison, *Ute Land Religion in the American West: 1879–2009* (University of Nebraska Press, 2017), 8–12; Sarah Dees, "An Equation of Language and Spirit: Comparative Philology and the Study of American Indian Religions," *Method & Theory in the Study of Religion* 27, no. 3 (2015): 195–219.

22. Yi-Fu Tuan, *Space and Place: The Perspective of Experience* (University of Minnesota Press, 2001).

23. Elliot West, *The Contested Plains: Indians, Goldseekers, and the Rush to Colorado* (University Press of Kansas, 2000); and by the same author, *The Way to the West: Essays on the Central Plains* (University of New Mexico Press, 1995).

24. Laurie F. Maffly-Kipp, *Religion and Society in Frontier California* (Yale University Press, 1994); Tisa Wenger, *We Have a Religion: The 1920s Pueblo Indian Dance Controversy and American Religious Freedom* (University of North Carolina Press, 2009); Joshua Paddison, *American Heathens: Religion, Race, and Reconstruction in California* (University of California Press, 2012); Quincy D. Newell, *Constructing Lives at Mission San Francisco: Native Californians and Hispanic Colonists, 1776–1821* (University of New Mexico Press, 2009); Brett Hendrickson, *The Healing Power of the Santuario de Chimayó: America's Miraculous Church* (New York University Press, 2017); Jennifer Graber, *The Gods of*

Indian Country: Religion and the Struggle for the American West (Oxford University Press, 2018).

25. Daniel K. Richter, *Facing East from Indian Country: A Native History of Early America* (Harvard University Press, 2001); Inés Maria Talamantez, "Seeing Red: American Indian Women Speaking About Their Religious and Political Perspectives," in *In Our Own Voices: Four Centuries of American Women's Religious Writing*, ed. Rosemary Skinner Keller and Rosemary Radford Ruether (Westminster John Knox Press, 1995); Gabriel Estrada, "Navajo Sci-Fi Film: Matriarchal Visual Sovereignty in Nanobah Becker's 'The 6th World,'" *Journal of the American Academy of Religion* 82, no. 2 (2014): 521–30; Philip J. Deloria, *Indians in Unexpected Places* (University Press of Kansas, 2004).

26. Paul Bramadat, Patricia O'Connell Killen, and Sarah Wilkins-Laflamme, eds., *Religion at the Edge: Nature, Spirituality, and Secularity in the Pacific Northwest* (University of British Columbia Press, 2022).

27. For another example of how this framing is used, see Jessica Lauren Nelson, ed., *Religion in the American West: Belief, Violence, and Resilience from 1800 to Today* (University of New Mexico Press, 2023).

28. Henry Nash Smith, *Virgin Land: The American West as Symbol and Myth* (Harvard University Press, 1950).

29. Robert Athearn, *The Mythic West in Twentieth-Century America* (University Press of Kansas, 1986), 252. See also David Wrobel, *Promised Lands: Promotion, Memory, and the Creation of the American West* (University Press of Kansas, 2002).

30. Joy S. Kasson, *Buffalo Bill's Wild West: Celebrity, Memory, and Popular History* (Hill and Wang, 2001), 62.

31. Jonathan Z. Smith, *Map Is Not Territory: Studies in the History of Religions* (University of Chicago Press, 1993), 297.

32. Judith Weisenfeld, *New World A-Coming: Black Religion and Racial Identity During the Great Migration* (New York University Press, 2018), 25.

33. Sarah Koenig, "The Legend of Marcus Whitman and the Transformation of the American Historical Profession," *Church History* 87, no. 1 (March 1, 2018): 99–121; Thomas S. Bremer, *Blessed with Tourists: The Borderlands of Religion and Tourism in San Antonio* (University of North Carolina Press, 2004); Roberto Ramon Sagarena, *Aztlán and Arcadia* (New York University Press, 2014).

34. Janne Lahti, *The American West and the World: Transnational and Comparative Perspectives* (Taylor & Francis, 2018); Rudy V. Busto, "Religion/Science/Fiction: Beyond the Final Frontier," *Implicit Religion* 17, no. 4 (2014): 395–404.

35. One example is the HBO adaptation of Michael Crichton's *Westworld*. See: Jane Lovell and Sam Hitchmough, "Simulated Authenticity: Storytelling and Mythic Space on the Hyper-Frontier in Buffalo Bill's Wild West and Westworld," *Tourist Studies* 20, no. 4 (December 1, 2020): 409–28, https://doi.org/10.1177/1468797620937912.

36. In his classic text, Sydney Ahlstrom refers to the British colonies and early republic as a "Protestant Empire." See Sydney E. Ahlstrom, *A Religious History of the American People* (Yale University Press, 1972).

37. For the argument that Native peoples formed empires, see Pekka Hamalainen, *The Comanche Empire* (Yale University Press, 2009), 1–17; and by the same author, *Indigenous Continent: The Epic Contest for North America* (Liveright, 2022).

38. Tisa Wenger and Sylvester A. Johnson, eds., *Religion and US Empire: Critical New Histories* (New York University Press, 2022), 7.

39. For a discussion of some of the religious aspects of these conflicts, see John C. Pinheiro, *Missionaries of Republicanism: A Religious History of the Mexican-American War* (Oxford University Press, 2014).

40. Julius W. Pratt, "The Origin of 'Manifest Destiny,'" *The American Historical Review* 32, no. 4 (1927): 795–98.

41. A few notable examples include Sylvester A. Johnson, *African American Religions, 1500–2000: Colonialism, Democracy, and Freedom* (Cambridge University Press, 2015); Willie James Jennings, *The Christian Imagination: Theology and the Origins of Race* (Yale University Press, 2010); and Tisa Wenger, *Religious Freedom: The Contested History of an American Ideal* (University of North Carolina Press, 2017).

42. In invoking care in relation to religion, some religious studies scholars might think of Russell McCutcheon's argument in *Critics Not Caretakers*, where he convincingly asserts the role of religious studies scholars as public intellectuals and cultural critics rather than defenders (or caretakers) of religious people, ideas, practices, and institutions. This book is not engaged in that conversation; rather, it employs critique to examine the cultural, social, and institutional power structures that flow through care discourses in the context of the American West. See Russell T. McCutcheon, *Critics Not Caretakers: Redescribing the Public Study of Religion* (SUNY Press, 2001).

43. Ann Laura Stoler, "Tense and Tender Ties: The Politics of Comparison in North American History and (Post)Colonial Studies," in *Haunted by Empire: Geographies of Intimacy in North American History*, ed. Ann Laura Stoler (Duke University Press, 2006); Anne F. Hyde, *Empires, Nations, and Families: A New History of the North American West, 1800–1860* (Ecco, 2012).

44. For an overview of the ethics of care, see Mercer E. Gary, "From Care Ethics to Pluralist Care Theory: The state of the field," *Philosophy Compass* 17, no. 4 (2022), e12814, https://doi.org/10.1111/phc3.12819.

45. See Andrew Power and Edward Hall, "Placing Care in Times of Austerity," *Social & Cultural Geography* 19 no. 3 (2017): 303–13; and Ann E. Bartos, "Stretching the Boundaries of Care," *Gender, Place and Culture* 26, no. 6 (2019): 767–77.

46. Carey-Ann Morrison, "A Personal Geography of Care and Disability," *Social & Cultural Geography* 23, no. 7 (2022): 104.

47. Uma Narayan, "Colonialism and Its Others: Considerations on Rights and Care Discourses," *Hypatia* 10, no. 2 (1995): 134.

48. Jonathan Boyarin, *The Unconverted Self: Jews, Indians, and the Identity of Christian Europe* (University of Chicago Press, 2009).

49. Jonathan Herring, "The Disability Critique of Care," *Elder Law Review* 8 (2014), 4.

50. Winnifred Fallers Sullivan, *A Ministry of Presence: Chaplaincy, Spiritual Care, and the Law* (University of Chicago Press, 2014), 19.

PART I

The Religious Making and Maintaining of the American Empire

The particulars of religious freedom as granted by the US Constitution have been a critical factor in spreading, enforcing, and legitimating the United States empire. Political and theological rhetoric about religious freedom in the American West takes two competing forms. First is the idea that the "openness" of the region poses an opportunity for the United States to bring its polity of "religious freedom" to the West. In this scenario, the Protestant tradition of voluntarism encounters the West as fertile territory for freewheeling religious competition. Second is the idea that the same "openness" of the West presents a pressing danger to the American nation. This section's chapters grapple with making and maintaining religious boundaries around the promises and perils of the West through the language of paternalistic care.

The section opens with Thomas Bremer's analysis of race and religion in the formation of the national park system. Bremer argues that the national parks created and sustained the racial ideologies of white Protestant America. He draws on Thomas Moran's landscape paintings, speeches, and legislation to demonstrate how the aesthetics of white supremacy melded with paternalistic care to create these natural sacred spaces. Bremer concludes his essay with a close reading of W. E. B. Du Bois's recollection of his visit to the Grand Canyon and echoes Du Bois's critique of and vision of hope for equality realized through the national parks.

The perceived religious tabula rasa of the West, broadly speaking, and California more specifically, became the focus of national anxieties and familial concerns about young adults being "lured" into anti-family new religious movements, specifically Thomas Lake Harris's Fountaingrove colony. Harris's life and the resulting opposition to him in print, Joshua Paddison argues, developed to develop the American West as a signifier for "cult activity" and as the originating source for anti-cult movements. As Paddison shows, this opposition was often racialized and gendered and very much the result of the migratory conditions of the American West.

Carleigh Beriont's essay analyzes a moment during World War II when US troops arrived on an atoll in the Marshall Islands, part of the watery

West. Media reports of this arrival observed that the native Marshallese islanders vocally identified themselves as "Boston Congregationalists" and asked the US forces if they could "pray now." The US media, in turn, presented this as evidence of the justness of US expansion into the Pacific—it was a means to liberate practicing Christians from the threat of un-American religious authoritarianism. However, it was a type of "protective care" that also came with extensive and irreparable environmental and social harm from aerial bombing.

In the final essay of the section, James Bennett shows that anxieties about religious experimentation and innovation in the American West, detailed by Paddison's essay, remained high into the late twentieth century. Under the aegis of care for vulnerable adults, Bennett documents the growth of a multifaceted "anti-cult movement" to combat various new religious groups, including the People's Temple, the Children of God, and the International Society for Krishna Consciousness. Bennett argues that the anti-cult movement's attempts to corral and criminalize religious practice show that the American West was not the site of explosive religious freedom that is sometimes portrayed.

Chapter 1

Icons of Whiteness

Race and Religion in US National Parks

THOMAS S. BREMER

Keywords: aesthetics, national parks, race, whiteness, conservationism, environmentalism, eugenics, Manifest Destiny, National Park Service, nationalism, Yellowstone, Yosemite

Mount Rushmore, with its enormous busts of George Washington, Thomas Jefferson, Abraham Lincoln, and Theodore Roosevelt carved into the stone of the sacred Black Hills in South Dakota, attracts millions of patriotic pilgrims and curious critics each year; it also shows up as a ubiquitous image of nationalist pride in American popular culture. Gutzon Borglum, who created this monolithic sculpture, envisioned his epic work as "a nation's memorial" that would portray the four former presidents in a way that conveys "a serenity, a nobility, a power that reflects the gods who inspired them and suggests the gods they have become."[1] This massive monument, though, represents far more than inspired patriotism honoring the national gods. Borglum, a member of the Ku Klux Klan who supported eugenic policies and was "unambiguous about the perils of miscegenation" as well as "the evils of the alien races" more generally, expressed his white supremacist views in much of his sculptural work.[2] For him, the racial elements in his vision of America steady the gaze of these Great White Fathers as they peer out across the western US landscape.

Mount Rushmore's monumental figures staring out across the mountainous terrain embed Borglum's glorification of whiteness in an inspired vision of American imperial triumph. By its location in sacred lands illegally taken from Native peoples, its choice of four US presidents who each loom large in the mythologies of national expansion, the magisterial positioning of their gaze from an "elevated vantage point—and the sense of mastery and control that vantage point inspires,"[3] Mount Rushmore reigns as a "homage to the ideology of Manifest Destiny."[4]

Now part of the US national park system as a "national memorial," Mount Rushmore is one of the 433 units managed by the National Park Service, a division of the US Department of the Interior. Borglum's memorial may be the most explicit expression of white racist ideology in the system, but all US national parks, and in fact the very idea of national parks itself as a celebrated value of the American nation, involve a history of racial ideologies. From their origins in the nineteenth century as products of postbellum "Manifest Destiny" to their widespread acceptance as sacred sites for the appreciation and enjoyment of pristine nature, as places of healing and renewal, US national parks embody the confluence of the "inextricably linked" categories of religion, race, and nation articulated in American landscapes.[5] More than stunning scenery and places of recreation, these parks throughout their histories have affirmed and furthered prevailing racial ideologies of Protestant white America in their religious and rhetorical roles as icons of US empire.

This essay discerns the racial elements in the logic of US national parks as sacred spaces of the American nation, spaces that have affirmed the aesthetics of white supremacy in the making of empire. Besides their gendered significance in the "masculine expectations" of wilderness preservation,[6] and often touted as places of healing from the rigors and traumas of modernity, the preservation of these extraordinary landscapes also contributed to evolving racial ideologies. Indeed, representations and experiences of national parks as sacred destinations have articulated both religious and nationalistic imperatives in racialized visions of empire.

Manifesting Destiny

Extending the earlier precedents of Hot Springs in Arkansas, set aside as a "federal reserve" by Congress in 1832, and Yosemite, granted by the federal government to the state of California in 1864 to "be held for public use, resort, and recreation . . . inalienable for all time,"[7] the Yellowstone plateau in the Rocky Mountains became the world's first national park in 1872, a product of Manifest Destiny. Rather than invented tales of prescient conservationists adamant on preserving a sacred land, Yellowstone and other early national parks were a consequence of the aspirations of East Coast capitalists seeking to convert American Indian lands into tourist destinations.[8] This expansionist mindset of capitalist ambition that transformed Yellowstone into a national park gained much of its moral authority and justification from the essentially religious discourse of Manifest Destiny, a concept articulating divine chosenness, with "origins both Protestant and liberal in nature," that fueled nationalist ambitions in the postbellum era.[9] With biblical justifications for dispossessing American Indian communities of their homelands, the US empire expanded westward.

Manifest Destiny names a national discourse on expansion and its unseemly ambitions, specifically the genocidal efforts to dispossess Native peoples of their homelands. The concept of Manifest Destiny, as Anders Stephanson asserts, warranted the inclusion of ethnic cleansing in the narrative of US national destiny. The nation's white Protestant majority turned to their Bible and to natural law for justifying the violence that expansionism entailed. Some US citizens objected to the genocidal treatment of American Indian communities and initiated efforts at Christian-humanitarian assimilation of Native peoples, but most of these initiatives failed. As Stephanson concludes, "Americans wanted land to exploit, not indigenous peoples to assimilate." Thus, in the minds of many US citizens, the choice was either "expulsion or extermination."[10]

The Civil War quieted expansionist ambitions of the Manifest Destiny discourse, but a resurgence in the postbellum period emboldened efforts to conquer, settle, and civilize western territories. This postbellum revival of Manifest Destiny included the creation of national parks. When President Ulysses Grant signed the Yellowstone Act on March 1, 1872, he effectively transformed the unclaimed space of "wilderness" into a "civilized" place of parkland, "from Wilderness to Wonderland."[11] This newly created place in a sparsely populated western territory far from the centers of national power had distinct potential to benefit eastern economic interests, but it also had clear symbolic significance as a representation of nationalistic visions of land, of nature, and more broadly of the United States as an exceptional, divinely endowed nation.

The founding of Yellowstone National Park as part of the national effort to claim, conquer, and settle the ever-expanding territories of the United States in the context of Manifest Destiny also contributed to racialized understandings of land and nation. The role of Yellowstone and other western national parks in racializing wild and scenic lands stemmed in large part from their participation in the production of a national identity as part of the US recovery from the Civil War when the nation's priorities shifted from the trauma of north–south divisions to the optimism of westward expansion. As early as 1865, the eminent landscape architect Frederick Law Olmsted Sr. proposed a management plan for Yosemite that would reorient national attention from the north–south divisions of the Civil War to an east–west axis of expansionism and Manifest Destiny.[12] More than western parklands, though, religious affiliations and racial identity served to reconcile regional differences. Indeed, postbellum national reunification relied to a large extent on the shared racial identity of white Christians, with northern US Protestants playing a central role in the process of reasserting whiteness to supersede sectional differences, such that by the end of the century "in the minds of many northerners, American nationalism, whiteness, and Protestant Christianity had been powerfully bound together once again."[13]

Abandoning the Reconstruction project of racial justice for formerly enslaved peoples, the United States instead aimed its ambitions on its western territories. Places like Yellowstone, Sequoia, Yosemite, and Mount Rainier (the nation's first four national parks) supported the image of the American West as a desirable region that, under the divine promise of Manifest Destiny, the United States was successfully incorporating into the civilized, Christian world of white America. Indeed, US national parks, with their beginnings in this destinarian context and its "historical logic of whiteness,"[14] have perpetuated nineteenth-century racial ideologies regarding land and nature.

Besides helping to redirect national attention to western expansion at the expense of racial justice for newly liberated African Americans, the postbellum establishment of national parks in the American West had severe consequences for Native peoples. Most ruinous was the removal of American Indian communities from their traditional homelands, in some cases "forcibly removed from their homes so tourists would feel comfortable contemplating a true 'wilderness.'"[15] The conquest and settlement of western territories required the "pacification," a euphemism for genocidal displacement, of American Indian communities who had previously occupied desired lands, with US religious groups playing a key role in these nationalist ambitions of white America. This included the removal from national parks of peoples whose ancestors had valued those places for generations. Moreover, besides dispossession and sometimes the actual genocidal mortality of Native bodies, transforming their traditional homelands into national parks also involved cultural genocide in the erasure of American Indian values, relationships, and histories with the land.

Many Euro-Americans in the United States regretted what they assumed would be the lamentable but inevitable demise of Native peoples. One of the earliest tourists to visit Yellowstone, Reverend Edwin J. Stanley, a Methodist circuit preacher in Montana, pondered the fate of the countryside he passed through on his way to the new national park in 1873, a land which previously had been, as he understood it, "the undisputed abode of the wild red-man; these streams, on the banks of which he was born, and by the side of which he was reared; these plains, over which he roamed at will with the wild beasts that he loved to chase—all must soon come under the influence of civilization, and yield to the scepter of the irrepressible white man."[16] Though lamenting the irrepressible advance of white civilization, Rev. Stanley also justifies cultural genocide as the inevitable fate of recalcitrant Indians, who, he argues, "must be made to feel the strong arm of the Government, and fear it, before they will respect 'the powers that be,' or before any progress can be made toward their civilization."[17]

Rev. Stanley's sentiments toward American Indians were widely shared in nineteenth-century US discourse. In the case of Yellowstone, such attitudes necessitated the literal removal from the park of Shoshone people who had for generations been living there year-round.[18] The derogation of Native peoples also involved mythologizing Yellowstone's origins in a way that excluded significant mention of the area's previous inhabitants. As the flagship national park of the US, an iconic site of white triumph in the religious and imperialist rhetoric of Manifest Destiny, Yellowstone bolstered the nation's resolve to claim and civilize the western territories as the well-deserved heritage of white Protestant Americans.

Yellowstone's reputation as an iconic destination in the American West quickly grew following the enactment of the 1872 legislation establishing the park. Its popularity relied to some extent on the nineteenth-century concept of the sublime, which regarded certain rare landscapes as places where one could "glimpse the face of God."[19] Sublime experience emerged as a vital concept of Romanticism, one that the German philosopher Immanuel Kant had explained as a paradoxical sensation of both terror and awe in confronting nature; in Kant's analysis, the sublime makes possible a regard for wild nature as "aesthetically agreeable" that suggests "the association of God and wild nature."[20] Virtually all of the early US national parks offered aesthetic experience of the sublime as their chief attraction.[21]

Yellowstone in particular as a place of sublime wonder gained widespread public enthusiasm in the 1870s through the artistic renderings of Thomas Moran, a late figure in the Hudson River School of landscape artists, who had joined the first official US government geological survey of the Yellowstone plateau in 1871. Not only did his paintings help convince members of Congress to preserve the region as a park, his monumental rendition of the Grand Canyon of the Yellowstone River (not to be confused with the much larger canyon in Arizona, which Moran also visited and painted in 1873), first exhibited in New York in May 1872, brought the Yellowstone wonders to the attention of a wider American public, contributing decisively to "the iconological emergence of Yellowstone."[22] Besides the breathtaking realism Moran achieved in his representation of the sublime immensity, textures, and coloring of the canyon, the painting made Yellowstone into a place "of magnificence and wonder that could stand as important symbols of America's uniqueness"; in short, Moran's depiction portrayed the American landscape as a land that "could speak for God," a place of white Protestant conquest claimed in the logic of Manifest Destiny.[23]

Part of the appeal of Moran's painting for nineteenth-century white Americans was its implicit racial messages. Despite his skillful depiction of the canyon's colors in his masterpiece, Moran painted Yellowstone as a place of

Figure 1.1 Thomas Moran, *The Grand Cañon of the Yellowstone*, 1872, 12-foot-by-7-foot oil on canvas mounted on aluminum. Smithsonian American Art Museum, lent by the Department of the Interior Museum, L.1968.84.1. Image courtesy of Steven Zucker. A full-color image of the painting is available online at https://upload.wikimedia.org/wikipedia/commons/1/1b/Thomas_Moran_-_Grand_Canyon_of_the_Yellowstone.jpg.

whiteness. His artistic rendering of the canyon utilized conventional landscape painting techniques that conformed to dominant nationalist and religious sentiments in American society as it portrayed a triumphant space of whiteness, exemplifying what Albert Boime describes as the "magisterial gaze" of nineteenth-century American landscape painting.[24] Moran includes in the foreground minuscule human figures dwarfed by the immensity of the canyon; art historian Joni Kinsey surmises that the central figure is geologist Ferdinand Hayden, leader of the expedition, shown beside the figure of an Indian, a generic representation of American Indians occupying western territories, standing together on an outcropping high above the gleaming blue rapids of the river at the canyon's bottom.[25] The white geologist points toward the river while the Indian faces away from the canyon, with his head turned back in the direction of Hayden's gesture.[26] A large tree frames the left edge of the scene, and dark pines stand in a line along the canyon sides like pious devotees in solemn reverence to the divine sanctuary. Towering cathedral spires rise toward the right, while the view focuses on the distant falls in the left-center portion of the painting. On the plateau in the background can be seen pillars of steam rising from far-off hot springs, and the snow-peaked range of the Teton Mountains is faintly visible in the far distance.

Moran's imaginative framing of the scene, which includes features not visible from the actual Grand Canyon of the Yellowstone, invites viewers to join the figures at the bottom in gazing on a redemptive space that symbolically highlights a story of white salvation. The majestic waterfall that captures the viewer's attention echoes a most powerful theme of Protestant Christianity: the Fall, the epic story of humankind's lapse and the source of the human condition under the spell of original sin. Meanwhile, the white "discoverer" of Yellowstone, Ferdinand Hayden, directs the Indian's view of the canyon in a metaphor of conquest and progress, with the Native figure turned away from the scene.[27] Moran positions the white geologist pointing toward the light-filled future, whereas the Indian figure turns toward the shadowed past, suggesting to Moran and his white contemporaries "the end of the 'savage state' and the arrival of 'civilization.'"[28] The positioning of the two figures also symbolizes, according to cultural geographer Gareth John, the imperialist relationship of US explorers and Native Americans, "as if the latter were conceding the territory in its pristine natural condition to the former."[29]

Moran's depiction of the canyon's vivid coloration amplifies the theme of empire in his painting by privileging white as the color of uplift, as the symbol of a redemptive whiteness rising toward a heavenly paradise above this wild terrestrial paradise. A cloud of white mist shrouds the waterfall and rises all the way to the upper edge of the canvas, where it spreads out as it enters the celestial realm. White columns also rise from steam vents along the canyon wall and from hot springs on the distant plain. The colorful walls of the canyon bleach white as they reach their highest point in the upper right corner of the painting, and the white peaks of the distant Teton Mountains stretch along the rear of the scene.

Following the convention of other Hudson River School painters before him, Moran infused his masterpiece with Christian themes that affirm the American landscape as a place of white Protestant conquest claimed in the beneficence of divine providence.[30] These themes were evident to viewers at the unveiling of *Grand Cañon of the Yellowstone* in 1872, which revealed the newly established national park as a place of sublime beauty that confirmed the providential claims of Manifest Destiny while affirming the hubris of white Protestant righteousness. It very quickly became a popular symbol of American progress and domination. The US Congress paid Moran an unprecedented sum for an American artwork, making it the first work of landscape art to hang in the US Capitol.[31] The painting also became a familiar icon for the nation's schoolchildren, with reproductions of Moran's masterpiece soon hanging in nearly every classroom across the country,[32] more ubiquitous in nineteenth-century American culture than John Gast's now-famous *American Progress* painting of the same year. Perhaps more than any other representation of the new national park, Moran's colossal rendition established Yellowstone as an affirmation of white destiny in the American West.

The popularity of Moran's painting also helped make Yellowstone an attractive destination for privileged nineteenth-century travelers, which in turn inspired other artists, photographers, writers, and promoters to spread the fame of the Yellowstone "Wonderland." Consequently, growing public support for preserving other western scenic wonders added three more national parks by the end of the nineteenth century: Sequoia National Park and the expansion of Yosemite, both established in 1890, plus Mount Rainier in 1899. However, as the significance of Manifest Destiny shifted in the late decades of the nineteenth century and the early years of the twentieth century from conquest and settlement of the American West to imperialist ambitions on the global stage,[33] the cultural meanings of national parks also gradually changed toward notions of pristine nature. This changing discourse on the divinely bestowed destiny of the United States also altered the racial ideology underlying the significance of national parks. With less concern about conquering Native peoples and claiming their homelands, the racial element of national parks turned more deliberately to concerns about threats to the white race from miscegenation, linking the conservation of nature to the preservation of whiteness. National parks in the first decades of the twentieth century became symbolic refuges against the specter of "race suicide."

Pristine Nature and White Supremacy

Theodore Roosevelt, as president of the United States, embarked on a cross-country "Great Loop" tour in April of 1903 that included a good deal of politicking, some outdoor adventure, and visits to national parks and other scenic destinations in the American West to gain support for his conservationist agenda. The president's itinerary included two weeks in Yellowstone National Park and a one-day stop at the Grand Canyon in Arizona, where he delivered a speech arguing for its protection. The California leg of his trip included a week in Yosemite National Park in the Sierra Nevada mountains.[34] There he enjoyed three nights of camping with naturalist and wilderness preservation advocate John Muir. Roosevelt had insisted on Muir to serve as his Yosemite guide, and Muir relished the opportunity to influence the president's environmental initiatives.[35] When the two met at the park, they quickly abandoned the pomp and adulation that accompanied the president everywhere he traveled and went alone (except for two guides, two packers, and three mules) into the Yosemite wilderness.[36]

These two luminaries of the American environmental movement, John Muir and Theodore Roosevelt, are often mistakenly identified as founding

Figure 1.2 President Theodore Roosevelt with naturalist John Muir at Glacier Point in Yosemite, 1903. Courtesy of the Library of Congress, control number 93503130.

figures of American national parks. Though neither played any part in the beginnings of the national park movement—Yellowstone had been established more than thirty years before they went camping together in Yosemite—their contributions in the closing decades of the nineteenth century and the early years of the twentieth century were enormously influential in defining the ways that many people would come to regard national parks as sacred treasures of the American landscape. Their influence also secured the legacy of national parks as white spaces of racial purity.

John Muir's importance as a naturalist and advocate for preservation of scenic landscapes is often associated with his relationship with Yosemite. Before arriving in California, though, the young John Muir had undertaken a "thousand-mile walk" that took him into the heart of the postbellum south.[37] Having avoided the military draft during the Civil War by fleeing to Canada,[38] Muir was no activist for racial justice, and his observations of southern life during Reconstruction, although perhaps more generous than most of northern white America, were rife with demeaning racial attitudes.[39] He depicted Blacks in Georgia as "very lazy [revised to 'easy-going' in the published version] and merry," claiming that a single white laborer could "easily pick as much cotton as half a dozen sambos and sallies."[40]

Initially intending to continue his long walk all the way to South America, Muir had his sights redirected westward after a bout of malaria in Florida. His arrival in California in March 1868 marked the beginning of a lifelong romance with the state's landscapes, especially its mountains. California became his permanent home, and the Yosemite Valley was "the spiritual center of that home."[41] He was not enamored, however, of the Native people who had inhabited those landscapes for generations. Much like his depictions of African Americans during his southern sojourn, Muir adopted an ambivalent view of American Indians. For instance, in describing an elderly Native woman he encountered during his first summer in Yosemite, Muir contrasts her unfavorably with "Nature's neat well-dressed animals," lamenting "that mankind alone is dirty."[42] More damaging, however, than his negative portrayals of Native inhabitants of the land was Muir's vision of the American landscape that erased Native presence entirely.[43] In his view, nature was an unpeopled paradise.

Muir's vision of an unpeopled wilderness exalted the holy purity of nature, and especially the mountains. He was not original in this but instead drew on a long Calvinist tradition of religious reverence of the natural world as God's creation—a tradition that led Muir, like others in the early environmental movement, "toward a spiritual (and not merely scientific) relationship to nature." His spiritual view of nature's beauty in all of its complexity and constant wonder revealed for Muir the ever-present reality of God.[44] Reverence for nature, though, came most clearly in solitude, in the absence of humans in wild places. While on a long autumn trek through the California mountains, Muir paused in a meadow where "every tree seemed religious and conscious of the presence of God. A free man revels in a scene like this and time goes by unmeasured. I stood fixed in silent wonder . . . exulting in Nature's wild immortal vigor and beauty, never dreaming any other human being was near." But then his reverie was interrupted by the sudden appearance of "a man and a horse [that] came in sight at the farther end of the meadow, where they seemed sadly out of place."[45] Claiming this meadow for himself alone, Muir's practice of wilderness piety seeks complete solitude for the worshipper to perceive a divine presence.

As an author exalting the holiness of nature in the sanctity of wild mountain landscapes, Muir had become a leading voice in the nascent environmental movement by the time Theodore Roosevelt brought his presidential politicking spectacle to California in 1903. As the leading apostle of American nature religion, as the foremost advocate for national parks as protected reservations of pristine wilderness, as an environmental activist displaying a passionate intimacy with the natural world, John Muir was an ideal companion for Roosevelt's visit to Yosemite. Their three days touring and camping in the park deepened the personal connection between these two figures who were the most visible public face of conservation in the first decade of the twentieth century.

The mutual admiration and personal bond between John Muir and Theodore Roosevelt relied on a shared environmental ethic that superseded important differences in their respective experiences of the natural nonhuman world. Roosevelt's interest in preserving wilderness came from strongly gendered adventures in nature that for him had clear nationalistic significance; above all, the hunting of wild animals in Roosevelt's estimation afforded the greatest opportunities for affirming one's virile manliness and ensuring the strength of the nation, a view that contrasted starkly to Muir's professed dislike of sport hunting.[46] Yet despite their differences, both Roosevelt and Muir interpreted the sanctity of nature through the lens of the Reformed traditions in their respective Presbyterian backgrounds, which tended, according to Mark Stoll, to produce Progressive conservationists committed to righteous activism.[47] Both were passionately committed to preserving nature, but while Muir envisioned the sacred purity of nature absent of a human presence (other than the recreational enjoyment of nature by a privileged class of travelers), Roosevelt tended more toward the pragmatic conservation ethos of his chief forester Gifford Pinchot, who insisted on conserving the nation's natural wealth "in such a way as to promote the greatest good of the greatest number for the longest time."[48] This conservationist philosophy regarded the preservation of scenic beauty strictly for its aesthetic value as, in Pinchot's words, "sentimental nonsense," which contrasted sharply with Muir's preservationist view.[49]

Pinchot's insistence on the rational management of natural resources for the good of society became a pillar of Progressive ideology and politics that motivated Roosevelt's unprecedented accomplishments in setting aside federal lands as national parks, forest reserves, wildlife sanctuaries, and national monuments, earning the president recognition for elevating conservation as a national priority.[50] But it also entailed a racial dimension. Alongside and connected to a concern about the wasteful depletion of the nation's resources was the perception of threats to the undisputed dominance of the white race. And just as conserving natural resources demanded rational, scientific management principles, averting "race suicide" required the scientific application of eugenic policies.[51]

Whereas a Calvinistic lens gained from his Reformed Protestant upbringing informed John Muir's idealization of nature, Roosevelt's Reformed background as a lifelong Presbyterian coincided with a thoroughgoing embrace of Darwinist principles.[52] The Darwinian evolutionary paradigm defined not only how Roosevelt viewed the natural nonhuman world, but it also provided a scientific justification for his advocacy of eugenics as the rational response to the threat of "race suicide" evident in the declining birth rates of white Protestants, paradoxically contradicting his demonstrated commitment to the ability of nationalism to transcend race.[53] He wrote in 1914, "I wish very much that the wrong people could be prevented entirely from breeding. . . . Criminals should be sterilized, and feebleminded persons forbidden to leave offspring behind them. But as yet there is no way possible to devise which could prevent all undesirable people from breeding. The emphasis should be laid on getting desirable people to breed."[54]

Roosevelt's interest in a eugenic solution to the perceived loss of white supremacy was not separate from his significant achievements in preservation and the conservation of natural resources. The entanglement of environmental conservation with the preservation of the white race can be seen perhaps most clearly in one of the last initiatives of Roosevelt's presidency, the three-volume National Conservation Commission report, compiled by the Commission's executive chairman, Gifford Pinchot, the president's closest and most trusted adviser on environmental issues. When he brought it to Congress in 1909, Roosevelt declared the report to be "one of the most fundamentally important documents ever laid before the American people."[55] Its importance, though, had a racial element. The report addressed key issues of Progressive politics with ten far-reaching recommendations that ranged from public health to labor regulation, to the elimination of poverty and crime. This broad range of social issues all pointed toward its tenth recommendation, which advocated for "eugenics, or hygiene for future generations," including forced sterilization and marriage prohibition for "degenerates generally" while establishing social norms to encourage eugenically preferable marriages. The report explicitly connected these eugenic policies to environmental concerns, concluding, "The problem of the conservation of our natural resources is therefore not a series of independent problems, but a coherent, all-embracing whole. If our nation cares to make any provision for its grandchildren and its grandchildren's grandchildren, this provision must include conservation in all its branches—but above all, the conservation of the racial stock itself."[56]

Though Congress took little interest in the lame-duck president's National Conservation Commission report, the linkage between protecting natural resources and conserving the white racial stock of the nation persisted as cornerstones of Progressive politics, with eugenics and environmentalism becoming "intimately connected in the minds of many during the first half of the twentieth century."[57] One of the more influential champions of this Progressive agenda for conserving nature and saving the white race was Madison Grant, a close associate of Theodore Roosevelt, who gained notoriety for his popular treatise advocating eugenic solutions to the nation's problems.

Many of his contemporaries knew him as an indefatigable warrior for wilderness preservation, but Grant's infamy today rests on his authorship of what was perhaps the most influential book on eugenics, *The Passing of the Great Race*, a racist tome that Adolf Hitler described as "my Bible."[58] The popularity of Grant's book exposed an underlying terror among white Americans confronted by "the specter of deterioration and degeneration of the human species—race suicide on the cultural level and an environmental wasteland on the other."[59] The solution to both, in the Progressive worldview, was rational, scientifically informed management to protect the nation's most cherished resources, both racial and natural.

This rationalistic, scientifically managed approach to the Progressive conservationist agenda was not shared by John Muir, who vigorously disputed Pinchot's view of managing natural resources, most famously in Muir's opposition to damming Yosemite's Hetch Hetchy Valley to provide water for San Francisco.[60] Instead, he viewed the stunning beauty and pristine quality of Yosemite and elsewhere as an American Garden of Eden, an idyllic image of sanctuary resembling the original paradise eloquently described in the poet John Milton's epic *Paradise Lost*.[61] Muir's euphoric accounts of the enchanted garden paradise in the California mountains inspired others to appreciate the spiritual qualities of the American landscape, but it also generated public concern for its vulnerabilities to the rapacious exploitations of industry and agriculture. Perhaps more than any other single figure, Muir established the sacredness of national parks in the cultural imagination of the American people, articulating an ethos of preservation to protect their sanctity for the posterity of future generations and the prosperity of the nation. His vision of wild nature, though, remained absent of people, especially people of color, whom he regarded as less human than white people.

Muir's racial views admittedly were never a prominent aspect of his advocacy for preserving wild nature and promoting national parks. His attitudes toward African Americans, American Indians, and other people of color appear clearly at various points in his published work and private writings, but they never were central themes in his essays. In contrast, the conservation of the white race was central to Theodore Roosevelt's environmental ideology and policies. For him and the Progressives that he associated with, conserving nature and the unique lands of the American nation was inextricably linked to perpetuating the dominance of the white race. In their American imaginary, the hallowed grounds of national parks were exemplary sites of white supremacy. Their significance as places of whiteness, though, did not go unchallenged. The religious and racial discourses of nationhood that regarded the US national parks as privileged precincts celebrating the superiority of the white race met with counter-discourses that celebrated instead the liberating ideology of democracy. One significant though rarely noticed example came from a leading African American intellectual and activist of the twentieth century.

Subverting the Whiteness of National Parks

W. E. B. Du Bois, a formidable intellectual in the first half of the twentieth century whose insights and critiques of race continue to resonate, recounts in his 1920 *Darkwater* collection of essays "a great journey" covering much of the midwestern and western regions of the United States.[62] In all of the wondrous and impressive sights he witnessed, Du Bois "saw one thing that lived and will live eternal in my soul,—the Grand Cañon." He describes this incomparable feature of the American landscape as "a sudden void in the bosom of the earth, down to its entrails—a wound where the dull titanic knife has turned and twisted in the hole, leaving its edges livid, scarred, jagged, and pulsing over the white, red, and purple of its mighty flesh, while down below—down, down below, in black and severed vein, boils the dull and sullen flood of the Colorado."[63] Standing at the rim of the Grand Canyon, the sight astonished Du Bois. On the one hand, the chasm that spread before him was "awful. There can be nothing like it. It is the earth and sky gone stark and raving mad. . . . It is a grim thing, unholy, terrible." On the other hand, however, "it cannot be a mere, inert, unfeeling, brute fact—its grandeur is too serene—its beauty too divine! It is not red and blue, and green, but ah! the shadows and the shades of all the world, glad colorings touched with a hesitant spiritual delicacy."[64]

Du Bois's confusing encounter of this bewildering land, its madness invoking in him a paradoxical sense of awe in confronting the grim, unholy, and terrible scene that at the same time radiates a serene and divine beauty, suggests the aesthetic power of sublime experience, reclaiming a prominent theme in the literature of nineteenth-century travelers seeking auspicious landscapes. But though the concept suffered from overuse in the popular media, becoming more a "domesticated sublime" absent its sense of terror in the omnipotent presence of divinity found in superlative landscapes, Du Bois rediscovers the paradoxical qualities of sublime reality on the rim of the Grand Canyon.

Du Bois's enigmatic experience of the Grand Canyon's sublimity and his poetic musings on its awful and divine qualities was itself an enigma in the white imagination of national parks. As heirs to centuries of systematic denial of African and African American humanity, most white Americans found it difficult, if not impossible, to conceive of an African American person capable of sublime experience that was the pinnacle of the white experience of

Figure 1.3 View of the Grand Canyon from Grand View Point, 1900–1902. Photo by Charles C. Pierce, digitally reproduced by the USC Digital Library from the California Historical Society Collection at the University of Southern California.

American national parks. Du Bois's writings, however, confound the assumption that only white people can appreciate sublime landscapes.[65]

By the time Du Bois's portrait of the Grand Canyon appeared in print, the great chasm of the American Southwest had only recently achieved national park status. President Theodore Roosevelt had protected the canyon as a national monument in 1908, five years after his own rapturous experience of its sublime immensity. The president had stopped there during his "Great Loop" tour of the American West for a quick visit between his trek through Yellowstone and his meeting with John Muir in Yosemite.[66] Overwhelmed by the breathtaking expanse of the Grand Canyon, Roosevelt admonished the American public "to keep this great wonder of nature as it now is." In his speech delivered at the canyon's rim, the president warned against constructing buildings or other improvements that would "mar the wonderful grandeur, the sublimity, the great loveliness and beauty of the Canyon." However, he continued, "What you can do is to keep it for your children, your children's children, and for all who come after you, as one of the great sights which every American if he can travel at all should see."[67] On that day in May 1903, preserving the Grand Canyon "as it now is" became a priority in the president's environmental agenda.

Though both were astounded by the magnificence of the Grand Canyon, W. E. B. Du Bois's journey to Arizona contrasted sharply with Roosevelt's. As president, Theodore Roosevelt arrived at the Grand Canyon in the luxury of an opulently appointed private train, "complete with barbershop, parlor, kitchen, sleeping compartments, and baggage chambers," surrounded by an entourage to do his bidding and care for his every need.[68] Though fancying himself a populist in touch with the lives of ordinary citizens, Roosevelt's insistence that every American "if he can travel at all" should visit the Grand Canyon ignores—in fact, remains willfully ignorant of—the obstacles that non-white travelers faced in the early part of the twentieth century. Du Bois, however, had no illusions about the difficulties of travel for a Black American. Framing his rhapsodies on experiencing the Grand Canyon are his descriptions of demeaning, difficult, often rude, and sometimes violent experiences that Black Americans routinely faced on the nation's highways, byways, and specifically on the railroads. He relates the humiliating treatment from railroad employees, and writes of the great discomforts, inconveniences, and unsanitary conditions endured in the so-called Jim Crow car for non-white railroad passengers. "The 'Jim-Crow' car," Du Bois explains, "is up next the baggage car and engine. . . . and often the car is a smoker cut in two and you must pass through the white smokers or else they pass through your part, with swagger and noise and stares. Your compartment is a half or a quarter or an eighth of the oldest car in service on the road. . . . The white train crew from the baggage car uses the 'Jim-Crow' to lounge in and perform their toilet."[69] Certainly, non-white travelers endured conditions that elite white leaders like Theodore Roosevelt could hardly imagine existed at all.

Despite the demeaning realities of travel that he faced, W. E. B. Du Bois nevertheless made his way to the Grand Canyon, and his portrayal of the great chasm reveals two visions. On the one hand it employs the trope of the sublime "to recuperate and represent an authentic encounter with nature," but at the same time it also "suggests the trauma of racial violence, specifically castration and ritual lynching."[70] Though his view of racial trauma does not explicitly encompass the traumas of American Indian people who had lived in and near the canyon for generations, Du Bois knew well how colonial disruptions and dispossessions had traumatized Indigenous peoples everywhere, including in America.[71] The grim unholiness he perceived as he took in the scene of the Grand Canyon suggested histories of violence exerted by colonizers everywhere.

The constant experience of racism that he endured in the United States affords Du Bois, in the estimation of John Claborn, "the advantage of second-sight and a challenge to the discourses of segregation," which in turn rescues him "from the white bourgeois tourist's commodified experience of nature." This second-sight faculty "not only grants African Americans access to the cultural nationalist project of the national parks but also interprets that project as integration rather than segregation."[72] Ultimately, for Du Bois, Claborn concludes, "there is no 'nature' without the baggage of the color line, no Grand Canyon without Jim Crow, and no wide-open landscapes without claustrophobic cityscapes."[73]

Du Bois's double envisioning of the Grand Canyon derives in part from a profound religious understanding that informs his critical interpretations. Though often misunderstood, unacknowledged, or entirely ignored by many who study his work and legacy, Du Bois's writings exhibit a deep religiosity.[74] One way his religious orientation becomes apparent is his adoption of the critical tradition of African American jeremiad preaching, perhaps most notably in his *Darkwater* collection. Joining a long line of African American critical commentary, Du Bois rebukes American triumphalism in favor of a vision of the United States that, according to Jeffrey Kahn, "emphasizes the democratic conditions of pluralistic dissent and difference" as he seeks redemption through the denunciatory technique of the jeremiad to bring forth "a language of affirmation."[75] Contrary to the traditional American jeremiad that worships the nation and affirms divine promises of America's destiny, Du Bois conceives of the nation as a site for realizing the promise of democracy, as a place, in Kahn's interpretation, "to enact the promise of the United States as one landscape among many in which humans can work to create political conditions to reflect godly virtues."[76] In this regard, his description of rapturous, sublime experience at the rim of the Grand Canyon enacts a critical stance far beyond the conventional, bourgeois interpretations and uses of the sublime. Du Bois appeals to the sublime to suggest the redemptive potential of national parks, not as places of whiteness but as sites that affirm the democratic virtues of pluralistic dissent and difference.[77] He reveals how the aesthetic power of auspicious landscapes invokes a deeply spiritual awareness of the moral possibilities for justice in a democratic nation.

His spiritual awareness and an astute moral vision are both implicated in Du Bois's depiction of the Grand Canyon. Unlike so many representations of the American landscape, Du Bois refuses to claim conquest of the canyon—his description never assumes a pose of superiority in a "magisterial gaze" of Manifest Destiny, nor does it romanticize the land as a place of providential blessings contributing to national prosperity. His representation of the Grand Canyon as a place of sublime experience conforms to much of conventional nature writing of the time, yet his emphasis on the canyon's inaccessibility, both physically and conceptually, coincides with a traditional African American ambivalence toward wilderness. As Claborn concludes, "The Grand Canyon, then, is the perfect landscape for a meeting between African American ambivalence and sublime representations of nature."[78] Accordingly, Du Bois exploits a convergence of the sublime and ambivalence in his jeremiadic double visioning of the awful, unholy, and terrible vista paradoxically radiating a serene and divine beauty that is both the Grand Canyon and the United States.

Conclusion

Like race, like religion, like cities and farms, like churches and homes, national parks are very human inventions. They have been created, developed, maintained, promoted, interpreted, and valued in complex cultural contexts of politics, economics, social relationships, aesthetic values, and nationalist sentiments. Certainly, these sites of exquisite natural wonders have no inherent determinants of racial or religious significance. People bring their own racial biases and religious orientations to plant in the soil of these wild places, to paint over the spectacular scenery with racial tints and religious colorings that define their own lives. In short, national parks are mirrors to those who love and value them.

From early on, national parks have been regarded as places of healing, where urban people can take refuge from the debilitating surroundings of their everyday lives and reconnect with something more authentic, more edifying, and more healthful in the natural world.[79] Their healing value in US culture, however, has been strictly circumscribed for the benefit of white America. Manifest Destiny cleansed the parks of the Native American communities who had inhabited those lands for generations.

An underlying racial logic has made US national parks places of whiteness where non-white visitors never quite feel welcome. As Carolyn Finney observes, the dominant environmental narrative in the United States has never adequately addressed the collective experiences of African Americans or other people of color in relation to natural landscapes, a reality that has been especially true of national parks.[80] Although a 2004 study concluded that the history of underrepresented subjects must be "retold in full and equal detail," it has been an elusive goal.[81] Much of the Park Service's progress in telling a more inclusive national story has been reversed during the second Trump administration. In an effort to undo decades of progress toward correcting the racial legacies of the past, Donald J. Trump has promulgated policies to reinstate white supremacy, including in the national park system.[82]

An ascendent white supremacy, however, will not be the last word for the American nation. Criticism is the foundation of hope, and W. E. B. Du Bois's blistering critiques of racism in America articulate a hopeful vision of the promises made in the logic of democracy. In his opening "Credo" at the beginning of *Darkwater*, for instance, Du Bois professes his belief in "liberty for all men: the space to stretch their arms and their souls, the right to breathe and the right to vote, the freedom to choose their friends, enjoy the sunshine, and ride on the railroads, uncursed by color; thinking, dreaming, working as they will in a kingdom of beauty and love."[83] To the extent that the United States does not live up to this promise, has never come close to fulfilling this vision of a land of liberty, a kingdom of beauty and love, Du Bois's critical voice instills a hope for national healing and reconciliation that may still come.

The hope in Du Bois's voice exposes and rejects the inherent racism featured in the preservationist orientation of earlier American environmentalism that has continued to haunt national parks as places of white racial identity. He exposes the traumas of American racial apartheid "by de-naturalizing segregation and naturalizing integration in defiance of Jim Crow and early environmentalist discourse"[84] in his representation of sublime experience at the Grand Canyon with a metaphor of hope that national parks might extend to the nation as a whole. "I have seen what the eye of man was never meant to see," he writes. "I have looked upon the dread disrobing of the Night, and yet I live." On the canyon's rim, Du Bois survives the dark dread of the Night's dream to witness the hopeful light of the "dim-dawn." With a problematic invocation of the male gaze, he exclaims, "Down dropped the black-blue robes, gray-pearled, and slipped, leaving a filmy, silken, misty thing, and underneath I glimpsed her limbs of light."[85]

This new light dawning in the Grand Canyon signals perhaps a hopeful path for a nation still ensconced in the heavy chains of slavery that a Civil War, a civil rights movement, a summer of racial reckoning, and ceaseless efforts by passionate activists have not been able to loosen, a nation unwilling to acknowledge the enormous injustices of its past. That hope might likewise extend to recognizing the long- standing spiritual, cultural, and economic connections of American Indians to lands incorporated as national parks. Beneath the dark robes of nationalist rhetoric and claims of racial supremacy bolstered with the authority of religious justification lies a hope that we, like Du Bois, may also find new "limbs of light" in the sacred healing places of the national parks.

Notes

Portions of this essay rely on material in Bremer, *Sacred Wonderland: The History of Religion in Yellowstone* (University of Nebraska Press, 2025), used by permission. I am grateful for the comments, questions, and suggestions from all participants in the Religion in the American West Symposium—their input has greatly improved this essay. I especially thank Carleigh Beriont, Lynne Gerber, Brennan Keegan, Quincy Newell, and Joshua Paddison, as well as the editors of this volume, Brandi Denison and Brett Hendrickson.

1. According to the sculptor's son, Lincoln Borglum, as quoted in Albert Boime, "Patriarchy Fixed in Stone: Gutzon Borglum's 'Mount Rushmore,'" *American Art* 5, no. 1/2 (1991): 142.

2. Albert Boime, "Patriarchy Fixed in Stone," 165; Iyko Day, "Tseng Kwong Chi and the Eugenic Landscape," *American Quarterly* 65, no. 1 (2013): 97.

3. Boime, "Patriarchy Fixed in Stone," 143.

4. Day, "Tseng Kwong Chi," 108–9.

5. Henry Goldschmidt and Elizabeth A. McAlister, eds., *Race, Nation, and Religion in the Americas* (Oxford University Press, 2004), 5.

6. Susan R. Schrepfer, *Nature's Altars: Mountains, Gender, and American Environmentalism* (University Press of Kansas, 2005), 5. For the role of women in the preservation, development, and interpretation of US national parks, see Polly Welts Kaufman, *National Parks and the Woman's Voice: A History* (University of New Mexico Press, 1996).

7. A copy of the 1864 Act creating the Yosemite park and granting it to the state of California is available online on the Library of Congress's site *The Evolution of the Conservation Movement, 1850–1920*, https://search.catalog.loc.gov/instances/cdd19e30-8ecd-5ff0-bb72-2f19a2580eb3?option=lccn&query=00529694.

8. Richard Grusin, *Culture, Technology, and the Creation of America's National Parks* (Cambridge University Press, 2004), 10–11. Day; "Tseng Kwong Chi," 106.

9. Anders Stephanson, *Manifest Destiny: American Expansionism and the Empire of Right* (Hill and Wang, 1995), xiii.

10. Stephanson, *Manifest Destiny*, 24–26.

11. Gareth E. John, "Yellowstone as 'Landscape Idea': Thomas Moran and the Pictorial Practices of Gilded-Age Western Expansion," *Journal of Cultural Geography* 24, no. 2 (2007): 4.

12. Grusin, *Culture, Technology, and the Creation of America's National Parks*, 23–24.

13. Edward J. Blum, *Reforging the White Republic: Race, Religion, and American Nationalism, 1865–1898* (Louisiana State University Press, 2005), 6–7.

14. Manning Marable, quoted in Carolyn Finney, *Black Faces, White Spaces: Reimagining the Relationship of African Americans to the Great Outdoors* (University of North Carolina Press, 2014), 95.

15. Philip Burnham, *Indian Country, God's Country: Native Americans and the National Parks* (Island Press, 2000), 9.

16. Edwin James Stanley, *Rambles in Wonderland: Or, Up the Yellowstone, and among the Geysers and Other Curiosities of the National Park* (D. Appleton, 1878), 20.

17. Stanley, *Rambles in Wonderland*, 37–38.

18. Peter Nabokov and Lawrence Loendorf, *Restoring a Presence: American Indians and Yellowstone National Park* (University of Oklahoma Press, 2004), 285–87.

19. William Cronon, "The Trouble with Wilderness; or, Getting Back to the Wrong Nature," in *Uncommon Ground: Rethinking the Human Place in Nature*, ed. William Cronon (W. W. Norton, 1996), 73.

20. Roderick Nash, *Wilderness and the American Mind*, 4th ed. (Yale University Press, 2001), 45–46.

21. Cronon, "The Trouble with Wilderness," 73.

22. John, "Yellowstone as 'Landscape Idea,'" 14. For the unveiling of Moran's painting on May 2, 1872, and the immediate responses, see Thurman Wilkins and Caroline Lawson Hinkley, *Thomas Moran: Artist of the Mountains*, 2nd ed. (University of Oklahoma Press, 1998), 3–5.

23. Joni Kinsey, "Thomas Moran's Surveys of Yellowstone and the Grand Canyon: The Coalition of Art, Business, and Government," in *Splendors of the American West: Thomas Moran's Art of the Grand Canyon and Yellowstone: Paintings, Watercolors, Drawings, and Photographs from the Thomas Gilcrease Institute of American History and Art*, ed. Anne Morand, Joni Kinsey, and Mary Panzer (Birmingham Museum of Art, 1990), 34; John Clayton, *Wonderlandscape: Yellowstone National Park and the Evolution of an American Cultural Icon* (Pegasus Books, 2017), 15.

24. Albert Boime, *The Magisterial Gaze: Manifest Destiny and American Landscape Painting, c. 1830–1865* (Smithsonian Institution Press, 1991), 20–21.

25. Joni Kinsey, *Thomas Moran and the Surveying of the American West* (Smithsonian Institution Press, 1992), 44.

26. Peter H. Hassrick, *Drawn to Yellowstone: Artists in America's First National Park* (Autry Museum of Western Heritage in association with University of Washington Press, 2002), 42.

27. Hassrick, *Drawn to Yellowstone*, 42.

28. Rebecca Bedell, *The Anatomy of Nature: Geology & American Landscape Painting, 1825–1875* (Princeton University Press, 2001), 134.

29. John, "Yellowstone as 'Landscape Idea,'" 18–19.

30. Regarding earlier artists in the Hudson River School of landscape painting who regularly produced art with "religious associations of landscape," see Mark Stoll, *Inherit the Holy Mountain: Religion and the Rise of American Environmentalism* (Oxford University Press, 2015), 58; and Joel Daehnke, *In the Work of Their Hands Is Their Prayer: Cultural Narrative and Redemption on the American Frontiers, 1830–1930* (Ohio University Press, 2003), 68. For Moran's propensity "to suggest the late nineteenth-century concept of the Far West as Eden" in his Yellowstone paintings, see Anne Morand, "Thomas Moran: Yellowstone and the Grand Canyon: In the Field and from the Studio," in *Splendors of the American West: Thomas Moran's Art of the Grand Canyon and Yellowstone: Paintings, Watercolors, Drawings, and Photographs from the Thomas Gilcrease Institute of American History and Art*, ed. Anne Morand, Joni Kinsey, and Mary Panzer (Birmingham Museum of Art, 1990), 18.

31. Wilkins and Hinkley, *Artist of the Mountains*, 5; Hassrick, *Drawn to Yellowstone*, 42.

32. Floramae McCarron-Cates, "The Best Possible View: Pictorial Representation in the American West," in *Frederic Church, Winslow Homer, and Thomas Moran: Tourism and the American Landscape* (Bulfinch Press, 2006), 107.

33. Stephanson, *Manifest Destiny*, xii.

34. For details on Roosevelt's 1903 Great Loop tour, see Douglas Brinkley, *The Wilderness Warrior: Theodore Roosevelt and the Crusade for America* (Harper, 2009), 502–53.

35. Brinkley, *The Wilderness Warrior*, 546.

36. Brinkley, *The Wilderness Warrior*, 545.

37. Muir recounts his sojourn to the American south in John Muir, *A Thousand-Mile Walk to the Gulf*, ed. William Frederic Badè (Houghton Mifflin, 1916).

38. Donald Worster, *A Passion for Nature: The Life of John Muir* (Oxford University Press, 2008), 91.

39. Worster contends, "Whatever Muir may have missed about the deeper turmoil of southern Blacks' lives, he met them more or less as equals and shared the intimacy of their homes to an extent that few white northerners, or white southerners, ever did." Worster, *The Life of John Muir*, 127.

40. Quoted in Worster, *The Life of John Muir*, 128.

41. Worster, *The Life of John Muir*, 149.

42. John Muir, *My First Summer in the Sierra* (Houghton Mifflin, 1911), 78.

43. Rebecca Solnit, "John Muir in Native America," *Sierra: The Magazine of the Sierra Club* 106, no. 1 (April 2021): 7.

44. Stoll, *Inherit the Holy Mountain*, 148; also see Donald Worster, "John Muir and the Religion of Nature," *Historically Speaking* 10, no. 2 (2009): 27. Regarding the Calvinist influence in the history of American environmentalism, see Stoll, *Inherit the Holy Mountain*, 2.

45. John Muir, *Our National Parks* (Houghton Mifflin, 1901), 303–4.

46. Brinkley, *The Wilderness Warrior*, 544; Worster, *The Life of John Muir*, 369.

47. Stoll, *Inherit the Holy Mountain*, 139–40.

48. Pinchot's approach to conservation appears in Roosevelt's 1908 announcement of a National Conservation Commission to be chaired by Pinchot, who likely penned the announcement. "The National Conservation Commission," *Science (New Series)* 27, no. 704 (June 26, 1908): 996.

49. Garland E. Allen, "'Culling the Herd': Eugenics and the Conservation Movement in the United States, 1900–1940," *Journal of the History of Biology* 46, no. 1 (2013): 42.

50. Steven Mintz, "'Taking Stock of Our Resources': A Request from Theodore Roosevelt, 1908," *OAH Magazine of History* 21, no. 2 (2007): 45.

51. Allen, "Culling the Herd," 62.

52. Brinkley, *The Wilderness Warrior*, 8–9.

53. Charles P. Wohlforth, *The Fate of Nature: Rediscovering Our Ability to Rescue the Earth* (Thomas Dunne Books/St. Martin's Press, 2010), 174. W. Paul Reeve's discussion of Theodore Roosevelt and "race suicide" includes a reprint of a 1904 cartoon showing Roosevelt applauding "No Race Suicide" among the Mormons in Utah. W. Paul Reeve, *Religion of a Different Color: Race and the Mormon Struggle for Whiteness* (Oxford University Press, 2015), 250.

54. Quoted in Wohlforth, *The Fate of Nature*, 171–72.

55. Quoted in Wohlforth, *The Fate of Nature*, 170.

56. Wohlforth, *The Fate of Nature*, 170–71.

57. Allen, "Culling the Herd," 61.

58. Brinkley, *The Wilderness Warrior*, 276–80; Wohlforth, *The Fate of Nature*, 174.

59. Allen, "Culling the Herd," 62.

60. Worster, *A Passion for Nature*, 437.

61. Mark Stoll, "Milton in Yosemite: Paradise Lost and the National Parks Idea," *Environmental History* 13, no. 2 (April 2008): 238.

62. W. E. B. Du Bois, *Darkwater: Voices from within the Veil* (Harcourt, Brace and Howe, 1920), 237.

63. Du Bois, *Darkwater*, 237–38.

64. Du Bois, *Darkwater*, 238–39.

65. John Claborn, "W. E. B. Du Bois at the Grand Canyon: Nature, History, and Race in 'Darkwater,'" in *The Oxford Handbook of Ecocriticism*, ed. Greg Garrard (Oxford University Press, 2014), 125.

66. Regarding Roosevelt's experience during the single day that he spent at the Grand Canyon, see Brinkley, *The Wilderness Warrior*, 526–29.

67. The original copy of Roosevelt's Grand Canyon speech, delivered May 6, 1903, is in the Library of Congress and can be viewed online at *Theodore Roosevelt Center Digital Library*, accessed May 10, 2023, https://www.theodorerooseveltcenter.org/Research/Digital-Library/Record?libID=o289796.

68. Brinkley, *The Wilderness Warrior*, 522.

69. Du Bois, *Darkwater*, 229.

70. Claborn, "Du Bois at the Grand Canyon," 126.

71. Kyle T. Mays, "Transnational Progressivism: African Americans, Native Americans, and the Universal Races Congress of 1911," *Studies in American Indian Literatures* 25, no. 2 (2013): 255.

72. Claborn, "Du Bois at the Grand Canyon," 127–28.

73. Claborn, "Du Bois at the Grand Canyon," 130.

74. Jonathon S. Kahn, *Divine Discontent: The Religious Imagination of W. E. B. Du Bois* (Oxford University Press, 2009), 6.

75. Kahn, *The Religious Imagination of Du Bois*, 89.

76. Kahn, *The Religious Imagination of Du Bois*, 103–4.

77. Claborn, "Du Bois at the Grand Canyon," 122.

78. Claborn, "Du Bois at the Grand Canyon," 125.

79. Thomas S. Bremer, "The Religious and Spiritual Appeal of National Parks," in *The Routledge Handbook of Religious and Spiritual Tourism*, ed. Daniel Olsen and Dallen J. Timothy (Routledge, 2021), 168–69.

80. Finney, *Black Faces, White Spaces*, 65–66.

81. Finney, *Black Faces, White Spaces*, 85. Also see the "Participant Guide" for a 2010 employee training course on "Locating and Recruiting Diverse Applicants for the National Park Service," accessed May 8, 2023, available at https://mylearning.nps.gov/wp-content/uploads/2016/08/Locating-and-Recruiting-Diverse-Applicants-for-the-National-Park-Service.pdf (URL no longer active).

82. See, for instance, executive order, Donald J. Trump, "Restoring Truth and Sanity to American History," The White House, March 27, 2025, accessed May 5, 2026, https://www.whitehouse.gov/presidential-actions/2025/03/restoring-truth-and-sanity-to-american-history/.

83. Du Bois, *Darkwater*, 4.

84. Claborn, "Du Bois at the Grand Canyon," 122–23.

85. Du Bois, *Darkwater*, 239–40.

Chapter 2

The Birth of the Cult Leader

Thomas Lake Harris, New Religions, and the American West

JOSHUA PADDISON

Keywords: cults, California, scandal, sexuality

On May 19, 1901, readers of the *San Francisco Call* found themselves face-to-face with Thomas Lake Harris, the infamous "prophet, seer, reformer, hypnotist, or what not." As drawn by *Call* illustrator Willis Thorndike, Harris sported long, unkempt hair and a pointed, graying beard. He wore the embroidered robes of a wizard, suggesting wealth, knowledge, and occult powers. His eyes were slightly crossed, making his gaze seem feverish or crazed. Arms outstretched, he appeared to be in a trance or perhaps in the middle of an arcane ritual. He stood in front of trees and a white-columned building, placing him at his Fountaingrove colony near Santa Rosa, California. Beneath each arm was an inset image of violence: a bullet whizzing by the head of Laurence Oliphant, Harris's former protégé—a near-miss Harris had supposedly prophesized—and the crumpled body of Harris's granddaughter Mary, who had killed herself at Fountaingrove in 1896. The illustrator, Thorndike, crammed in two more portraits: one, a profile of Harris wearing a more respectable-looking suit; the other, an image of "Prince Tokuma Konoye" (a misspelling of Kanaye Nagasawa), another of Harris's disciples.

Thorndike's dramatic, nearly full-page illustration accompanied an article marking "the passing of the world-famous 'Primate' Harris colony." After moving to New York City, Harris and his wife Jane Lee Waring Harris had transferred ownership of the Fountaingrove lands to several colonists. Hardly ground-shaking news, but the *Call* and other California newspapers had been providing the public with a steady diet of Fountaingrove-related stories for a decade, taking any opportunity to linger over details of what the *Call* article labeled "the weirdest communal scheme ever perpetrated." For Harris was "no ordinary man," the article reminded readers. "He was a human magnet who drew after him thousands of converts who were as clay in his hands, turning over to him all their worldly goods and obeying his dictates as humbly as a slave."[1]

The Passing Of The World Famous "PRIMATE" HARRIS COLONY

PRINCE YOKUMA NAGAOYE

A BULLET GRAZED HIS HAIR.

THOMAS LAKE HARRIS

ONE DAY SHE ATTEMPTED TO GAIN HER LIBERTY BY JUMPING FROM A TWENTY FOOT WINDOW

Figure 2.1 *San Francisco Call*, May 19, 1901.

Before Charles Manson, before Jim Jones, and before Father Yod, there was Thomas Lake Harris, California's first notorious cult leader. Beginning in 1891 and continuing until Harris's death in 1906, periodicals from San Francisco to London published thousands of articles attacking him, his movement, his theology, and even his poetry. Outsiders insisted that Harris was laughably bizarre yet powerfully charismatic, using occult powers of hypnotism to take financial and sexual advantage of his followers. Sometimes viewed as a calculating fraud and at other times as a delusional fanatic, Harris was always seen as dangerous, especially to young white women. Portrayed as a figure of violence and immorality, he twisted notions of family, perverted notions of spirituality, and defiled notions of community. His brainwashed victims deserved pity, but he deserved nothing but scorn (and prison). The presence of Japanese immigrant men at Fountaingrove only further cast Harris's movement as un-American, un-Christian, and racially suspect.

In all of these ways, press portrayals of Harris helped create and solidify modern notions of cults and cult leaders that were emerging in the early 1890s. The media firestorm around Harris did not singlehandedly create the modern conception of the cult leader, but it helped establish a set of signifiers that would come to define it in the popular imagination. These signifiers included important visual elements—most notably Harris's long beard, his robes, and his intense, "hypnotic" gaze—as well as traits that would thereafter be associated with cult leaders: his California commune, his dangerous charisma, his "bizarre" religious beliefs, his Orientalist "harem," his willful disruption of traditional marriage and family, and the danger he supposedly posed to young white women. The scandal surrounding Harris demonstrates how the term "cult" has always been a marker of race, sexuality, and religion, placing groups labeled cults outside the bounds of whiteness, acceptable family and sexual relations, and normative Protestant religion. As California's first example of a cult leader, Harris became a prototype for a category that would long be associated with the American West, emerging from and serving the needs of US empire-building.

The term "cult" is derived from the Latin word *cultus* and originally referred simply to religious veneration. For most of the nineteenth century, Americans used the word "cult" infrequently as a neutral synonym for sect, denomination, or religion.[2] It was in the early 1890s that "cult" began to take on derogatory meanings, applied to "primitive" or "heathen" religions practiced in Asia, Africa, and the Caribbean. British and American missionaries, scholars, and other writers began speaking of "Shinto cults," "Buddhist Tibetan cults," "Hindu cults," and "voodoo cults."[3] The demands of the British and US empires fueled this new concept of cults, working alongside and replacing older religio-racial categories of "heathen" and "pagan."[4] Unlike those broad categories, the term "cult" acknowledged differences between religious groups—a Shinto cult was different from a Hindu cult—while still casting them as illegitimate.

In the early 1890s, newspaper writers in the United States also began applying the word "cult" to certain homegrown religious movements outside the mainstream. Cyrus R. Teed, a colorful occult scientist, utopianist, and self-styled messiah in Chicago, inadvertently gave new religious movements like his a new name when he told a reporter from the *Chicago Daily Tribune* in 1890 that his was "a complete system of cult, universal in its scope." He used "cult" in its traditional meaning of religious veneration. The *Daily Tribune* ran "In Short, a 'Cult'" as a mocking subhead in the article, one of the first uses of the word in its newly emerging, derogatory definition.[5] Other newspapers around the United States reprinted the article, helping to spread the new meaning of the word.[6] A month later, the *Daily Tribune* complained of the "kaleidoscopic cults and crazes in this departing century," and soon cults seemed to be everywhere.[7] Christian Science, Theosophy, and the Church of Jesus Christ of Latter-day Saints became labeled as cults.[8] So did spiritualism.[9] Episcopalian minister Arthur Barrington published *The Anti-Christian Cults* in 1898, solidifying the term in the public consciousness. Barrington argued that Christian Science, Theosophy, and spiritualism were "false, subversive of the Christian faith, and totally unable to afford true comfort and consolation."[10]

Just as the new connotations of the word "cult" furthered the goals of US imperialism, they also proved useful for conservative Protestants attempting to consolidate an American Protestant identity and body politic. As such, the category of the "cult leader" began to supplant older terms like "enthusiast," "prophet," and "fanatic" to suggest—in the words of religion scholar Jennifer Graber—"fakery, deception of hapless followers, and promotion of dangerous politics."[11] Unlike older categories of religious demarcation, cults were, by definition, threats to the public; their existence demanded not missionization, as had been the case with "heathens," but suppression or even obliteration.

From the moment the modern category of cults was being formed, the American West—and California in particular—would be especially associated with cult activity. Just as Thomas Lake Harris moved his colony from upstate New York to California in 1875, many other communal and innovative religious movements moved west in search of freedom, cheap land, healthy climates, and escape from persecution. In so doing, they ironically became agents of the US empire, hastening Native dispossession alongside mainstream Christian churches. Most famously, Brigham Young led a group of Saints from Illinois to Utah in 1846 following the assassination of founder Joseph Smith. Decades earlier, both the Harmony Society and the Society of Separatists of Zoar had relocated from Pennsylvania to the then-frontier territories of Indiana and Ohio, respectively. Utopianist William Keil and his followers moved from Pennsylvania to Missouri to Oregon Territory, where they founded Aurora colony in 1856.[12]

As California's population exploded after 1848, it became a prime destination for all manner of spiritual groups. Perhaps the most religiously and ethnically diverse state in the nation, California earned a reputation for unorthodox thinking and heterogeneity despite the best efforts of Protestant missionaries and ministers.[13] Seeking a "way station" for Saints on the Pacific coast, Brigham Young authorized the formation of a colony at San Bernardino in 1851.[14] Spiritualism flourished in California, taking advantage of what one spiritualist deemed the state's unique "spirit of universal freedom of thought, expression, and action."[15] Touting California's salubrious "climate, soil, and scenery," a group of spiritualists founded the Summerland colony near Santa Barbara in 1888 as a haven for those seeking spiritual and physical restoration.[16] By the late 1880s, dozens of Theosophists, Christian Scientists, and other metaphysicians were lecturing, offering classes, and founding associations in the state.[17] California's reputation for freedom, opportunity, and innovation attracted new religious movements and placed the state at the center of emergent conceptions of cults and cult leaders.

Immigrants from China, and later from Japan and Korea, brought with them to California a variety of Asian religions that added to the state's singular religious landscape. The arrival of "joss houses" and Buddhist temples sparked widespread concerns about religio-racial "contamination" among many white Christians, but others were intrigued.[18] A Swedish-born metaphysician named Herman Vetterling founded the nation's first Buddhist newspaper, *The Buddhist Ray*, in Santa Cruz in 1888, drawing in elements from Swedenborgianism, Theosophy, and spiritualism. In the early 1890s, Theosophists sponsored lectures on Buddhism in San Francisco and Los Angeles, prompting a Protestant backlash.[19] "Buddhism is inferior to Christianity not only in that it is unprogressive, but in that it is highly personal and selfish," exclaimed the *San Francisco Examiner* in 1893.[20]

With its strong Asian presence and history of religious hybridity and experimentation, California would be ground zero for battles over "cults" from the very beginning of the category's existence. California had been militarily conquered, Protestantized, and "tamed" during the mid-nineteenth century, but those processes remained ongoing in the 1890s as cults emerged as the state's newest threat to America's moral order. Like the concept of the frontier—"the meeting point between savagery and civilization," according to Frederick Jackson Turner—the concept of the cult created a line between safe and dangerous, normative and deviant, and American and foreign.[21] It should be no surprise that many of the first groups labeled cults were in the West, for that is where white Protestant American control was most contested and where margins of race, religion, and sexuality required the most policing. As James Bennett shows elsewhere in this volume, the American West would remain a central arena of cult controversies well into the twentieth century and beyond.

The media scandal that surrounded Thomas Lake Harris in the 1890s occurred just as new ideas of cults were forming. California was by that point well on its way toward gaining a reputation for what Carey McWilliams would soon call its "fabled addiction to cults and cultists."[22] Newspapers were undergoing rapid changes in the 1890s as more and more papers began emulating Joseph Pulitzer's *New York World*, which pioneered the use of the "scandal story" to boost circulation. All scandals were good, explained Pulitzer's top editor, John Cockerill, but those involving a "fracture of the Vth, VIth, VIIth, VIIIth, or IXth Commandments" were best. By the early 1890s, publishers Charles and Michael de Young had made the *San Francisco Chronicle* the largest newspaper in the American West through often sensationalistic tactics, attacking public figures in proto-muckraking fashion. The *Chronicle* was locked in a circulation battle with William Randolph Hearst's *San Francisco Examiner*, which he had taken over from his father in 1887.[23] San Francisco had a reputation for being a "wide open town" in terms of personal freedoms, especially sexual freedoms, as discussed by Lynne Gerber in this volume.[24] However, historian Amy Sueyoshi has shown that mainstream newspapers generally enforced the "overwhelming white supremacy and heteropatriarchy that rigidly structured residents' imaginations and lived realities." Scandal stories sold newspapers and tended to reinforce the status quo by policing society's sexual, religious, and racial borders.[25]

The Harris scandal provided all the things Hearst, Pulitzer, the de Youngs, and other newspaper editors knew would make a compelling story: unusual religious doctrines shrouded in secrecy; unsavory sexual practices featuring white women and Asian men; and, in Harris, an evil villain with mysterious mental powers—all located in a peripheral setting, California, already associated with Asian culture, unruly behavior, and frontiers of religion, race, and sexuality. Harris became the quintessential California cult leader, establishing the basis of a pattern that would be repeated by the media throughout the twentieth century and beyond.

In addition to feeding this new, scandal-focused journalism, the Harris controversy also served the needs of certain onlookers. Surprisingly, it was Theosophists, spiritualists, Swedenborgians, and members of other metaphysical movements—rather than Protestant, Catholic, and Jewish leaders, who most hotly debated the scandal—with some voices defending Harris but most hastening to explain why their group was immune to such vulgarities lest they be similarly targeted as dangerous and un-American.[26] By policing the boundaries of their movements and distancing themselves from Harris, members of marginalized religions joined journalists, reformers, and Protestant ministers in creating the category of cults.

Thomas Lake Harris, Pivotal Man

Well before his rise to international infamy in the 1890s, Harris had been a polarizing figure within spiritualist circles for decades. Born in England in 1823, he grew up in Utica, New York, a focal point of the Second Great Awakening. At age fifteen he attended a revival meeting where "the presence of the Lord was manifested with a sense of quickening as of a new birth," he recalled later. He became filled by an "overflowing love of Christ," vowing to "devote my life to him."[27] After studying to be a Baptist minister, he broke with traditional Protestantism and embraced Universalism, in 1845 becoming pastor of a Universalist Church on Elizabeth Street in New York City. From there he dabbled in mesmerism before moving on to spiritualism, joining the small circle that surrounded the charismatic young medium Andrew Jackson Davis.[28]

Unlike most spiritualists, Harris rarely used the language of science to explain the supernatural. He considered himself a poet and seer, not a scientific investigator. Rather than framing his metaphysics in terms of empiricism, natural science, or the Enlightenment, Harris embraced the arcane, the emotional, and the erotic. This put him often out of step with other religious liberals and spiritual seekers. As Harris came into his own as a medium in the 1850s, his increasingly bold pronouncements about his divine powers further alienated many of his fellow travelers. In a series of cosmic trance poems, he declared himself a visionary who could tour the heavens at will and whose destiny it was to "shed / Celestial light on Earth." Throughout the remainder of his life, Harris—who began calling himself a "pivotal man"—would enter trance states to converse with God, commune with fairies, and do battle with demons.[29] Mainstream spiritualists responded by dubbing him a "fanatic."[30] Religion scholars have shown how a wide range of nineteenth-century religious movements—from Methodism to Adventism—used the concept of "fanaticism" as a means of boundary marking. Charges of fanaticism provided a language with which gatekeepers policed their ranks and purified their theologies. As such, Harris the fanatic was a precursor to Harris the cult leader.[31]

In the 1850s, he began establishing a doctrine that would later become notorious: "counterparts." According to Harris, "every human soul" had a match-soul—a counterpart—with which it was destined to be "conjoined / In sacramental marriage of the heart." Unlike other spiritualists, who often spoke of "soul mates," Harris insisted that people's (inevitably heterosexual) counterparts were not living people but spirits, those who had died and gone over to the celestial plane. Harris's counterpart was named Lily Queen, with whom he entered a spiritual marriage in 1854. Harris's poetic descriptions of Lily

Queen were rife with erotic undertones. "I began to glow in her sweet presence," Harris recorded. "My head on her translucent breast was pillowed. . . . I trembled as a dew-drop."[32]

Harris described his marriage to Lily Queen as akin to his experience as a teenager at the Utica revival: "I felt a new-born life in me begin." His mystical bond with Lily Queen would be a lifelong source of inspiration and authority for Harris. What Mary Van Arnum, his earthly wife since 1845 and the mother of his two sons, thought of this development is unknown, for during the composition of these works she grew gravely ill from tuberculosis and died. In 1856, Harris got remarried to a New Orleans spiritualist named Emily Isabella Waters, but at his insistence, Harris and Waters would never consummate the marriage.[33] In fact, after his marriage to Lily Queen, Harris became an advocate of strict celibacy; all sexual impulses were to be directed toward heavenly counterparts. "When a man is no longer entangled with women, he begins to long for a Social Kingdom of God," Harris would later explain. Human reproduction "must cease, 'til the sons and daughters of God are prepared for the higher generation, by evolution into structural, bisexual completeness, above the plane of sin, of disease, or of natural mortality." Celibacy helped "redeem" the body, Harris believed, by restoring it to a prelapsarian state that Adam and Eve had possessed before the fall.[34]

Harris's embrace of celibacy was a bigger departure from mainstream spiritualism than his belief in fairies or his grandiose prophesies. With their celebration of companionate marriage and procreation, spiritualists tended to be more "sex-positive" than the broader culture. But Harris was not alone in championing sexual self-control as a means of spiritual advancement. Sexual desire's potential to disrupt piety was in fact a widespread concern in nineteenth-century America. Catholic priests and nuns and Shakers practiced celibacy; many others, from Protestant minister Lyman Beecher to diet reformer Sylvester Graham, urged sexual restraint. Yet celibacy was transgressive; in the words of historian Kara French, proponents of celibacy "denaturalized the assumed naturalness of sex within marriage," and they—like the Fountaingrove colonists—found themselves facing accusations that "unmentionable sexual deviance" went on behind closed doors.[35]

What made Harris unique was his combining of celibacy with his doctrine of counterparts. On one hand, he urged total sexual self-control; on the other, he effused about the delights of counterpartal sex. "Soul-life and sex-life are at one, in the Divine their pulses run," he wrote. In another poem, he declared, "Unsexed existence weaves but desolation." Sex between people on earth was mere "bodily pleasure"—a fool's gold that distracted and corrupted the spirit. Sexual urges in themselves were not immoral, according to Harris, but they became so unless directed heavenward, to counterparts. Perhaps as a result of this sublimation, Harris's writings were more unabashedly erotic than most spiritualists even as he condemned carnal desires between the living. This unusual combination of sexuality and mysticism would eventually prove explosive.[36]

In 1859, Harris left New York for London, where he quickly raised the ire of British spiritualists because of his public lectures warning people away from séances, which he viewed as dangerous unless presided over by an "experienced self-crucified disciple of Christ" such as himself.[37] He then moved on to Scotland, where he founded the Brotherhood of the New Life, a name he would use thereafter to refer to his international group of followers. "Brotherhood" suggested the broad equality of all people; "new life" carried echoes of the "new birth" Harris had experienced as a teenager in Utica. Long interested in the Advent, Harris viewed the emergence of the Brotherhood of the New Life as a fulfillment of Biblical prophecy and a harbinger of the coming apocalypse. Rather than engage with this wicked world, the Brotherhood of the New Life would set itself apart: communal rather than competitive, rural rather than urban, sacred rather than profane.

Over the next six years, Harris established three agrarian colonies in succession in New York state, each larger than the previous: first at Wassaic, then in nearby Amenia, and finally in Brocton on the banks of Lake Erie. Members of the Brotherhood of the New Life pooled their finances to buy the land. Several, but by no means all, of Harris's followers were wealthy, most prominently Laurence Oliphant, the British diplomat who left politics to join Harris's movement. Other than Harris, who generally devoted his time to study, writing, and spiritual journeys, everyone in the Brotherhood engaged in physical labor. "Upon this base of industry, the temple of our spiritual work is now to stand," Harris explained.[38]

Harris continued to view celibacy as central to spiritual advancement, and most colonists embraced it. "They have become, in the natural sense, celibate as I am: some entering from a state of monogamic marriage, but others virginal from the first," Harris claimed.[39] He instructed his followers in a spiritual practice called "divine respiration"—a combination of deep breathing, prayer, and meditation—that helped practitioners overcome sexual desire and free their impulses from being "exaggerated and perverted to cupidities and lusts."[40] Most families lived together as a unit in the three New York colonies, but Harris at times urged family members to live separately when he thought their devotion to each other was a spiritual hindrance. "'Familism' was an evil to be broken down," one colonist later explained.[41] Some of the younger children present were raised communally: "They feel they have many Fathers and Mothers who all love them or are trying to do so, with an equal devotion," recorded Oliphant.[42]

While composing another of his trance-poems, Harris had a vision of himself, "in future time, as dwelling in the vicinage of the great forests of sequoia, near the Pacific, where, mingled with the sighing winds among the evergreens, might be heard the murmur of the not far distant ocean."[43] Like so many others, Harris looked westward for spiritual renewal and a chance to create heaven on earth. In February 1875, Harris and a few trusted acolytes took the overland railroad to California, purchasing a tract of land outside Santa Rosa for $20,000.[44] It supported itself at first as a dairy and poultry farm and then as a vineyard, helping to establish Sonoma's reputation as a top-notch wine area.[45] Harris named the new colony Fountaingrove. Here, unlike in earlier colonies, men and women were segregated into separate living quarters, with men in a building named the Commandery, women in the Familistery.[46] Fountaingrove also saw another innovation: communal bathing. In addition to its restorative physical effects, communal bathing encouraged a breaking down of people's feelings of modesty, embarrassment, and lust. "Our father says that before we can be in any true condition we must all be so innocent that we can stand naked before each other without a thought of shame, and wash and dress each other," wrote one woman at Fountaingrove.[47]

Among the initial colonists who traveled to California with Harris in 1875 were Kanaye Nagasawa and Ōsui Arai, two of the nearly twenty Japanese men who spent time in Harris's colonies in the late 1860s and 1870s. When Nagasawa was thirteen years old, he had been chosen by the Japanese government to be a part of a secret overseas mission to travel to Great Britain to learn about Western military strategy, agricultural practices, politics, and technology. In London, Nagasawa and the other Japanese student-spies met Laurence Oliphant and, through him, Harris, who offered to pay their passage to New York if they wanted to join the Brotherhood of the New Life. In 1867, Nagasawa and five other students gave up spying and took Harris up on his offer, becoming some of the very first Japanese immigrants to move to the United States. Ōsui Arai, who like Nagasawa hailed from a wealthy samurai family, joined the Brotherhood in 1871, and the two men became among Harris's most trusted and devoted disciples. At Fountaingrove, Harris put Nagasawa in charge of the planting and operation of the vineyard, and Arai ran the colony's print shop, which produced Harris's works of poetry and theology.[48]

Altogether, about thirty colonists lived at Fountaingrove during the 1880s, down from the Brotherhood's peak of nearly one hundred members at Brocton. They kept to themselves and attracted little attention from neighbors during these years, other than earning occasional positive coverage of their popular wines and general industriousness. In a local history of Sonoma County published in 1889, Harris won praise for "converting the apparently barren hills into lands teeming with wealth and abounding in beautiful homes."[49]

Fountaingrove, along with the rest of the Santa Rosa region, had once been part of a land grant given by Mexico to Maria Ygnacia Lopez de Carrillo in 1841. She had employed local Pomo men and women as laborers to herd cattle and grow wheat, corn, and beans. Like other Californio families, the Carrillo family slowly but surely lost title to their lands after the US military takeover and invasion.[50] Whatever else he was, Harris was part of the Anglo-Americanization of California as his efforts to create utopia overwrote the local Pomo and Mexican landscape.

Sex Scandal

The scandal that exploded in 1891 was initiated by two individuals who were, like Harris, spiritual seekers outside America's Protestant mainstream: a mental healer named Alzire Chevaillier and a Swedenborgian named Alfred Manning. Chevaillier was a moral reformer, suffragist, and mental healer from Boston who had taken classes in Christian Science from Mary Baker Eddy. Mentally and physical exhausted by her political reform work, she decided in 1891 to go to California to "seek the mysteries of God and of our own being on the mountain tops of the Sierra Nevadas." Intrigued by Harris's poetry, she wrote to him, hoping to "obtain board near him and receive the benefit of his instructions for a few months, that I might both become holier and be able to do more wisely a consecrated work for Humanity."[51] She and her mother, Sarah, spent the summer of 1891 in a mountain cabin on Harris's lands near Fountaingrove. She met with Harris several times that summer and left for Oakland in September, happy to have had what she called a "priceless privilege, a privilege never before extended, to be the guest of this man of God for nearly four months."[52]

Then she met Alfred Manning, vice president and librarian of the Swedenborg Library and Tract Society in San Francisco. Formally called the Church of the New Jerusalem, the Swedenborgians were a small but vocal Protestant sect, active in Europe and the United States, organized around the eighteenth-century Swedish mystic's writings. Since the 1850s, when Harris claimed to communicate directly with Emanuel Swedenborg's spirit, Swedenborgians had denounced Harris and mocked his "visits to Mars and the 'heaven girls.'"[53] Like many Swedenborgians, Manning had studied and ultimately rejected the visions of Harris as contrary to the writings of Swedenborg and the Bible. Manning had spent the past decade speaking to ex-members of the Brotherhood of the New Life and gathering their accounts and affidavits. He asked questions about finances—how much money and property they gave over to Harris. He asked about labor arrangements—how much they toiled compared to Harris. And he especially asked about sex—were the colonists truly celibate, as Harris maintained? Or did secret debauchery go on behind closed doors?

Virtually every utopian colony and new religion in nineteenth-century America faced insinuations of licentiousness at one point or another. Sensationalized books such as John B. Ellis's *Free Love and Its Votaries; or, American Socialism Unmasked* had made the Oneida colony in upstate New York—and utopianism more broadly—synonymous with sexual immorality and the destruction of Christian marriage.[54] During the 1880s, attacks on Mormon polygamy had reached a fever pitch as hundreds of Saints were imprisoned after passage of the Edmunds Anti-Polygamy Act of 1882. This persecution was done in the name of saving women from polygamous "slavery" as well as saving the nation from religious defilement.[55] Harris's colonies had encountered much less hostility from outsiders compared to members of the Oneida community and Saints but some rumors about sexual improprieties had circulated among neighbors in New York. At Brocton in 1869, Laurence Oliphant mentioned in a letter that "attacks upon the purity of the life continue to reach us from various directions. The 'movement' is said to be 'more odious in its character than that of Brigham Young.'"[56]

Manning turned over his stack of letters and affidavits to Chevaillier, which she reluctantly agreed to read. She read, and she believed. Her public gushings of praise for Harris and for the "happy and harmonious" people at Fountaingrove now made her burn with "humiliation." She had made a terrible "blunder," she now saw, "in so widely commending this remarkable two-sided man, an angel of light and an angel of darkness, bringing moral wreck and ruin."[57] As so many other pioneers—spiritual and otherwise—had discovered, going West brought not just freedoms and opportunities but moral dangers and corruptions. Chevaillier now saw the California dream of spiritual renewal to be a California nightmare of moral ruin.

She spent the next six months in a single-minded crusade to expose Harris as a dangerous "hypnotist" who took advantage of the "dupes" he lured into his Fountaingrove "lair." Initially in the pages of the *San Francisco Chronicle* and other publications, and then in public lectures, she informed the world that while Harris dined on "oysters and champagne," his colonists ate the "plainest kind of food." His followers had turned over great sums of money to Harris and had to live "under his severe ordinances." But the most explosive charges Chevaillier made revolved around sex, specifically how Harris's ideas of counterparts led to unholy acts of sexual license. "This accursed doctrine of the counterparts is worse than anything ever revealed as to the Utah and Oneida practices," she said. "It is a new sexology, holding the virus of a refined and subtle sensualism in whose web many a pure soul has become hopelessly entangled." According to Chevaillier, Harris "permitted" people's spiritual counterparts to "descend and take material form in whatever woman he may see fit." This led to "horrible immorality": communal bathing, orgies, and partner swapping, all overseen by Harris, including "a boy of seventeen being ordered by Mr. Harris to co-habit six times a day with a married woman"; "old men with young women and young men with old women"; and, to hide pregnancies, "kneading and pounding [of] the women to produce abortion."[58]

Chevaillier's talk of "Hypnotist Harris" played on public concerns about mesmerism and hypnotism that had simmered for decades. Newspapers routinely roused fears of villainous hypnotists who misused their occult powers to take financial or sexual advantage of, usually, women.[59] For example, the *San Francisco Call*, chasing the *Chronicle* and *Examiner* in circulation, had recently published an article with titillating illustrations describing how hypnotists could take complete control of women's bodies.[60] In California, stage hypnotists were coming under suspicion for causing madness and imbecility; legal experts debated how to handle crimes committed by hypnotized people as if this was a common occurrence; and Protestant ministers speculated about whether it was "divine power" or "purely magnetic or psychological forces" at work. These cultural concerns would soon take fictional form in the character of Svengali, the hypnotist villain of George du Maurier's wildly popular novel *Trilby*, serialized in *Harper's Monthly* in 1894.[61]

In fact, Harris had rejected mesmerism after dabbling in it in the late 1840s. However, because he seemed to have powerful influence over others, Chevaillier and the media labeled him a hypnotist. The figure of the evil hypnotist was powerful in part because it offered an explanation for why people like Laurence Oliphant—wealthy, educated white people—devoted years of their life to communal living and a strange religion. Decades later, a similar explanation would be offered by anti-cultists and the media in the 1970s: namely, that people who joined new religious movements were "brainwashed" by cult leaders. The assumption behind both the hypnotism and brainwashing tropes was that no one—especially well-to-do white people—would willingly join a colony or movement outside the religious mainstream.[62] As historian Rebecca Davis has observed, concerns about hypnotism and brainwashing revealed wider anxieties about "possible weaknesses within the American psyche that exposed the mind to subjugation."[63] If anyone could be brainwashed, no one was safe.

Chevaillier reassured readers that she herself "saw no impurities at Fountaingrove." However, she was satisfied that "ninety-nine out of every hundred girls who might be drawn under the spell of this wonderful and unscrupulous hypnotizer and mesmerist could by no means on earth escape from his power, and they would be dragged down to ruin." Only the presence of her mother, together with a "will that is stronger than that of most girls," saved Chevaillier from that ruin. "I trusted myself in the lion's den, and with these great safeguards I could defy the beast," she reported. "This lion's den is still open, and into it may be thrust many other women."[64] Her focus on protecting young white women from ruin was consistent with older anti-Mormon and anti-Catholic narratives as well as Chevaillier's own history of moral reform work. In Boston and New York, Chevaillier had striven to protect society's most vulnerable members—the mentally ill, prisoners, workers, the poor, children, and women. Her ongoing work in the female-dominated field of mental healing was also part of these endeavors. By presenting herself as a caretaker of California's young white women, Chevaillier put herself in the role of maternalistic protector of virtue and purity.

The idea of saving young white women from sexual and moral peril also resonated with cultural anxieties about prostitution that were rising in the 1890s. Anti-prostitution reformers were beginning to use the term "white slavery" to dramatize the plight of urban female prostitutes "enslaved" by corrupt male pimps and traffickers. This new focus on "saving" young white women from a life in sex slavery was a shift in rhetoric from earlier campaigns that had demonized prostitutes, often portrayed as racialized immigrants, as threats to public health and morality.[65] In San Francisco, the Pacific Society for the Suppression of Vice would soon form in 1893 to curb prostitution due to mounting concerns that "white slavery" was "dragging, driving, drawing, duping" the city's "daughters" to "infamy."[66] Chevaillier's focus on saving young white women from the "lion's den" of sex and sin at Fountaingrove drew power from these broader fears of unchecked male power and fragile white womanhood, fears that journalists were amplifying during this period through high-profile exposés of prostitution similar to Chevaillier's campaign.[67] "Already I think I have saved a number of girls from going there to be introduced to his licentious system of counterparts," she boasted.[68] This shows that cults have always been defined not just by their leaders but by their followers. From Fountaingrove to the Manson girls to NXIVM, white women, tragically misled and endangered by a corrupt male leader, were an essential part of what comprised a cult.

Chevaillier's allegations about Fountaingrove quickly garnered headlines across the Atlantic world. To ensure maximum exposure, she gave an interview to a reporter from Joseph Pulitzer's *New York World*, which ran it under the headline "Worse than Mormons." Versions of her account appeared in newspapers large and small, from Galveston, Texas, to Wheeling, Pennsylvania.[69] In Britain, where Laurence Oliphant's fame had been much larger than in the United States, at least twelve newspapers ran summaries of Chevaillier's account in the first week of the scandal alone.[70]

Several news accounts employed the word "cult" in its newly emerging, modern sense. An editor for the *Patriot* of Harrisburg, Pennsylvania, took the Harris scandal as an opportunity to lambast all the "cults and isms" that had proliferated in nineteenth-century America. "Nine-tenths of such communities, wherever found, are either blasphemous or lewd," thundered the *Patriot*. "The leaders of these communities are all swindlers, and some of them a curse to society and a shame to the name of religion."[71] The *London Anti-Jacobin* announced with concern that the "Harris cult is amazingly on the increase, and that the cult is likely to take on the proportions of a boom." This piece, reprinted in the *San Francisco Chronicle*, stirred up fears that the "Harris cult" was spreading, preying on "that motley crowd of zealots who revel in the new and strange."[72] According to the *New York Times*, cults led by "Harris and other prophets of his sort" could reliably be identified by "the absence of clothes in both sexes."[73]

As Fountaingrove became "the Harris cult," some editors put the blame on not cult leaders but followers for their naivete, upon which "such impostors as Harris count."[74] The *San Francisco Wave* righteously called for the Grand Jury of Sonoma County and the governor of California to investigate the "iniquitous debaucheries" of Fountaingrove, where "both sexes of one family bed together like dogs in a kennel."[75] According to the *Kalamazoo Gazette*, Harris's teachings threatened to destroy "the sanctity of Christian marriages" and the "Christian family relation."[76]

As the story spread from newspaper to newspaper, an artist added an illustration of Harris that became appended to many accounts. He is shown dining on raw oysters and champagne. He wears a Moroccan-style fez hat with tassel, reminiscent of Ottomans as well as semi-secret masonic groups in the United States such as the Shriners, founded in 1872, who wore the fez. With his decadent meal, fez, and long beard—a style of facial hair often associated with Eastern Orthodox Christianity, Islam, and Hinduism—Harris was portrayed as an Asiatic sultan complete with harem. At the same time, the illustration mocked Harris as foolish—a laughable false prophet "not like Christ," as a common headline trumpeted.[77]

Reflecting the new 1890s religio-racial connotations of the term "cult," media accounts portrayed Fountaingrove in Orientalist terms. According to Chevaillier, "Fountaingrove was no fit place for any one who had not first been a follower of Mohammed or other sensualist of equal power."[78] Colonists, she said, dressed "in the most Sybaritic fashion imaginable," straight out of Frederic Leighton's 1880 Orientalist painting *The Light of the Harem*.[79] By calling Harris specifically "fakir" and "prophet," the media drew on a tradition of Islamophobic discourse that linked Harris to the original "false prophet," Muhammad.[80] Similarly, by comparing Fountaingrove to Mormon Utah, the media tapped into a long history of anti-Mormon rhetoric that frequently depicted Mormons as Orientalized agents of interracial mixing due to their religious and sexual practices.[81] As scholar K. Mohrman has argued, Protestant outsiders labeled the Mormons "'peculiar,' 'barbaric,' and 'foreign,' consequently constructing them as racially and civilizationally inferior."[82] Calling Fountaingrove "worse than Mormons" conjured up powerful religious, racial, and sexual associations.

The presence of Japanese men at Fountaingrove added an element of potential miscegenation to the scandal, invoking more fears of racial impurity. If unbridled "free love" was happening at Fountaingrove, then must not interracial sex between white women and Japanese men be happening as well?[83] In 1880, California had banned intermarriage between whites and "Mongolians," a term that proved broad enough to apply to both Chinese and Japanese Americans.[84] Public concern would soon rise about Japanese "houseboys" who were supposedly seducing white women in their homes.[85] In the Fountaingrove scandal, media reports made much of the co-ed bathing, often called "Japanese bathing," that went on there. In Meiji Japan, mixed bathing was on the decline by the 1890s, but the practice had appalled American visitors for decades.[86] The specter of Japanese men bathing and potentially having sex with white women intensified public scrutiny on Fountaingrove while casting the colony as deviant. As Chrissy Yee Lau's essay in this volume demonstrates, these religio-racial fears about Japanese immigration would remain central to California politics for decades.

The Fountaingrove scandal was started by a mental healer and a Swedenborgian in Chevaillier and Manning, and it was extended through the efforts of other metaphysicians who leaped into the media fray. Seeking publicity, Cyrus Teed—the Chicago messiah who had helped popularize the new meaning of "cult" in his 1890 interview—defended Harris's honor and even paid a visit to Fountaingrove in 1892 in the hopes of forming a "confederation" with the Brotherhood of the New Life.[87] On the other side, the *New Church Pacific*, San Francisco's Swedenborgian journal, went on record to back up Chevaillier's accusations. According to its editor, Harris's "rottenness" was "long known" to Swedenborgians. Only Chevaillier's "innate purity" and "sublime effort of will which few are able to use" had saved her from his hypnotic powers.[88]

Theosophists likewise joined the chorus against Harris. A Theosophist named Jerome Anderson introduced Chevaillier before her lecture in San Francisco and supported her charges against Harris in his journal, the *New Californian*.[89] British Theosophists had previously criticized Harris's "false mysticism" and complained when outsiders put movement founder Helen Blavatsky and Harris "side by side as guides and prophets."[90] In the wake of

Chevaillier's new charges, national Theosophist leader William Q. Judge in New York lambasted Harris's "disgusting doctrines" and emphasized that "the Theosophical Society has nothing in common" with Harris. "Our Society must be kept as free as possible from being mixed up with these enterprises," Judge insisted.[91]

Spiritualists likewise publicly distanced themselves from Harris, the culmination of his troubled relationship with mainstream spiritualism dating back to the 1850s. Chicago's *Progressive Thinker* printed Chevaillier's accusations, adding, "Verily, what next?"[92] Henry Lafayette Williams, leader of the Summerland colony near Santa Barbara, felt compelled to affirm his community's commitment to keeping it "free from all sensualists." With Harris's spiritualist colony now dominating the headlines, Williams wanted to address the "numerous inquiries I have received, as to whether this is a free-love colony." Summerland, he insisted, housed only "those whose aspirations are higher than the gratification of the animal nature." He tolerated no "free-lovers," nor "confirmed sots," a reference to Fountaingrove's vineyards.[93]

All of these movements, from Christian Science and its offshoots, with which Chevaillier was involved, to Theosophy and spiritualism, had been targeted at one time or another with charges of practicing "free love" and undermining Christian family values. The US government had criminalized the circulation of "obscene" and "immoral" materials in 1873, especially targeting spiritualist-inspired sex radicalism for prosecution. For years, US postal inspector Anthony Comstock hounded Victoria Woodhull, a spiritualist, woman's rights activist, and "varietist" who sanctioned serial monogamy in the pursuit of true love. Dubbed "Mrs. Satan" by cartoonist Thomas Nast, Woodhull and free love were caricatured in the press as dangerous and demonic.[94] By the 1880s, most spiritualists, freethinkers, and feminists were distancing themselves from the taint of free love.[95] The Harris scandal provided a new opportunity for marginalized groups to affirm their dedication to mainstream American values of monogamy, marriage, and family. Meanwhile, California's Protestant press refrained from commenting on the scandal.[96] Though it is safe to assume that Protestant leaders disapproved of Harris and his teachings, they felt no danger of being tainted by association in the way that metaphysical movements clearly did.

Conclusion

The initial phase of the scandal ended in March 1892 when Harris left California, never to return. Chevaillier moved on to other issues, eventually moving to Los Angeles and becoming involved in prison reform and what was then being called the New Thought movement. California newspapers remained interested in the goings-on at Fountaingrove, however, and a new scandal erupted in 1896 when Harris's fifteen-year-old granddaughter Mary was found dead from strychnine poisoning at Fountaingrove. Media reports speculated that she had killed herself because she "loathed free love" and preferred death to being assigned a counterpart by her grandfather. The *San Francisco Chronicle* blamed her suicide on her forced isolation and the physical labor she supposedly endured at Fountaingrove, concluding, "The blood of this child is upon the heads of those at Fountaingrove who were responsible for trying to break her spirit."[97] According to the papers, Kanaye Nagasawa—whom the *San Francisco Call* labeled Fountaingrove's "little, shrewd-faced, black-eyed manager"—drove the girl to her death by enforcing Harris's rules.[98] Taken together, the stories swirling around Mary's death warned that cults like Fountaingrove took more than young women's chastity and freedom—they could take those young women's lives as well.

By the time of Harris's death in 1906, California newspapers were becoming filled with accounts of "cult leaders" using their "hypnotism" to defraud and seduce followers, especially young white women. Some of those labeled cult leaders in the early twentieth century were white but many were African Americans or Asian immigrants, further solidifying the racial and religious dimensions of the category.[99] From the Fountaingrove scandal onward, the category of the cult operated as a way of demonizing certain groups as dangerous in terms of religion, race, gender, and sexuality. The category was created and sustained by newspapers chasing readers, activists striving to "rescue" victims, ministers condemning "false" religions, authorities protecting what they consider public morality, and members of minority religions hoping to avoid being labeled a cult themselves. The modern concept of the cult began in the early 1890s, grew in power throughout the early twentieth century, erupted into a public "crisis" in the 1970s, and shows no sign of diminishing in the twenty-first century. Lurking on the perilous margins of religion, sex, gender, race, and nation, cults continue to frighten and fascinate us in equal measure.

Notes

1. *San Francisco Call*, May 19, 1901, 5. This essay is adapted from Joshua Paddison, *Unholy Sensations: A Story of Sex, Scandal, and California's First Cult Scare* (Oxford University Press, 2025).

2. Hugh G. Urban, *New Age, Neopagan, and New Religious Movements: Alternative Spirituality in Contemporary America* (University of California Press, 2015), 8; Timothy Miller, "Are the Cult Wars Over? And If So, Who Won?," in *"Cult Wars" in Historical Perspective: New and Minority Religions*, ed. Eugene V. Gallagher (Routledge, 2017), 33–42.

3. Philip Jenkins, *Mystics and Messiahs: Cults and New Religions in American History* (Oxford University Press, 2000), 48–49; *Raleigh Christian Advocate*, January 17, 1894, 1; Lafcadio Hearn, *Glimpses of Unfamiliar Japan*, vol. 2 (Houghton, Mifflin, 1894), 385; *Baptist Missionary Review* 4 (1898): 404; L. Austine Waddell, *The Buddhism of Tibet* (Luzac & Co., 1899); *Tacoma News Tribune*, March 7, 1891, 8; *Literary Digest*, December 11, 1897, 983.

4. On "heathen," see Joshua Paddison, *American Heathens: Religion, Race, and Reconstruction in California* (University of California Press, 2012); and Kathryn Gin Lum, *Heathen: Religion and Race in American History* (Harvard University Press, 2022). I agree with Jolyon Baraka Thomas that American notions of religion were profoundly shaped by "imperial encounters in the American West and the Pacific"; see Jolyon Baraka Thomas, *Faking Liberties: Religious Freedom in American-Occupied Japan* (University of Chicago Press, 2019), 79.

5. *Chicago Daily Tribune*, July 20, 1890, 26.

6. *Cincinnati Enquirer*, July 16, 1890, 6; *Spokane Falls Review*, July 7, 1890, 11.

7. *Chicago Daily Tribune*, August 3, 1890, 26.

8. On Christian Science becoming a cult, see *San Francisco Call*, December 14, 1891, 1; J. J. Taylor, *The Christian Science Cult* (American Baptist Publication Society, 1894); *Coconino Weekly Sun* (Flagstaff, AZ), November 21, 1895, 6; and *Copper Country Evening News*, May 6, 1896, 1. On Theosophy, see *Indianapolis Journal*, March 9, 1891, 4; *Spokane Review*, August 15, 1891, 4; *York Daily* (York, PA), July 25, 1893, 2; and *Madison Daily Leader*, March 2, 1894, 4. On Mormons, see *Calgary Weekly Herald*, August 6, 1890, 2; *London Pall Mall Gazette*, June 16, 1893, 11; and *Minneapolis Journal*, October 30, 1899, 4.

9. *Seattle Post-Intelligencer*, February 3, 1895, 7; *New York Sun*, December 27, 1895, 5; *San Francisco Call*, May 27, 1896, 10.

10. A. H. Barrington, *The Anti-Christian Cults* (Young Churchman Co., 1898), 9.

11. Jennifer Graber, "Beyond Prophecy: Native Visionaries in American Religious Studies," *American Religion* 2 (2020): 44.

12. Paul Kagan, *New World Utopias: A Photographic History of the Search for Community* (Penguin Books, 1975); James J. Kopp, *Eden Within Eden: Oregon's Utopian Heritage* (Oregon State University, 2009), 34–50.

13. Sandra Sizer Frankiel, *California's Spiritual Frontiers: Religious Alternatives in Anglo-Protestantism, 1850–1910* (University of California Press, 1988); John K. Simmons and Brian Wilson, *Competing Visions of Paradise: The California Experience of 19th Century American Sectarianism* (Fithian Press, 1993); Laurie F. Maffly-Kipp, *Religion and Society in Frontier California* (Yale University Press, 1994).

14. Edward Leo Lyman, "The Rise and Decline of Mormon San Bernardino," *Brigham Young University Studies* 29 (1989): 43–63.

15. *Banner of Light*, June 30, 1866, 3.

16. *The Problem of Life*, 1 no. 1 (January 1890): 41; Molly McGarry, *Ghosts of Futures Past: Spiritualism and the Cultural Politics of Nineteenth-Century America* (University of California Press, 2008), 60–63.

17. *Sacramento Daily Union*, September 28, 1886, 3; *Los Angeles Daily Herald*, May 20, 1888, 3; *San Francisco Daily Alta California*, June 4, 1888, 2; *San Jose Daily Mercury*, October 15, 1888, 3; *Harmony* 1, no. 1 (1888); *San Francisco Daily Alta California*, June 11, 1889, 5; Rolf Swenson, "Pilgrims at the Golden Gate: Christian Scientists on the Pacific Coast,

1880–1915," *Pacific Historical Review* 72 (2003): 229–63; Frankiel, *California's Spiritual Frontiers*, 68–78.

18. Laurie Maffly-Kipp, "Engaging Habits and Besotted Idolatry: Viewing Chinese Religions in the American West," in *Race, Religion, Region: Landscapes of Encounter in the American West*, ed. Fay Botham and Sara M. Patterson (University of Arizona Press, 2006), 60–88; Paddison, *American Heathens.*

19. *Buddhist Ray* 1, no. 1 (January 1888); *San Francisco Call*, September 28, 1891, 8; *Los Angeles Herald*, May 9, 1892, 8; *San Francisco Call*, December 16, 1894, 11; Thomas A. Tweed, *The American Encounter with Buddhism, 1844–1912: Victorian Culture and the Limits of Dissent* (Indiana University Press, 1992), 31–32.

20. Reprinted in *Auburn Placer Argus*, August 19, 1892, 6.

21. Frederick Jackson Turner, "The Significance of the Frontier in American History," *Annual Report of the American Historical Association for the Year 1893* (Government Printing Office, 1894), 200.

22. Carey McWilliams, *Southern California: An Island on the Land* (Duell, Sloan & Pearce, 1946), 249.

23. Gray Brechin, *Imperial San Francisco: Urban Power, Earthly Ruin* (University of California Press, 2006), 173–78; Christopher B. Daly, *Covering America: A Narrative History of a Nation's Journalism* (University of Massachusetts Press, 2012), 123, 130–31; Dennis Brian, *Pulitzer: A Life* (John Wiley & Sons, 2001), 2.

24. Nan Alamilla Boyd, *Wide-Open Town: A History of Queer San Francisco to 1965* (University of California Press, 2005); Clare Sears, *Arresting Dress: Cross-Dressing, Law, and Fascination in Nineteenth-Century San Francisco* (Duke University Press, 2015).

25. Amy Sueyoshi, *Discriminating Sex: White Leisure and the Making of the American "Oriental"* (University of Illinois Press, 2018), 32.

26. On the category of "metaphysical," see Catherine L. Albanese, *A Republic of Mind and Spirit: A Cultural History of Metaphysical Religion in America* (Yale University Press, 2007), 6–16.

27. Richard McCully, *The Brotherhood of the New Life and Thomas Lake Harris* (John Thomson, 1893), 1–20; Arthur A. Cuthbert, *The Life and World-Work of Thomas Lake Harris, Written from Direct Personal Knowledge* (C. W. Pearce & Co., 1908), 86; Thomas Lake Harris, "An Autobiographic Letter from T. L. Harris," 1896, reel 7, item 55, *Thomas Lake Harris and the Brotherhood of the New Life: Books, Pamphlets, Serials and Manuscripts, 1854–1942*, microfilm (New York Times, 1974).

28. *Utica Evangelical Magazine and Gospel Advocate*, October 18, 1844, 334; *Boston Universalist Miscellany* 3 (April 1846): 404; *Boston Trumpet and Universalist Magazine*, September 12, 1846, 49–50; Andrew Jackson Davis, *The Magic Staff: An Autobiography* (J. S. Brown & Co., 1857), 342.

29. Thomas Lake Harris, *A Lyric of the Morning Land* (Partridge and Brittan, 1854), 208, 244, 246.

30. Ephraim W. Capron, *Modern Spiritualism: Its Facts and Fanaticisms* (Bela Marsh, 1855), 131; Emma Hardinge, *Modern American Spiritualism: A Twenty Years' Record of the Communion Between Earth and the World of Spirits* (1870), 58–59, 207–13.

31. Ann Taves, *Fits, Trances, and Visions: Experiencing Religion and Explaining Experience from Wesley to James* (Princeton University Press, 1999), 165; Robert Wuthnow, *American Misfits and the Making of Middle-Class Respectability* (Princeton University Press,

2017), 101–34; Jeffrey Wheatley, "Nat Turner and the Affective Power of Religious Fanaticism," *Political Theology* 25 (2023): 171–85; Jeffrey Wheatley, *American Fanatics: Religion, Rebellion, and Empire in the Nineteenth Century* (New York University Press, 2026).

32. Harris, *A Lyric of the Morning Land*, 48–49.

33. Thomas Lake Harris, *A Lyric of the Golden Age* (Partridge and Brittan, 1856), 4; Samuel Byron Brittan, ed., *The Spiritual Telegraph*, library ed. (Partridge and Brittan, 1854), 405; Herbert W. Schneider and George Lawton, *A Prophet and a Pilgrim: Being the Incredible History of Thomas Lake Harris and Laurence Oliphant* (Columbia University Press, 1942), 20; Melissa Daggett, *Spiritualism in Nineteenth-Century New Orleans: The Life and Times of Henry Louis Rey* (University Press of Kentucky), 2017, 25.

34. Thomas Lake Harris, "Some Ways of the Evil Woman," n.d., reel 8, item 203, *Thomas Lake Harris and the Brotherhood of the New Life: Books, Pamphlets, Serials and Manuscripts, 1854–1942*, microfilm (New York Times, 1974); William Alfred Hinds, *American Communities* (Office of the American Socialist, 1878), 146.

35. Kara M. French, *Against Sex: Identities of Sexual Restraint in Early America* (University of North Carolina Press, 2021), 3–4.

36. Thomas Lake Harris, *Veritas: A Word Song* (C. W. Pearce & Co., 1910), 2; Thomas Lake Harris, *The Marriage of Heaven and Earth* (C. W. Pearce & Co., 1903), 234.

37. Thomas Lake Harris, *Modern Spiritualism: Its Truth and Errors* (W. White, 1860); *London Morning Advertiser*, January 16, 1860, 5.

38. *The Herald of Light*, November 1861, 12.

39. Hinds, *American Communities*, 143–46.

40. Thomas Lake Harris, *Brotherhood of the New Life: Letter from Thomas Lake Harris, with Passing Reference to Recent Criticisms* (Fountaingrove Press, 1891), 4.

41. *International Psychic Gazette*, July 1916, 312.

42. Laurence Oliphant to Georgina Cowper, July 18, 1869, *Harris–Oliphant Papers*, Rare Book & Manuscript Library, Columbia University.

43. Thomas Lake Harris, "Localities: March of Events," n.d., *Harris–Oliphant Papers*, Rare Book & Manuscript Library, Columbia University.

44. *San Francisco Daily Alta California*, February 24, 1875, 1; *Sonoma Democrat*, July 31, 1875, 5; *Santa Rosa Daily Democrat*, November 23, 1875, 3.

45. *Pacific Rural Press*, February 14, 1880, 109; Thomas Pinney, *A History of Wine in America: From the Beginnings to Prohibition* (University of California Press, 1989), 334.

46. Schneider and Lawton, *A Prophet and a Pilgrim*, 301.

47. "Experiences of a Sister in the New Life," in Schneider and Lawton, *A Prophet and a Pilgrim*, 519.

48. Ivan Parker Hall, *Mori Arinori* (Harvard University Press, 1973); Gaye LeBaron, *The Japanese "Baron" of Fountaingrove* (Santa Rosa Junior College, 1976); Paul Akiria Kadota and Terry Earl Jones, *Kanaye Nagasawa: A Biography of a Satsuma Student* (Kagoshima Prefectural Junior College, 1990); Andrew Cobbing, *The Satsuma Students in Britain: Japan's Early Search for the "Essence of the West"* (Curzon Press, 2000); John E. Van Sant, *Pacific Pioneers: Japanese Journeys to America and Hawaii, 1850–80* (University of Illinois Press, 2000), 79–96; Chinami Oka, "Arai Ōsui and the Transnational Reimagination of Civilization in the Late Nineteenth-Century United States," *Historical Journal* 65 (2022): 1–21.

49. *An Illustrated History of Sonoma County* (Lewis Publishing Company, 1889), 366.

50. *Sonoma County Journal*, August 14, 1857, 3; *Santa Rosa Democrat*, October 31, 1889, 3.

51. *Chicago New Church Independent*, July 1892, 335.

52. "Editorial Notes," *Problem of Life and International Magazine of Truth*, September–October 1891, 395.

53. *Springfield Republican*, August 28, 1858.

54. John B. Ellis, *Free Love and Its Votaries; or, American Socialism Unmasked* (United States Publishing Company, 1870); Carol Faulkner, *Unfaithful: Love, Adultery, and Marriage Reform in Nineteenth-Century America* (University of Pennsylvania Press, 2019), 136–39.

55. Sarah Barringer Gordon, *The Mormon Question: Polygamy and Constitutional Conflict in Nineteenth-Century America* (University of North Carolina Press, 2002).

56. Laurence Oliphant to William Cowper, January 3, 1869, *Harris–Oliphant Papers*, Rare Book & Manuscript Library, Columbia University.

57. Alzire A. Chevaillier, "An Open Letter to William Dean Howells," *California Illustrated World*, March 1892; Alzire A. Chevaillier, "Laurence Oliphant and the Primate," *International Magazine of Truth*, January 1892, 6.

58. *San Francisco Chronicle*, December 13, 1891, 10; Chevaillier, "An Open Letter to William Dean Howells."

59. *New York Times*, January 11, 1891, 2; Edward M. Brown, "Neurology and Spiritualism in the 1870s," *Bulletin of the History of Medicine* 57 (1983): 563–77.

60. *San Francisco Call*, July 13, 1890, 6.

61. *Sacramento Daily Union*, April 3, 1890, 2; May 4, 1890, 2; June 12, 1890, 2; *Santa Rosa Daily Democrat*, September 30, 1891, 1; *San Francisco Evening Bulletin*, December 15, 1891, 1. On broader cultural concerns about hypnosis in the transatlantic world, see Andreas-Holger Maehle, "History of Hypnotism in Europe and the Significance of Place," *Notes and Records: The Royal Society Journal of the History of Science* 71 (2017): 119–23; Alan Gauld, *A History of Hypnotism* (Cambridge University Press, 1992); Alison Winter, *Mesmerized: Powers of Mind in Victorian Britain* (University of Chicago Press, 1998); Daniel Pick, *Svengali's Web: The Alien Enchanter in Modern Culture* (Yale University Press, 2000); Fred Nadis, *Wonder Shows: Performing Science, Magic, and Religion in America* (Rutgers University Press, 2005), 97–112; W. Hughes, *That Devil's Trick: Hypnotism and the Victorian Popular Imagination* (Manchester University Press, 2015); and Emily Ogden, *Credulity: A Cultural History of U S. Mesmerism* (University of Chicago Press, 2018).

62. On the origins and historiography of "brainwashing" in cults, see Benjamin Zablocki, "Towards a Demystified and Disinterested Scientific Theory of Brainwashing," in *Misunderstanding Cults: Searching for Objectivity in a Controversial Field*, ed. Benjamin Zablocki and Thomas Robbins (University of Toronto Press, 2001), 159–214; and Elizabeth Aileen Young, "The Use of the 'Brainwashing' Theory by the Anti-Cult Movement in the United States of America, pre-1996," *Zeitschrift für junge Religionswissenschaft* 7 (2012): 5–19.

63. Rebecca L. Davis, *Public Confessions: The Religious Conversions That Changed American Politics* (University of North Carolina Press, 2021), 90.

64. *San Francisco Chronicle*, December 20, 1891, 4.

65. John D'Emilio and Estelle B. Freedman, *Intimate Matters: A History of Sexuality in America*, 2nd ed. (University of Chicago Press, 1997), 208–15; Alex Smolak, "White Slavery, Whorehouse Riots, Venereal Disease, and Saving Women: Historical Context of Prostitution Interventions and Harm Reduction in New York City during the Progressive

Era," *Social Work in Public Health*, 28 (2013): 496–508; Jessica R. Pliley, *Policing Sexuality: The Mann Act and the Making of the FBI* (Harvard University Press, 2014), 9–31; Jessica R. Pliley, "From White Slavery to Anti-Prostitution, the Long View: Law, Policy, and Sex Trafficking," in *Human Bondage and Abolition: New Histories of Past and Present Slaveries*, ed. Elizabeth Swanson and James Brewer Stewart (Cambridge University Press, 2018), 190–218.

66. *San Francisco Call*, March 20, 1891, 2; October 22, 1893, 13; November 29, 1893, 2; Sueyoshi, *Discriminating Sex*, 74–80.

67. Gretchen Soderlund, *Sex Trafficking, Scandal, and the Transformation of Journalism, 1885–1917* (University of Chicago Press, 2013).

68. *San Francisco Chronicle*, December 27, 1891, 1.

69. *New York World*, December 13, 1891, 7; *New York Tribune*, December 13, 1891, 4; *Wheeling Register*, December 15, 1891, 1; *Galveston Daily News*, December 17, 1891, 3.

70. These include *London St. James Gazette*, December 14, 1891, 11; *London Pall Mall Gazette*, December 14, 1891, 6; *Manchester Courier and Lancashire General Advertiser*, December 19, 1891, 17; and *London Weekly Dispatch*, December 20, 1891, 1.

71. *Harrisburg Patriot*, December 14, 1891, 4.

72. *San Francisco Chronicle*, January 4, 1892, 7.

73. *New York Times*, January 10, 1892, 4.

74. *Springfield Republican*, December 20, 1891, 4.

75. *San Francisco Wave*, February 13, 1892.

76. *Kalamazoo Gazette*, February 13, 1892, 7.

77. *Lincoln Evening News*, January 9, 1892, 4; *Topeka Daily Capitol*, January 19, 1892, 7; *Kalamazoo Gazette*, February 13, 1892, 7.

78. *San Francisco Chronicle*, December 25, 1891, 7.

79. *San Francisco Chronicle*, December 13, 1891, 10; Mary Roberts, *Intimate Outsiders: The Harem in Ottoman and Orientalist Art and Travel Literature* (Duke University Press, 2007), 90.

80. Robert Battistini, "Glimpses of the Other before Orientalism: The Muslim World in Early American Periodicals, 1785–1800," *Early American Studies* 8 (2010): 446–74; Graber, "Beyond Prophecy," 53–54.

81. Terry L. Givens, *The Viper on the Hearth: Mormons, Myths, and the Construction of Heresy* (Oxford University Press, 1997), 121–52; Martha M. Ertman, "Race Treason: The Untold Story of America's Ban on Polygamy," *Columbia Journal of Gender and Law* 19 (2010): 287–366; Richard V. Francaviglia, *Go East Young Man: Imagining the American West as the Orient* (Utah State University Press, 2011), 87–125; J. Spencer Fluhman, *"A Peculiar People": Anti-Mormonism and the Making of Religion in Nineteenth-Century America* (University of North Carolina Press, 2012), 110–17; W. Paul Reeve, *Religion of a Different Color: Race and the Mormon Struggle for Whiteness* (Oxford University Press, 2015); Peter Coviello, *Make Yourselves Gods: Mormons and the Unfinished Business of American Secularism* (University of Chicago Press, 2019); Konden Smith Hansen, *Frontier Religion: Mormons and America, 1857–1907* (University of Utah Press, 2019); Amanda Hendrix-Komoto, *Imperial Zions: Religion, Race, and Family in the American West and the Pacific* (University of Nebraska Press, 2022).

82. K. Mohrman, *Exceptionally Queer: Mormon Peculiarity and U.S. Nationalism* (University of Minnesota Press, 2022), 49.

83. For more on the racial dimensions of the scandal, see Joshua Paddison, "Disorderly Doctrines: Religion, Race, and the Fountaingrove Sex Scandal of 1891–1892," *Journal of the Gilded Age and Progressive Era* 14 (2015): 475–502.

84. Theodore H. Hittell, ed., *Supplement to the Codes and Statutes of the State of California*, vol. 3 (A. L. Bancroft and Company, 1880), 209; Peggy Pascoe, *What Comes Naturally: Miscegenation Law and the Making of Race in America* (New York: Oxford University Press, 2009), 87–89; Sueyoshi, *Discriminating Sex*, 33–44.

85. *San Francisco Call*, March 24, 1909, 2; June 20, 1910, 12; September 23, 1910, 8.

86. George Henry Preble, *The Opening of Japan: A Diary of Discovery in the Far East, 1853–1856* (University of Oklahoma Press, 1962), 181; Joseph M. Henning, *Outposts of Civilization: Race, Religion, and the Formative Years of American-Japanese Relations* (New York University Press, 2000), 23–24; Scott Clark, *Japan: A View from the Bath* (University of Hawai'i Press, 1994), 33–35.

87. *Chicago Flaming Sword*, January 2, 1892, 1–2; *San Francisco Chronicle*, February 26, 1892, 5.

88. *San Francisco New Church Pacific*, January 1892, 214.

89. *San Francisco New Church Pacific*, January 1892, 214; *San Francisco Call*, February 17, 1892, 8; *San Francisco New Californian: A Theosophic Journal*, February 1892, 287–88.

90. *London Lucifer*, September 15, 1891, 62.

91. *New York Path*, February 1892, 346–47.

92. *Chicago Progressive Thinker*, December 26, 1891, 6.

93. *Chicago Religio-Philosophical Journal*, January 2, 1892, 512.

94. Joanne E. Passet, *Sex Radicals and the Quest for Women's Equality* (University of Illinois Press, 2003); Barbara Goldsmith, *Other Powers: The Age of Suffrage, Spiritualism, and the Scandalous Victoria Woodhull* (Alfred A. Knopf, 1998); Helen Lefkowitz Horowitz, *Rereading Sex: Battles over Sexual Knowledge and Suppression in Nineteenth-Century America* (Alfred A. Knopf, 2002), 342–85; D'Emilio and Freedman, *Intimate Matters*, 156–67; Amanda Frisken, *Victoria Woodhull's Sexual Revolution: Political Theater and the Popular Press in Nineteenth-Century America* (University of Pennsylvania Press, 2004), 40–41; McGarry, *Ghosts of Futures Past*, 94–101.

95. Alex Owen, *The Darkened Room: Women, Power, and Spiritualism in Late Victorian England* (University of Chicago Press, 1989), 37–38; Paul C. Kemeny, *The New England Watch and Ward Society* (Oxford University Press, 2019), 99–101.

96. Frankiel, *California's Spiritual Frontiers*, 140.

97. *San Francisco Chronicle*, February 15, 1896, 6.

98. *San Francisco Call*, February 15, 1896, 3.

99. *Los Angeles Herald*, January 6, 1907, 8; *San Francisco Call*, February 9, 1909, 1; July 21, 1912, 45; *Imperial Valley Press*, July 22, 1924, 4; *Madera Tribune*, April 3, 1937, 1.

Chapter 3

Ever Westering

Religion, Freedom, and US Empire in the Twentieth-Century Pacific

CARLEIGH BERIONT

Keywords: Pacific, World War II, Micronesia, Marshall Islands, religious freedom, US military, Christianity

> The time has come for historians—especially western historians, whatever their proclivity—to acknowledge forthrightly and to study "westering" as it extended overseas.
>
> —Paul Sabin, "At Home and Abroad: The Two 'Wests' of Twentieth-Century United States History"

"May We Pray Now?" read the headline of a short article in the May 1, 1944, issue of *Time* magazine.[1] The piece described a United States flag-raising ceremony on an unnamed atoll in the Marshall Islands, the first part of Japan's prewar empire captured by US troops during World War II. *Time* reported that the question came from "an old chief" native to the island where the ceremony occurred. It came *after* US officials announced that the US military was formally occupying the atoll and extending its rule over the Marshallese people who lived there.

"May we pray now?" The man's question broke the silence among the Marshallese gathered to observe the occasion. The American officer in charge answered, "The US guarantees freedom of worship."

Yes, his response seemed to indicate, they could pray now. The article concluded with the crowd's response: "The Marshall Islanders, who are pious Christians (dominant variety: Boston Congregationalists), broke into cheers, [and] struck up a Christian hymn in the soft-flowing native dialect." They cheered the arrival of US military occupation, *Time* informed readers, as it would enable them to resume practicing Christianity.

Only 140 words long and with no byline, *Time*'s account of the introduction of United States occupation—and American religious freedom—to "one of the outer atolls of the Marshall Islands" helped introduce American readers to the distant and unspecified atoll as it became part of the United States' protean Pacific empire. The article also acquainted American audiences with these new subjects of US rule. *Time* readers learned the people who lived in this breezy, palm-filled paradise were "Boston Congregationalists." Thousands of miles away from the US "mainland," on the war's front line, lived a community of pious Protestants with an explicitly American connection.

The exchange between the Marshallese man and the US official illustrates what historian and religious studies scholar Tisa Wenger has referred to as "religious freedom talk."[2] Religious freedom talk, she explains, "delineated what counted as religion and so helped map the distinctions of race, nation, and religion across the cultural landscapes of the imperial world."[3] On its surface, the question and the answer suggest, as Wenger argues, that "the dominant varieties of American religious freedom talk were configured more often than not in ways that enabled imperial forms of domination."[4] Religious freedom was the scaffolding for the US empire in the Marshall Islands. It was also a way for Marshallese people to remake themselves—and be remade by the US military and American media—as "Boston Congregationalists."

As Wenger and Sylvester Johnson discuss in their recent volume on religion and US empire, and as the introduction to this book makes clear, religious freedom, as an ideal (however murky) and practice (however incomplete), has long been used by representatives of the United States to spread, legitimate, and enforce US empire. In the Marshall Islands, the US military occupation was explained to the Marshallese—and legitimated to American audiences—as necessary for religious freedom.[5] Phrased as "freedom of worship" and practiced as Protestant Christianity, the religious freedom the US official promised to the Marshallese epitomized one of the main political-ideological justifications for the United States' involvement in the war. As outlined by US president Franklin Roosevelt in his January 1941 State of the Union Address, "the freedom of every person to worship God in his own way" was one of what had become known to the American public as the Four Freedoms.[6] The *Time* piece, as a showcase for religious freedom talk, depicted one of the Four Freedoms at work in the US-occupied Marshall Islands. At the same time, the article emphasized the Marshallese people's "Boston Congregationalist" lineage to link them to American Protestantism and to square the acquisition of new territory and subjects—an imperial endeavor—with the potent anti-imperial rationales given by the US government for fighting the war.[7]

What can the Marshallese man's question, the US official's response, and *Time*'s depiction of the flag ceremony tell us about the multifaceted roles played by religion and religious freedom, American media and historical memory, and Indigenous and imperial actors in the making of US empire in the Pacific during this period? About "westering," to borrow from Paul Sabin, as it extended overseas? This essay considers what we might learn about religion and the American West—and about religious freedom and US empire—when viewed from the maritime and militarized Pacific. This region was deemed a "new frontier" by a prominent US senator and considered by many in the wartime and postwar United States to be "American soil" because of the American blood spilled there during the United States' war with Japan.

Often, discussions about religion and the American West remain bounded geographically by the Pacific Ocean and temporally by the turn of the twentieth century. But, as Quincy Newell has cautioned—and as other contributors to this volume, including Max Greenberg, Nicole Kirk, and Andrew Klumpp, have demonstrated—our conversations need not remain landlocked by specific, and limited, presuppositions about who, what, when, and where makes the West "American." In this essay, I explore how a twentieth-century, archipelagic vantage point might help to unmoor or dissolve some of the imagined yet rigid lines that often delineate the American West and US empire, home and abroad, and religion and religious freedom, as these designations were cocreated by, conferred on, and frequently contested by people overseas and under the US flag.

The Significance of the Flag

On April 13, 1944, *Time* correspondent Robert Martin cabled his editors a story from "Somewhere in the Marshall Islands."[8] Fighting between the United States and Japanese armed forces for control of the Japanese Mandated Islands in Micronesia had been underway since 1942. By April 1944, US forces had claimed several significant victories on Japanese-held Marshallese atolls, including Kwajalein, Majuro, and Enewetak.

These victories were significant because the Marshallese archipelago—a constellation of twenty-nine atolls and five islands sprinkled across seven hundred and fifty thousand square miles of ocean—formed the eastern perimeter of Japan's Pacific Empire. Just as control of the region had put Japanese forces within striking distance of the US Territory of Hawaii and, American officials feared, the mainland United States, US control of the archipelago afforded US forces a foothold in the Pacific that would enable them to attack Japan's Pacific holdings—including the US territories of the Philippines and Guam—and mainland Japan.

Some of the battles were bloodier than others. At Kwajalein, for instance, US forces bombed the islands around the clock in the days leading up to the land invasion. The *New York Times* reported that it was "the heaviest air and sea bombardment the world has ever seen."[9] By the time the Americans declared victory, one US soldier reported the "entire island looked as if it had been picked up 20,000 feet and then dropped."[10] More than eight thousand Japanese and Koreans, three hundred and fifty Americans, and two hundred Marshallese were dead.[11] One Marshallese man recalled that there were so many bodies strewn about the reef, the beaches, and the interior of the islands that you "had to walk on the bodies" to get from place to place.[12] At Majuro, by contrast, the Japanese armed forces had already evacuated, leaving only a handful of personnel to meet the US invasion.[13]

To mark each conquest, the US military staged a flag-raising ceremony. On some islands, the American flag was raised amid sniper fire and smoldering remains, the battle for control not quite complete. On other islands, ceremonies occurred amid rows of white crosses: the newly constructed, coconut palm–covered gravesites of American and Marshallese casualties of the war.

On atolls captured without opposition, the Americans raised their flag with little fanfare. On Ailuk Atoll, for example, the Commanding Officer's report presented a perfunctory timeline: "0715—Landed troops . . . followed by Civil Affairs party and provisions for natives. 0930—Flag raised, proclamation published, American sovereignty established. No enemy or enemy installations were found. No casualties were sustained in landing. 1030—Reembarked all troops and equipment."[14] In a little more than three hours, the Americans had come, claimed the atoll, raised their flag, distributed supplies, and set off for their next destination.

Regardless of the circumstances, on each of the Marshallese islands where they occurred—accompanied by spoken and posted proclamations of indefinite US military rule that enjoined the Marshallese people to assist the Americans and informed them that treason would be punishable by death—the ceremonies marked a transition from Japanese occupation to United States occupation. As one US official explained, these ceremonies were intended to communicate to the Marshallese people that they were "now under American protection."[15] In practice, American "protection" meant a variety of different things. It meant liberation from Japanese rule, which had grown increasingly harsh on many atolls as supplies ran low and Japanese anxieties about the likelihood of a US invasion and the outcome of the war grew. It meant the cessation, for the most part, of the bombardments by US warplanes where Japanese armaments and opposition had been destroyed. And it meant the Marshallese people who lived on those islands were free to pray and practice Christianity. Liberation, however, did not mean independence for the Marshallese.

Although it did not make it into *Time*, war correspondents on the ground and military sources emphasized that the significance of the American flag for Marshallese communities also derived from the tangible protection that it offered the people under its sway. According to Martin, the correspondent whose colorful cables from the Marshall Islands formed the foundation for the flag-raising story that ultimately appeared in *Time*, the Marshallese were instructed to observe the ritual of raising and lowering the flag to ensure their security on islands that had been captured or claimed by the United States but on which no American forces were stationed. He explained, "The American flag was left on every atoll and the natives, when told, 'There is no danger of United States bombings if you fly this flag,' faithfully promised to observe the ritual of sunset lowering and sunrise raising."[16] The American flag did not just communicate to the Marshallese that they were under American occupation but also indicated this to American bombers in an effort to deter them from harming the people who were under their flag.

The Sacrifice of American Blood and Transformation of the Newest Frontier

A number of influential US officials wanted to make the occupation of the Marshall Islands—or at least the atolls they designated as strategic, such as Kwajalein, Majuro, and Enewetak—permanent. Before the war's end, Ernest King, the commander in chief of the US fleet, was insisting that "the sacrifice of American blood" rendered the atolls US property in perpetuity.[17] The Pacific territory that the United States occupied during World War II, including the Marshall Islands, the Caroline Islands, the Marianas, Palau, the Bonins, and the Ryukyus, together comprised a terraqueous region greater in size than the continental United States. Hugh Butler, a Republican senator from Nebraska and member of the Committee on Territories and Insular Affairs, described the region as a "new frontier."[18]

Butler characterized the archipelagos and island chains as a geopolitical new frontier because they represented an expansion of the US presence in the Pacific Ocean *and* as a cultural new frontier because of the religious and racial diversity of their inhabitants—to whom, to be sure, he did not advocate extending the rights and protections of US citizenship. Nor did Butler want to make these "frontier" areas into states with representation in Congress. King and Butler asserted that the islands (and islanders) belonged *to* the United States, not *in* the United States.

Butler and King, along with other influential American policymakers, wanted these islands and atolls primarily to serve as US military bases.[19] Although Butler asserted that they could also function as "fueling stations, airports, [and] recreational spots," he was adamant that the United States gain and maintain control over these islands for national security.[20] As Martin, the *Time* correspondent, wrote from where he was stationed in the Pacific, "History has placed the Marshalls in a unique position: the United States has come not as a liberating nation but as an occupying nation because the islands occupy a strategic position."[21] Stories like the one in *Time* collapsed the distinction, or at least smoothed the transition, between the United States military as a liberating force and the United States as an occupying power.

"All of these must be ours," Butler stated in a Senate hearing. Echoing King, he continued, "We owe it to our destiny. We owe it to those who have secured them for us by the payment of their own life's blood."[22] Butler wanted the United States to permanently occupy *all* the Micronesian islands where American blood had been shed during the war. In part, this was to ensure that American blood would never again be spilled to gain control of territory that was crucial for the United States' war against Japan and to the United States' ascendency in the Pacific. It was also a politically salient rationale for a war-wary American public, a majority of whom considered the United States to be fundamentally anti-imperial.[23] If the United States were to relinquish control over these strategically located and resourced islands, what meaning would the American public ascribe to the blood shed by their sons and brothers?

Going forward, men like King and Butler asserted, these islands would provide the United States with an essential "line of defense," even in peacetime, by solidifying the United States' presence in the Pacific.[24] Butler also attempted to persuade his colleagues that maintaining control over the islands under the US flag would be advantageous if the United States were to go to war again. Technological advances in the range and impact of weapons, he cautioned, could enable enemies to strike the interior of the United States. In the future, the Pacific and Atlantic oceans would no longer suffice as a buffer; it would be prudent to establish a defensive perimeter far beyond the contiguous United States. Situated across the International Date Line, the Marshall Islands could join Guam (and the rest of Micronesia) as tomorrow's US frontier. Far from the "mainland"—and linked by an increasingly traversable ocean—these imperial peripheries would ensure the United States' security and power in the Pacific in the present *and* in the future.

This rationale for US expansion and occupation was not novel. As Butler himself pointed out during a congressional hearing, his explanation for the necessity of permanent US control over a place like the Marshall Islands had ample historical precedent. It echoed the rationales deployed by US officials during the acquisition of the Louisiana Territory and Pearl Harbor.[25] As literary and cultural historian Nicole Waligora-Davis has argued, these kinds of justifications were often circular; places that the United States occupied in the guise of "benevolent protector" were crucial for the protection of the United States and its satellite centers of imperial power, particularly US military bases.[26] Nor was it a new idea that the United States needed to militarily occupy a place and a people in order to establish religious freedom. This was familiar to anyone who recalled the interventionist rhetoric that accompanied the US occupation of the Philippines.[27] What was unique in this instance was how the Marshallese people were represented to the American public: as "Congregationalists from Boston." And as such, they were worthy of American religious freedom, but not self-determination or US citizenship.

Public Perceptions: Marshallese Christianity and American Religious Freedom

In the United States, most Americans learned about the US occupation of the Marshallese archipelago and about Marshallese people via newspaper stories, newsreels, and articles in publications like *Time* or, for the particularly Protestant- and missionary-minded, the *Missionary Herald*. By and large, then, the stories that the papers and magazines chose to tell (and, of course, what military censors allowed them to reveal) informed the American public's perceptions of the Marshall Islands and Marshallese people as well as their perceptions of the role that the United States was playing in the region.

Headlines like "Marshall Natives Ready to Help Us; Show No Hostility as We Enter Upon Program of Control," "Missionary Effort Pays Dividends," and "Cheers for Prayers" told American audiences, hungry for news about the war's progress, that the United States military was being received favorably in the Marshall Islands.[28] During a period of anti-imperial fervor, the US military's and American media's portrayals of the Marshallese as embracing American soldiers and cheering the onset of the US occupation drowned out political and economic critiques of the legitimacy of the United States' occupation of the archipelago.

Within the United States (and the Marshall Islands), narratives circulated that portrayed the US occupation of the Marshall Islands as anti-imperial. Religious freedom was central to the anti-imperial portrayal of what was happening throughout the archipelago. The reported exchange between the old man and the US military official provided editors with an opportunity to showcase the United States military's orientation toward religion—and occupation—in the Marshall Islands. "May we pray now?" Each of the four words in the Marshallese man's question was important, but perhaps none more than "now." With it, the man—and through him, the American editors at *Time*—drew a sharp contrast between the US and Japanese occupations of the Marshall Islands. Coverage of the US occupation neglected to mention that the United States was not the first occupying power to "free" religion in the Marshall Islands. Following World War I, when the League of Nations designated the Marshall Islands a Japanese Mandate, the Japanese government implemented a policy of "religious freedom" in the region.

While the *Time* story did not give readers much in the way of Japanese- or American-Marshallese history, its descriptions of the Marshallese people as "Boston Congregationalists" and as "pious Christians" pointed to a longer and shared history between Marshallese and American Protestants. By the time American forces landed in the Marshall Islands in 1944, Protestant Christianity had been present in the Islands for almost a century.[29] The American Board of Commissioners for Foreign Missions dispatched the first American missionaries from Boston to the Marshall Islands in December 1856. In 1857, they were invited by Kaibuke, a Marshallese *iroij*, to establish a mission on Ebon, one of the atolls in his dominion. Over the ensuing decades, a handful of American missionaries, Native Hawaiian missionaries, and Marshallese Protestants carried the gospel throughout the archipelago.

In the 1920s, the Japanese government viewed Christianity—and continuity—as beneficial. Convinced that Christian Marshallese people would be easier to rule than non-Christians, the Japanese government endorsed the presence and, at times, supported the ongoing work of American Board missionaries in the Marshall Islands. By the 1930s, a Japanese visitor reported that over 80 percent of the populace was Protestant.[30]

In the lead-up to the US invasion of the Marshall Islands, US officials recognized and sought to leverage the strategic value of these relationships, coupled with the robust and organized presence of Marshallese Protestant Christianity throughout the archipelago. The US Civil Affairs Handbook for the Marshall Islands, first compiled and published in August 1943—six months before the initial invasion—described the people's "Attitude toward Americans" as "generally favorable" owing to "the strong influence of American missionaries."[31] By this time, Japanese officials had soured on the few American Board missionaries who remained as well as on Marshallese Christian leaders, suspecting them of, if not directly supporting the United States, being unsupportive of the Japanese cause because of their close religious and historical association with the American Board. Stories like the one in *Time* therefore surfaced a seeming tension: The United States military was in the Marshall Islands to liberate the islands and the people and to return them to the sphere of American hegemony.

The Importance of Christianity for the US Occupation

The US occupation provided US military and civil affairs personnel with a chance to hone their approach toward people characterized by commentators and correspondents like Martin as "United States wards," a status that many thought would be permanent for the Marshallese and likely to apply to other Pacific peoples whose territories the United States might occupy over the course of the war. As Martin explained, "experiments in government conducted here will form the pattern for future United States occupation on the long sea-lanes leading to the [Japanese] homeland."[32] He continued, "There is little question but that what the United States does here will reflect on her position in the eyes of other peoples. There is less question that what is being done here is almost certain to be permanent."[33] Not only would the US occupation in the Marshall Islands be a model for other prospective US occupations in the Pacific, but as the first prewar Japanese-controlled island to be occupied, it would draw the attention—and perhaps the scrutiny—of the rest of the world.

The US military also sought to take advantage of returned American Board missionaries' knowledge of the language, culture, and connections with people in the Marshall Islands. During the invasion, occupation, and in later reflections, military officials concluded that "the friendliness of the Marshallese people toward the American military forces was due in no small part to the respect and affection with which American Protestant missionaries had been held for almost a century in the islands."[34] On the ground, Martin judged the Japanese armed forces' efforts to "suppress religious activities" during the war to have been a major blunder, backfiring and leaving the United States forces free to "collect more than full payment for the friendship and efforts" of the American missionaries.[35]

The US military's confidential World War II reconnaissance reports from atolls throughout the Marshallese archipelago reflected the same underlying assumptions. By and large, they attributed the warmth of the welcome US forces and news of the US Occupation received to the Marshallese people's Boston Christianity. As one report noted, "The work of American missionaries . . . has inculcated the feeling among them that Americans are a good, kindly people. This high regard being of great advantage to the US Forces." It continued, "Many of the natives were discontented with the official discouragement by the Japanese of Christianity, and now they are happy to be under a government where they may worship as they choose."[36]

As part of the coverage of the US invasion and occupation of the Marshall Islands, the *Time* article communicated clearly that religious freedom and Christianity—both American and Marshallese—as well as the history between American Protestant missionaries and Marshallese people, played a pivotal role in the success of the US military's operations there. The American Board was quick to claim credit for easing the occupation. In June 1944, the *Missionary Herald* published an excerpt from a letter written by a US Navy chaplain stationed in the Marshall Islands expressing gratitude for the groundwork laid by the American Board's missionaries. It said, "The work of your Board is simply magnificent. If the missionaries had not laid so deep a foundation for American friendship, the people could cause the armed forces a great deal of trouble under present conditions. But nothing but respect and friendship greeted the Americans here, as far as the natives were concerned."[37] What the *Time* article only alluded to, the *Missionary Herald* made clear: Boston Christianity was both the foundation and justification for the US occupation of the Marshall Islands.

One of the first and most important tasks the US military government sought to undertake in the Marshall Islands was to "provide not only for [the people's] physical well-being but for their religious and educational needs."[38] To do this, the US military government in the Marshall Islands adopted what they claimed was an "impartial" stance toward "representatives of all faiths" and guaranteed "complete religious freedom." According to US military sources, this entailed "encouraging" Marshallese "religious leaders to . . . continue their work" where possible and to use US military chaplains in instances when "native evangelists were not available," which was largely the case prior to 1946, when the military allowed American missionaries to reenter the region.[39]

The dominant interpretation of religious freedom in the Marshall Islands was explicitly pro-religion, with support for Protestant Christianity on the basis that it represented continuity with the Marshallese people's past. In coordination with US Christian organizations like the American Board of Commissioners for Foreign Missions and American Bible Society, "Bibles and hymnals in Marshallese were procured and distributed and assistance given the Marshallese in rebuilding their churches."[40] Although US military officials emphasized that they did not want the "native peoples" to think that the missionaries and religious literature were "sponsored by military government," they were frequently paid for by donations collected from among the US troops stationed there and disseminated by military personnel.[41]

One US admiral who oversaw the implementation of US rule in the Marshall Islands explained the value of religion, and Christianity in particular, to the US occupation. He wrote, "Christianizing the natives will tend to bind them to us and to separate them from Japan, as will teaching them English."[42] But, he added, there were limitations to what fell within the purview of the

US military, "Please do not think, however, that I am trying to put undershirts on any native belles who are not accustomed to wearing them."[43]

In his reports, Martin noted that the Marshallese who were present for the flag ceremony and the proclamation of military rule watched "passively" as the flag fluttered up the staff and an American lieutenant enjoined the Marshallese people "to help the United States."[44] He attributed their initial reaction to a lack of understanding. Even though the proclamation was "translated by native interpreters," Martin believed "they did not comprehend thoroughly the meaning of the sudden changes."[45] While the people may have been reflecting on the consequences of the transition from Japanese to US occupation, depending on where the flag ceremony occurred, it is possible that they were uncertain how to respond given the overwhelming military power of the Americans and the magnitude of the violence they had unleashed on Kwajalein and Enewetak.[46] Or, perhaps the people assembled were waiting to see how *their* leaders reacted, and they, in turn, wanted to learn more about how the US occupation would impact their lives and their social and political status. In other words, there were likely a number of different factors—some more apparent to Martin and US officials than others—that informed and constrained the Marshallese crowd's reaction to the US declaration as it was narrated by Martin.

But when the crowd heard that "the US guarantees freedom of worship," Martin wrote, their demeanor changed abruptly. He concluded, "That one statement virtually unraveled the Jap[anese] propaganda net woven in the past 30 years and ensured native cooperation."[47] The guarantee of religious freedom, to Martin's eye, was the key to securing the assistance of this community in the United States' war effort and military occupation.

Conclusion

Although Martin's cables give little indication, it is almost certain that the story published in *Time* was a composite of events that occurred in two different places in the Marshall Islands. Lieutenant Galen Sturgeon, the US official quoted in the *Time* article, visited multiple atolls in the Marshall Islands. As a Navy civil affairs officer, he was "responsible for all dealings with the local population."[48] During the first week of April 1944, Sturgeon led reconnaissance missions to Ailuk Atoll, Likiep Atoll, and Mejit Island on the Ratak or sunrise side of the archipelago. On Ailuk, his report noted, the US military government proclamations "were posted on the church . . . and the American flag raised just east of the church."[49] As he observed in an earlier reconnaissance report, "The work of American missionaries in this region has not only brought about the conversion of a large part of the natives to at least nominal Christianity, but has inculcated the feeling among them that

Americans are a good, kindly people."[50] Surely, his decision to post the US military government proclamations on the Protestant church and raise the American flag nearby was due to his assessment that the church—and by extension Christianity—occupied a prominent place on that island. And that choice in turn likely reified the association of Christianity and American power in the minds of the people.

Unlike on Kwajalein Atoll, a major Japanese military base where many of the islands were decimated by US bombs, the US occupied Ailuk without firing a single shot. "No Japanese have lived on this atoll for the last three years," Sturgeon's report stated. The absence of Japanese settlers also likely contributed to the warm welcome the Americans received there. When the US tank landing ship entered the lagoon, the atoll's leader, a man named Typhoon, reportedly sailed out to meet the US military vessel "and invited the American Forces to come ashore, stating that the sight of the American Ensign on the ship was a welcome sight."[51] On Ailuk, where the landing, proclamation, flag raising, provisioning, and departure took place over a little more than three hours, Sturgeon noted that "the question was raised as to whether the people could now pray again, and considerable pleasure was expressed when they were assured that they could."[52] The next island that Sturgeon visited with his team of Civil Affairs Officers, medical personnel, and a small contingent of US troops was Mejit. There, Sturgeon wrote, "during explanation of the proclamations the announcement that the people were now free to worship as they please was greeted with a burst of applause." According to Martin, the anonymous Marshallese community that he wrote had cheered the US occupation—although a model—was not exceptional. "Everywhere [the lieutenant] emphasized the point [about freedom of worship] and was greeted by bursts of spontaneous applause and the singing of Christian hymns in the soft native dialect."[53]

Well before American readers of *Time* learned about the US flag flying "somewhere in the Marshalls" over a community of Boston Congregationalists, US officials were working to ensure their flag would never come down. US admiral Alva Bernhard told reporters, "It would be unthinkable to ever haul down the Stars and Stripes from over these islands." He continued, "We have freed the native population, who have been living in a state of slavery. Of course, we must keep the Marshalls and allow no one to interfere with us."[54]

US empire—like the American West—is a space of defining rather than definition.[55] Throughout the twentieth century, caretakers and critics have used religious freedom to define US empire. If the *Time* article sought to convey to American readers that the Marshallese people's Christian identity and connection to American missionaries—and their cheerful reception of the news of US occupation—rendered them worthy of consideration by

American readers, the strategic and central location of the Marshall Islands in the north Pacific Ocean and the blood shed there by American soldiers during the US invasion was what made them American.

Notes

1. Paul Sabin, "Home and Abroad: The Two 'Wests' of Twentieth-Century United States History," *Pacific Historical Review* 66, no. 3 (August 1997): 332; "May We Pray Now?," *Time*, May 1, 1944, 68.

2. Tisa Wenger, *Religious Freedom: The Contested History of an American Ideal* (University of North Carolina Press, 2017), 1.

3. Wenger, *Religious Freedom*, 2.

4. Wenger, *Religious Freedom*, 2.

5. Tisa Wenger and Sylvester Johnson, eds., *Religion and US Empire: Critical New Histories* (New York University Press, 2022).

6. Franklin D. Roosevelt, "Annual Message to Congress," January 6, 1941, Records of the United States Senate, SEN 77A-H1, Record Group 46, National Archives, www.fdrlibrary.org/documents/356632/390886/readingcopy.pdf/42234a77-8127-4015-95af-bcf831db311d.

7. "Cairo Conference, November 1943," released December 1, 1943, Avalon Project, Yale Law School, https://avalon.law.yale.edu/wwii/cairo.asp.

8. Robert Martin, "Cable #2," April 13, 1944, 1, in *Dispatches from Time Magazine Correspondents: First Series, 1942–1955*, Time, Inc. Houghton Library, Harvard University.

9. Robert Trumbull, "Our Guns Exploded Marshalls Myth," *New York Times*, February 8, 1944, 3.

10. Burton Wright, *Eastern Mandates: The US Army Campaigns of World War II* (US Army Center of Military History, 1993), 14.

11. Wright, *Eastern Mandates*, 16; Suzanne Falgout, *Memories of War: Micronesians in the Pacific War* (University of Hawaii Press, 2008), 88.

12. Falgout, *Memories of War*, 92.

13. Atoll Commander, "Naval Air Base Majuro Historical Report, 1 January 1944–1 March 1945," 9, NAB, MAJURO–War History 13, *World War II War Diaries, Other Operational Records and Histories*, Record Group 38, Records of the Office of the Chief of Naval Operations, National Archives, NAID 77636573 [hereafter cited as WWII Diaries].

14. Commanding Officer, "Report of Reconnaissance of Ailuk Atoll, Mejit Island, and Likiep Atoll, 6 April 1944," 1, Civil Affairs Section, COM KWAJALEIN ATOLL–Act Rep, *Rep of Occupation of Ailuk & Likiep Atolls & Mejit & Jemo Is in Marshalls, 30 March–5 April 1944*, 8, WW II Diaries.

15. Chief of Civil Affairs Section, "Report of Reconnaissance of Wotho, Ujae, and Lae Atolls (Confidential), March 15, 1944," 3, Civil Affairs Section, COM KWAJALEIN ATOLL–Rep of Occupation of Wotho, Ujae & Lae Atolls, Marshalls, *Report of Occupation of Wotho, Ujae & Lae Atolls, Marshalls, 8–13 March 1944*, 13, WWII Diaries.

16. Martin, Cable # 2, 3.

17. "Keep Bases, Admiral King Asks US," *Seabee News Service*, April 10, 1945, 1.

18. 79 Cong. Rec. S4397 (daily ed. May 10, 1945).

19. 79 Cong. Rec. S4399 (daily ed. May 10, 1945).

20. 79 Cong. Rec. S4398 (daily ed. May 10, 1945).

21. Martin, Cable #2, 5.

22. 79 Cong. Rec. S4398 (daily ed. May 10, 1945) (statement of Sen. Butler).

23. Huntington Gilchrist, "The Japanese Islands: Annexation or Trusteeship?," *Foreign Affairs*, July 1, 1944, 642.

24. 79 Cong. Rec. S4399 (daily ed. May 10, 1945).

25. Franklin D. Roosevelt, "Message to Congress on Exchanging Destroyers for British Naval and Air Bases," September 3, 1940, The American Presidency Project, www.presidency.ucsb.edu/documents/message-congress-exchanging-destroyers-for-british-naval-and-air-bases.

26. Nicole Waligora-Davis notes this trope of the US as the benevolent "protector of the Western Hemisphere . . . does little to mask a propriety imperative fueled by a long history of US dependency on [places like] the West Indies." Nicole Waligora-Davis, "Myth of the Continents," in *Archipelagic American Studies: Decontinentalizing the Study of American Culture*, ed. Brian Russell Roberts and Michelle Stephens (Duke University Press, 2017), 193.

27. "US Senator Albert Beveridge Speaks on the Philippine Question," US Senate, Washington DC, January 9, 1900, USC US-China Institute, https://china.usc.edu/us-senator-albert-j-beveridge-speaks-philippine-question-us-senate-washington-dc-january-9-1900.

28. "Marshall Natives Ready to Help US: Show No Hostility as We Enter Upon Program of Control—Past Is Studied," *New York Times*, February 10, 1944, 4; Wynn Fairfield, "Late Overseas News," *The Missionary Herald: At Home and Abroad* 140, no. 5 (June 1944): 38; Martin, Cable #2, 3.

29. Carleigh Beriont, "The 'Children's Mission Ship': The 1856 American Board Mission to Micronesia and the Making of a New American West," *Pacific Historical Review* 92, no. 3 (Summer 2023): 333–364.

30. Tadao Yanaihara, *Pacific Islands Under Japanese Mandate: A Report in the International Research Series of the Institute of Pacific Relations* (Greenwood Press, 1940), 234.

31. *Military Government Handbook OPNAV 50E-1 Marshall Islands*, Office of the Chief of Naval Operations, August 17, 1943, 31.

32. Martin, Cable #2, 1.

33. Martin, Cable #2, 5.

34. Dorothy Richard, *United States Naval Administration of the Trust Territory of the Pacific Islands* (Office of the Chief of Naval Operations, 1957), vol. 1: 400–401. See also letters from chaplains stationed in Marshalls, ABCFM archive, Eddy, George, etc.; Letter from 7th Infantry Division G-1 report from Kwajalein operation cited in Richard, vol. 1, 401.

35. Martin, Cable #2, 3, 2.

36. Lieut. G. H. Sturgeon, USNR, "Report of Reconnaissance of Ebon and Namorik Atolls and Kili Island (Confidential), April 6, 1944," 8, Civil Affairs Section, COM KWAJALEIN ATOLL–Act Rep, *Rep of Occupation of Ebon & Namorik Atolls & Kili Is in Marshalls, 21–29 March 1944*, 38, WWII Diaries.

37. Fairfield, "Late Overseas News," 38.

38. Richard, *United States Naval Administration*, 1:402.

39. Richard, *United States Naval Administration*, 1:402.

40. Richard, *United States Naval Administration*, 1:402.

41. Rear Adm. C. A. Pownall, USN, "Missionaries—Policy Regarding, Speedletter from ComMarianas, December 31, 1946," reproduced in Richard, *United States Naval Administration of the Trust Territory*, 2:544, appendix 19.

42. Adm. Raymond Spruance, USN, letter to Captain Moore, February 14, 1945, quoted in Richard, *United States Naval Administration of the Trust Territory*, 2:78.

43. Spruance, letter to Captain Moore, 2:78.

44. Martin, Cable #2, 2.

45. Martin, Cable #2, 2.

46. Martin described the inhabitants of the islands as "grateful that the United States had spared them the bombardments which devastated Kwajalein and Eniwetok" in Cable #2, 2.

47. Martin, Cable #2, 2.

48. Rear Adm. Alva Bernhard, USN, "Periodic Inspection of Certain Atolls and Islands of the Lesser Marshalls Operation Plan Number 13–44 (Secret), May 25, 1944," 4 COM MARSHALL IS SUB AREA—*War Diary, 5/1–31/44*, 81, WWII Diaries.

49. Lieut. G. H. Sturgeon, USNR, "Report of Reconnaissance of Ailuk and Likiep Atolls and Mejit Island (Confidential), April 7, 1944, 2," Civil Affairs Section, COM KWAJALEIN ATOLL–Act Rep, *Rep of Occupation of Ailuk & Likiep Atolls & Mejit & Jemo Is in Marshalls, 30 March–5 April 1944*, 11, WWII Diaries.

50. Lieut. G. H. Sturgeon, USNR, "Report of Reconnaissance of Ebon and Namorik Atolls and Kili Island (Confidential), April 6, 1944," 8, Civil Affairs Section, COM KWAJALEIN ATOLL—Act Rep, *Rep of Occupation of Ebon & Namorik Atolls & Kili Is in Marshalls, 21–29 March 1944*, 38, WWII Diaries.

51. Lieut. G. H. Sturgeon, USNR, "Report of Reconnaissance of Ailuk and Likiep Atolls and Mejit Island (Confidential), April 7, 1944," 6, Civil Affairs Section, COM KWAJALEIN ATOLL–Act Rep, *Rep of Occupation of Ailuk & Likiep Atolls & Mejit & Jemo Is in Marshalls, 30 March–5 April 1944*, 15, WWII Diaries.

52. Sturgeon, "Report of Reconnaissance of Ailuk and Likiep Atolls," 6.

53. Sturgeon, USNR, "Report of Reconnaissance of Ailuk and Likiep Atolls," 6.

54. Frazier Hunt, "Kwajalein Becomes a Mighty Base," *Saturday Evening Post*, March 25, 1944, 106.

55. Greg Dening, *Readings/Writings* (Melbourne University Press, 1998), 86.

Chapter 4

California Cultbusters

The West Coast Origins of the Modern Anticult Movement

JAMES B. BENNETT

Keywords: anticult movement, cult, Southern California, deprogramming, brainwashing

Kay Rambur, a twenty-two-year-old registered nurse in San Diego, spent the first part of her 1971 summer vacation in the San Francisco Bay Area. She was visiting her boyfriend, after which she planned to meet her parents in North Dakota. While biking on the UC Berkeley campus, she heard a group singing on the street and stopped to learn more. The singers were part of the Children of God (COG), a communal bible-based religious movement that began in Huntington Beach a few years earlier. Kay never made it to North Dakota. Instead, she left her job and boyfriend and moved to a COG missionary training center in Texas. Kay told her parents about her decision by mail and limited her contact with them. The abrupt conversion and lack of communication led Kay's parents to believe the COG had used brainwashing to coerce her into joining and remaining in the group. "None of this made any sense," Kay's mother wrote. She described Kay as one who "seemed happy and well adjusted . . . certainly not anticipating making a drastic change in her life style." Kay's parents made multiple deprogramming attempts to get her to leave the COG. None were successful. Kay remained in the COG, married a fellow member, started a family, and moved to South America as a missionary.[1]

As Bill and Betty Rambur struggled to understand their daughter's choice, they connected with other parents in the San Diego area who were also in shock over their adult children's decision to join the COG.[2] Their networking marked the beginnings of the modern anticult movement. Within a year of Kay's conversion, the Ramburs and similarly affected parents formalized their efforts and took the name The Parents Committee to Free our Sons and Daughters from the Children of God Organization, known as FREECOG. A colleague in these early efforts recounted that Bill Rambur's strategy "was to organize parents, try to rescue children and spread the word that the *Children of God* was a destructive organization." FREECOG also facilitated contact with deprogrammers, who tried to persuade converts to leave, often using force. Parents with similar experiences formed anticult groups elsewhere in Southern California and the San Francisco Bay Area. Following the FREECOG model, these grassroots organizations became national clearinghouses for parents seeking information about new religious movements and strategies to get their children back. Based on the range of inquiries, Rambur's San Diego group soon expanded its focus beyond the COG and renamed itself Citizens Freedom Foundation (CFF). By the early 1980s, the California movement had grown into a national anticult organization, adopting the name Cult Awareness Network (CAN). Still, even with the formation of a national organization, the California chapters remained preeminent in size, influence, and as centers of information.[3]

The 1970s Southern California anticult movement demonstrates the tensions and complexities that characterize religion in the American West. The West has long been a place of mythic possibility, though the reality often contradicted the myth. On the one hand, many who settled in the West experienced it as a place of religious creativity and tolerance.[4] On the other hand, religious experimentation did not always meet with toleration and acceptance, especially from those who considered new religious movements a danger to their families and the nation. For these opponents, the story of religious diversity and experimentation was one of peril, not promise. Taken together, these simultaneous yet contradictory narratives point to the dialectic between acceptance and opposition that has been a recurrent theme in the history of religion in the American West, especially in California

As early as the nineteenth century, California had become a center of the tension between toleration and hostility and of the use of the word "cult" to describe those conflicts. As Joshua Paddison's analysis of Thomas Lake Harris and the media's sensationalist coverage of his Fountaingrove Community in the 1890s demonstrates, the Golden State played a crucial role in solidifying the connotations of the word "cult" and conceptions of cult leaders that also characterized the language of the modern anticult movement nearly a century later. Although they were unaware of the connections and believed they were combatting something new, the anticultists in the mid-twentieth century were utilizing an interpretive framework that had been in use for nearly a century. It provided ready-made vocabulary to warn of the dangers that such groups posed to families, the nation, and Christianity. In both the late nineteenth- and the mid-twentieth-century episodes, this cult framework advanced the American imperial project as it used religious, racial, and sexual boundaries to cordon off groups from acceptable American identities and to mark them as unworthy of citizenship and constitutional protections. Like its predecessors, the modern anticult movement would leave a lasting impact that survived the demise of the organizations that had originated it.

Still, even as the anticult movement formed part of the long history of religious intolerance in California examined in this volume's chapters by Chrissy Lau and Joshua Paddison, the modern anticult also took on a particular shape that reflected its time and place. The large-scale migrations to Southern California in the mid-twentieth century fueled the dialectic between toleration and antagonism that led to debates about the limits of religious freedom and the boundaries of American citizenship. Perched on the western edge of the United States, California was central to the defense and expansion of the post–World War II American Empire. The aerospace and defense industries proliferated in California, attracting those whose work supported the effort to increase American influence across the Pacific. As a result, Californians had a front-row view of the real and perceived threats of the Cold War.

This large-scale relocation to Southern California also reconfigured care networks as migrants left community roots and family connections behind, only to feel threatened by new religions where they settled. The resulting sense of precarity led them to prioritize both the safety of their families and the security of the nation. On the heels of this internal migration, immigrants from Asia began arriving following the 1965 Immigration Act, which ended prohibitions that had been in place since 1924. That new wave of immigration increased California's religious and racial diversity. It also exacerbated the sense of familial and national insecurity for the small group of white parents whose children became involved in the movements they labeled "cults," many of which had Asian origins. Forged in this context, the anticult movement was an expression of these fears, bridging the projects of American Empire building and care—particularly paternalistic care—that are the foci of this volume.

The anticult movement also illustrates how the dialectic between tolerance and intolerance produced contesting definitions of religion that resulted in debates about who is entitled to the protections the category of religion is supposed to provide in the United States. While not exclusive to the West, these contests did play out in ways that reveal California to be both distinct from and representative of the nation as a whole. These disputes also point to the conflicting legacies of the anticult movement. New religious movements and their members emerged victorious in their legal and legislative battles to be defined as religions and claim the protections of the First Amendment. Still, theirs was not a total victory. Anticultists prevailed in the court of popular opinion. They leveraged the news and popular media to preserve and expand the use of the word "cult" and its connotations that such groups were dangerous. They also popularized terms like "brainwashing" and "mind control" to explain why people joined such groups, and they invented the term and practice of "deprogramming" as the way to rescue them. Decades after the anticult movement's collapse, these terms still carry fluency in the popular imagination despite being rejected in the legal and legislative realms.

Also contributing to these debates about the definition of religion were concerns about communism in the context of the Cold War. The precarity of family relationships was also of concern in this context, especially for those who were unable to assert control over their adult children's religious choices. For some, the anticult movement encapsulated those fears and offered a solution. Ironically, their methods often contradicted the national and familial values they claimed to defend, as their opponents were quick to point out. The anticult movement that emerged from California's distinctive context exerted an influence that lasted beyond the movement itself, as it perpetuated the complexities and contradictions of the dialectic between acceptance and opposition that remains a major theme of religion in the American West.

Religious Innovation in Twentieth-Century California

Fears about the explosion of new religions catalyzed the emergence of the anticult movement in the 1970s. Such concerns were hardly new. By 1946, journalist Carey McWilliams could trace over a century of religious experimentation in an *Atlantic Monthly* article entitled "The Cults of California."[5] Academics, adherents, and antagonists all shared journalists' assertions of California's religious fertility. The Center for the Study of New Religious Movements, founded at the Graduate Theological Union in Berkeley, California, in 1977, justified its mission with the claim that "California has historically been a center for the development and practice of non-traditional or alternative religious movements."[6] That same year, San Francisco historian Charles A. Fracchia linked religious creativity to California's location as a crossroads of the world: "California is the laboratory—'the great crucible,' so to speak, where these new religious forms are being forged, where the revival of traditional Christianity, the importation of the ancient religious beliefs of the Far East and the psychological insights of the 'new consciousness' are blending to create a new form of religious experience."[7] In more concise fashion, sociologists Anson Shupe and David Bromley called Southern California America's "cult capital."[8] Anticult activists agreed. San Diego–based deprogrammer Ted Patrick claimed the rash of new movements had been "nourished . . . by that strange climate of religious hysteria that seems endemic to California."[9] Henri Crampton, who was a leader in the early Southern California parent groups along with the Ramburs, claimed in a letter to her state Assembly representative that "there are

Figure 4.1 Frank Interlandi, © 1979. Los Angeles Times.

probably more religious cults in California than in any other state."[10] In Northern California as well, the Corresponding Secretary of the Bay Area anticult affiliate noted in a cover letter for a media kit that "Unfortunately, Northern California is still one of the most fertile areas for cult activity."[11]

California's history of religious creativity was a product of its settlement patterns. New religious movements appear most frequently where there are fewer churches and where ties to organized religion are weakest, as scholars of new religious movements and of California history have noted.[12] Migration is a significant contributing factor to these weak religious ties, as it severs multigenerational family connections to traditional churches and religious organizations By the mid-1950s, one thousand people a day were moving to California, over two-thirds of them to the Southern California counties of Los Angeles, Orange, and San Diego.[13] With this rapid growth, denominations and ecumenical organizations could not replicate the density they had achieved elsewhere in the United States. Only one-third of Southern Californians belonged to a church by the late 1950s, compared to 60 percent nationwide. Once they arrived in California, migrants tended to adapt to their new home's less engaged religious participation rather than recreating what they left behind. In the words of political scientist John Compton, this pattern led to "an environment where religious authority was stretched unusually thin" and resulted in a "uniquely lax religious culture."[14]

New religious movements in California emerged due to this relative scarcity of institutional churches, which lacked the numerical and cultural dominance to stifle religious invention. Some innovators worked within a Protestant framework. Robert Schuller started what would become the Crystal Cathedral at a drive-in theater in Garden Grove, while Chuck Smith's work among hippies in the Orange County beach communities of Costa Mesa, Corona del Mar, and Newport Beach gave rise to Calvary Chapel.[15] By the late 1960s, other new religious movements were moving beyond traditional Christian beliefs and practices. Many in this latter group became targets of anticult groups, including Scientology, which began in Los Angeles in the 1950s; the COG, which started in Huntington Beach in 1968; and the Susan and Tony Alamo Foundation, which formed in Hollywood in 1969 and soon relocated to Newhall, north of Los Angeles.[16]

California and the West also became home to religious movements from Asia. Many of these groups arrived first on the West Coast, following the Immigration and Nationality Act of 1965, which reopened immigration from Asia for the first time since the Asian Exclusion Act of 1924. As historian Laurie Maffly-Kipp has observed, religion arriving from the West across the Pacific, rather than from the East across the continent, distinguishes religion in the American West from elsewhere in the United States.[17] The International Society for Krishna Consciousness (ISKON or Hare Krishna) recruited followers in San Francisco's Haight District, and the Unification Church ("Moonies") established missions in San Francisco and Oakland, as well as retreats in Napa Valley and Mendocino County.[18] Other movements that originated in Asia before establishing a presence in California and the American West included the Divine Light Mission, Transcendental Meditation, and the Rajneesh movements. With homegrown and imported new religious movements, mid-twentieth-century California lived up to its reputation as a land of religious innovation. As it did so, these waves of spiritual creativity and resulting religious affiliation challenge assumptions about secularization in the American West and the consequences of declining religiosity.[19]

Religious Intolerance in California

Not all Californians celebrated the mid-century burst of religious creativity. What some welcomed, others feared, and where some found hope, others saw danger. FREECOG founder Bill Rambur exemplified the danger perspective, insisting that the "COG was anti-society and subversive in nature," as were "the hundreds of other pseudo-religious cults" like it.[20] While hostility to new religious movements is a universal phenomenon, the modern anticult movement was also a product of the social patterns of mid-century California, no less than the "cults" it opposed.

By the 1960s, despite California's progressive reputation, it was also home to a burgeoning conservative ethos, especially in the coastal counties stretching from Los Angeles to San Diego.[21] The massive post–World War II migration of Midwesterners and Southerners to work in the aerospace and defense industries fueled this conservativism. Defense was the nation's largest business in this era, and California received more than twice as many defense contracts as any other state, most of them in Southern California. These young families moved for economic security and to contribute to the nation's defense during the Cold War, not for the region's sunshine or religious diversity. These were the same people who would make suburban Southern California the birthplace of conservatism in the 1960s, beginning with the nomination of Barry Goldwater in 1964 and culminating in Ronald Reagan's election as President in 1980. Many of these migrants had been stationed in California or passed through it on their way to military sites across the Pacific, including anticult founder Bill Rambur, who had been a Navy pilot. In Orange County alone, half of its male civilian residents in 1960 had served in the military, compared to the national average of 37 percent.[22]

This postwar migration also increased racial homogeneity in suburban Southern California. Families who relocated to the Golden State were almost entirely white, further marginalizing the small communities of color, particularly Mexican Americans, whose presence predated the mid-nineteenth-century arrival of Anglo-American settlers. By 1960, non-white residents comprised less than 10 percent of the population in Orange County.[23] Suburban building patterns reinforced racial uniformity in a region where over two-thirds of the population owned their homes. The housing boom benefited white residents, as the new housing was beyond the means of those below the middle class.[24] The resulting segregation meant that suburban whites had limited interaction with people different from them—and they preferred it that way. When non-white buyers could afford houses, white owners often refused to accept their offers. Such was the fate of Korean American Dr. Sammy Lee, a two-time Gold Medal Olympic diver and USC-trained physician. Two different sellers rejected Lee's offers to buy a home in Garden Grove. Not far away, more than fifty neighbors opposed a sale to Harold Bauduit, an African American US Air Force Lieutenant, and raised funds to buy him a house elsewhere in order "to keep undesirable elements out of the neighborhood."[25] By 1960, the suburbs of Southern California were the most segregated in the nation. Later that decade, those same counties played a significant role in passing Proposition 14, a state constitutional amendment to overturn the 1963 Rumford Act, which authorized investigations into racial discrimination in housing sales and rentals. Two-thirds of Los Angeles County voters and three-quarters in Orange County supported Prop 14. Although the US Supreme Court soon struck it down, its passage demonstrated the region's resistance to outlawing segregation and its unwillingness to assist those on the economic margins.[26]

White suburban concerns about racial mixing contributed to a sense of unsettled precarity, with fear often directed toward Asian immigrants, many of whom made California their home. Anti-Asian sentiment had a long history in California, as Lau and Paddison's chapters demonstrate. These concerns, coupled with this xenophobia, led white suburban parents to worry about the influx of new religions from across the Pacific. Early anticult groups filled their newsletters with accounts of Asian immigrants' supposedly subversive activities. One such report, from conservative San Diego journalist Ann Watson warned that "a new faith called Soka Gakkai is spreading from Japan to America to the rest of the world." She continued, "This new religion is sweeping country after country. It lures the young and the naïve and even coerces businessmen into membership." She was especially concerned that members had been welcomed in San Diego "in spite of the fact they were responsible for vandalism and numerous acts against the law-abiding people in the communities where they established themselves."[27]

Through such outcries, Southern California's anticult movement was participating in the national project of empire that protected whiteness by using religion as a marker of race and citizenship. However, most converts to groups such as the Unification Church, Hare Krishna, and the Divine Light Movement were white, middle-class suburban young adults, even though the religions had originated in Asia. In response, anticult materials coded the religious groups they opposed as non-white, regardless of the racial composition of their membership. Even groups that began in the United States were framed as racially "other," such as a warning that lumped the COG and Scientology together with Hare Krishna and Transcendental Meditation as "guru sects" that "beguiled young Americans."[28]

Cold War anxieties joined with anti-Asian bias to produce the widespread claim that new religious movements used mind control to gain members. What earlier opponents had called hypnotism, magnetism, or mesmerism was most often called brainwashing by the 1970s. It was a concept borrowed from the Cold War to depict the convert as a victim of irresistible manipulation. It was also a term, "firmly associated with Asian villains," as historian Philip Jenkins notes.[29] These ideas drew upon the popular but debunked idea that

Chinese communists recruited party members through brainwashing, which was an attempt to explain why a handful of American POWs in the Korean War expressed sympathy for communism. The accusation that religious groups in the United States used brainwashing suggested that what had once been contained across the Pacific was now infiltrating the United States.[30] It also shifted the blame for the supposed "cult crisis" from individuals and families to the new waves of Asian immigration. Anticult publications and media events were rife with accusations of brainwashing. A 1977 CFF press conference in Los Angeles "presented evidence that brainwashing and mind control are utilized by the cults to recruit and hold their members."[31] At another press conference a year later, the same LA CFF chapter included a former Unification Church member as evidence of their claims. When asked why she followed the church's teachings, she responded, "I personally believe I was brainwashed."[32] The ex-member's response revealed another advantage of the brainwashing explanation in a time of increased anxiety about the disintegration of the family unit. By insisting on the victim's passivity, brainwashing absolved both parents and converts of responsibility for the child's unwelcome religious activity.[33]

In anticult rhetoric, "cult" functioned as shorthand for the fears that worried parents projected onto new religious movements. It was a familiar playbook used by previous generations of white Californians, as Joshua Paddison's analysis of the term in the late nineteenth century demonstrates. "Cult" connoted a long list of dangers, including secrecy, dishonesty about the group's beliefs and practices, authoritarian leaders with irresistible charisma, control of members' assets, unconventional family and sexual arrangements, the potential for violence, and loss of mental autonomy. With this predetermined meaning, "cult" functioned as a code that operated in lieu of specific information about a particular group. A group's beliefs and practices were irrelevant once labeled a cult.[34] This designation was also a tool of US imperialism in its efforts to police the religious, racial, and national boundaries of American identity.

Family Fragility

In a 1975 anticult fundraising appeal, Bill Rambur claimed there were five thousand cults in the United States.[35] About the same time, fellow San Diegan and deprogrammer Ted Patrick claimed cult membership was over three million. Neither leader provided evidence to back up his claims. For the parents in the anticult movement, the growth of new religious movements created a crisis that threatened the stability and future of their families. Exaggerated claims about the size of the threat were one way they tried to provoke a sense of urgency.[36] Warnings about widespread vulnerability were another.

Headlines like "No One is Immune," which appeared above a story about a Congressman's daughter's involvement with the Unification Church in San Francisco, were intended to stoke fears about the reach of new religious movements.[37] Blaming conversions on brainwashing was another way to stress vulnerability and suggest that cults' mind control efforts were irresistible.

Parents who participated in the anticult movement offered their children's experience as evidence that anyone could be affected. Henri Crampton, leader of a Los Angeles area parents' group, warned at the end of an account of her daughter's involvement that "your children and grandchildren may be as easily ensnared."[38] Crampton's account also illustrated how parents used specific examples to extrapolate generalized warnings. Writing about the commune her daughter joined and its leader, Love Israel, she insisted that "we can equate Love Israel to Charles Manson point by point."[39] Another anticult parent opined that Patty Hearst's treatment while kidnapped by the Symbionese Liberation Army (SLA) "reads as if it might be a page torn from a book describing the treatment . . . by one of the many cults."[40] Following the 1978 Jonestown tragedy, anticult advocates compared nearly every group they opposed to the People's Temple.[41] Despite the small number of actual examples the anticult movement could use, these atrocity tales were a favorite tactic in the effort to create a sense of crisis.[42]

Assumptions about the fragility of youth and young adults fueled this sense of danger. A brochure titled "The Cult Crisis," published by the Northern California CFF chapter, claimed, "Hundreds of parents have been rudely awakened to the fact that cults are actively recruiting our young people now." A psychologist quoted in the same pamphlet warned that "almost any young adult can be recruited into a cult."[43] Parents' concern for their children was why most members joined the anticult groups. They were not mistaken that new religious movements focused on recruiting young adults, who tend to be spiritually curious. Youth had become inquisitive about spiritual alternatives to what they experienced in their white middle-class suburbs, where they were raised by parents who embraced an individualist, materialistic, and militaristic orientation and who either held a low religious commitment, or, if they were religious, joined churches that were theologically and politically conservative.[44] California offered many promising fields for finding groups seeking young converts, with its vibrant beach scene, a hippie culture drawing young people from across the country, and two large state university systems whose campuses had developed a reputation as hospitable places for experimentation, rebellion, and countercultural movements. Many new religious movements worked in those fields to gain members, from Protestant groups like Campus Crusade and the Jesus People to groups often labeled as cults, such as the Unification Church, the Hare Krishnas, and Transcendental Meditation.[45]

When children joined a new religious movement, their parents often experienced the decision as a rejection of their family and its values. Dr. Jerome Millman, a Los Angeles physician, filed a $150 million lawsuit against the Unification Church after his son joined during his freshman year at UC Berkeley. According to Millman, his son became a "psychological prisoner" who had redirected his "natural affection" away from his father and toward the church.[46] The loss was especially acute when converts limited or cut off communication or adopted new identities, as when Kathe Crampton moved in with her new "God-centered family" and changed her name to Corinth.[47] To their parents, these converts were repudiating their parents' caretaking role, which intensified the isolation for those who had migrated to California and were geographically distant from extended family.[48] They were depending on their children, whose educational, professional, and economic success would position them to provide support—to care for them as they aged. In this context, their children's choices were incomprehensible, so they pointed to "severance of family ties" and "irrational change from love to hatred of family" as evidence that a religious movement relied on brainwashing to recruit and retain members.[49]

Fear of communism also drove the anticult movement's warnings about the precarity of the nation's families. Activists claimed that cults and communism shared an anti-American, anti-family ideology. A child's decision to leave a job, drop out of college, or turn over financial resources to a new religious movement came as a rejection of their parents' economic caretaking and the values that underpinned it.[50] Financial security was the reason many of these parents had relocated to Southern California. They had brought with them an unwavering commitment to capitalism, placing a high value on individual hard work and affirming the economic self-interest that sustained it. This economic perspective was grounded in the anticommunist and Cold War ideology of the aerospace and defense industries that had drawn them to the West.[51] Anticommunist activism was widespread in Southern California, which was home to almost a third of the national membership of the stridently anticommunist John Birch Society in the 1960s. It was also where Fred Schwarz's Christian Anti-Communism Crusade attracted its largest crowds during that decade.[52] Along with Southern California's growing conservative base, the anticult movement was critical of any group that had the appearance of communist leanings. A frequent critique of the Unification Church was that it fostered group dependence by requiring members to turn over money they had solicited rather than retain it.[53] While the anticult movement expanded these economic concerns to questions about preserving American ideals, they remained, at their core, anxieties about economic security for individual families.

This emphasis on family was why the anticult movement struggled to achieve numerical and financial stability. Parents who joined anticult groups wanted to restore their fractured relationships with their children, and once those were repaired, most parents left the movement. As a result, the revolving door of anticult membership mirrored the pattern seen in those same religious groups the parents opposed.[54] This instability strained the volunteer groups financially and in terms of workload, even in the relatively strong chapters in California. A 1984 report from the Los Angeles chapter noted that despite a heavy workload of answering inquiries and making presentations, the "work [was] carried out by 3 or 4 couples," they had "no acting chairman," and they had been unable to hold any meetings recently.[55] In their efforts to broaden support, the anticult movement claimed there was no line separating the fragility of families and the precarity of the nation. They characterized families as the basic building blocks of the nation and its social order, echoing an argument that dated back to nineteenth-century anti-Catholicism and anti-Mormonism. Families at risk imperiled the nation, the movement insisted.[56] However, the movement struggled to transform the problems of a small, ever-shifting group of parents into a national crusade, leaving it unable to achieve the stability it needed.

A Nation Imperiled

When anticult arguments moved beyond their focus on family relationships, activists most often claimed that these new religious movements undermined American ideals of freedom and liberty. The anticult movement portrayed itself as loyal to the United States, fighting against un-American groups that threatened the nation. A steady stream of articles in the newsletter of the Southern California CFF outlined these opposing perspectives between the nation and the "cults." One column claimed, "Thousands of concerned people want to know why so many cults can flourish while advocating the destruction of America."[57] The most commonly invoked evidence of opposition to freedom was the way new religious movements supposedly controlled their members.

The anticult movement drew on the long-standing cult stereotype of an authoritarian leader who dictated members' sexual, marriage, and family relations to support their claims of control. Such leaders also required members to relinquish their economic assets to the leader to manage on behalf of the organization. Anticult advocates denied that any American would freely choose to live under such conditions. "Any program which depicts cult membership as the result of free and independent decision making instead of coercive persuasion, brainwashing, behavior modification, etc. does a disservice to the public," declared a critic of a television show that featured a convert to Hare Krishna."[58] A leader's coercive tactics also demonstrated disregard for freedom of religion, which the anticult movement defined as one's ability to choose their religion freely. "The effectiveness of our established institutions," a *CFF News* column cautioned, and "even our Constitution is being eroded by these treacherous and seditious groups and affects all of us."[59] Twenty years after he began the modern anticult movement's first organization—and with his daughter still a part of the Children of God (since renamed the Family International)—Bill Rambur explained his goals: "We wanted to educate the public on how to recognize when cults posed a threat to the basic freedoms and rights we enjoy in this country and to encourage responsibility among other Americans for protecting these freedoms and rights."[60] The parents who founded the anticult movement assumed this line of reasoning about religious liberty was self-evident, especially from their position on the front lines of the Cold War. Perched on the West Coast, and often employed in the region's defense industry or themselves veterans, they took it as a given that freedom, especially freedom of religion, was essential to American democracy. This was in contrast to its antithesis: authoritarianism, and godless communism.[61]

As a result, these threats to family and nation were a crisis of the highest order. Extreme danger required an extreme response. As Bill Rambur insisted four years after his daughter joined the COG, "the severe threat imposed by these cults justifies action taken by these parents to save their children . . . [and] is why such drastic action is necessary."[62] In the California context of fractured families and an imperiled nation, caretaking could take uncomfortable and even violent forms. While parents hoped their movement would gain support from law enforcement and government agencies, many did not wait and took measures into their own hands. Deprogramming was the most visible and controversial of those actions. San Diego resident Ted Patrick claimed to have invented the practice based on his encounter with and supposed escape from the COG.

While deprogramming could mean different things, in its original and most familiar form, developed by Patrick, it involved removing converts from the group, often employing deception or physical force, and isolating them in a motel or remote home. Once there, deprogrammers denied them sleep and bombarded them with negative information until they agreed to leave the group.[63] Brainwashing was the justification for deprogramming. Supporters of deprogramming insisted it reversed the effects of mind control and freed the former cult member "to take their rightful place in society, free from further threats to their peace and security."[64] While anticult publications claim deprogramming was an effective tool, it is impossible to determine how many attempted deprogrammings took place and what percentage were successful, as reliable statistics are not available, leaving only general assertions that disagree widely.[65] Some former members credited deprogramming for their decision to leave a group. Others managed to evade or deceive their deprogrammers and returned to their religious community, sometimes multiple times. Although forcibly removing people from religious communities was not new, the particular vocabulary and process of deprogramming was distinctive and made it one of the defining characteristics of the modern anticult movement.

Deprogrammers and their supporters soon found themselves on the defensive. Not only was it illegal to remove adults from a community they had chosen, but it was also antithetical to the principles of religious freedom that the anticult movement insisted it upheld. Opponents pointed to the logical inconsistency of claiming to free someone by taking away their freedom. They also noted that deprogramming appeared no different from the brainwashing that the anticult movement criticized. Anticultists countered that their antagonists had it backward: The new religious movements had taken away freedom. The anticult movement linked deprogramming to their rhetoric of religious liberty. It was the means to restore freedom. Because "cults are controlling and abusing behind a façade of religion," concerned parents insisted, "the victims are unable to free themselves." As a result, extracting them "from the influence of cult leaders" was a way to ensure the member was "exercising their own free will."[66] Going further, anticult groups insisted that the groups they targeted had forfeited any claim to constitutional protections because of their unwillingness to ensure freedom within their communities. In this back and forth, both sides of the deprogramming debate participated in the ongoing dialectic between toleration and resistance characteristic of the experience of religion in California and the American West.

The anticult movement insisted that the vast deficiencies in the groups they opposed proved they were not real religions and therefore not entitled to constitutional protection. To anticultists, groups that undermined families and the nation stood outside the bounds of religion, at least in the United States. They used labels such as "counterfeit," "false," and "pseudo" to signal that distinction.[67] The so-called fake religions, they contended, only called themselves religions to shield their destructive practices under the guise of religious freedom. A typical allegation was that there were a "large number of counterfeit religions functioning under the protective cloak of the Constitution." The column went on to claim "conclusive evidence . . . showing that many of these pseudo-religions are fraudulently thriving and no action is taken because they claim to be religions."[68] In this schema, cult and religion were mutually exclusive categories. Real religion was worthy of constitutional protection; illegitimate religion was not. As anticult groups used labels like "pseudo" and "cult" to stigmatize a group and insist it was outside the bounds of authentic religion, they theorized the category of religion and policed its boundaries. They were also participating in a long history of battles about the definition of religion in California and the West.[69]

Going National

While efforts to nationalize the anticult movement faltered during the 1970s, the California chapters remained relatively strong. This regional strength enabled them to play a significant role during the movement's first decade and in the national organization that emerged in the 1980s. The first effort to create a national organization occurred in 1972 in Detroit, when a group of parents formed a national FREECOG modeled on the chapter that Bill Rambur and others had started in San Diego. The national group proved unable to expand beyond the work the San Diego chapter was already doing, and "parents were still coming to San Diego for help." As a result, the national organization folded when "after a number of months it became apparent that we were national in name only."[70]

A second effort to form a national organization occurred in Denver in 1974, taking a broader focus beyond just the COG. They adopted the model of an umbrella organization with local chapters around the country and chose the name Citizens Freedom Foundation, as had the San Diego and Los Angeles chapters when they expanded their efforts beyond the COG. Most chapters in the national organization struggled with both membership and finances. But not in California. The several California organizations, both Northern and Southern, were among the largest in the nation. *CFF News*, started by Rambur in 1974, functioned as the national newsletter throughout the decade, even though it was technically the newsletter of the Southern California chapters. California chapters met regularly; had a clear leadership structure and bylaws; maintained a reliable slate of speakers from medical, legal, educational, and law enforcement fields; and publicized their concerns to the media contacts, resulting in coverage that drew national attention. Based on their accomplishments, leaders from California often took on roles in the national organization. In the early 1980s, when the national organization that would finally endure was formed, it was initially headquartered in Los Angeles, "where it could rely on the superior organization and larger number of members of the CFF, undoubtedly still the most stable and largest ACM organization in America at that time." Even when CAN relocated its national office to Chicago, it continued to depend on California affiliates to answer many of the inquiries that came into the national office.[71]

The strategies the California chapters used become models for CAN, the national organization, and for other local anticult groups nationwide. A common approach was working with legislatures. The first step was often hearings by a legislative committee whose members had been lobbied by concerned parents. State Senator Mervyn Dymally, chair of the California Senate's Committee on Children and Youth, held a hearing in Los Angeles in 1974 "to determine whether legislation was needed to deal with alleged instances of teen-agers being 'brainwashed' into joining some cults." The Committee heard from former members of religious communal movements such as the COG and the Susan and Tony Alamo Foundation (a communal movement located 30 miles north of Los Angeles) about their experiences in and difficulty leaving those groups.[72] Many other states would hold similar hearings in subsequent years, especially following the People's Temple tragedy in Jonestown in November 1978.

Three months after the events at Jonestown, Senator Bob Dole of Kansas sponsored a national hearing. Dole had also organized a session three years earlier to hear complaints about the Unification Church. As the meeting approached, national leaders from nine Protestant denominations and one Jewish organization wrote Dole asking for more balance in the views of the scheduled speakers. They warned that "the hearing you are co-sponsoring next week can do nothing but inflame the public and obscure the complex issues which surround the activities of minority groups." Despite assurances in his opening remarks, Dole did not schedule additional hearings, reflecting the unexpected level of opposition the session attracted.[73] While the national stage of Dole's hearings provided a higher profile, it remained the exception as most followed the California model of focusing on state legislatures.

Anticult activists went beyond pushing for hearings to advocate legislation restricting new religious movements. These efforts usually took an indirect approach, given the likelihood of constitutional challenges to laws that explicitly named the targeted groups. A bill proposed in the California Assembly in 1977 (AB2058) would have required those soliciting funds to register with the state and forced charities to disclose certain information about their organizations. They would also be subject to outside review of their books if they had revenue exceeding $100,000.[74] In 1980, California also changed its corporations code, allowing the state attorney general to investigate religious groups under certain conditions. But after only a year on the books, it was repealed with strong support from a wide range of religious groups, including long-established religious institutions as well as the new religious movements that were the intended targets of the legislation.[75]

The most common legislative proposals focused on expanding conservatorship and guardianship laws. An early success in using conservatorship laws occurred in California in December 1976. The parents of a woman in the Unification Church convinced a Superior Court judge in Alameda County to appoint her mother as a conservator, enabling them to forcibly remove her and return her to her family and home.[76] When a higher court determined that the conservatorship law was not applicable to such cases, state legislatures across the country started proposing amendments to their conservatorship and guardianship laws that would make them applicable to those who had joined new religious movements. Most attempts occurred in the years following the tragedy in Jonestown.[77] Anticult activists hoped to provide legal cover for deprogramming, since people who were conserved lost their ability to make their own decisions, including undergoing deprogramming. Ultimately, neither California nor any other state succeeded in passing such laws. The New York state legislature came the closest, passing bills in both houses in consecutive years (1980 and 1981). The governor vetoed both because of concerns about the First Amendment.[78] Even these vetoes did not discourage efforts in California. Seeking help, a member of the Los Angeles CFF chapter wrote to an advocate for the New York bills, explaining, "There are so many cults in California that the need for legislation that would help curb their strength is very great."[79]

One of the more distinctive strategies that Southern California chapters pursued was leveraging their location to enlist celebrity support. Steve Allen, the first host of *The Tonight Show*, was their most frequent ally. Allen's son Brian was a member of the Love Israel Family for several years, and the elder Allen wrote a book about this experience.[80] Allen did not fight his son's choice and maintained communication with him, unlike the more confrontational approaches many parents in the anticult movement pursued. Eventually, Brian left of his own volition and joined his father in the anticult movement. The elder Allen did not share all of CAN's views and often asked for explanations of its activities. Still, he remained grateful for the support he and his family received from anticult organizations while his son belonged to the Love Israel Family. Unlike other parents, Allen remained connected to the anticult movement after Brian left the group. He served on CAN's Advisory Board, provided financial support, spoke at events, signed his name to fundraising letters, wrote an introduction to a book by the national director of CAN, and agreed to appear in an anticult documentary.[81] Another celebrity whom the Los Angeles chapter frequently relied upon was Mike Farrell, best known for his role as B. J. Hunnicutt in the television series *M*A*S*H*. As a well-known activist and spokesperson for progressive causes, Farrell's support was a publicity coup for CAN. Like Allen, Farrell provided financial support, attended conferences, and appeared at fundraising events.[82] He also offered introductions to other potential celebrity supporters in the Los Angeles area. Allen and Farrell's work paved the way for celebrities elsewhere to lend their influence and support to the anticult movement. In the 1980s, when Scientology became the anticult movement's biggest opponent, the celebrity support for CAN countered Scientology's celebrity members such as Tom Cruise, John Travolta, and Kirstie Alley.

Various other organizations in the Golden State reinforced its preeminence as a hub of anticult advocacy. The Freedom Counseling Center in Burlingame, though not an explicitly anticult organization, described its client base as families whose lives have been disrupted by "cults."[83] Others were explicitly Christian organizations whose primary emphasis was the heretical character of new religious movements, although they also warned of the dangers around mind control and brainwashing that were the focus of anticult parent groups. Walter Martin's Christian Research Institute, which relocated to Southern California from New Jersey in 1974, collected information and resources about groups they identified as "cults" and trained Christian leaders in counter-cult activity. In Northern California, the Spiritual Counterfeits Project in Berkeley emerged at the same time. It emphasized a scholarly approach to the study of new religious movements, including publication in the *Journal of Cultic Studies*, although it still operated from an underlying evangelical motivation and engaged movements from a theological perspective. When the national anticult organization CAN finally found success in the 1980s, it followed the example of the Spiritual Counterfeits Project by forming the American Family Foundation (AFF) to provide the appearance of academic and professional support for CAN's work.[84] Long after its founding, California organizations continued to play a critical role in an anticult movement that had gone national.

Conclusion

Although the anticult movement had some success, it never achieved the status its founders hoped. Portraying the supposed cult crisis as a threat to families had not resonated with most Americans. Only a few families had experienced a child's decision to join a new religious movement. Nor did all parents object to a child's conversion, even to one of the groups the anticult movement labeled a cult. Concerns about religious freedom further compounded the anticult movement's challenges. As Senator Dole learned at the 1979 hearing he sponsored, many Americans opposed the anticult movement's legislative and regulatory efforts, even in the wake of the Jonestown tragedy. The same was true at the state level. In Washoe County, Nevada, on the border of California and home to Reno, 61 percent of registered voters in 1984 disagreed with the state legislature's effort to impose restrictions on new religious movements.[85] By the 1990s, the growing opposition to anticult efforts overwhelmed CAN. The national organization lost most of its remaining credibility when its anticult perspective contributed to the federal government's decision to raid the Branch Davidian compound outside Waco in 1993, resulting in the death of seventy-four Branch Davidians and ten federal officers.[86] CAN was also the defendant in numerous criminal and civil cases stemming from its connections to deprogramming, leading to its bankruptcy in 1996.[87] Although some smaller anticult organizations continued, none rose to the level of CAN, or even its predecessor organizations that had begun in Southern California twenty-five years earlier.

Despite its challenges and eventual demise, the California-founded anticult movement had a national impact. Its consistent use of "cult" as a one-word-fits-all label for unwelcome or threatening religious groups and as a racially inflected marker of difference, ensured continued awareness and utilization of the term and its negative connotations. In the two and a half decades since the institutional anticult movement ended, the word "cult" has been used as frequently as ever to discredit groups, including Islam (especially after 9/11), supporters of Donald Trump, followers of Q-Anon conspiracies, and participants in the January 6 insurrection.[88] In entertainment, the category of cult, as well as terms such as "brainwashing" and "deprogramming," remain common plot devices that require no explanation for audiences to understand. Anticult members' media savvy was crucial to this ongoing cultural impact, even as those terms and those who advocated their use were increasingly discredited in legal and legislative contexts. Anchored in the media hub of Southern California, the early anticult movement used its proximity to and connections with members of the news and entertainment media and their interest in sensational stories to promulgate the anticult message on networks that had national and even international reach. Anticult members appeared on radio and television talk shows, in popular magazines, and in the news media, which raised their profile and made them the default experts on "cults." Nor was this impact limited to the United States. Like much of what begins in California, the anticult movement expanded to become not just national but international in scope. The success of this global expansion was a product of differing approaches to religious freedom and expanding patterns of international migration that new religious movements and their members followed.[89]

The modern anticult movement had deep roots and broad branches in California, not only in its origins but also for its duration. In the absence of religious hegemony, the Golden State had long been conducive to religious innovation. Such was the case in the mid-twentieth century, especially in Southern California. But the same region that fostered experimentation was also resistant to it. The founders of the modern anticult movement drew upon that resistant context to create opposition to the groups they labeled cults, by which they meant groups that transgressed the boundaries of acceptable religion and citizenship that the anticult movement had created. The Californians who founded the anticult movement viewed the religious groups they attacked as threats to their family and the nation. As recent transplants to California in the Cold War context, they experienced the precariousness of those responsibilities in their "daily lives and livelihoods."[90] Even in a region historically characterized by pluralism, Southern Californians were navigating a new level of religious and cultural pluralism by the 1960s.[91] The modern anticult movement was an expression of that challenge. The story of its emergence, growth, and struggles is a case study in the complicated ways that religious creativity is both present and contested in an ongoing dialectic in the American West.

Notes

1. Betty Rambur, "Kay Rambur Joins the Children of God," in "Legal Issues—Dole Hearings," Cults/Anti-Cult, Box 234, American Religions Collection, ARC Mss 1, Special Research Collections, UC Santa Barbara Library; Flo Conway and Jay Siegelman, *Snapping: America's Epidemic of Sudden Personality Change*, 2nd ed. (Stillpoint Press, 1995), 74–78; "Cult Awareness Network Co-founder's Claims Fraudulent," in *The Family—A Fellowship of Independent Christian Missionary Communities*, Baptist and Religious, Institute of Church-State Studies Vertical File Collection, J. M. Dawson Institute of Church-State Studies, Research Files Collection, Baylor University; "Parents Join to Combat Radical Youth Sect," *New York Times*, February 21, 1972; Larry Eskridge, *God's Forever Family: The Jesus People Movement in America* (Oxford University Press, 2013), 191.

2. Unless otherwise specified, "children" in this chapter refers to adult children (e.g., those age eighteen and older).

3. Henrietta Crampton, "Citizens Freedom Foundation," *Who We Are and What We Do: A Handbook for Newcomers*, Folder 6, Box 136, Cult Awareness Network (CAN) Collection, ARC Mss 19, Department of Special Collections, Davidson Library, University of California, Santa Barbara; William Rambur, letter, Folder 7, Box 136; Priscilla D. Coates, "The History of the Cult Awareness Network," in *Anti-Cult Movements in Cross-Cultural Perspective*, ed. Anson Shupe and David Bromley (Garland Publishing, 1994), 93–101; Eugene V. Gallagher, *The New Religious Movements Experience in America* (Greenwood Press, 2004), 4–13; J. Gordon Melton, "Anti-Cultists in the United States: An Historical Perspective," in *New Religious Movements: Challenge and Response*, ed. Bryan Wilson and Jamie Cresswell (Routledge, 1999), 216; Anson D. Shupe and David G. Bromley, *The New Vigilantes: Deprogrammers, Anti-Cultists, and the New Religion* (SAGE, 1980), 89–93; Anson D. Shupe and Susan E. Darnell, *Agents of Discord: Deprogramming, Pseudo-Science, and the American Anticult Movement* (Transaction Publishers, 2006), 34–35.

4. Lisa McGirr, *Suburban Warriors: The Origins of the New American Right*, Politics and Society in Twentieth-Century America (Princeton University Press, 2001), 20–21; John W. Compton, *The End of Empathy: Why White Protestants Stopped Loving Their Neighbors*

(Oxford University Press, 2020), 200–16; Wade Clark Roof, "Pluralism as a Culture: Religion and Civility in Southern California," *The Annals of the American Academy of Political and Social Science* 612 (July 2007): 84; Eldon G. Ernst, "The Emergence of California in American Religious Historiography," *Religion and American Culture: A Journal of Interpretation* 11, no. 1 (Winter 2001): 35, 42, 48.

5. Carey McWilliams, "The Cults of California," *The Atlantic Monthly* 177 (March 1964): 105–10.

6. "Agency History," New Religious Movements Organizations: Vertical Files Collection Graduate Theological Union Archives, Berkeley, CA. For similar claims by historians who participated in the Center's first major conference and publication, see Sydney E. Ahlstrom, "From Sinai to the Golden Gate: The Liberation of Religion in the Occident," and John Dillenberger, "Roots of the American Ethos," both in *Understanding the New Religions*, ed. Jacob Needleman and George Baker (Seabury Press, 1981), 22, 25; Lorne L. Dawson, *Comprehending Cults: The Sociology of New Religious Movements* (Oxford University Press Canada, 1998), 26–27; Philip Jenkins, *Mystics and Messiahs: Cults and New Religions in American History* (Oxford University Press, 2000), 175.

7. Charles A. Fracchia, "The Western Context: Its Impact on Our Religious Consciousness," *Lutheran Quarterly* 29 (February1977): 13–20. I am grateful to Joshua Paddison for drawing my attention to this article.

8. Anson Shupe and David G. Bromley, "The Modern Anti-Cult Movement 1971–1919: A Twenty-Year Retrospective," in *Anti-Cult Movements in Cross Cultural Perspective*, ed. Anson Shupe and David G. Bromley (Garland, 1994), 11.

9. Ted Patrick and Tom Dulack, *Let Our Children Go!* (Dutton, 1976), 62.

10. Henrietta Crampton to Assemblyman Gerald Felando, February 1, 1986, Box 104, Affiliates-Calif-Los Angeles, CAN Collection.

11. Judith M. Weber, Corresponding Secretary, to Media, cover letter to media kit, 1991, Box 105, "Nor California," CAN Collection.

12. Among histories of Southern California, see Compton, *End of Empathy*; and McGirr, *Suburban Warriors*. Among scholars of religion, see Dawson, *Comprehending Cults*, citing Rodney Stark and William Sims Bainbridge, *The Future of Religion: Secularization, Revival and Cult Formation* (1985); and Chris Bader and Alfred Demaris, "A Test of the Stark and Bainbridge Theory of Affiliation with Religious Cults and Sects," *Journal for the Scientific Study of Religion* 35, no. 3 (1996): 285–303.

13. Darren Dochuk, *From Bible Belt to Sunbelt: Plain-Folk Religion, Grassroots Politics, and the Rise of Evangelical Conservatism* (W. W. Norton, 2011), xv–xvi, 171.

14. Compton, *End of Empathy*, 11, 207–8, 214–16; Ernst, "Emergence of California," 42; McGirr, *Suburban Warriors*, 85–86.

15. Dochuk, *From Bible Belt to Sunbelt*; Eskridge, *God's Forever Family*, 69–75; McGirr, *Suburban Warriors*, 242.

16. David G. Bromley and Anson D. Shupe, *Strange Gods: The Great American Cult Scare* (Beacon Press, 1981), 82; Eskridge, *God's Forever Family*, 61–63.

17. Laurie Maffly-Kipp, "Eastward Ho!," in *Retelling U.S. Religious History* (University of California Press, 1997), 127–48.

18. Barbara Underwood, "What Is There to Fear from the State's Religious Cults?" *California Journal* 12, no. 12 (December 1981): 431.

19. Dawson, *Comprehending Cults*, 26–27.

20. William Rambur, "Statement from CFF's President," *CFF News* 1 (November 1974): 1–2.

21. The emergence of this conservative moment and its religious dimensions are the focus of Compton, *End of Empathy*; Dochuk, *From Bible Belt to Sunbelt*; and McGirr, *Suburban Warriors*.

22. McGirr, *Suburban Warriors*, 8–9, 20–21, 25–26, 45; Compton, *End of Empathy*, 207.

23. McGirr, *Suburban Warriors*, 8, 43–44.

24. Dochuk, *From Bible Belt to Sunbelt*, 172; George Lipsitz, *How Racism Takes Place* (Temple University Press), 25–46; David Delaney, "The Space That Race Makes," *Professional Geographer* 54, no. 1 (February 2002): 6–7.

25. Charlotte Brooks, "Sing Shen vs. Southwood: Exclusion, Residential Segregation, and Chinese American Resistance in Postwar California," *Pacific Historical Review* 73, no. 3 (August 2004): 490–97; Scott Kurashige, *The Shifting Grounds of Race: Black and Japanese Americans in the Making of Multiethnic Los Angeles* (Princeton University Press, 2010), 247; McGirr, *Suburban Warriors*, 42–45; Dochuk, *From Bible Belt to Sunbelt*, 106–9, 172.

26. Compton, *End of Empathy*, 209–12, 219–25.

27. Ann Watson, *The Ann Watson Report* (January 1975), reprinted in *CFF News* 2 (January–February 1975): 3.

28. "Western Europe Watching Sects," *CFF News* 3 (November 1978): 3; J. Gordon Melton, "The Modern Anti-Cult Movement in Historical Perspective," in *The Cultic Milieu: Oppositional Subcultures in an Age of Globalization*, ed. Jeffrey Kaplan and Heléne Lööw (AltaMira Press, 2002), 266–67.

29. Jenkins, *Mystics and Messiahs*, 189; Shupe and Bromley, *New Vigilantes*, 70–71.

30. On earlier examples of the "fear of internal subversion" from religious groups labeled foreign, see David Brion Davis, "Some Themes of Counter-Subversion: An Analysis of Anti-Masonic, Anti-Catholic, and Anti-Mormon Literature," *Mississippi Valley Historical Review* 47, no. 2 (September 1960): 205–24.

31. "Press Conference a Success," *CFF News* 2 (October 1977): 1.

32. "Fraser Committee—CFF News Conference," *CFF News* 3 (November 1978): 2.

33. Elizabeth Aileen Young, "The Use of the Brainwashing Theory by the Anti-Cult Movement, Pre-1966," *Zeitschrift für junge Religionswissenschaft* 7 (2012): 5–19; Conway and Siegelman, *Snapping*, 78–83; Bromley and Shupe, *Strange Gods*, 95; Shupe and Bromley, *New Vigilantes*, 29–30, 71–72; Shupe and Darnell, *Agents of Discord*, 38–39, 65, 126–28.

34. Eugene V. Gallagher, "'Cults' and 'New Religious Movements,'" *History of Religions* 47, no. 2/3 (November 2007–February 2008): 205–20. Jenkins, *Mystics and Messiahs*, 10, 14; James D. Tabor and Eugene V. Gallagher, *Why Waco? Cults and the Battle for Religious Freedom in America* (University of California Press, 1995), 139, 159–65.

35. William Rambur," CFF Fund-Raising Appeal," February 1975, in Citizens Freedom Foundation [3/5], Box 232, ARC Mss 1.

36. Bromley and Shupe, *Strange Gods*, 3, 24–25.

37. "No One Is Immune," *CFF News* 3 (April 1978): 2.

38. Henrietta Crampton, "Killing Her Softly with His Love," undated typescript in "Citizens Freedom Foundation—Corr. [4/5]," Box 232, ARC MSS 1.

39. Henrietta Crampton, "Kathe Crampton's Story," *CFF News* 3 (April 1975): 2–3.

40. Jack Eckhardt, "Religious Cult or Radical Revolutionary," *CFF News* 3 (January 1976): 1–2.

41. Melton, "Anticultists," 221.

42. Shupe and Bromley, *New Vigilantes*, 153–64; James R Lewis, "Apostates and the Legitimation of Repression: Some Historical and Empirical Perspectives on the Cult Controversy," *Sociological Analysis* 49, no. 4 (1989): 386–96.

43. "The Cult Crisis," in "Affiliates—Calif—Nor Cal," Box 204, CAN Collection.

44. Compton, *End of Empathy*, 206–7; Dochuk, *From Bible Belt to Sunbelt*, 309; McGirr, *Suburban Warriors*, 242; Shupe and Bromley, *New Vigilantes*, 72.

45. Eskridge, *God's Forever Family*, 2–3, 10–93; McGirr, *Suburban Warriors*, 242; Melton, "Anticultists," 214–15.

46. "$150 Million Suit Filed Over 'Moonie' Follower," *CFF News* 3 (April 1978): 2.

47. Henrietta Crampton, "Kathe Crampton's Story," *CFF News* 3 (April 1975): 2–3.

48. Compton, *End of Empathy*, 207; McGirr, *Suburban Warriors*, 309, 48, 53.

49. William Rambur, "'How Can You Get at Somebody Who Controls a Kid's Mind? Asked One Unhappy Father (A Letter to Our Legislators)," *CFF News* 2 (January–February 1975): 1–2.

50. Shupe and Bromley, *New Vigilantes*, 38–42.

51. Compton, *End of Empathy*, 212; Dochuk, *From Bible Belt to Sunbelt*, 170; McGirr, *Suburban Warriors*, 8, 29, 51–53.

52. Compton, *End of Empathy*, 211.

53. Shupe and Bromley, *New Vigilantes*, 40–42.

54. Shupe and Darnell, *Agents of Discord*, 29, 118; Bromley and Shupe, *Strange Gods*, 4, 91.

55. "Quarterly Activity Report: CFF Cult Awareness Network," in "Affiliates-Calif-Los Angeles," Box 104, CAN Collection; Shupe and Bromley, *New Vigilantes*, 8, 95.

56. Davis, *Themes of Counter-Subversion*; James B. Bennett, "'Until This Curse of Polygamy Is Wiped out': Black Methodists, White Mormons, and Constructions of Racial Identity in the Late Nineteenth Century," *Religion and American Culture* 21, no. 2 (Summer 2011): 183; Bradley B. Onishi, *Preparing for War: The Extremist History of White Christian Nationalism—and What Comes Next* (Broadleaf Books, 2023), 30.

57. William Rambur, "Statement from CFF's President," *CFF News* 3 (February–March 1976): 1.

58. "Lou Grant / Hare Krishna Show," *CFF News* 3 (January 1978): 1.

59. "Whose Burden—Yours or Mine?" *CFF News* 3 (April 1975): 1.

60. Bill Rambur to CAN Supporters [n.d.], Folder 7, Box 136, CAN Collection.

61. Compton, *End of Empathy*, 209–12; Onishi, *Preparing for War*, 30, 51–56. This language illustrates how the ideas that informed the logic of American Empire in an earlier period through what Tisa Wenger calls "religious freedom talk," persisted into the mid- and late twentieth century. Tisa Joy Wenger, *Religious Freedom: The Contested History of an American Ideal* (University of North Carolina Press, 2017).

62. William Rambur, "Kidnap or Rescue?," *CFF News* 2 (March 1975): 1.

63. Patrick, *Let Our Children Go!*, 37–60; Shupe and Bromley, *New Vigilantes*, 121–44; Bromley and Shupe, *Strange Gods*, 181–83.

64. William Rambur, "What Is Deprogramming?" *CFF News* 1 (November 1974): 1; Young, "Use of Brainwashing Theory," 5–6.

65. For example, David G. Bromley, a scholar critical of the practice claims the success rates were high, in "Deprogramming as a Mode of Exit from New Religious Movements: The Case of the Unificationist Movement," in *Falling From the Faith*, ed. David G. Bromley (SAGE, 1988). In contrast, some analysis by anti-cult organizations, such as the International Cultic Studies Association, suggest over a one-third failure rate; see Michael D. Langone, "Deprogramming: An Analysis of Parental Questionnaires" *Cultic Studies Journal* 1 (1984): 63–68.

66. Rambur, "Kidnap or Rescue?," 1.

67. James B. Bennett, "Pseudo Religion and Real Religion: The Modern Anti-Cult Movement and Religious Freedom in America," in *The Lively Experiment: Religious Toleration in America from Roger Williams to the Present*, ed. Chris Beneke and Christopher S. Grenda (Rowman & Littlefield, 2015), 287–303.

68. William Rambur, "Statement from CFF's President," *CFF News* 3 (February–March 1976): 1.

69. On ways ordinary Americans in the West have theorized religion, see David Walker, *Railroading Religion: Mormons, Tourists, and the Corporate Spirit of the West* (University of California Press, 2019), 7.

70. William Rambur, "Statement from CFF's President," *CFF News* 1 (November 1974): 1–2.

71. Shupe and Bromley, *New Vigilantes*, 93, 105; Shupe and Bromley, "The Modern Anti-Cult Movement," 6; Shupe and Bromley, *Agents of Discord*, 79.

72. "Senator Dymally Hosts Hearing on Religious Cult Tactics," *CFF News* 1 (November 1974): 3.

73. Robert Z. Alpern, J. Elliott Corbett, et al. to Robert Dole, January 30, 1979, Folder 39, Box 228, ARC Mss 1; "Dole Announces Justice Department Meeting with 'Brainwashing' Experts," October 14, 1976, Robert J. Dole Senate Papers, Folder 11, Box 302, Robert and Elizabeth Dole Archive and Special Collections, Robert J. Dole Institute of Politics, University of Kansas; "Senator Dole's 'Expert' Witnesses Exposed," Folder 23, Box 50, Dole Senate Papers; "Dole Announces Justice Department Meeting," October 14, 1976, Folder 24, Box 50.

74. "California Bill AB 2058," *CFF News* 3 (January 1978): 4.

75. California Senate Bill 1044, "An Act to Amend Section 9230 of the Corporations Code, Relating to Religious Corporations" (1980); "Petris Bill Update—California," *Citizens Freedom Foundation Information Services News* 5 (June 1980): 1.

76. Morton A. Eden to Speaker of the House, May 12, 1981, Box 135, "Misc. Leg," CAN Collection.

77. Chart of State Resolutions, "Legis.—State Laws," Box 135, CAN Collection.

78. Veto Jacket #127 (1980) and Veto Jacket #27 (1981), "Veto Jackets," New York State Library, Albany, NY.

79. Janet Baranet to Priscilla Coates, July 19, 1981, "Proposed Other States," Box 135, CAN Collection.

80. Steve Allen, *Beloved Son: A Story of the Jesus Cults* (Indianapolis: Bobbs-Merrill, 1982).

81. Listed on proposed conference program for Inglewood 1992; Pat Quinn to Cynthia Kisser, October 30, 1991, "Steve Allen," Box 87, CAN Collection; Steve Allen to Carlos Cornier, December 22, 1992, "Steve Allen," Box 87, CAN Collection; Allen to Kisser, April 25, 1991, "Allen, Steve," Box 87, CAN Collection; Steve Allen to Friend, July 25, 1988, Folder 6, Box 136, CAN Collection.

82. Wine and Cheese fundraiser flyer, Folder 10, Box 136, CAN Collection.

83. "Freedom Counseling Center," Folder 33, Box 13, New Religious Movements Organizations: Vertical Files Collection, GTU 99-8-1, Graduate Theological Union Archives, Berkeley, CA.

84. On the Christian Countercult Movement and its difference from the Anticult Movement, see Douglas E. Cowan, *The Christian Countercult Movement*, Cambridge Elements: New Religious Movements (Cambridge: Cambridge University Press, 2023); Melton, "Anti-Cultists," 222–23.

85. James T. Richardson and Barend Van Driel, "Public Support for Anti-Cult Legislation," *Journal for the Scientific Study of Religion* 23, no. 4 (December 1984): 412–13.

86. Tabor and Gallagher, *Why Waco?*

87. Melton, "Anti-Cultists," 213, 230–32; Shupe and Darnell, *Agents of Discord*, 179–80.

88. Benjamin E. Zeller, "The Cult of Trump? What 'Cult Rhetoric' Actually Reveals," *Religion & Politics*, October 29, 2019; Shupe and Bromley, *New Vigilantes*, 170, 241.

89. Shupe and Darnell, *Agents of Discord*, 195–238; Shupe and Bromley, *Anti-Cult Movement in Cross-Cultural Perspective*, 129–219; Marat S. Shterin and James T. Richardson, "Effects of the Western Anti-Cult Movement on Development of Laws Concerning Religion in Post-Communist Russia," *Journal of Church and State* 42, no. 2 (Spring 2000): 247–71.

90. McGirr, *Suburban Warriors*, 51–52.

91. Roof, "Pluralism as Culture," 84.

PART II

Caretaking and Imperial Enclaves

In the vast expanses of the trans-Mississippi West, much of which had also been the northern reaches of the Spanish Empire, religio-ethnic groups sometimes found locations to gather and create their communities of care and control. However, these religious islands in an expanding empire were hardly immune to the explicit and implicit forces that empires exert on their subjects to assimilate and to function within licit bounds. In this section of the volume, we see quite different examples of ethnic and religious enclaves that defy and are ultimately beholden to surrounding powers. The examples here, the remnants of the Spanish empire, Dutch Calvinists, and the Church of Jesus Christ of Latter-day Saints, all represent groups that maintained strong institutions, even as they were surrounded by the US State. These groups, unlike the communities discussed in section 3, aimed not just to respond to the imperial aspirations of the US but to enact their own imperial aspirations. In each case, we see that caregiving and caretaking play a key role not only in meeting the needs of members of the community but in defining the boundaries around the community.

Jon Garcia's chapter opens a new window on the Hermanos de Nuestro Padre Jesús Nazareno, better known as the Penitentes of northern New Mexico and southern Colorado. This long-lived Catholic lay brotherhood developed in relative isolation from Spanish and Mexican centers of control and cared for Hispano communities for centuries, serving as lay religious leaders and village caretakers. After the US takeover of New Mexico during and following the US–Mexican War (1846–1848), the region received sharp new Catholic ecclesiastical oversight under Bishop Jean Lamy, a French missionary. His and his successors' open opposition to the Penitentes and their acts of bodily penitence forced the order to the margins for decades. Drawing on performance theory, Garcia convincingly argues that the Penitentes' persistent self-flagellation declared the Hispano people's racial and religious identity in defiance of the bishops' opposition.

The section continues with Andrew Klumpp's chapter on Dutch Calvinist enclaves in northwestern Iowa in the nineteenth century. Calvinist churches created a backbone of support and organization for rural Dutch communities even as they provided a theological rationale for occupying Indigenous lands. Klumpp's analysis shows how this experience of religiously sanctioned settlement served as a kind of training for eventual Dutch missionary efforts abroad. The chapter also examines the complex influence that the Boer War between Afrikaans and English rivals in South Africa had on Dutch-speaking immigrants in the United States. Dutch Calvinists in the United States made common cause with the Boers against the British Empire even as they forged their own settlements (and missionary pretensions) in Iowa.

Chapter 7 turns to Quincy Newell's discussion of Latter-day Saint responses to the 1918 influenza pandemic. The "gathering of Zion" in the American West, the unique customs and polities of the LDS Church, and the bloody history of repression against them set the Saints apart. One aspect of this separate religious identity pertained to customs of metaphysical and revelatory healing practices going back to Joseph Smith. Yet, health officials in Utah and elsewhere in the LDS heartland were eager for Church members to adopt scientifically proven preventative measures against the flu pandemic both to save LDS lives and to move them closer to mainstream US biomedical culture in ways that had serious implications for LDS identity in the nation. Newell ultimately contends that the LDS flu response exposes the extent of Latter-day Saint secularization and accommodation to white Protestant norms.

Chapter 5

There Will Be Blood

Reimagining Penitente Bodily Rituals as Performative Hispano Culture

JON M. GARCIA

Keywords: Penitentes, Hispano, Catholicism, performance, ritual

In 1889, a journalist for the *Rocky Mountain News* arose early on Good Friday to witness a religious procession in Taos, New Mexico. The annual flagellation ceremony involved crosses, music, and nudity:

> Now there were three Brothers using the lash, and two carrying crosses; while two more strode unconcernedly along, each with a burro-load of entrana (buckhorn cactus) lashed upon his naked back. The entrana is one of the most depraved of all its diabolical family. Its spines are long, slenderer and sharper than the sharpest needle, yet firm enough to penetrate any ordinary boot. Get one entrana needle into the hide of a steer, and the maddened animal will gallop bellowing over the landscape till it falls from exhaustion. Yet these two fanatics wore huge bundles of it, held on by half-inch hempen ropes drawn so tightly about chest and arms and waist that they cut the skin and stopped the circulation; each must have had thousands of the thorns burrowing into his flesh, but he gave no sign. There was no sham about it . . . The cruel needles pierced his shoulders so deeply that the heavy branch hung there, yet he never winced nor turned his head![1]

The whipping ritual occurred every hour of the day over a third of a mile. Crowds gathered from distant towns to witness the public floggings. For many spectators, the Holy Week ritual was a bizarre spectacle. Yet, for the participants, it was a profound act of devotion, marking them as committed followers of Christ.

Los Hermanos de Nuestro Padre Jesús Nazareno, or the Penitentes, were a lay Roman Catholic confraternity that rose to prominence in New Mexico during the late 1840s.[2] The male-dominated brotherhood excluded women from participating in its public rituals but allowed them to assume subordinate roles within the community.[3] The Penitentes practiced physical mortification to reenact the Passion of Christ during Holy Week. Scholars widely believe that

Spanish Franciscan priests introduced these traditions to the Americas during the colonial era. This has led most historians to conclude that the brotherhood's origins are linked to the Third Order of Saint Francis of Assisi.[4] Although flagellation ceremonies eventually vanished from Spain, the Penitentes revived these medieval practices throughout the nineteenth century to preserve their Spanish heritage.[5] Like most scholars, I assume that the brotherhood was composed of Hispanos[6] who drew inspiration from Spanish customs.

In this chapter, I offer a fresh perspective on the Penitentes by analyzing their rituals through the lens of performance theory. Past scholars have often reduced the brotherhood's corporeal liturgies to historical narratives or folkloric spectacles, which flattens their cultural significance and portrays them as either archaic traditions or the imaginative rituals of uneducated folk.[7] This scholarly interpretation is further complicated by the brotherhood's vow of secrecy, which limits access to primary sources from the Penitentes themselves.[8] Most of the information available on the confraternity comes from outside observers, including reporters and local witnesses. Marta Weigle, a leading historian on the Penitentes, underscores this tension, arguing that we cannot fully understand the "ethnoperspective" of the brotherhood because they have not directly articulated the meaning behind their art, music, and rituals.[9] I argue Penitente rituals should be viewed as performative liturgies that provide new analytical insights into a context marked by archival silences. These customs extend beyond mere ritualistic order, functioning as theatrical displays of Hispano identity. The brotherhood's dramatic performances drew inspiration from Spanish religious plays of the fifteenth through seventeenth centuries, which were performed during Christmas, Epiphany, Easter, and feast days for the saints.[10] Their practice of bodily penance represented a metamorphosis—one that altered the lived reality of the performers. Performance theory enables us to examine flagellation as a multifaceted transformation that impacts the story, the performer, and the audience. As Richard Schechner argues, theatrical drama enacts visible changes in all three domains.[11] Applying this framework reveals how the Penitentes used self-flagellation not only as a religious act but as a cultural performance to preserve their Hispano identity. These transfigurations affected their bodies, influenced their spectators, and contributed to historical narratives that challenged dominant portrayals of Catholicism in the Americas.

Public and private flagellation ceremonies granted the confraternity agency to resist external religious influences. Following the US acquisition of Mexican territories after the Mexican–American War, non-Hispano Catholic ideologies became more prevalent in the region. The brotherhood viewed these foreign theologies as a threat to their cultural identity. In response, the Penitentes embodied their cultural legacy through religious performances, using visual and auditory rituals to defend their heritage from being erased or redefined by outsiders. Ultimately, Penitente bodies served as a political force of visual power against institutional authority. As Judith Butler notes, performativity extends beyond human language, becoming its own form of "discourse" that wields power.[12] By theologizing their physical suffering, the Penitentes enacted racial and cultural agency, using their bodies to resist the encroachment of Americanized institutional Catholicism. The brotherhood's existence, therefore, was as much about preserving Hispano cultural memory as it was about religious devotion. Their rituals represented both a spiritual and cultural defiance—a testament to their resilience and a reminder of the enduring power of religious performance in the preservation of communal identity.

Constructing Catholicism in a Contested Land

On May 11, 1872, the *Christian Register*, a Boston newspaper, published a letter from a woman living in Fort Sumner, New Mexico. Her correspondence aimed to "give information through the Register for the good of mankind." She believed Bostonians thought little of the Southwest and sought to provide the East Coast with a different narrative. In particular, she wanted to dispel misconceptions by demonstrating that religion was alive and well in New Mexico. Taking it upon herself to "avail" wisdom "in lessons of patience and religious earnestness," she described the Penitente rituals of nudity, self-flagellation, and the symbolic consumption of bread and vinegar. Her letter also contained a curious observation: "Each of the 'Penitentes,' for such these suffering men are called, has his head covered with a black cloth, and is not supposed to be recognized by the crowds which witness the ceremonies. They seemed like Africans, their skin dark, between the color of an Indian and a negro."[13] Although the Penitentes concealed their faces from view, they publicly displayed their "dark" bodies for all to see. This paradox raises an important question: Why would they choose to do this? Beyond the element of secrecy, what can we learn from the public display of self-inflicted suffering? To answer this, we must first contextualize the history of the Southwest.

In August 1846, Mexican rule in New Mexico collapsed under US military forces. The region erupted into turmoil as Mexicans feared the loss of their land to American settlers. On the morning of January 19, 1847, a Hispano insurgency rose in defiance of US authority during what became known as the Taos Revolt. Led by Pablo Montoya and Tomás Romero, guerrilla soldiers stormed the home of Charles Bent, the newly appointed governor of New Mexico. The rebels brutally attacked Bent, shooting him with arrows, scalping him alive, and ultimately killing him.[14] This violent uprising was a final, desperate attempt to reclaim what insurgents viewed as their stolen land. A little over a year later, Mexico ceded its northern territories to the United States under the Treaty of Guadalupe Hidalgo, ending the Mexican–American War. The treaty's aftermath left Hispanos in a complex position. While some welcomed change, believing that US governance might bring stability, others feared it would come at the cost of Mexico's newly acquired independence.[15] Despite efforts to accommodate the influx of Anglo settlers, Hispanos soon found themselves engaged in a cultural and ideological conflict over history and identity—a battle steeped in patriotism and racial sensitivity against American hegemony.[16]

At the same time, it is important to remember that New Mexico was never only a contest between Mexicans and Anglos. Long before either Spain or Mexico claimed jurisdiction, the region was home to Navajo, Pueblo, Tewa, and many other Indigenous nations whose ties to the land were both ancestral and ongoing.[17] By the nineteenth century, Indian communities remained a significant presence. Yet when the Penitentes spoke of ancestral land or claimed continuity with their forefathers, they framed their belonging through a distinctly Spanish imaginary that elided Indigenous claims. Their liturgies did not simply resist American hegemony; they also asserted a version of history in which Hispano identity displaced Indian presence and recast the land as Spanish Catholic terrain.

In 1850, the United States established the territory of New Mexico, though its early governance was marred by disorder. The region became a contested space, claimed by both the Union and Confederate governments during the Civil War. As New Mexico evolved, American officials sought to impose social order, laying the foundations for new traditions, identities, and historical narratives.[18] In the process, Hispanos were forced to reconcile their ancestral histories with rapidly shifting sociopolitical realities.

Although the US takeover disrupted Hispano ways of life, religious tensions in New Mexico had existed long before the territory's annexation. During the late sixteenth and early seventeenth centuries, the region's religious landscape was dominated by Franciscan missions established by the Order of Friars Minor.[19] Spanish friars clashed with Indigenous groups as they sought to impose Catholic rule. For generations, Franciscan missionaries operated autonomously, without oversight from the broader Catholic hierarchy.[20] It was not until the mid-eighteenth century that Pedro Tamarón y Romeral, the sixteenth bishop of Durango, sought to extend his jurisdiction over New Mexico. Franciscans in New Mexico refused to yield to the bishop's decree, claiming he had overstepped his authority and was imposing upon their governing responsibilities.[21] These disputes resulted in numerous failed attempts by the church to install a bishop in the region. After Mexico's independence from Spain in 1821, New Mexico was considered isolated and dangerous. Episcopal battles over territorial jurisdiction eventually resulted in the lion's share of Catholic clergy departing the area by the 1830s.[22] Ecclesial absence from the region was noticeable: The area did not have a resident bishop; it suffered from a shortage of priests; and it lacked a seminary.[23]

Religious deprivation forced remaining Catholics in the area to pursue their faith with little direction from the church. In time, a remnant of believers formed and learned to practice Catholicism without the formal oversight of any governance. The Penitentes rose to popularity during this period of religious liminality in the Southwest. Their practices gained prominence at a time when the rites and rituals of Catholic salvation were largely absent from the daily religious life in New Mexico.[24] The Penitentes filled this void by preserving Catholic traditions through acts of physical devotion that reenacted the Passion of Christ. Their public rituals—rooted in pain, penitence, and performative faith—symbolized a collective effort to retain their Hispano identity amid social and political upheaval.

The genesis of the brotherhood offered hope and solace to Hispanos grappling with the upheaval of their world. In the absence of institutional Catholicism, the confraternity emerged as a vital force, tending to the spiritual and social needs of an isolated community in New Mexico. Their yearlong commitments extended beyond the bounds of religious observance, encompassing the practicalities of daily life: teaching catechism to children, officiating funeral rites, caring for the sick, supporting widows, feeding the poor, upholding moral standards, and even maintaining law and order.[25] Deeply rooted in generational ties to the region, Hispano culture saturated their customs and shaped the very spaces in which their faith was practiced. Their chapels, known as *moradas*, embodied this cultural distinctiveness in both form and function. Built by hand from adobe, these structures adhered to an L- or U-shaped design and were often surrounded by small cemeteries, a sacred marker of the past that reinforced communal memory. Unlike other religious sanctuaries, the *moradas* were exclusively male spaces, defined by their secret contemplative practices and their intense Lenten devotions—penitential acts that reaffirmed their collective identity and spiritual resilience.[26] As cultural epicenters of Hispano identity, the *moradas* became iconic symbols of faith and solidarity, their adobe walls standing as steadfast witnesses to endurance and belonging.[27] Their presence extended beyond religious ritual, functioning as sanctuaries of care and social welfare. For many, the *morada* was not simply a place of worship—it was the heart of a community, a spatial embodiment of the Hispano imaginary, where memory, faith, and survival converged.

The Penitentes further consolidated a Hispano identity by drawing inspiration from fourteenth-century Spanish flogging rituals to reconstruct a distinct form of Catholicism. Scholars trace the revival of Spanish flagellation practices in what would be the United States to as early as the seventeenth century—two centuries before the formal emergence of the Penitentes.[28] Thus, Holy Week flagellation was not merely an act of devotion; it was a performative remembrance that allowed the Penitentes to honor and embody elements of their threatened Hispano identity. Theologically, the ritual also provided a visceral connection to the suffering of Christ. In the absence of priestly absolution, bodily penance became a means of securing redemption for Hispanos seeking atonement for their sins, both past and future.[29] When clergy thinned, bodies kept the calendar. The act of flogging offered spiritual assurance of deliverance from death, transforming the pain of the body into a sacred testament of faith. Through the physical uniting of Hispano bodies to Christ's suffering, the brotherhood enacted a salvific union between the created and the Creator—an embodied performance of atonement that not only redeemed the soul but also reaffirmed cultural survival through a theology of shared suffering.

Penitente bodily identification with the crucified Christ united the brotherhood to God; it also connected them to their ancestors through performance. Flogging ceremonies reinforced the sacred rituals of their forefathers, merging Hispano bodies with Spanish bodies in a continuum of devotional practice. This act of "transportation," as Richard Schechner describes it, allowed Penitente performances to leave the "ordinary world" and enter the "performative world" where their ritual roles became embodiments of something beyond themselves.[30] In this space, liturgical mimesis became a display of ontology, an enactment where the visualization of material and immaterial realities constructed culture, heritage, and ethnicity through the medium of performance. As Diana Taylor asserts, the repertoire of performance embodies memory in gesture, orality, movement, and dance. These embodied practices allow scholars to trace cultural traditions and historical influences through the lens of performativity.[31] Examining the brotherhood through this framework reveals that corporeal mimesis was not merely an act of devotion but also a reenactment of racial and cultural identity. The visual spectacle of bodily suffering enabled the Penitentes to remember and reclaim their Hispano identity, a recognition that epitomized their ancestral religion. This ancestral connection was pivotal, as the Penitentes saw themselves as caretakers of the Catholic faithful in New Mexico, much like their Franciscan predecessors. Their devotion was heightened by a profound sense of cultural continuity, where their faith became a vessel for preserving Hispano heritage, a sacred lineage spanning centuries and steeped in religious endurance.

By emphasizing Spanish ancestry and ritual inheritance, the Penitentes staged their bodies as vessels of an explicitly Hispano lineage. This performative choice was not neutral. In a landscape where Indigenous ritual life was vibrant and visible, the Penitentes' insistence on Spanish devotion marked a deliberate distancing from Indian cosmologies and practices. Many members of the confraternity almost certainly had Indigenous ancestry, yet their rituals narrated themselves otherwise: as heirs to Spain rather than kin to nearby Indian communities. In this sense, the brotherhood's liturgies were racial performances as much as they were religious ones, inscribing Spanishness onto bodies to define cultural boundaries. Performance theory helps us see that the Penitentes were not merely preserving tradition but actively drawing lines of differentiation, resisting Anglo encroachment on one side and resisting identification with Indigenous peoples on the other.

Repetitive flagellation rituals reinforced identity-making practices that tied the Penitentes to their Hispano relatives of the past. Annual Holy Week processions were more than customary—they were memorization tools. Maren Wehrle argues as much, noting that identity is developed at a bodily level by forming habits.[32] Hence, to command and train the body to regularly experience penance was to ceremonialize racial scripts through reiteration. Penitente bodies reinforced Spanish heritage and culture by means of unremitting performative liturgies. Judith Butler contends performativity is always an operation of iterability—a theatrical process in which the ritual is not an act or singular event but a taboo production operating in "constraint" and "prohibition."[33] The brotherhood's performances repeatedly constructed Spanish religion in the absence of a formal ecclesial presence by creating memories of the past. This directly challenged American attempts to reconstruct Hispano spaces and rewrite history. Further, Penitente productions thwarted Anglo ideologies by embodying religious expressions that transmitted knowledge, culture, and history.[34] Through corporeal liturgies, the brotherhood established agency and resistance against Americans.

The Penitentes continued their rituals in the absence of a formal governing ecclesial institution. They hid their faces but displayed their "dark"-skinned bodies so that observers might know who they really were. They observed these customs for years, until the arrival of a new bishop in New Mexico threatened their existence. The hierarchy of the Catholic Church was not fond of the Penitentes, and ecclesial authorities set out to make that abundantly clear. While the brotherhood labored to order their liturgical rituals, Rome made it a priority to disorder these practices. This created a contentious relationship between the Mexican band of brothers and their religious authorities. In time, the institutional church would set out to disband what it considered to be fanaticism. Religion in New Mexico was about to be transformed, as the road to Rome would no longer go through Spain.

Embodied Resistance to Ecclesial Authority

The Penitentes practiced their yearly spectacles in public. Although this schedule allowed others to appreciate their religious observances, it often yielded criticism from skeptics. A local journalist from Denver noted their displeasure with these rituals: "I had heard much about the 'Penitentes' of New Mexico, and desired to see with my own eyes if there were human beings living so close to civilization who, during the 40 days of Lent, were as heathenish as had been reported . . . my attention was called to a gang of men just across the river, who were doing penance by carrying heavy wooden crosses and whipping themselves . . . It was too much to witness long and I turned away sickened by the horrible sights."[35] The brotherhood's practices were described as visually hideous by many in attendance. As word of these barbaric liturgies spread throughout the country, observers labeled the rituals as blasphemous and semipornographic.[36] The United States government soon pressured the Catholic Church to put an end to Penitente customs after ecclesial authority was transferred to Americans in the wake of the Mexican-American War.[37] The Catholic Church responded in kind by turning to an unlikely ally to carry out the task.

In 1851, Jean Baptiste Lamy, an ordained priest from France, arrived in Santa Fe, New Mexico as the newly consecrated bishop of the region. His appointment came as a surprise to many since he was unfamiliar with New Mexico and did not speak Spanish.[38] Giovanni Maria Mastai-Ferretti, Pope Pius IX, favored the United States in the aftermath of the Mexican-American War. His commissioning of Lamy to govern New Mexico, an outsider from France, was fueled by a lack of sympathy toward Mexicans in the region.[39] The new bishop, who had previously served as a missionary in Ohio and Kentucky, was welcomed by Juan Felipe Ortiz, one of the rural deans in New Mexico. They maintained a cordial relationship until Ortiz refused to acknowledge Lamy's authority. Ortiz was operating under the jurisdiction of José Antonio Laureano de Zubiría y Escalante, the bishop of Durango, Mexico. Zubiría had informed Ortiz that Rome had given Mexican bishops permission to "continue to exercise their episcopal authority north of the border."[40] Accordingly, Ortiz refused to yield his leadership to Lamy without a formal notice from Zubiría communicating a transfer of power in the region. Curiously, Ortiz resisted Lamy despite his apathy toward his own administrative duties in New Mexico—including upkeep of the churches, keeping parish records, observance of liturgy, care for sick priests, visits to parishes, and an annual report to his bishop.[41] Ortiz was just one of several Hispano Catholics who resisted Lamy's jurisdiction in what amounted to a battle of ideological warfare.

The French bishop had his work cut out for him. His diocese spanned approximately two hundred and thirty-six thousand square miles.[42] The territory of New Mexico, an area larger than France, had lacked a diocese for years. This prompted Lamy to reestablish the formal presence of the Catholic Church in the region by replacing the existing Hispano chapel in Santa Fe, built in the 1700s, with a new cathedral inspired by French architecture.[43] Lamy further concentrated his efforts on creating organization and structure. His initial concern was education (religious and otherwise) because he considered the state gravely immoral. He declared a need for schooling "since the Mexican national vice" was ignorance.[44] He recruited French clergy to help him build schools, hospitals, orphanages, and cathedrals to establish his vision for a visible religious presence in New Mexico. By Lamy's self-conducted census, the territory had sixty-eight thousand Catholics, two thousand heretics, thirty to forty thousand infidels, eighteen missions, twelve Hispano priests native to New Mexico, twenty-six churches, and forty chapels.[45] As previously stated, Lamy's overhaul of the region caused tension with the local priests. For example, Father Antonio José Martínez was angered by an 1853 precept which required parishes to tithe because he believed this order violated local New Mexico laws. He was eventually excommunicated from the church for his refusal to pay the requisite tithes.[46] Consequently, Lamy established himself as an authority over existing Catholic practices in New Mexico. He ruled with an iron fist and frequently expressed his power. But amid Lamy's vision for reordering the religiously volatile land, one problem remained—the presence of the Penitentes.

On October 27, 1856, Lamy turned his attention to the brotherhood. He claimed to have received orders from the Pope to disband the Penitentes (although no formal records exist of such a request).[47] Lamy issued the brotherhood twelve mandatory rules they were to observe if they wished to remain faithful Catholics. His plan was to formalize his authority and reorder what he perceived to be an unruly group of fanatics. Rule nine exemplified his approach:

> All and every one of the individuals of the brotherhood shall obey and respect the legitimate Supreme pastor of this territory, His Grace, the Most Reverend Catholic Bishop, Juan Lamy, and his successors in all matters which he may be pleased to ordain, whether it be this or any other matter and likewise in the same manner the parish priest, whom he may be pleased to place in this or any other point of his diocese without complaining or grumbling regarding dispositions of these

> matters which the prelate may be pleased to ordain and anyone who having been duly advised should insist in so doing he shall be expelled from the brotherhood as unworthy of being a member of a Catholic congregation, the fundamental basis of which is obedience and charity.[48]

An angered Lamy was intent on reimagining Penitentes practices. His first order of business was to exert control over how their bodies displayed religious ceremonies. He set about to erase their long-standing New Mexican theological liturgies that he believed were contrary to Catholic orthodoxy. The Penitentes, however, doubled down on their religious customs. While Lamy's theological convictions offered something new, the Penitente rituals symbolized something old—a deeply rooted heritage from the past. This is important because the brotherhood's refusal to cease their practices upon Lamy's arrival meant they did not believe the new bishop understood the importance of their rituals. Thus, the brotherhood's insistence on maintaining Holy Week liturgies demands a deeper investigation.

The brotherhood had labored for years to cultivate their relationship with the land and religious ideology, so it was important for them to maintain their rituals. Their acts of holy remembrance were performances that altered profane space. Alberto López Pulido argues as much, stating that the Penitentes transformed the region of New Mexico into "a sacred place by the sacred sentiments of the people."[49] Their practices established a world in which Hispano communities produced and reproduced Spanish memory through ritual theatrics tied to the land. These religious customs connected them to a group identity they hoped to never forget (especially considering Mexico's partial annexation to the United States).[50] As such, the brotherhood was bound together through the physical rehearsing of hallowed stories and liturgies as they searched for a faith without a priest. Embodied religion became a means of rehearsing culture—an ideological construction of memory and identity rooted in survival.[51] These experiences allowed the Penitentes to find faith outside the walls of the institutional church by giving them agency over the telling of their story. They were not going to surrender their commemoratory presentations and yield to a foreign ecclesial authority.

Furthermore, space-crafting liturgies enabled the Penitentes to preserve knowledge of their racial identity. Corporeal rituals gave the brotherhood access to these epistemologies by means of embodied cultural memories. Lawrence Sullivan argues this point saliently, stating that the "reproduction, consumption, and exchange" that the body encounters in religious settings is a knowledge that is sustained through experience.[52] For the Penitentes, their land united their bodies to Spanish religion and heritage from the past. This allowed them to reorder their displaced religious reality in the wake of Lamy's threat to displace them. Perhaps more importantly, corporeal liturgies reenacted their history. The brotherhood's practices were productions of transmitted epistemology—a distant impression of the former self.[53] Performances concretized race and being via ritual. As Jan Assmann notes, this type of evocation is, "characterized by its distance from the everyday . . . fateful events of the past, whose memory is maintained through cultural formation (texts, rites, monuments) and institutional communication (recitation, practice, observance)."[54] As Penitente bodies hosted historical recollections, they constructed race by recalling the past and reordering the present.[55] When the body was engaged in rituals, it was an act of embracing identity to liberate the self from oppressive Anglo racialization. This energized the brotherhood to assert agency over their realities by training their bodies to ceremonialize new racial scripts on ancestral land.

Penitente liturgies were performance imaginaries committed to uniting bodies and spaces. Lamy's edict threatened to "expel" anyone who continued to partake in bodily rituals. His actions communicated a desire to reimagine Hispano space, and in doing so, displace their bodies from the land. Willie Jennings argues that bodies are intimately connected to land because it unites them to imaginaries of existence. For Jennings, reconfiguring bodies and spaces is a theological concept in which displacement distorts and reimagines doctrinal trajectories.[56] The Penitentes, like their Hispano forefathers, believed they were the rightful spiritual overseers of New Mexico. While Catholic bishops from bordering territories had long attempted to govern the region, it was Hispanos who had ruled the land. As a result, the Penitentes were battling to maintain their bodily right to exist in a space that belonged to their Hispano heritage. Lamy's theologizing of the land was yet another attempt to reimagine Hispano space. But years of abandonment at the hands of the Catholic Church had conditioned the brotherhood to know better. Under these circumstances, they established holy connections to the land that their forefathers had constructed when the Catholic Church deserted the region.[57] Consequently, Lamy's actions hearkened back to the Hispano traumas of the past in which they were forced to live on the margins of society as not fully Mexican nor fully European. His ordinance was a theological mandate intent on reconfiguring the space they had worked so hard to establish. The Penitentes responded to this threat through performative imaginaries in which bodies and spaces were theatrical displays of theological rebellion. Schechner's description of these types of performative spaces helps communicate how agency is possible with such theatrics. He writes, "Humans have a special facility for materializing dreams, desires, projections, imagos (identifying with the collective unconscious), and all kinds of not-yet-real or not-real-now projects."[58] The Penitentes combatted Lamy's orders with a response that reflected a different desired reality. These objections amounted to ideological warfare over the ownership of space and land.

As the Penitentes continued to partake in forbidden religious rituals, Lamy fought desperately to drive them from public sight. In 1857, he issued five additional rules targeting the confraternity, one of which would require the practice of penance to be done "as hidden as possible, without giving scandal, to the rest of the faithful according to the spirit of the Church and without doing it with vain-glory; for such penance is disapproved by the Holy Mother, the Church."[59] Following the publication of Lamy's new directives, the flogging fellowship was forced to live in secrecy. Three years later, the Penitentes responded by drafting an official constitution for their members that reinforced the brotherhood's commitment to secrecy. The Penitentes went into hiding for the next few decades. Although they still existed, they had disappeared from the visible Catholic imagination.

Two decades later, Lamy published another edict regarding the Penitentes. This act marked the finale of his battle against the brotherhood. His letter, published in 1879, was written for Lent in *La Revista Católica*, a Spanish Catholic weekly. This epistle was the bishop's sharpest critique of the brotherhood, fully rebuking the Penitentes' disobedience:

> Finally, we would be failing in our duty if we did not allude to another abuse that unfortunately is too common in some places. We are talking about the Penitentes . . . they have continued their cruel practices and customs in deserted regions, and at night, giving themselves such terrible lashes that many have not only fallen ill as a result of these penances, but some have also died . . . All these are great abuses that the church does not approve of, but rather reproves. We strongly exhort you not to allow yourselves to be deluded by a false kind of devotion, which far from pleasing God, rather offends Him because it is not done according to the obedience due to the church . . . Obedience matters more than sacrifice. If you obey the authority of the church in all that it commands and forbids from God, it will be worth more to you than all those penances that some practice out of order and with excessive rigor, of which God will not take into account, because they are not done according to obedience in addition to the fact that they have given and continue to give rise to blasphemy of our religion. We could add that many of the most zealous of these confraternities do not behave as exemplary Christians.[60]

Lamy demanded obedience from a group that was not used to formal oversight. He was frustrated that the Penitentes refused to submit to his authority. They were frustrated that the bishop was trying to erase their history.

While scholars have debated whether Lamy intended to eliminate the Penitentes or not, they agree that Hispano Catholicism ran contrary to his vision for institutional Catholicism.[61] The bishop considered their rituals ungodly and disobedient to the faith, prompting him to refuse to give the sacraments to anyone in the brotherhood.[62] His disapproval of the secret society's practices signified his failure to understand why they deemed them necessary. Abandoned by the Catholic Church, Hispanos in New Mexico were forced to create novel ways of identifying with God. Hispanos in the region had a long ancestral history tied to religious oversight in the region, so they felt compelled to remember those liturgies. Hence, Penitente ceremonies were marked by religiosity as much as they were by race. Moreover, the involvement of the body in these religious customs united them to Spain through performative memory. By recalling the past, the brotherhood was able to craft a future. Although Lamy issued decrees forbidding the confraternity's flogging traditions, they refused to take orders from a French bishop who did not understand their ways.[63] For the Penitentes, decades of New Mexico religion signified a way of life. More importantly, it denoted Spanish identity.

Survival Through Secrecy

On Thursday, April 5, 1883, the *Bennington Banner*, a daily periodical, published a piece documenting the status of the Penitentes following Lamy's ordinances: "They were originally Roman Catholics, but archbishop Lamy banished them from the communion. Great care is taken to prevent the discovery of their identity, all being masked while conducting their annual penance . . . During the march not a groan was heard nor a word spoken . . . As the torture grew more terrible the chant grew louder and the thongs fell with more vigor."[64] When the Penitentes were forced into secrecy, their resistance became more apparent. While their masks hid their physical appearance, their chants revealed their Spanish heritage. The *alabados* (hymns) that accompanied the Holy Week processions were an important part of the brotherhood's culture. Further, this music presented a distinctly Catholic worldview through imagery.[65] These hymns closely resembled a flamenco style and introduced a uniquely Spanish sound into the Southwest. Instead of singing, the brotherhood wailed to reflect raw and honest emotions. These cries invited listeners to participate in an empathetic conversation.[66] Penitente music became an auditory experience of Spanish heritage, performed amid withdrawal from the public eye. Although the Catholic Church succeeded in hiding the brotherhood's physical appearance, it could never silence their Hispano pride.

On July 18, 1885, Jean Baptiste Salpointe succeeded Lamy as the bishop of Santa Fe, New Mexico upon Lamy's retirement. The new French bishop had previously served as the Vicar General of the Arizona Missions. His reputation preceded him as he was admired throughout the region and renowned for his work in Arizona.[67] He immediately picked up where Lamy left off and turned his attention to the church's greatest challenge yet—the Penitentes. By this point in time, Salpointe was not alone in his desire to rid Catholicism of the secret society. In March of 1886, he distributed copies of Pope Leo XIII's *Regla de los Socios de la Tercera Orden de San Francisco* (Rule for Members of the Third Order of St. Francis). The circular stated the brotherhood had come from the Third Order of St. Francis and were to recant their religious practices and return to the Third Order to obtain indulgences promised by the pontiff. The correspondence stressed the brotherhood should stop its flogging practices and instead observe obedience to God and his earthly vicar.[68] While the letter did allow for certain types of penance as proper and good, it forbade other forms. Specifically, it prohibited all public flagellations and cross-bearing ceremonies. Salpointe obliged with the mandate and appointed himself as the authority who would enlist members from the confraternity to the Third Order should they choose to do so.

On May 17, 1888, Salpointe condemned the Penitentes "as not to be fostered in the least" at Santa Fe's first Synod of the Archdiocese.[69] Additionally, he encouraged priests to refuse to celebrate Mass with the brotherhood and deny them the opportunity to partake in the sacraments.[70] Just under a year later, on March 31, 1889, Salpointe issued another mandate, once again denouncing acts of flagellation or cross-carrying in public. All who disobeyed this order were to be denied the sacraments.[71] The Penitentes refused to obey the church's wishes and continued to practice their rituals. The bishop reminded the confraternity of an earlier church ruling that led to the demise of the fourteenth-century flagellants. He warned the brotherhood that failure to heed his warnings would result in a discipline like that experienced by their Spanish forebears.[72]

The Penitentes responded to Salpointe's request in kind. In October of 1891, they delivered a letter to the bishop requesting to be considered an official Catholic confraternity.[73] The document stressed the brotherhood's loyalty to the church and explained that flagellation was a means of honoring the passion of Christ.[74] They also expressed their desire to be blessed by the church and end the conflict between themselves and the institution.[75] The bishop offered to honor the appeal with a few addenda of his own. Unfortunately, the two sides could not come to an agreement. On February 7,

1892, Salpointe issued another circular threatening the brotherhood. This epistle was much harsher than his previous correspondence, stating, "Not only do we not progress, but we are perceptibly retrogressing year by year, with the passing of time."[76] The Penitentes had succeeded in frustrating Salpointe despite his best efforts to disband the movement. For the brotherhood, they simply wanted to be acknowledged as the rightful overseers of the ancestral religion in New Mexico.

The Penitentes continued to battle the Catholic Church for decades as they practiced forbidden rituals despite the wishes of numerous bishops. Their secret ceremonies of bodily mortification, Spanish hymns, and prayer were in direct disobedience to the institutional church. The confraternity's initiation process, a laceration to the back with a sharp stone, differentiated Hispano bodies from American bodies.[77] Only those worthy to be called Penitentes would receive this badge of honor, a symbol of resistance against American Catholicism. The open wound served as a physical reminder that the brotherhood came from a religious tradition dating back to the fourteenth century. Scars of mortification bore witness to the passion of Christ as his agony and sorrow became embodied in the agony and sorrow of the Penitentes—a Hispano brotherhood determined to never be forgotten.

Conclusion

In the summer of 1940, Juan B. Rael, an ethnographer and professor at Stanford University, traveled to northern New Mexico and southern Colorado to record the musical and religious traditions of Spanish Americans.[78] Upon observing his subjects, Rael discovered the Penitentes and documented his observations:

> The members of the society of flagellants are, with rare exceptions, Spanish-speaking . . . Although many of them have Indian blood in their veins, their culture is genuinely Spanish, as indicated by their language and their rich heritage of Spanish traditions, customs, and folklore . . . the Spanish inhabitants of New Mexico and Colorado held tenaciously to their ancestors' way of life, resisting almost entirely the cultural influences of the Indian tribes which surrounded them . . . The Spanish inhabitants of New Mexico, extremely conservative as they were . . . continued to live in a manner of their sixteenth- and seventeenth-century forefathers. Hence, it is not surprising that the processions of the New Mexican flagellants are almost identical to the Spanish penitent processions of the seventeenth, eighteenth, and nineteenth centuries.[79]

Rael's study of the Penitentes led him to conclude that the brotherhood's language, music, and practices were reflective of Spanish tradition. He noted the brotherhood had held fast to their ancestors' way of life despite the cultural influences of others around them. Rael's interpretation crystallizes a dynamic of differentiation. He observed that although many Penitentes had "Indian blood in their veins," they "resisted almost entirely the cultural influences of the Indian tribes which surrounded them."[80] This framing underscores how Hispano identity was constructed not only in opposition to Anglo power but also through contrast with Indian traditions. The brotherhood's claim to a Spanish religious lineage was as much an act of erasure as it was of preservation, reimagining New Mexican land as ancestrally Hispano while overlooking its deeper Indian roots. In this light, Penitente flagellation emerges as a double performance: a remembrance of Spanish Catholic heritage and a repudiation of Indian presence.

The Penitente movement began in the nineteenth century when Hispanos feared the erasure of their culture. Their movement spawned during a period of religious uncertainty for Catholics in New Mexico. The region lacked ecclesial hierarchy and oversight, prompting the brotherhood to reimagine religion by reviving fourteenth-century flogging practices to express religious solidarity with their Spanish heritage. By examining their rituals through a performance theory analytic, we gain valuable insight into their commitment to preserving their Hispano identity. Flogging theatrics boldly proclaimed a desire to preserve religious traditions from their Spanish forefathers. Additionally, by situating Penitente liturgies as performative practices, we gain a historical perspective as to how Hispanos in New Mexico constructed their racial imaginary. Corporeal rituals reified the connection between Spanish heritage and Catholic identity by rehearsing and memorizing old ways. The confraternity's ongoing disobedience to the institutional church stemmed from a desire to preserve its Hispano identity. They feared that Anglo Catholicism threatened their Spanish heritage, so their rituals served as performances of identity to resist American Catholicism.

On January 28, 1947, Archbishop Edwin V. Byrne conceded what Hispano devotion had already secured. In four decrees, he named the Penitentes a pious society of obscure origins, and in the last clause, claimed no authority over the confraternity.[81] Recognition without rule made them Catholic enough to count yet free enough to endure. After a century of skirmish, their penance had become their claim to legitimacy. Byrne's ink merely traced the lines their bodies had already drawn. The lash wrote the charter.

Notes

1. "Brothers of Light," *Rocky Mountain News* (Denver, CO), May 5, 1889.

2. Although the movement originated prior to the late 1840s, sources are sparse. See Michael P. Carroll, *The Penitente Brotherhood: Patriarchy and Hispano-Catholicism in New Mexico* (Johns Hopkins University Press, 2002), 11–14.

3. Marta Weigle, *Brothers of Light, Brothers of Blood: The Penitentes of the Southwest* (University of New Mexico Press, 1976), 145–46.

4. Although this is the majority position held by historians, there are some scholars who don't hold this position. For example, see Fray Angelico Chavez, "The Penitentes of New Mexico," *New Mexico Historical Review* 29, no. 2 (1954); Norman Toby Simms, *Marranos on the Moradas: Secret Jews and Penitentes in the Southwestern United States from 1590 to 1890* (Academic Studies Press, 2009).

5. Chavez, "The Penitentes of New Mexico," 97.

6. The term "Hispano" is fraught with complicated histories of conquest, dominance, and segregation. It is difficult to employ terms such as "Hispano," "Spanish," or "Mexican" without acknowledging the convoluted past of the Southwest. I use the term "Hispano" in this article but acknowledge its imperfections in fully capturing Spanish conquest in the Americas. I borrow from Jeffrey Smith who notes that "Hispano" refers to long-term residents of the Upper Rio Grande region of New Mexico who trace their ancestry back to Spain and distinguish themselves from Mexicans. While the term "Nuevomexicano" is becoming an increasingly popular term for its cultural inclusivity, I land on Hispano for purposes of continuity with the literature. For a more detailed explanation, see Jeffrey Smith, "Penitente Moradas: A Vestige of the Nuevomexicano Cultural Landscape," *Material Culture* 47, no. 2 (2015): 23–40.

7. Norman Toby Simms, *Marranos on the Moradas: Secret Jews and the Penitentes in the Southwestern United States from 1590 to 1890* (Academic Studies Press, 2009), 95–96.

8. Michael Wallis's work is an exception to this. His research on Penitente Moradas quotes anonymous members. See Michael Wallis, *En Divina Luz: The Penitente Moradas of New Mexico* (University of New Mexico Press, 1994).

9. Marta Weigle, *The Penitentes of the Southwest* (Ancient City Press, 1970), 39.

10. Weigle, *The Penitentes of the Southwest*, 6.

11. Richard Schechner, *Performance Theory* (Routledge, 2003), 191.

12. Judith Butler, *Bodies That Matter: On the Discursive Limits of Sex* (Routledge, 2011), 139.

13. "Mexican Practices," *The Christian Register* (Boston, MA), May 11, 1872.

14. "From New Mexico: Headquarters Army in New Mexico," *Wilmington Journal* (Wilmington, NC), April 30, 1847.

15. Brett Hendrickson, *The Healing Power of the Santuario de Chimayó: America's Miraculous Church* (New York University Press, 2017), 78.

16. Fray Angelico Chavez, "The Penitentes of New Mexico," *New Mexico Historical Review* 29, no. 2 (1954): 101.

17. Adolph F. Bandelier and Madeleine Turrell Rodack, "History of the Colonization and Missions of Sonora, Chihuahua, New Mexico and Arizona to the Year 1700," *Journal of the Southwest* 30, no. 1 (1988): 83.

18. Roberto Ramón Lint Sagarena, *Aztlán and Arcadia: Religion, Ethnicity, and the Creation of Place* (New York University Press, 2014), 14.

19. France Scholes, "Problems in the Early Ecclesiastical History of New Mexico," *New Mexico Historical Review* 7, no. 1 (1932): 34.

20. Paul Horgan, *Lamy of Santa Fe* (Wesleyan University Press, 2003). 72.

21. Eleanor B. Adams, "Bishop Tamarón's Visitation of New Mexico, 1760," *New Mexico Historical Review* 28, no. 2 (1953): 83.

22. Alberto López Pulido, *The Sacred World of the Penitentes* (Smithsonian Institution Press, 2000), 11.

23. Robert Sprott, *Making Up What Is Lacking: Towards an Interpretation of the Penitentes* (University of New Mexico Press, 1984), 3.

24. Pulido, *The Sacred World*, 39.

25. Jeffrey Smith, "Penitente Moradas: A Vestige of the Nuevomexicano Cultural Landscape," *Material Culture* 57, no. 2 (2015): 27.

26. Smith, "Penitente Moradas," 24; 30–31.

27. Alvar W. Carlson, *The Spanish-American Homeland: Four Centuries in New Mexico's Río Arriba* (John Hopkins University Press, 1990), 142.

28. Simms, *Marranos on the Moradas*, 123.

29. "Painful Fanaticism: Practices of the Penitentes," *New York Times*, April 22, 1876.

30. Richard Schechner, *Between Theater and Anthropology* (University of Pennsylvania Press, 1985), 125–26.

31. Diana Taylor, *The Archive and the Repertoire: Performing Cultural Memory in the Americas* (Duke University Press, 2003), 20.

32. Maren Wehrle, "Bodies (That) Matter: The Role of Habit Formation for Identity," *Phenomenology and the Cognitive Sciences* 20 (2021): 366.

33. Butler, *Bodies That Matter*, 60.

34. Taylor, *The Archive and the Repertoire*, 16.

35. "*A Peep Into Heathenism*," Rocky Mountain Presbyterian (Denver, CO), June 1, 1873.

36. Jeffrey Smith, "Penitente Moradas: A Vestige of the Nuevomexicano Cultural Landscape," *Material Culture* 47, no. 2 (Fall 2015): 28.

37. Ray John De Aragón, *New Mexico in the Mexican-American War* (History Press, 2019), 103.

38. Aragón, *New Mexico in the Mexican-American War*, 103.

39. Aragón, *New Mexico in the Mexican-American War*, 103.

40. Horgan, *Lamy of Santa Fe*, 113.

41. Horgan, *Lamy of Santa Fe*, 115.

42. Horgan, *Lamy of Santa Fe*, 116.

43. Aragón, *New Mexico in the Mexican-American War*, 104.

44. Horgan, *Lamy of Santa Fe*, 127.

45. Horgan, *Lamy of Santa Fe*, 127.

46. E. K. Francis, "Padre Martínez: A New Mexican Myth," *New Mexico Historical Review* 31, no. 4 (1956): 284.

47. Horgan, *Lamy of Santa Fe*, 204.

48. Weigle, *Brothers of Light*, 203.

49. Pulido, *The Sacred World*, 69.

50. Pulido, *The Sacred World*, 69.

51. Jeanette Rodriguez and Ted Fortier, *Cultural Memory: Resistance, Faith, and Identity* (University of Texas Press, 2007), 4.

52. Lawrence Sullivan, "Body Works: Knowledge of the Body in the Study of Religion," *History of Religions* 30, no. 1 (1990): 87.

53. Taylor, *The Archive and the Repertoire*, 2.

54. Jan Assmann, "Collective Memory and Cultural Identity," *New German Critique* 65 (1995): 129.

55. Rodríguez and Fortier, *Cultural Memory*, 14.

56. Willie James Jennings, *The Christian Imagination: Theology and the Origins of Race* (Yale University Press, 2010), 24–25.

57. Simms, *Marranos on the Moradas*, 116.

58. Richard Schechner, *Performed Imaginaries* (Routledge, 2014), 81.

59. Weigle, *Brothers of Light*, 205.

60. "Carta Pastoral," *La Revista Católica* 5, no. 6 (1879): 66.

61. Pulido, *The Sacred World*, 42.

62. Weigle, *Brothers of Light*, 57.

63. Francis, "Padre Martínez," 271.

64. "Horrible Exhibition," *Bennington Banner* (Bennington, VT), April 5, 1883.

65. Anna Maria Cardinalli-Padilla, "El Llanto: A Liturgiological Journey into the Identity and Theology of the Northern New Mexican Penitentes and Their Spiritual Siblings" (PhD diss., University of Notre Dame, 2004), 155.

66. Marion Papenbrook, "The Sacred World of Flamenco," in *Flamenco: Gypsy Dance and Music from Andalusia*, ed. Claus Schreiner, trans. Mollie Comerford Peters (Amadeus Press, 1990), 53–54.

67. John G. Bourke, *On the Border with Crook* (Charles Scribner's Sons, 1902), 77.

68. Weigle, *Brothers of Light*, 60.

69. Edward Mary Zerwekh quoting Synods Sanctae Fidei Prima, May 17, 1888, Archdiocesan Archives, Santa Fe, New Mexico.

70. Edward Mary Zerwekh, "John Baptist Salpointe, 1825–1894," *New Mexico Historical Review* 37, no. 2 (1962): 154.

71. Weigle, The *Penitentes of the Southwest*, 15.

72. Weigle, *Brothers of Light*, 61.

73. Zerwekh, "John Baptiste Salpointe," 154.

74. Weigle, *Brothers of Light*, 61.

75. Weigle, *Brothers of Light*, 61.

76. Weigle, *Brothers of Light*, 61.

77. Carroll, *The Penitente Brotherhood*, 19.

78. Juan B. Rael, *The New Mexican Alabado, with Transcription of Music by Eleanor Hague* (Stanford University Press, 1951), 19.

79. Rael, *The New Mexican Alabado*, 11.

80. Rael, *The New Mexican Alabado*, 11.

81. Weigle, *Penitentes of the Southwest*, 18.

Chapter 6

Dutch Calvinist Imperials

Community Building and Global Engagement in the Nineteenth-Century Trans-Mississippi West

ANDREW KLUMPP

Keywords: Dutch immigration, global imperialism, community building, Iowa

In 1846, a cohort of secessionist Calvinists in the Netherlands fixed their gaze on the American West. Frustrated by the heavy-handed reassertion of state power under the newly installed King William I, these clergymen and many of their congregants, referred to as Seceders, had left the Dutch state church and intended to establish new Dutch colonies outside the reach of the king. In a pamphlet published that year, they made their case for moving to the West, especially appealing to those who would have preferred to relocate to Dutch colonies in present-day Indonesia rather than the forests and prairies of Michigan, Iowa, and Wisconsin.[1]

In their treatise, the Revs. Albertus Van Raalte and Antonie Brummelkamp explained that six questions informed their choice of the United States: "Who will lead the colonist there, or enable him to make up for the heavy travel expenses? Who will show him the ground to live on? What could he do? Where to settle? And we who view the matter from a Christian point of view?"[2] These queries focused on three primary concerns: livelihood, logistics, and leadership. In their answers, Van Raalte and Brummelkamp vaunted the American West, which to them meant the nation's midsection, as the best choice for prospective immigrants.

As the pamphlet reached its crescendo, the authors looked back on the golden age of Dutch colonialism, lamenting the loss of New Netherland to the English in 1664, and suggested to their kin that their best hopes lay in building new homes for themselves in the United States. "Oh, how much we would like to see another New Netherland arise in the East or West. Our people are now eager for migration. Thousands are willing to go." Having spent two dozen pages dismantling the case for moving to "the East," clearly the authors believed that "the West," by which they meant the United States, was the only reasonable option. Finally, they bathed their appeal in patriotic and religious rhetoric: "We beseech the God of our Fathers, to the salvation of the Netherlands and the blessing of its colonies, that the wish of the nation and the prayer of the children of God may be fulfilled."[3] This group of schismatic Calvinists had made their case for emigration and draped it in a fervent devotion to being Dutch and building Dutch colonies yet without a hint of irony claimed that the only way forward was to leave Dutch-controlled territory and head to the American West.

In 1847, the first waves of Dutch immigrants made their way to the eastern edges of the American West and over the next seven decades, hundreds of thousands of Dutch men, women, and children followed.[4] Although they built communities in what became known as the American Midwest, in the sources they left behind, they consistently define themselves as westerners. If we take that self-professed identity seriously, we see that it reflected not only their place in the United States but also their position within their denomination and the global Dutch empire. While some recent work has proposed unifying midwestern identity during this period, distinct insights about Dutch immigrants' own regional, national, and global perspectives would be lost if we overlooked their own self-professed western identities and imputed a more modern midwestern identity onto them.[5]

A shared religious faith tethered the local, national, and international in the minds of those living in these rural Dutch colonies.[6] They pointed to their faith as the reason for their exodus from their homeland; the justification for the clearing of the Odawa, Meskwaki, and Dakota people from the land; the motivation for sending the next generation out from their upstart colonies even further west; and a call to arms to defend Dutch Calvinists globally. This tightly bound religious community fits some expectations of the immigrant experience while subverting others. As non-Anglophone immigrants, they never occupy the apex of power in the United States, yet unlike the Japanese immigrants studied by Chrissy Lau, their race and religion afford them some agency. From this middle position in a social hierarchy, they shrewdly politick, build communities, and reach out globally. These immigrants also cut against the stereotypes of religion in the American West, suggesting that the Mormons, who were making a contemporaneous flight even farther westward, were not the only religious outsiders to utilize the space and freedom of the West as a destination, incubator, mission field, launching pad, and soapbox.

Building Dutch Communities

Trusting that they would find land on which to settle, Van Raalte and fellow Seceder minister Henrik Scholte led the first two groups of Dutch colonists across the Atlantic. When they departed in 1847, they set their sights firmly on the eastern edge of the American West. Although they departed the Netherlands separately, they hoped to combine their followers into one large colony in Iowa or Wisconsin once they arrived. When Van Raalte opted for the forests of West Michigan, Scholte balked at the proposed site, preferring Iowa's tall grass prairies.[7] He believed that Iowa's abundant farmland offered a surer future and a more immediate source of income. With more money in its coffers, Scholte's immigration society purchased thousands of acres of land in Marion County, in south central Iowa. Scholte named his new settlement Pella, meaning "city of refuge," which assured that the religious strife that had motivated his flight from the Netherlands became a permanent part of the colony's founding mythology.

The faith that drove and shaped these communities did not just mean right belief and correct practice but also connoted a sense of community belonging. Many of the first Dutch Calvinists to cross the Atlantic in the nineteenth century brought a long list of grievances against the Dutch state church, focused largely on a lack of fidelity to their three confessions—*The Belgic Confession, The Heidelberg Catechism*, and *The Canons of Dort*—a perceived lack of piety, and the state's meddling in church affairs.[8] They wanted more stringent adherence to these statements of faith and argued that piety, as an aspect of faith, reflected correct application of orthodox belief.[9] Critically, they believed that regenerated and converted Christians should live together in a covenant community, nurturing a life together that reflected their shared beliefs.[10]

The appeal to covenant community gestures toward a critical aspect of religious and ethnic identity for these immigrants: group identity. Despite theological squabbles and persistent factionalism within Dutch colonies in the United States, their shared connection to the Dutch Calvinist tradition became a central component of Dutch immigrants' identities.[11] Dutch Calvinist churches remained at the center of Dutch social life and cultivated cultural, social, religious, and political traditions. Their shared religious tradition, though split into two factions in many communities, still managed to unite early immigrants' social, cultural, economic, and political aims as newly minted Americans. Faith meant not only belief and practice but also belonging.[12]

A year before leaving the Netherlands, in yet another treatise, Brummelkamp and Van Raalte described what they hoped to find in the United States: "Our hearts' desire and prayer to God is that on one of those uninhabited regions there may be a spot where our people . . . may find their temporal subsistence secured."[13] They wanted to build communities centered on their shared faith and a common ethnic heritage, and they were prepared to settle in remote areas of the West in order to assure that they had ample land for their new homes. Thousands of Dutch Calvinist emigrants left the Netherlands during the latter half of the nineteenth century and most settled in colonies under the leadership of clergymen like Van Raalte and Scholte. The majority of Dutch emigrants headed first to the rural areas of Michigan, Iowa, and Wisconsin and then later to the Dakotas, Mountain West, Pacific Northwest, and California's Central Valley.[14] Immigrants coordinated colonization societies to manage logistics and ensure that immigrants settled among their kin, could purchase land near other Dutch Calvinists, and participated in the building of a network of churches and schools.[15]

In their pamphlets, Dutch leaders appealed to an empty, untamed wilderness in the West that was just waiting for Christian settlers to conquer it.[16] In doing so, these pro-immigration propaganda pieces mischaracterized the West, erasing the lingering presence and memory of the Native people who had lived in the region for centuries. Despite this rhetorical move, most settlers knew Native Americans had lived on the land they now claimed. Even prospective immigrants in rural villages in the Netherlands understood that Native Americans lived on the American frontier.[17] At times, these early settlers noted their fear of the land's original inhabitants, but at others, they just mentioned Native people in passing, as if they were a part of the scenery.[18]

Dutch colonists rarely worried about conflicts with Native Americans because the US government had continually pushed Native nations off of their lands to make way for white settlement. Van Raalte, for instance, established his colony in West Michigan virtually on top of the only space in the area where the government permitted Chief Wakazoo's Odawa band to live. The two groups avoided open conflict; however, the Dutch tendency to take maple sugar–making kettles and troughs that they presumed to be abandoned caused tensions. Within three years, the Odawa left, moving north due to the severe disruption of their way of life caused by the Dutch colony.[19]

In Iowa, the US government had pushed most American Indians out of the new state prior to the arrival of the Dutch. The Sac and Fox Treaty of 1842 forcibly removed the Meskwaki people and their Sauk allies west of the Missouri River, though the Meskwaki returned to Iowa in 1857 to establish an independent settlement just 60 miles north of Pella. In Northwest Iowa, the Wahpekute Dakota lived in and around the Little Sioux River Valley until violence erupted in 1857; however, the rapidly expanding US frontier pushed them ever farther to the west, especially after the Sioux Wars. When Henry Hospers led the first group of Dutch immigrants to build a colony in Northwest Iowa in 1870, talk of lingering Native American bands still worried some settlers, but the last small bands of Dakota had left nearly a decade earlier.[20] Nevertheless, the justifications for settler colonialism buttressed Dutch society building at home and abroad. In their view, they took the land to build their own rural enclaves as havens for like-minded immigrants and to perpetuate their specific cultural and religious traditions.

When the first Dutch immigrants arrived in the United States in 1847, they settled in concentrated areas. The familial, religious, and community associations that made some Dutch citizens more likely to emigrate also contributed to a sense of shared identity and desire to stay together as a group. This pattern of clustering gave them an outsized influence in particular areas like West Michigan or Northwest Iowa. In 1870, 90 percent of the Dutch immigrants were spread throughout only eighteen American counties in just seven states. In these dense settlements, the belonging engendered by their faith led to shared religious, cultural, and social priorities, which blended a desire to maintain Dutch distinctiveness and to strategically engage with the culture and politics of their new American home.[21]

In the early years (1846–49), over half of all Dutch immigrants were Seceders, although they accounted for only 5 percent of all Calvinist adherents in the Netherlands, and almost 80 percent of all Seceders left the Netherlands during this period. Later arrivals, primarily members of the state church, had to adjust to the Seceders' pious and orthodox ways, or they had to leave these communities entirely, an option few chose.[22]

From 1846 to 1880, 62 percent of the immigrants were from the state church, 7 percent more than the national population. Catholics comprised only 17 percent, half of their share of the Dutch population, because their leaders discouraged immigration. Dutch Jews composed 2 percent of Dutch immigrants, which was equivalent to their share of the Dutch population.[23] Because of the shared Latin liturgy, Dutch Catholic immigrants more easily worshiped with non-Dutch communities in the United States. As Dutch historian Henry Lucas noted, "Religion encouraged dispersal [among Dutch Catholics], while it tended to keep Seceders together."[24] Dutch Calvinists, then, were not the only Dutch immigrants to the United States, but their religious convictions often held Dutch Calvinists together while the faith of Dutch Catholics and Jews enabled them to integrate more easily with non-Dutch coreligionists in the United States.

Colonial Control and Conflict

Despite the national turmoil in the United States and occasional internal squabbling among Dutch colonists during the 1850s and 1860s, the initial Dutch colonies flourished. They participated in American life while continuing to guard their own religious and cultural distinctiveness and remained unwavering in their efforts to build and control their own Dutch colonies. The growth of their colonies, however, resulted in a dilemma. After waning before and during the Civil War, immigration from the Netherlands increased in 1867, and by 1869, affordable farmland nearby their original settlements in West Michigan and Central Iowa became scarce.[25] Squeezed out by high prices, the second generation took advantage of the 1862 Homestead Act and established new settlements. From these initial settlements, the Dutch consistently looked farther west.[26] In the strategic colonial development of these communities, their settlements along the West's easternmost edges functioned as the first outposts in a network that, at least in theory, could continue to hive off new communities farther into the expanding western United States.

The development of the Dutch colony in Sioux County, Iowa, along the state's western border, provides a fitting example of how daughter (and even granddaughter) colonies adhered to the initial Dutch immigrant vision. By 1870, Dutch farmers owned 98 percent of the land surrounding Pella, Iowa, and prospective farmers started to look west.[27] In keeping with the Dutch immigrant tradition, they intended to find a site where they could live together, maintain their distance from outsiders, secure sufficient land for future Dutch settlers, and keep non-Dutch officials from meddling in their affairs. Henry Hospers, then Pella's mayor, led the way.[28] Like their predecessors who crossed the Atlantic, these Pella immigrants formed an immigration society to coordinate the move across over 250 miles of tall grass prairie.

As soon as the colonists arrived in Northwest Iowa, they shored up their control over local politics. Within two years of the first Dutch wagon rolling onto the prairies, Dutch settlers violently clashed with their Yankee neighbors in the nearby town of Calliope (then the county seat,) deftly used local elections to win outright majorities in county boards, hobnobbed with politicians in Des Moines to pass laws that facilitated Dutch control in the county, and eventually relocated the entire county government to their colony's central town.[29] A decade later the editor of *The Sioux County Herald* simply quipped: "Any question, political or financial for years thereafter, was decided by the colony."[30] Within two years of arriving in Sioux County, through violence, skilled politicking, and leveraging connections to international immigrant communities, the Dutch had secured their position as the dominant community and constituency in the county.

Tensions still flared between the Dutch colony and its American neighbors, yet the tightly knit religious nature of the Dutch kept them united, and their coordinated colonization strategy meant they shrewdly maintained a key numerical advantage. For decades, Sioux County's newly established Dutch newspaper, *De Volksvriend*, advertised a colony slate of nominees for county and township offices without regard for party affiliation, often including members of both major parties.[31] The editor reminded the colony that the results showed, “We may be able to mobilize the Dutch people for the cause, the interests of our colony.”[32] The Dutch intentionally continued to differentiate between themselves and their neighbors.

On the eve of an important local election in 1876, the editor of *De Volksvriend* in Orange City, Iowa, fretted that political differences within the Dutch colony threatened to fracture the Dutch vote and undermine their majorities in local government. He encouraged his readers to “obtain a full voice, in order to show that the Dutch are one! ONE! **ONE!**”[33] The same year, Henry Hospers, a perennial political powerbroker in the county, entered the fray and reminded the colony that the perpetuation of their Christian society relied on Dutch voters flexing their political muscle.[34] The colony did not disappoint, and as they had done since their arrival in the county in 1870, they swept more of their own into office. These naked appeals to religious and ethnic distinctiveness—possibly emboldened by their publication in a Dutch periodical that few non-Dutch could read—critically relied on the same sense of cultural superiority and justified their settler colonialism.

In 1882, an anonymous incendiary pamphlet titled “The Free Voter” circulated in the small non-Dutch communities on the county’s periphery, lambasting Dutch political control. It scandalized the colony. “The Free Voter” bemoaned that, in a cunning move of political calculus, Dutch Republicans had withdrawn their own candidate in a local election to avoid siphoning votes from an incumbent Dutch Independent candidate and inadvertently handing the election to the non-Dutch candidate.[35] It also laid bare the simmering tensions between the colony and its neighbors. The author excoriated the culture and religion the Dutch had carried with them across the Atlantic, disparaging both: “We do not want to live where wooden-headed and wooden shod have absolute control of public affairs, where the people are a hundred years behind the time. . . . We want to live in a community controlled by public spirited, progressive men—men who are abreast with the century.”[36] “The Free Voter” described the Dutch as “clannish” and objected to Dutch conservatism, culture, religion, and political dominance.[37] In the author’s view, the Dutch had remained an unassimilated band of conservative immigrants who had no business controlling the county.

The “Free Voter” positioned the Dutch as un-American outsiders, signaling that their ethnic and religious distinctiveness could be wielded against them, yet unlike the accommodating approach taken by the Japanese immigrants discussed by Chrissy Lau in this volume, the Dutch were far more confrontational and exhibited much more agency. Moving to its rhetorical climax, the pamphlet called for a united multiethnic coalition to oppose the Dutch political machine: “Now is the accepted time for every American, German, Irishmen, and Scandinavian in Sioux County to make a united effort to throw off the supremacy of the Dutch. It has been tolerated too long, and a more odious and unbearable curse it has seldom been the lot of any people to bear."[38] The call focused squarely on the ethnicity of the dominant Dutch colony. This was a clear attack on the Dutch that portrayed their religion, culture, and politics as backward, opposed to progress, and simply un-American.

Unsurprising given the county's demographics, the Dutch incumbent rolled to reelection with 58 percent of the vote due to his large margins of victory in the Dutch-dominated townships.[39] The *Sioux County Herald* gloatingly printed the pamphlet the week following the election and credited its publication with energizing the Dutch base to "rise in their might" and "crush [the non-Dutch ticket] beneath their feet, killing it so completely that there is no hope of its ever reviving."[40] The county's most salient lines were drawn by ethnicity and by extension, religious faith. In the wake of the 1882 county elections, *De Volksvriend* had even announced, "We, therefore, all agree to vote together."[41] The importance of maintaining their Christian society kept the Dutch united, but it enraged their opponents, who pointed to ethnicity and religious and cultural backwardness in an attempt to ouster local Dutch officials. The election of 1882 reflected tensions the colony encountered with some of its neighbors as well as how the broader Dutch colonization model overcame those challenges and enabled immigrants to maintain control over their local governments.

Zwemers in the Middle East and American West

The Zwemer clan was among the most prominent Dutch immigrant families to eventually put down roots in these rural Dutch colonies. They exemplify how the West provided an ideal site from which Dutch immigrants could both extend their vision of the global Dutch Empire and also embrace rapidly expanding American imperialism. The patriarch, Adrian Zwemer, had been among the initial Dutch immigrants to make the trans-Atlantic journey. He was a committed Seceder and eagerly followed his pastor to Holland, Michigan.[42] Because of the dire need for Dutch-speaking ministers and his sizable family, including seven children, he had been one of the few men to receive a special dispensation from his denomination to become a minister without attending seminary.[43] Adrian spent his ministerial career building connections throughout Dutch colonies in Iowa, Wisconsin, Minnesota, and Michigan, which kept him in contact with men and women throughout the region and an ever-expanding missionary network throughout the globe; however, the careers of three of his sons—Samuel, James, and Frederick—exhibit how Dutch colonies on the eastern edges of the American West facilitated Dutch expansion westward, local community building, and global missions.[44] Each man was heralded as a paragon of Christian faithfulness and seen as undertaking central work in the development of the Dutch community, broadly conceived, but their work differed markedly.

Samuel Zwemer became perhaps the most prominent missionary to progress through the Dutch immigrant educational system in the 1870s and 1880s, becoming a well-known missionary to the Middle East. In time, he attracted attention far beyond the densely networked Dutch Calvinist community. For thirty-five years, he published the *Moslem World*, which attempted to share critical knowledge about Islam with supporters in the United States and Europe. In addition to this periodical, he wrote unceasingly, often focusing his attention on the need for missionary work to Muslims. One biographer noted that Samuel was likely a rather poor evangelist, winning few converts; however, he was a formidable booster of missions in the Islamic world, founding four different mission sites and recruiting dozens of missionaries to the field.[45] This success led historian Thomas Kidd to claim, "It is difficult to overstate Zwemer's importance in American missions to Muslims, or his role in popularizing religious knowledge about Islam among American Christians. He was certainly the most influential American Christian missionary to Muslims of his time, if not ever."[46] After thirty-nine years in Bahrain, Egypt, and other Middle Eastern countries, Samuel eventually returned to the United States, taking up a post as professor of missions at Princeton.

In 1890, though, Samuel stood alongside a coterie of Dutch immigrant missionaries who shared a common background in rural Dutch colonies and were headed to China, Japan, and India. These men and women had been educated within a tradition that prized evangelism, linked education to faith, fretted about the salvation of non-Christians, and rhapsodized about efforts to "civilize" the rest of the world.[47] He kept up a lively correspondence with his family, friends, and contacts back in the United States from the moment he left for the Middle East in 1890. In August of that year, while he was still learning Arabic, he wrote to his brother Frederick, who was a pastor in Middleburg, Iowa, a hamlet within the Dutch colony in Sioux County. He trusted that his brother, who was a church planter with eyes on extending his ministry to more Dutch colonies in South Dakota, would share his note with others as Frederick traveled. Although Samuel was himself newly arrived in the Middle East, he offered brief snippets of life, mostly reporting that travel was difficult and done primarily on foot and that he hoped to tag along with the mission's doctor on a "medico-camping trip among the Bedouins."[48] Samuel had no intention of breaking off connections with his robust support network back home, and his frequent letters became a vital source of information about the Middle East.

Samuel excellently publicized his mission. He maintained frequent communication with John Karsten—the editor of the Dutch-language weekly *De Hope*, which circulated widely in Dutch colonies in Michigan, Wisconsin, and Iowa. Karsten dutifully translated Samuel's English-language updates into Dutch and shared them.[49] In his first year in the Middle East, he took up the practice of writing frequently to the Hope College Mission Band in the Dutch immigrant settlement of Holland, Michigan.[50] Samuel's rising star in the missionary and Dutch communities was due at least in part to his dogged commitment to frequent communication.

Throughout the 1890s, these updates shared a trove of information with the people back home. Everyday residents in Dutch colonies read about daily life in the Middle East and the longing for "Christian fellowship" that Samuel acutely felt.[51] He shared harrowing tales of converts being placed under police surveillance in Baghdad and failed efforts to entice locals to purchase Christian books.[52] He also announced his increased evangelization efforts: "I am just back from a preaching tour of 700 miles up to Bagdad [*sic*] and down the Euphrates. The latter river was never before visited by a missionary, as far as I could learn."[53] These updates characterized Samuel's work as a pioneering missionary in the Middle East. Enthusiastic readers in American Dutch colonies responded excitedly to these updates.[54]

Ultimately, Samuel's work in the Middle East received mixed reviews, with his Dutch kin and US-based mission boosters celebrating his work and his colleagues in the Middle East and Muslims themselves viewing him more harshly. Later in his life, when stationed in Cairo, Egypt, Zwemer caused controversy for his militant evangelistic style, leading historian Heather J. Sharkey to describe other missionaries as being fearful that Samuel would be "dangerous" and to observe that he advocated for a particularly strident form of Christian militancy.[55] He disparaged Islam as being of human origins (rather than divine) and expressed low views of Muslims. While potentially out of line from his colleagues in the Middle East, these very ideas resonated in the immigrant communities he called home. As a missionary who had grown up in, been educated by, and drawn support from Dutch colonies in the West, he enacted a critical part of the vision that had justified their immigration and community building.

In the same year that Samuel departed for the Middle East, his brothers James and Frederick took on leadership positions in the growing Dutch colonies in Iowa and South Dakota. In that year, James became the principal of Northwestern Classical Academy in Sioux County, and Frederick moved farther west to young Dutch colonies in South Dakota, hoping to plant churches there.[56] These brothers never received the national recognition heaped upon their younger brother, yet within the broader Dutch community, they modeled other important elements of their vision to build Christian communities and evangelize the world.

James had served as a pastor in the Sioux County colony since 1886 and had also been appointed to serve as a booster for the RCA's educational institutions "in the West," by which the denomination meant Northwestern Classical Academy in Orange City, Iowa, and Hope College and Western Theological Seminary in Holland, Michigan.[57] Even late into the nineteenth century, these Dutch colonists explicitly viewed Iowa, South Dakota, and even Michigan and Wisconsin as "the West," a region ripe for Dutch colonial expansion and development. James helmed Northwestern throughout the 1890s, and despite the difficult economic times brought about by the Panic of 1893, he managed to expand the school. New buildings popped up on campus and enrollments grew.[58] Graduates from the young academy made a trek across Iowa's prairies to Hope College to receive an education, with many heading to western Dutch colonies as ministers and teachers or leaving the country as fresh-faced missionaries.

Eventually, James followed many of his students and became an administrator and booster for both Hope College and Western Theological Seminary in western Michigan. Under his watchful eye, students received rigorous training from a Dutch Calvinist perspective and took that with them to Dutch colonies and global missions. No less so than his brother's caravan rides to Bedouin camps, James's role as the principal of Northwestern Classical Academy was a vital position in the broader landscape of these rural Dutch colonies. In the 1890s, while Samuel wrote frequent appeals begging for new missionaries to enter the fray, James, from his post in Orange City, was preparing them.

Samuel and James's older brother, Frederick—possibly the least well documented of the trio—embraced a different element of the Dutch evangelistic impulse by heading farther into the West, to South Dakota in order to build new churches. The hiving off of colonies had always played an important role in the growth of these rural Dutch enclaves.[59] As they often did, the Dutch followed in the wake of the US Army, pushing out Native American populations. After the Wounded Knee Massacre in 1890, white settlement and the US government managed to force Native Americans even farther west, making way for men like Frederick to lead new colonies onto the northern Great Plains. Frederick, more than either of his brothers, demonstrates that the West remained a promising destination for colonial development until at least the eve of the twentieth century.

The Zwemer brothers in the Dutch American West kept track of their younger brother in the Middle East, receiving letters from him and sending updates of their own. Samuel's frequent reports in newspapers like *De Hope*, which was a staple of their colonies' media diets, kept Samuel close to their minds and hearts.[60] Their letters told of life events, new children and the death of friends and family, yet they also captured a sense of the common mission they shared. These men never equated the work of being a missionary in the Middle East, church planting in South Dakota, and being an educational administrator in Iowa. They knew their work differed; yet they also shared a common sense of purpose. They believed that each brother played a role in a Christian drama that extended far beyond the rural Dutch enclaves that dotted Iowa's tall grass prairies. For the Zwemers, the Dutch colonies in the West were mission fields, training grounds, and launching pads for global outreach.

A South African War, Dutch Immigrant Outrage

For Dutch men and women in the American West, their faith had justified settling on Native Americans' land, encouraged them to train young people, and propelled many to undertake missions throughout the world, yet it also tied them to Dutch Calvinist kin in the remnants of the declining Dutch Empire. From the outset, leaders viewed the American West as a site that promised to be "the salvation of the Netherlands and the blessing of its colonies," and that commitment to the global Dutch diaspora did not wane in the subsequent decades.[61] Furthermore, their new homes, situated outside of the Dutch Empire's formal borders, also allowed them to lobby their adopted government on behalf of their coreligionists. For instance, when the Dutch-descended Boers clashed with the British in a battle for control in South Africa during the Second Boer War (1899–1902), much of the American public paid only passing attention to the conflict nearly half a world away. The Dutch immigrant settlements in Iowa, however, took notice and lobbied their neighbors—and even the US government—to defend the Dutch-descended Boers.[62]

In October of 1899, Dutch newspapers in Iowa announced the outbreak of war in Africa. That month *The Sioux County Herald* featured twenty-six scenes spread across a single page of paper that introduced the major players and events in the conflict. British leaders like Queen Victoria and Alfred Milner, the governor of the Cape Colony, appeared alongside the Boer leadership. President of the Boer South African Republic, Paul Kruger and the leader of the South African Parliament, referred to as the Volksraad, Franz Vogel Gesang also took positions of prominence in these early discussions of the war.[63] In the feature, the Boers far outnumbered the British, and the *Herald*'s captions often praised them for their work and nobleness while the British figures got basic descriptions of an individual's title or role.

Sioux County's coverage of the war skewed heavily in favor of the Boers, indicating the favorable treatment that the Dutch newspapers provided concerning the conflict, and in doing so, it also revealed the clear connection that ethnicity and religion played in informing how these Dutch immigrants interpreted the conflict.[64] In the brief profile of Gezina Kruger, President Kruger's wife, the paper described her as "a simple Dutchwoman" and noted that she was "as old fashioned as she was before her husband became great." Although the Krugers were born in South Africa, the paper insisted on referring to them as Dutch. This identity appealed to the heritage the Dutch immigrants in America still claimed for themselves. It yoked the Dutch in the American West with their kin in South Africa. Far from a slight, describing Gezina as "old-fashioned" and boasting of her maintaining her character despite the political ascendency of her husband marked her as a stalwart and respectable woman.

These early profiles placed key South African figures in familiar religious and political roles. One portrait depicted Kruger in an elevated and clearly Dutch Reformed pulpit. The caption read, "President Kruger now and then enters the pulpit and preaches a sermon. He knows his Bible as well as he knows diplomacy."[65] Unlike the British leaders in this feature and elsewhere throughout the Dutch papers' coverage of the war, this portrait presented Kruger as a pious and biblically literate leader. The Boers became associated with faithfulness and a dedication to a biblically based faith. The British, in contrast, appeared devoid of religious leadership, especially in South Africa.

Dutch coverage of the Boer War employed gendered and racial language to position the Boers as sympathetic defenders of their homes and the British as enemies who had wrongly invaded land held by "civilized" Christians. All of these characterizations became particularly apparent in an October 1899 article published in *The Alton (IA) Democrat* titled, "Women will Fight: Mothers in the Transvaal Will Shoot Englishmen, They Sleep on Their Rifles, Ready Always to Defend Themselves and their Homes."[66] The article, somewhat unexpectedly, began with a shot across the bow of American rather than British imperialism: "Like the Filipino women, who fight for their homes in our war of imperialism and criminal aggression, so it is with the brave Dutch mothers in the Transvaal."[67] The association of Dutch mothers and Filipino resistance fighters cut against popular tropes about the people who found themselves living within the American Empire after the end of the Spanish–American War. At one level, this article presented the fight of the Dutch-descended Boers as a battle against an aggressive and invading imperialistic foe. It conveniently overlooked the Dutch acts of imperialism that resulted in the presence of the Boers in Africa in the first place. On another level, this piece reads as a broader critique of the trans-Pacific expansion of American

Empire. By ignoring Dutch imperialism in South Africa and American imperialism in the American West, the author conveniently disregarded centuries of imperialism that had benefited the Dutch immigrants. Yet by equating the sympathetic Dutch mother with Filipinos, the author encouraged his readers to think critically about the McKinley administration's imperialistic policies, either suggesting a limit to how far the West might expand or warning against the United States pursuing its own imperial ambitions too close to Dutch holdings in Indonesia.

The article presented these women as victims who, through no fault of their own, found themselves being assaulted by the British Empire, perhaps in a way that recalled the clashes between Dutch colonies and their American neighbors. The author described them as "imbued with that spirit of ferocity and hatred which springs up in the harmless animal when driven back inch by inch from its haunts deeper into the heart of the wilderness." He continued, "In order to protect its own, the boer [*sic*] women, stirred by the deepest feelings of womanhood, will fight to defend their fireside." The description accomplished two critical tasks: First it again reinforced the characterization of the Boers as defenders of their homes against the imposing British. Second, it justified their actions and bitter hatred. In no uncertain terms, they believed that the Boers were the victims in this conflict, and the newspaper cast its lot with them. Third, this characterization presented the Boers as noble, fierce, and, most importantly, justified in their fight. Like a good-natured animal cornered by a predator, the Boers intended to fight back and defend themselves.

Although the author initially associated the Boer women with Filipinos, later in the same article he relied on important racial attitudes to position these same women as models of racial superiority. The author described them as "magnificent specimens of humanity." He noted that they were "tall, finely formed and very robust. . . . They are perfect in physique . . . nearly all of whom are blond, with full, well-built figures and clear pink complexions."[68] To top it all off, he boasted that they were excellent housekeepers and accomplished cooks.

At the very end of his article, the author highlighted the importance of religion and associated the Boers with religious fighters. "With prayers and fasting, with the rifle in one hand and the bible [*sic*] in the other, the boer [*sic*] women are on the alert. . . . They are ready to defy the whole British nation. And here's hoping she will win!"[69] The author of this piece left no doubt about his loyalties. He found himself squarely aligned with the Boers and the rifle-toting, Bible-wielding, pink-faced women defending their homes from the invading British. Here, again, though, religion played a critical role. While the British rushed pell-mell into battle, the Boers—with their Bibles and sharpshooting housewives—were the ones who deserved the Dutch Americans' sympathy and support.

A few months later, in April of 1900, local newspapers made it even more apparent that they viewed the struggle between their Dutch coreligionists the Boers and their British foes as a religious battle. In earlier pieces, authors had featured religion as an element of the broader justification for the Boers' fight and the reason why Dutch Americans should support their coreligionists in Africa. Here, however, religion took center stage in casting the British as their foes and the Boers as righteous defenders of their homeland. The center of the front page of the *Alton Democrat* featured an article titled "The Struggle for Liberty," which led off with the Catherine Markham poem, "A Sorrowful Christ." In the article, the author described the British troops' lack of religion and alleged that their all-out assault on faithful Christians marked them as the enemies. In particular, this article described how the British attacked religious figures in a way that revealed their faithlessness. When listing the victims of British aggression, the article included Dutch women, professors of divinity, other Boer civilians, and an irreverently sullied effigy of President Kruger.[70] The destruction of theological schools, attacks on divinity professors, and assaults on Boer women clearly marked the British as disrespectful of religion, and more specifically the Dutch Calvinism practiced by the Boers. The Boers' church was under assault by the British, and by extension, these Dutch Americans might also conclude that their own broader church body was being threatened.

When the Dutch American Protestants living in Iowa observed the Boer War in South Africa at the turn of the twentieth century, they did not see it simply as foreign conflict driven by capitalistic or imperialistic ambitions. Instead, they considered it to be a religious struggle by fellow Dutch people fighting to defend their homes. These writers, as might be expected, persistently ignored the fact that the Boers themselves had taken their "homeland" from the Africans who lived there prior to Dutch colonization—a group that received no mention in the articles. By casting the British as faithless and attackers of the Dutch Calvinism of the Boers, these newspapers revealed how Dutch Americans perceived the attacks of the British as an attack on the broader Dutch Calvinist tradition that they shared.

At the turn of the twentieth century, war dispatches in Dutch newspapers throughout Iowa offered weekly reminders that their church was under attack. While most Americans basked in the victory of the US over Spain in the Spanish-American War (1898), a constellation of rural Dutch American communities fretted over a different conflict in South Africa. The colonies remained unapologetically Dutch, yet just as these men and women had shrewdly used their US citizenship to succeed electorally and leverage key connections with state and national legislators to achieve their goals, they pled, in vain, with representatives, senators, and even President Roosevelt to intervene. With rapt attention, they watched the Second Boer War unfold, cheering on their coreligionists, the insurgent Boers, and vilifying their British foes.

This episode exhibits the persistent sense of kinship throughout the Dutch Calvinist diaspora and that from their position in the American West, these immigrants spoke boldly in defense of their kin. Furthermore, the community had complicated feelings about imperialism, sharply critiquing the expanding British Empire and even sending a barb toward US imperialism while papering over the long-standing Dutch and American empires that benefited them. Their own complex dual identities as Americans with deep loyalties to the Dutch appeared yet again as they tried to spur action from their adopted home on behalf of Dutch-descended people abroad.

Conclusion

Religion was the bedrock for these Dutch immigrant communities, and their location in and identification with the American West were critical elements to forging their complex identities. The religious mandate that they claimed nurtured a deep conviction about the importance of their community-building and missionary efforts. It also provided justification for displacement of the Odawa in Michigan and the Meskwaki and Dakota in Iowa, Calvinist community development, and global engagement. They parlayed their Dutch identities and fervent faith to conceive of the trans-Mississippi West as both a destination and a springboard. It knit communities together locally, regionally, and globally and united them against both pesky neighbors and global superpowers. Their adopted American identities gave them (limited) political clout and made them a force in local elections. Far from urban centers and relatively isolated from other settler communities, these colonists could urgently build communities that reflected their religious convictions while continuing to decide for themselves when and how they claimed their Dutch identity, American identity, or both.

With major settlements in Iowa and the Dakotas, in the nineteenth century, they were both the westernmost Dutch colonies in the US and the westernmost outposts of the Dutch Empire. Religion informed almost every part of their lives. It justified building colonies on Native land, wove together a cohesive community, and propelled men and women from that community into the world. Their faith, as practiced and conceptualized on the prairies and plains, allowed them to look at the Odawa, Meskwaki, and Dakota with indifference, Middle Eastern people with evangelistic hope, the Boers as persecuted victims, and themselves—crucially—as righteous western Dutch American saviors both at home and abroad.

Notes

1. Antonie Brummelkamp and Albertus Van Raalte, *Landverhuizing, of Waarom bevorderen wij de volksverhuizing en wel naar Noord-Amerika en niet naar Java?* (Hoogkamer, 1846).

2. Brummelkamp and Van Raalte, *Landverhuizing*, 16.

3. Brummelkamp and Van Raalte, *Landverhuizing*, 24.

4. Robert Swierenga, "Exodus Netherlands, Promised Land America: Dutch Immigration and Settlement in the United States," in *A Bilateral Bicentennial: A History of Dutch American Relations, 1782–1982* (Octagon Books, 1982), 127.

5. Jon K. Lauck, "Soft, Democratic, and Universalist: In Search of the Main Currents of Traditional Midwestern Identity and a Grand Historiographic Synthesis," *Middle West Review* 6 (2019–2020): 63–134.

6. This chapter intentionally uses the language of "colony," "colonizing," and "colonialism" not only to reflect the larger processes taking place but also, importantly, because these men and women consistently used this language themselves. They explicitly saw their community building efforts as colonization.

7. Robert P. Swierenga, "Van Raalte and Scholte: A Soured Relationship and Personal Rivalry," *Origins* 27, no. 1 (1999): 21–35.

8. Gerrit J. ten Zythoff, *Sources of Secession* (Wm. B. Eerdmans, 1987), 117.

9. Heideman, *The Practice of Piety: The Theology of the Midwestern Reformed Church in America, 1866–1966* (Wm. B. Eerdmans, 2009), xii.

10. Heideman, *The Practice of Piety*, 119.

11. Eugene Heideman, *Hendrik P. Scholte: His Legacy in the Netherlands and in America* (Wm. B. Eerdmans, 2015), 212; Hans Krabbendam, *Freedom on the Horizon: Dutch Immigration to America, 1840–1940* (Wm. B. Eerdmans, 2009), 106–107, 113, 119.

12. Dutch Calvinist immigrants split between the Reformed Church in America and the Christian Reformed Church in America. The former tended to Americanize more quickly (relatively speaking), and the latter preferred to hold onto Dutch traditions more strongly. Later the latter group would also be influenced more heavily by Dutch theologian and politician Abraham Kuyper. Peter Ester, "Religion and Social Capital Bonding and Bridging in Dutch-American Calvinist Communities: A Review and Research Agenda," in *Dutch Immigrants on the Plains*, ed. Paul Fessler, Hubert R. Krygsman, and Robert P. Swierenga (Joint Archives of Holland, 2006), 187.

13. Antonie Brummelkamp and Albertus C. Van Raatle, "Appeal to the Faithful in the United States of America," May 25, 1846, in *Dutch Immigrant Memoirs and Related Writings*, ed. Henry S. Lucas (Wm. B. Eerdmans, 1997), 17–18.

14. Krabbendam, *Freedom on the Horizon*, 5.

15. Nederlandsche Vereeniging ter Verhuizing naar de Vereenigde Staten van Noord-Amerika, Henry S. Lucas Papers, 1846–1930, Reel 3, Bentley Historical Library, the University of Michigan.

16. Jan J. Boersema and Anthonia Boersema-Bremer, "All but the Saloon: Nineteenth Century Dutch Immigrants, the Wilderness, and Ideas of Progress," in *Dutch Reformed Education: Immigrant Legacies in North America*, ed. Donald A. Luidens, Donald J. Bruggink, and Herman J. De Vries Jr. (Van Raalte Press, 2020), 384–88.

17. Pieter Hovens, "Moccasins and Wooden Shoes: Dutch Missionaries, Settlers, and Indians in Wisconsin, 1834–1940," in *Diverse Destinies: Dutch* Kolonies *in Wisconsin and the East*, ed. Nella Kennedy, Mary Risseeuw, and Robert P. Swierenga (Van Raalte Press, 2012), 2–22; James Calvin Schaap, "Native Lakota and Dutch-American Settlers in Early South Dakota," in *Dutch Immigrants on the Plains*, ed. Paul Fessler, Hubert R. Krygsman, and Robert P. Swierenga (Joint Archives of Holland, 2006), 56–75.

18. See, for instance, E. J. G. Bloemendaal, *My America* (Wright Place, 2009), 95; Brian W. Beltman, "A Dutch Immigrant's Success Story: E. J. G. Bloemendaal's Sojourns and Settlement in Northwest Iowa," *Annals of Iowa* 62 (Spring 2003): 203.

19. Robert P. Swierenga, "Introduction," in *Old Wing Mission: Cultural Interchange as Chronicled by George and Arvilla Smith in Their Work with Chief Wakazoo's Ottawa Band on the West Michigan Frontier*, ed. Robert P. Swierenga and William Van Appledorn (Wm. B. Eerdmans, 2008), 46–53.

20. Paul Beck, *Inkpaduta: Dakota Leader* (University of Oklahoma, 2008), 20–24, 74–75; Douglas Firth Anderson, "'Kerk en School': Henry Hospers and Iowa's Second Kolonie," *Origins* 41, no. 1 (2023): 25.

21. Swierenga, "Exodus Netherlands," 127–47; Brian W. Beltman, "Ethnic Territoriality and the Persistence of Identity: Dutch Settlers in Northwest Iowa, 1869–1880," *Annals of Iowa* 55, no. 2 (1996): 103.

22. Robert P. Swierenga and Elton Bruins, *Family Quarrels in the Dutch Reformed Church in the Nineteenth Century* (Wm. B. Eerdmans, 2000), 6–7.

23. Robert P. Swierenga, "Religion and Immigration Patterns: A Comparative Analysis of Dutch Protestants and Catholics, 1835–1880," *Journal of American Ethnic History* 5, no. 2 (Spring 1986): 23–45, esp. 27; Hans Krabbendam, *Freedom on the Horizon*, 9.

24. Henry Lucas, *Netherlanders in America: Dutch Immigration to the United States and Canada, 1789–1950* (University of Michigan Press, 1955), 444–59, at 459.

25. Hans Krabbendam, *Freedom on the Horizon*, 73.

26. Hans Krabbendam, "The Return of Regionalism: The Importance of Immigration to the Plains for the History of the Dutch in America," 1–21, in *Dutch Immigrants on the Plains*, ed. Paul Fessler, Hubert R. Krygsman, and Robert P. Swierenga (Joint Archives of Holland, 2006); Robert Schoone-Jongen, "Churches Bigger Than Windmills: Religion and Dutchness in Minnesota, 1885–1928," in *Going Dutch: Holland in America, 1609–2008*, ed. Joyce D. Goodfriend (Brill, 2008), 157–78.

27. Brian W. Beltman, "A Dutch Immigrant's Success Story," 203.

28. G. Nelson Nieuwenhuis, *Siouxland: A History of Sioux County* (Pluim Publishing, 1983), 110.

29. Antonie J. Betten, Jr., "Legal Notice," *The Sioux County Herald*, September 20, 1872; Charles L. Dyke, *The Story of Sioux County* (Verstegen, 1942), 136; "What Shall We Say?," *Sioux County Herald*, November 9, 1872.

30. "Sioux County! The Fairest Land Under the Sun," *Sioux County Herald*, October 5, 1887.

31. "Plaatselijk Nieuws," *De Volksvriend*, October 8, 1874.

32. "Plaatselijk Nieuws," *De Volksvriend*, October 22, 1874.

33. "Ons County Ticket," *De Volksvriend*, November 2, 1876. Formatting original. "Republican County Ticket," *Sioux County Herald*, October 26, 1876.

34. Henry Hospers, "Township Conventie," *De Volksvriend*, October 19, 1876.

35. "The Free Voter," *Sioux County Herald*, November 16, 1882.

36. "The Free Voter."

37. "The Free Voter."

38. "The Free Voter."

39. "Election Returns," *The Sioux County Herald*, November 16, 1882. The final tally was 716 votes for the Dutch candidate, Henry J. Lenderink, and 530 votes for the American candidate, Fred Stone.

40. "Editor's Note," *The Sioux County Herald*, November 16, 1882.

41. "Zij Zouden 'T Ontgelden," *De Volksvriend*, November 9, 1882.

42. Adrian Zwemer to Family, August 22, 1859, trans. Harry Boonstra, Elton Bruins Research Collection, Van Raalte Institute, Holland, Michigan.

43. Zwemer to Family.

44. James F. Zwemer is most commonly referred to with both his first and middle names, James Frederick, and his brother, Frederick James Zwemer is also mostly commonly referred to as Frederick James. Despite this common practice, for the sake of clarity, James Frederick will be referred to as James and Frederick James will be referred to as Frederick.

45. Ruth A. Tucker, *From Jerusalem to Irian Jaya: A Biographical History of Christian Missions*, (Zondervan Academic, 2004), 241.

46. Thomas S. Kidd, *American Christians and Islam: Evangelical Culture and Muslims from the Colonial Period to the Age of Terrorism* (Princeton University Press, 2009), 58.

47. John H. Karsten, "Our Educational Institutions," unpublished speech, May 15, 1888, W88-060, John H. Karsten, Box 1, Joint Archives of Holland, Holland, Michigan (hereafter JAH); John A. Otte, "Civilization," *Excelsiora* 9, no. 12 (May 1879): 546–49; P. Hollerman, "Civilization," *Excelsiora* 12, no. 2 (November 1881): 55–58; Peter Huyser, "Civilization," *Excelsiora* 18, no. 1 (October 1888): 12–15; Henry Hospers, "Eene beknopte geschiedenis van de vestiging der Hollandsche Kolonie in Sioux County, Iowa," *De Volksvriend*, June 25, 1874.

48. Samuel Zwemer, Postcard to F. J. Zwemer, August 20, 1890, W88-0212.5, Zwemer Collection, JAH.

49. Samuel Zwemer, to J. H. Karsten, March 12, 1891 (from Aden, Arabia), W88-060, John H. Karsten Collection, Box 1, JAH; Samuel Zwemer to Karsten, September 14, 1892, W88-060, John H. Karsten Collection, Box 1, JAH; S. M. Zwemer to Karsten, November 16, 1895 (from Busrah to Oostberg, WI), John H. Karsten Collection, JAH.

50. Hope Missionary Band Minutes, 1890–95, Hope College Collection, JAH.

51. Zwemer to Karsten, March 12, 1891.

52. Zwemer to Karsten, September 14, 1892.

53. Samuel Zwemer, *The Missionary Review of the World* 6, no. 1 (January 1893): 54.

54. Zwemer to Karsten, September 12, 1892. In fact, the women of a Dutch church in the colony in Alto, Wisconsin, purchased a communion set for Samuel's mission in the Middle East after receiving his updates.

55. Heather J. Sharkey, *American Evangelicals in Egypt: Missionary Encounters in an Age of Empire* (Princeton University Press, 2008), 112–13.

56. In the twentieth century, Northwestern Classical Academy transitioned into a junior college before eventually becoming a four-year institution. It exists today as Northwestern College and remains in Orange City. Gerald F. De Jong, *From Strength to Strength: A History of Northwestern, 1882–1982* (Wm. B Eerdmans, 1982), 20; Jacob Van Hinte, *Netherlanders in America: A Study of Emigration and Settlement in the 19th and 20th Centuries in the United States of America*, ed. Robert P. Swierenga, trans. Adriaan de Wit (Baker, 1985), 518, 564–65.

57. Jennie Dubbink, "News," *Excelsiora* 17, no. 3 (December 1886): 226–27; Douglas Firth Anderson, "'The Joyous, Jolly Academy Days': Northwestern Classical Academy, 1882–1928," in *Dutch Reformed Education: Immigrant Legacies in North America*, ed. Donald A. Luidens, Donald J. Bruggink, and Herman J. De Vries Jr. (Van Raalte Press, 2020), 111–12.

58. Anderson, "'The Joyous, Jolly Academy Days,'" 112.

59. Hans Krabbendam, *Freedom on the Horizon*, 73; Ester, "Religion and Social Capital Bonding and Bridging in Dutch-American Calvinist Communities."

60. Samuel Zwemer, Postcard to F. J. Zwemer, August 20, 1890, Zwemer Collection, JAH.

61. Brummelkamp and Van Raalte, *Landverhuizing*, 24.

62. Michael Douma, "Ethnic Identities in a Transnational Context: The Dutch American Reaction to the Anglo-Boer War 1899–1902," *South African Historical Journal* 65, no. 4 (April 2013): 481–503.

63. "Portraits of the Boer War," *The Sioux County Herald*, October 25, 1899.

64. Douma, 486.

65. "President Kruger in the Pulpit," *Sioux County Herald*, October 25, 1899.

66. "Women Will Fight," *Alton Democrat* (Alton, IA), October 7, 1899.

67. "Women Will Fight."

68. "Women Will Fight."

69. "Women Will Fight."

70. "The Struggle for Liberty," *Alton Democrat*, April 21, 1900.

Chapter 7

Somewhat Secular Saints

Enacting and Resisting Modernity in the Church of Jesus Christ of Latter-day Saints During the 1918 Influenza Epidemic

QUINCY D. NEWELL

Keywords: influenza, Latter-day Saints, secularization, modernity, healing

Joseph F. Smith died in November of 1918 of pneumonia.[1] At the time of his death, Smith was the president, prophet, seer, and revelator of the Church of Jesus Christ of Latter-day Saints (popularly known as the Mormon Church, and hereafter referred to as the LDS Church).[2] Smith's death marked the end of an era: He was the last church president who had known the founder and first prophet, Joseph Smith Jr. (Joseph F. Smith was Joseph Smith Jr.'s nephew.) He was the last church president born before the church established itself in what became Utah. He was the last church president to have multiple living wives while in office. And just over a month before his death, he had described to church members the visions he had received that detailed the redemption of the dead, a crucial feature of Latter-day Saint theology that distinguished the church from other forms of Christianity. These visions became the last section added, to date, to the LDS Church's *Doctrine and Covenants* (hereafter D&C)—an ongoing record of God's communications with his people.[3] Smith's death—which brought with it the end of Smith's tenure as the living prophet of the church—was a big deal.

Normally, the funeral of a church president is a major event for the institution. In the nineteenth and twentieth centuries, church presidents' funerals normally included a service in the Salt Lake Tabernacle, packed to the gills with mourners, a long funeral cortege through streets crowded with believers turned out to pay their last respects, and a burial service attended by hundreds, if not thousands, of people.[4] Joseph F. Smith's funeral, in contrast, was small and private. The *Deseret News*, a newspaper owned by the church and published in Salt Lake City, printed a lengthy article announcing Smith's death, accompanied by a short notice from church leaders informing the public that

> at a meeting of the general authorities of the Church and representatives of the family this morning, it was unanimously decided that in view of existing health conditions in the community it would be improper to hold public funeral services for the late President Joseph F. Smith. This decision, though regretfully adopted, is a measure of prudence which will meet with general approval, we feel sure. Such services as shall be held at the time of interment in the city cemetery will therefore be brief. At a later date, however, announcement of which will be duly made, memorial services will be held throughout the whole Church for the beloved leader whose loss we so sincerely, but perforce silently, mourn[.][5]

The mention of "existing health conditions in the community" was a veiled reference to the influenza epidemic that was ravaging the city.

On November 11, 1918, the Allied powers' victory in World War I inspired a general outpouring of public celebration in Salt Lake City, as elsewhere in the United States. As a reporter for the *Ogden Standard* put it, "It was a merger of the wildest New Year's eve demonstration when John Barleycorn wielded the scepter, with the biggest Labor day and Fourth of July manifestations and the greatest of all festivals and carnivals ever witnessed in Salt Lake."[6] The "happy chaos" the reporter described predictably resulted in community spread of influenza in Salt Lake and elsewhere in Utah, triggering measures to control the outbreak: Health officials imposed quarantines, marked the homes of influenza patients with placards, restricted the number of people who could ride on streetcars, and established business hours for a variety of commercial establishments in an effort to reduce crowding and prevent large numbers of people from congregating. They also prohibited social gatherings and limited funeral services to half an hour, with a maximum of four vehicles—including the hearse—in a funeral procession.[7] Smith died as these measures were being put in place. A public funeral like those mounted for church presidents before and after him would have violated the regulations imposed by public health authorities.

The influenza epidemic of 1918–19 had arrived in Utah only a month before World War I ended. It was intimately linked to that conflict: Spread first in the United States among soldiers preparing to go to battle, the flu soon made its way out of military installations and into the public. The disease killed approximately 675,000 Americans, and between fifty million and one hundred million people worldwide.[8] It was particularly scary because, unlike previous strains of influenza, this strain seemed to target those in the prime of life: About half of those who died were between the ages of eighteen and forty-five.[9]

The LDS Church's response to the 1918 flu epidemic provided an opportunity for the church to demonstrate its modern, secular character—and, by implication, its legitimacy as an American religion. For religious traditions, "modernization" generally takes the form of what scholars call "secularization." By this term we mean, as religious studies scholar Gustavo Benavides puts it, the "differentiation and narrowing of the institutional religious realm."[10] Secularization "does not result in the disappearance of religion but rather in its consolidation," Benavides writes. He continues, "Similarly, the rationalization of economic and other types of behavior, exemplified by the denunciation of certain rituals, helps to delimit a subjective realm, one whose importance increases in direct proportion to the rationalization and instrumentalization of the social world."[11] When I say that Latter-day Saints were secular, this is what I mean: not that church members gave up their religious identity or practice, but that in public, at least, they separated the category of religion from the category of medicine and subordinated that "subjective realm" (as Benavides describes it) of religion to the rationalized, scientific realm of medicine—the latter, largely translated into society in the form of public health. At the same time, Latter-day Saints separated their participation in the public sphere from their participation in the religious sphere, allowing them to cooperate with those of other religious convictions in the common goals of limiting the spread of influenza and caring for those ill with the disease.

Scholars have pinpointed Latter-day Saints' secularization at several moments in the church's history. The decision of church leadership to work with—even court—non-Latter-day Saint business interests as early as 1868 demonstrated and facilitated the church's integration into the US capitalist system and encouraged the church and its members to cordon off religious imperatives from business decisions so as to keep the economic sphere separate from the religious one.[12] During the nineteenth century as well, the church worked hard to be recognized as white, and therefore as belonging to the American nation. These efforts culminated with the early twentieth-century whitewashing of the church's history in the minds of leaders and members, suppressing memories of Black priesthood holders and their full participation in the church's early history.[13] The end of polygamy also supported the church's aspirations to whiteness.[14] The first and second manifestos, in 1890 and 1904, which ultimately ended the practice of polygamy, are moments when the LDS Church seemed to accept the supremacy of the state and acquiesce to white Protestant constructions of "civilized" marriage and family.[15] As these developments suggest, and as numerous scholars have shown, Latter-day Saints knew that whiteness was not, or not only, a matter of skin color. Rather, both Latter-day Saints and outsiders understood whiteness to depend as well on a host of other factors including (but by no means limited to) religious practices, family structures, gender roles, and employment.[16] Many of these characteristics were also related to secularism, so Latter-day Saints' secularization project and their efforts to achieve whiteness overlapped significantly.[17]

As the church transitioned away from polygamy, it rewrote gender norms for men and women, using these to further cement the church's belonging in the United States. The new gender norms for women mirrored Protestant models that limited women's authority in the public sphere. As historian Joan Wallach Scott has shown, the construction of the public–private divide, and the relegation of women to the domestic realm, was a crucial, if often unnoticed, element of the secularization process.[18] By curtailing women's public activity, Latter-day Saints aligned with the prevailing white Protestant norm that relegated women, emotion, and religion to the domestic realm, leaving the public sphere for men, rationality, and politics. For men, Latter-day Saints emphasized successful participation in business and patriotism—the Boy Scouts of America and, with the onset of the Great War, enlistment in the armed forces.[19] The church thus wove itself into the American imperial project, moving from target of imperial power to representative of it, as missionaries fanned out across the globe carrying the gospel of this deeply American church. The 1918 influenza epidemic was another opportunity for the LDS Church to pursue this secularization project on multiple fronts.

I decided to write this essay on Latter-day Saints and the 1918 influenza epidemic as a first step toward a book on religion and the 1918 flu in the United States. I was curious about religious responses to the epidemic, and I went into the archive expecting to see Latter-day Saints theologizing the flu epidemic discursively, asking questions like "Why is God doing this?" and "What is the spiritual meaning of this event?" and ruminating on the answers. Like other major disasters, and other major disease events, in American and European history, the 1918 flu epidemic seemed ripe for theodicy.[20] For the most part, I did not find evidence of this sort of overt theologizing. Instead, I found Latter-day Saints responding to the epidemic by cooperating with largely non-Latter-day Saint secular authorities and relying, at least in public, on scientific theories of disease. This, in itself, is a kind of theology.[21] It illuminates Latter-day Saints' thinking about how to do religion "right": In their case, this was largely by removing from the public sphere any claims to divine intervention or supernatural aid; limiting public view of religious rituals (a process that was started decades earlier when important rituals were moved into temples that barred the general public); and otherwise at least appearing to conform to the norms set by white Protestant Americans.

In one sense, the Latter-day Saints' struggle to make themselves over in the model of the modern, secular American citizen is not a Western story at all, except in that it occurred largely in Utah and surrounding states, a place generally acknowledged to be located in the West. In another sense, however, as many of the chapters in this volume demonstrate, the task of theorizing religion was an ongoing, and especially urgent, activity in the West. Latter-day Saints' efforts to work out the parameters of acceptable religious belief and practice at this point in time illustrate one moment in this continuing project that engaged Westerners in a variety of ways throughout the nineteenth and twentieth centuries and into the twenty-first century.

In this essay, I use four episodes—Joseph F. Smith's death (which I discussed at the beginning of this chapter), a woman's decision to drink consecrated oil, the celebration of soldiers' return to Salt Lake, and a sermon given at the LDS Church General Conference in June 1919—to consider from different angles Latter-day Saints' secularity and resistance to secularism in their response to the flu.

As they navigated the 1918 flu epidemic, Latter-day Saints strove to embody a vision of the modern white American citizenry toward which they had been working since at least their arrival in the Great Basin in 1847. But even in this crucial moment, the church's achievement of secularity was uneven. In marking Joseph F. Smith's death, the church demonstrated its submission to the state, forgoing even a ceremony that included all of Smith's immediate family members, let alone his extended family or the broader church community. But Latter-day Saints would later meld white Protestant norms regarding heteronormative monogamous nuclear family structures with earlier understandings of the family as a public structure to create metaphorical public families to which Utah soldiers would return.[22] The public celebration of those soldiers' arrival was thus as much a family affair as a civic event. The adoption of white Protestant norms of "civilized behavior" entailed the subordination of women to men and women's organizations to those headed and staffed by men. This was especially obvious in the arena of healing during the 1918 flu epidemic: Women were on the front lines of caring for the ill, but men's work as health authorities, doctors, and scientists received most of the attention.

Latter-day Saints' resistance to the white Protestant consensus about the efficacy of science and biomedicine in managing the flu was apparent in how they treated the disease at both an individual and societal level. While Latter-day Saints used standard public health strategies like masking and quarantining, they also used a range of alternative therapies and religious techniques, consistent with the church's history and theology. These were rarely visible to those outside the church. Instead, in public, Latter-day Saints put aside sectarian differences and sought to work with those of other religions, finding a "lowest common denominator" in efforts to end the epidemic that allowed Latter-day Saints to join the broad Protestant secular consensus in the nation. Latter-day Saints worked hard to construct and maintain their belonging in that consensus, downplaying obvious markers of difference and emphasizing their whiteness and patriotic Americanness. The 1918 flu epidemic, and Latter-day Saints' responses to it, illuminate a range of ways that Latter-day Saints, in what they had once thought of as their "Great Basin Kingdom," were modulating their religious practice and working out how to do religion "right" in a modernizing United States—while not fully surrendering their identity as a distinctive religious group.

A Drink of Consecrated Oil

A Latter-day Saint woman from Malad, Idaho, recalled: "During the flu epidemic in, I think, about 1918, all of the family except Mother was ill. Mother said she was so busy caring for Dad and the children that she couldn't even find time to do the dishes. At one point, she started to feel ill herself. She was terrified that she might not be able to care for her sick family and, in desperation, she drank some of the consecrated oil that was always in the home[.] She felt it must have worked because she did not contract the flu."[23] This memory, recorded well after the events it recounted, points us to a number of important aspects of the Latter-day Saint response to the flu epidemic. Whereas the war was largely the domain of men, the flu invaded American homes and demanded the labor of women, who most often acted as healers in those private spaces.[24] At every turn, however, Latter-day Saint women's work against the epidemic was subjected to a dual subordination: First, women's work was subordinated to men's. Although women were on the front lines of the epidemic, serving as nurses in hospitals and in private homes (their own and those of relatives, friends, neighbors, and employers), their work was consistently made invisible in favor of the work done by men. These included public health officials, scientists working on vaccines, and doctors working in local contexts—hospitals, medical offices, and so on. One exception was Myrtle Swainston, a recent graduate of the LDS Hospital School of Nursing in Salt Lake City, who was named the head of a temporary hospital in Ogden, Utah.[25] Nevertheless, though Swainston was charged with running the hospital—hiring and supervising nurses, recruiting volunteers, and soliciting donations—her opinions were not sought regarding public health measures in the local community.

This subordination of women in the realm of medical practice was not inevitable: in the late nineteenth century, Latter-day Saint women had trained as regular medical doctors, and the community had respected their authority in that role. Historian Benjamin Cater locates the turning point in the early twentieth century, with the establishment in Salt Lake of Dr. W. H. Groves Latter-day Saints Hospital supported by the institutional LDS Church, in 1905. It was at this moment, Cater argues, that the hospital's trustees chose to reshape Latter-day Saint gender norms so that they conformed more closely to those of wider American society by "denying female Saints positions as medical doctors and surgeons, but training them mainly, if not exclusively, as nurses."[26]

Groves-LDS did not completely conform to the norms of secular hospitals, or even the other hospitals in Salt Lake run by religious groups. Its leaders allowed Latter-day Saint healing rituals, including anointing with oil and healing blessings, performed by priesthood holders.[27] Here, too, women's healing work had been subordinated to men's: Although women had participated in religious healing rituals throughout the church's nineteenth-century history, by the turn of the twentieth century LDS Church leaders began to curtail women's roles in healing rituals. Women were still allowed to pray for the sick, lay hands on them, and anoint them with oil, activities they had done for both male and female patients and in both all-female and mixed-gender groups during the nineteenth century. In 1900, however, church leaders started teaching that women could not "seal" such healings, but could only "confirm" them. This shift in language was crucial. As scholars Jonathan A. Stapley and Kristine Wright note, "the shift from 'sealing' to 'confirmation' enforced the view that ritual healing by Melchizedek Priesthood holders [who were all men] was liturgically superior" to healing performed by women.[28] Only a couple years after the influenza epidemic in 1921, the Relief Society General Board—the governing body for the LDS Church's women's organization—ruled that women should only perform healing rituals for pregnant women, and then only when priesthood holders were unavailable.[29]

The Relief Society positioned Latter-day Saint women's work against the flu as secondary in another way at the organizational level by subordinating itself, as a religious organization, to a secular organization. The Relief Society had first been organized in Nauvoo, Illinois, in 1842. Although the central organization more or less dissolved when the Latter-day Saints left Illinois, small groups of women continued to meet and work on relief projects throughout the 1850s and into the 1860s. In 1867, LDS Church President Brigham Young called for the Relief Society to be organized in every ward (local congregation) of the church, and it has existed as an element of the LDS Church since that time.[30] In 1918, the Relief Society was basically autonomous: It collected its own dues, managed its own funds, and controlled its own activities. It counted the majority of Latter-day Saint women as its members. And it was able to mobilize rapidly around the causes that fell under its purview, which included issues having to do with health. Rather than working directly on epidemic relief, though, the Relief Society channeled the majority of its resources—material, money, and people—to the American Red Cross (ARC) for relief efforts. Founded in 1881, the ARC was charged by the US surgeon general with coordinating efforts against the influenza epidemic in the United States. By focusing on supporting the ARC, rather than providing aid directly, the Relief Society placed itself in a subordinate position to a congressionally chartered organization, implicitly positioning the LDS Church as subordinate to the US government.[31] As a result, the LDS Church enacted a relationship to the secular state that was recognizable to outsiders as the "proper" ordering of social relations for the modern secular nation.

Thus, in the public and semipublic spaces of hospitals and other medical establishments, as well as in public rhetoric, women and religious organizations were subordinated to men and quasi-governmental organizations. Within the LDS Church, women's healing work was also subordinated to men's. Nevertheless, the day-to-day nursing care of family members and friends in both public and private spaces often fell to women. The Malad woman's decision to drink consecrated oil to protect her own health so that she could continue to care for her family members demonstrated her sense of imperative—she *had* to care for her family, and she had to stay healthy to do so. In consuming the oil, she drew on an extensive Latter-day Saint tradition of using material objects—or substances, in the case of oil—for healing. Historically, Latter-day Saints had seen such objects and substances as a medium through which divine healing could be conveyed, even in the absence of the recitation of the proper ritual formula or the invocation of the specific religious authority that church leaders insisted was necessary to "seal" the healing blessing.

Latter-day Saints had never required that healing be accomplished through religious means alone. Instead, members of the tradition leaned heavily on Thomsonian and similar theories of healing. Thomsonianism was a markedly democratic system of medicine that valued the common sense of ordinary people rather than relying on highly trained practitioners like orthodox medicine. It used herbal remedies and steam treatments to purge the body of cold and restore and augment the body's natural heat.[32] Scholar Thomas J. Wolfe notes the prevalence of Thomsonian healers among the leadership of the early LDS Church and points out that the Utah Territorial Legislature passed laws that favored Thomsonian practitioners over "regular" medical doctors.[33] Wolfe writes that by the turn of the twentieth century, "Thomsonianism had all but disappeared from Utah" because the formerly isolated western location had become increasingly interconnected with the rest of the United States.[34] Nevertheless, the influence of Thomsonianism remained, inclining Latter-day Saints to look favorably on botanical medicines and the gentler healing techniques of alternative medicine systems well into the twentieth century.[35]

When the woman in Malad drank the consecrated oil, she illustrated multiple aspects of Latter-day Saints' response to the 1918 flu epidemic. Her need to stay healthy was rooted in her identity as the primary caregiver for her family. Drinking the oil, rather than seeking care from a regular medical doctor, drew on traditions of alternative healing that continued to hold sway in Latter-day Saint communities. It also drew on religious healing practices. Indeed, Stapley and Wright note, "Drinking consecrated oil was . . . a common Mormon practice [that continued] into the twentieth century."[36] A half-century earlier, the woman might have called on other Latter-day Saint women nearby to perform a healing ritual, but by 1918, women's authority in religious healing had been almost entirely eroded, and such practices required male priesthood holders. The oil had already been consecrated, though, and perhaps that was enough. The woman's conclusion that "it must have worked because she did not contract the flu" betrayed a subtle resistance to the authority of men and science: Here was a way for a woman, subordinated to men, to protect her health when scientifically based remedies and male healers were ineffective or unavailable.

A Celebration of Soldiers

The return of Utah's soldiers from World War I was celebrated with parades in several Utah cities, culminating in Salt Lake City on January 24, 1919. Anguished debate preceded every parade: Utah's citizens wanted to celebrate the arrival of "their boys," but would the massive events result in another surge of flu infections? In Salt Lake City, the debate played out in the pages of local newspapers, including the LDS Church–owned *Deseret News*. As a committee planned a parade and reception, the editors of the paper pointed out the inconsistency in policy in an editorial. "There is no question of the desire of the citizens to give the heroes a reception worthy of the record they have made," they wrote, "but there is grave question of the wisdom of laying out a program which implies the participation of indiscriminate multitudes, with the thousand-fold liability of the spread of the epidemic." Observing that influenza's character as a "'crowd' disease" had led to regulations against public gatherings, they concluded, "these inhibitions have been right loyally observed by the great majority, though oftentimes at much sacrifice of sentiment and convenience. But if they are no longer necessary, or if they have no further efficacy, as would seem to be inferred from the plans now in contemplation, by all means let the fact be known, so that we may feel either that the danger is over, or that nothing we can do will enable us to control and escape it."[37] The day before the parade was to take place, the opposition of health authorities finally triumphed. An article in the *Deseret News* explained that, on the "urgent recommendation" of the city and state health boards, the committee in charge of planning the event had passed a resolution to abandon the parade and celebration. Despite this decision, the streets would still be decorated and "it is understood [that] a band will be at the station to welcome the soldiers." The article acknowledged that private celebrations might well occur, but said that "the public officials . . . will not assume responsibility for a gathering which it is feared might cause a further spread of the influenza."[38] Nevertheless, this decision was reversed the following day, and the parade was held as originally planned. At the same time, Latter-day Saint churches stayed closed—regular church services for Latter-day Saints did not resume until early February in Salt Lake.

Although Brigadier General Richard W. Young, who led the Utah troops, was a grandson of Brigham Young, the LDS Church's second prophet, the varying decisions about the parade for the 145th Artillery included no obvious religious reference, nor did the LDS Church become involved in the debate in any official way. Nevertheless, religion shaped the conversation thoroughly. Historian Dean L. May estimated that Latter-day Saints comprised 61 percent of Utah's population in 1910 and 55 percent in 1920.[39] With the remaining Utahns split among a variety of other religious traditions, the LDS Church was by far the largest religious body in the state in 1918 and 1919. The LDS Church and Latter-day Saint religious sensibilities thus had a significant impact on Utahn culture and society.

In previous decades, Latter-day Saints had conceived of their church community as a family, rejecting the limitations of the nuclear family in favor of a large, tightly bonded, public-facing familial structure.[40] By the time of the influenza epidemic, however, Latter-day Saints had thoroughly "Americanized," reshaping their families to conform to the white Protestant norm of nuclear families with monogamous, heterosexual couples as their nuclei. The welcome of soldiers in January 1919 put Salt Lake's achievement of what white Americans had come to understand as "civilized behavior" on display, demonstrating how thoroughly Latter-day Saints had remodeled their society to conform to white Protestant secular standards.[41] However, the "public family" of earlier times was not entirely gone. Instead, that family was metaphorized, shaping how Salt Lakers framed their roles in society.

The last page of the *Salt Lake Tribune* on January 24, 1919, included an article about the "Utah War Mothers" and their campaign to sell "Welcome Home" posters and have them displayed throughout the city. The organization's name framed its work as maternal: These women worked on behalf of the troops in their capacity as mothers, because the soldiers were their sons. Members of the Delta Epsilon sorority from the University of Utah assisted the War Mothers of Salt Lake in their campaign to distribute "Welcome Home" posters throughout the city, acting the part of dutiful daughters of the War Mothers and of sisters and sweethearts to the returning men. Businessmen took on the paternal role. Latter-day Saint men had learned, in the early twentieth century, to value individual hard work and success in the economic world as aspects of Latter-day Saint masculinity.[42] Purchasing "Welcome Home" posters allowed businessmen to model another aspect of Latter-day Saint masculinity, connecting their religious identities to their American identities through the patriotic displays, much as soldiers themselves did.[43] "Men of the 145th artillery who returned to Salt Lake yesterday were highly pleased with the banners," the article concluded, "and it is considered important that all the business houses in the city display the welcome to the men who were ready to give their lives to the cause. Indifference or neglect to show the welcome posters is looked upon as a lack of interest by the returning soldiers. The Utah War Mothers are emphatic in their wishes to display a banner in every business house in the city."[44] The campaign to distribute these posters thus emphasized the roles both women and businesses played in welcoming soldiers back to civilian life and familial contexts.

When the troops finally arrived, "the soldiers clambered from the car steps with the largest smile on their faces that they have cracked for months. There seemed to be someone there for each man—a pair of arms to fall in and lips to kiss—and the soldiers found them eagerly. The health warnings were forgotten and forced into the background as the men fell into the warm embraces of their loved ones," reported the *Salt Lake Tribune*.[45] The *Tribune*'s reporter framed the celebration in terms of family reunification—a different tone than had accompanied reports of the raucous celebration of the war's end a few months earlier.

The contrast between this celebration and the observance of Joseph F. Smith's death just two months earlier is striking: Although public officials voiced legitimate concerns about the potential for mass gatherings to spread influenza in both cases, the LDS Church complied with the guidance of public health authorities in November 1918, whereas military leaders and elected officials pushed back on, and ultimately disregarded, the guidance from local and state boards of health in January 1919. This difference points us to questions about who was deemed deserving of the kinds of extravagant care demonstrated in public events and processions. Joseph F. Smith's funeral and the parade for the soldiers both celebrated institutions larger than the individuals for whom the events were ostensibly planned—the LDS Church and the American state, respectively. In both cases, the concern for public health was weighed against the value of celebrating these institutions. The decision to go ahead with the parade, then, provides a clear indication that the American state took priority over the LDS Church.

A Conference Sermon

By June 1919, the United States was breathing a sigh of relief. The epidemic had waned enough that the LDS Church felt it appropriate to hold its spring General Conference, which had been postponed indefinitely from its usual date at the beginning of April. The first day of the conference did double duty, serving as an extended memorial service for Joseph F. Smith, the church president who had died in November 1918. On the second day, speakers turned their attention to exhorting the Saints to live the gospel. Apostle Melvin J. Ballard, a member of the Quorum of the Twelve Apostles (the church's highest governing body), dwelled at length on a religious interpretation of the influenza epidemic in the talk he gave at the General Conference.[46] He pointed his listeners to a Latter-day Saint scripture that prophesied that "there shall be men standing in that generation, that shall not pass until they shall see an overflowing scourge; for a desolating sickness shall cover the land" (D&C 45:31). Ballard told his listeners, "We stand at the zenith of our knowledge; never before have men known so much about bacteriology and sanitation; and yet coming from unknown quarters, and making its way—men do not know how—from city to city, from individual to in[d]ividual, there has come upon the world this dread affliction that has affected us so that our general conference had to be postponed. I believe in my soul that it is the Lord speaking, even as he has spoken before."[47] Ballard continued to point out the gap between human and divine knowledge and ability, and described what he viewed as physicians' utter helplessness in the face of the disease.

Yet despite that helplessness, Ballard told his listeners, "I believe that I am safe in saying that no community in the world has been touched so lightly as the Latter-day Saints." Ballard went on to contrast the effects of the pandemic on the church with its effects first in India and then in Portland, Oregon:

> Recently we learned that in India alone there have been more than six million persons who have died with this affliction. . . . There are three hundred thousand people living in Portland, Oregon, and I remember that it was reported that two thousand persons perished there during the influenza epidemic. So there were twice as many deaths from that cause in Portland, last year, as there were in the entire Church of Jesus Christ of Latter-day Saints, and its population is certainly greater than three

hundred thousand. Yet Portland had a record, according to the statistics, lower than most of the cities in the United States.[48]

The work this comparison performs is arresting. By setting the members of his church apart, first from those of a country that epitomized foreignness to his listeners and then from a city in which many of them might have lived or had relatives, Ballard stabilized Latter-day Saints as successfully white and legitimately American—and on top of that, as favored by God.

The work Ballard did to shore up Latter-day Saints' identity was yet another contribution to an ongoing effort to construct and maintain Latter-day Saints as modern white American citizens. For more than half a century, Latter-day Saints had worked hard to be recognized as white. By the twentieth century (and indeed well before that time), that achievement of whiteness was tied up with the enactment of modernity.[49] During the epidemic, this work frequently was accomplished by marking other ethnic groups as behaving incorrectly with regard to the flu.

As Ballard's general conference speech demonstrated, discussions of the influenza epidemic contrasted the epidemic's effects on Latter-day Saint, or Utahn, people with its effects on those perceived as non-white, non-American, or both. In late October 1918, the *Deseret News* reported several arrests for the violation of a state board of health order that prohibited the gathering of more than three people at a time in a public place. "Men Are Arrested for Gathering in Greek Coffee House," shouted one headline. A total of twenty-one men were arrested, the article reported, and it provided their names. With the exceptions of Boyer and Jones, the men's surnames were easily coded as Mediterranean in origin: Angelo, Barias, Callas, Colas, Karas, Kofenas, Konbarkass, Lois, Mehmet, Morapokas, Pappas, Paulos, Poulis, Regos, Saris, Spiros, and Stamelus. The article noted that "several of the men who were arrested last night were among those taken into custody for the same offense" a few days earlier.[50] By emphasizing that the location was a *Greek* coffee house, and providing the ethnically distinctive names of the detained individuals, the newspaper built a connection between Greek ethnicity and disdain for legal authority, a connection it continued to cement in later reporting. "One source of influenza infection is abroad, probably in Salt Lake City, that can easily contribute largely to spreading the disease, since the patient has shown a disposition to disregard all authority in the matter," reported the *Deseret News* at the beginning of November 1918. It continued, "A Greek escaped from the emergency hospital at the Magna plant, and was traced to the train for Salt Lake City, after which all efforts to find him have been futile."[51] The newspaper reported no name or other identifying information for the man—only that he was "Greek." A few weeks later in Ogden, Utah, the *Deseret News* reported, a "Greek barber" named James Serras was arrested "for alleged persistent refusal to wear the gauze mask while attending customers, as required by the city health board."[52]

Greek people were not the only ethnic group to be characterized as a threat to public health: Some of the first cases in Salt Lake City were reported to be "among an Italian family" living near the center of the city. A visitor from Idaho was believed to have spread the flu among them.[53] That visitor died the following day, and the *Deseret News* reported his death under the headline "Italian Succumbs to Spanish Influenza."[54] In Ogden, Japanese Americans were also singled out. Overwhelmingly, reportage in the church-owned *Deseret News* represented those violating public health orders as different in race, ethnicity, or nationality from the presumed white American newspaper reader. This contrast consolidated the whiteness of Latter-day Saints, aligning them again with the Protestant secular consensus in the United States. Latter-day Saints were not alone in using the arena of public health to draw a racial contrast between themselves and perceived ethnic others, nor was this strategy specific to the 1918 flu epidemic.[55] Indeed, Latter-day Saints had used this strategy before as they worked to consolidate their whiteness.[56] Its reappearance during the 1918 flu epidemic is an indication that Latter-day Saints found this strategy useful in establishing and maintaining their belonging in white America.

Ballard's use of Portland, Oregon, as a comparison to the LDS Church is more puzzling. The city had no place to speak of in Latter-day Saint history, nor any particular reputation among Latter-day Saints. At the time Ballard spoke, Portland did not have a Latter-day Saint population of meaningful size; the LDS Church did not open its first chapel in Oregon until a decade later.[57] It may be precisely this blankness that made Portland an attractive point of comparison to Ballard: It was a city with a similar racial profile as the church (largely white) and a similar sense of distance from the cultural center of the nation. It also was not one of the places hardest hit by the influenza epidemic: As historian Christopher McKnight Nichols notes, Portland did pretty well in avoiding large surges of infections, but its public health response was not effective enough to prevent the epidemic from dragging on well into 1919.[58] The main difference between Portland and the LDS Church, Ballard implied, was in the two entities' relationship to God: Members of the LDS Church had it right, while Portlanders did not.

Having shored up and stabilized the category of Latter-day Saints—as white, in contrast to Indians, and as correctly faithful, in contrast to Portlanders—Ballard turned his attention to the question of theodicy: "Why the Latter-day Saints—why should they be afflicted?" he wondered aloud. To answer this question, he turned to another revelation that predicted that "the

Lord's scourge shall pass over by night and by day, and the report thereof shall vex all people; yea, it shall not be stayed until the Lord come" (D&C 97:23).[59] A few verses later, though, the revelation offered Ballard some hope: "Nevertheless, Zion shall escape if she observe to do all things whatsoever I have commanded her" (D&C 97:25).[60] Ballard used this glimpse at the possibility of safety as the launching point for a jeremiad. "My brethren and sisters," he said, "why should we hope to escape, who have been baptized into this Church, yet ignore the commandments of the Lord? . . . I have received a witness to my soul that the innocent children and faithful Latter-day Saints were not taken because they were wicked, nor because the families that were touched needed to be chastised more than others, but that the Lord was speaking through those who have been taken. . . . The Lord is speaking through them to the whole Church, crying repentance unto us, calling us to set our houses in order, to keep the commandments of the Lord."[61]

Ballard's conference talk may have been the most overt Latter-day Saint theologizing of the influenza epidemic, but it was not the only time Latter-day Saint leaders invoked the divine in their thinking about the epidemic. On December 20, 1918, members of the church's First Presidency (the Church president and his two counselors) placed a short notice in the *Deseret News*: "To meet a general desire among the Latter-day Saints," they wrote, "Sunday afternoon, Dec. 22, is designated as a special time for fasting and prayer by all members of the Church, for the arrest and speedy suppression by Divine power of the desolating scourge that is passing over the earth." They continued, "The Saints are exhorted to meet, fasting, as families in their respective homes (public assemblies being postponed for a time), and supplicate our Heavenly Father for the speedy relief of His people and of all who are suffering from this great affliction. Presidents of Stakes and Bishops of Wards are directed to convey this announcement to all the members under their supervision."[62] Following that instruction, the presidents of the five Latter-day Saint stakes (geographic groups of wards) in Salt Lake City placed a "Notice" in the same issue of the *Deseret News*: "Attention of all members of the Church residing in the five Salt Lake City stakes is respectfully called to the request of the First Presidency as appearing in The Deseret News regarding the observance of a prayer and fast service in their respective homes on Sunday next for the purpose of importuning the Deity to remove from the earth the pestilence that has caused so much suffering and sorrow."[63]

The day after the fast day, the *Deseret News* reported that "Thousands Pray[ed] That Scourge Be Banished." The newspaper offered the family devotional held in the home of Frank W. Penrose as an example of the services it said were held "even in far distant country settlements, and in far-off mission fields." The Penrose service started with "musical selections . . . given by the children" and continued with a prayer offered by President Charles W. Penrose (Frank Penrose's father and a member of the LDS Church's First Presidency). President Penrose "also spoke quoting Revelations, which tells of the plagues that shall come in the last days. He urged that all follow the admonitions and principles of the gospel. Obeying the Word of Wisdom, he said, and trying to keep the body clean and pure will assist in overcoming disease." The article noted that two women, Mrs. Elizabeth P. Jensen and Mrs. Frank W. Penrose, "also spoke briefly."[64] The same issue also carried news of the fast being observed in Ogden, Utah.

Interestingly, a man named John Said had written a letter to the *Deseret News* two weeks earlier, urging "the Latter-day Saints especially . . . but also . . . all Christians, Jews, or others who accept the Bible as the Word of God" to fast and pray. Said's letter is jarringly apocalyptic: "It goes without saying," he opened, "that we are living in the last days—a time seen by seers of old and pointed out by prophetic pen. These are days when predicted judgments are poured out upon all nations."[65] Said's own religious affiliation was not clear, though his hope that "temples might again be open for ordnance [*sic*] work" suggested he was a Latter-day Saint. But unlike Latter-day Saint leaders, who directed their recommendation only to other members of their tradition, Said attempted to make common cause with a wide range of religious people—"all Christians, Jews, or others who accept the Bible as the Word of God." Said's formulation described a potential ecumenical coalition and placed Latter-day Saints squarely at its center. This inclusive ecumenism mirrored the outlook of liberal Protestants of the time, though it did not fit easily within a liberal Protestant framework. Matthew Bowman writes that, unlike Said, who emphasized a conservative, apocalyptic interpretation of the Bible, liberal Protestants "clung to Christian republicanism . . . with a particularly optimistic and ecumenical twist. [They] emphasized human autonomy, were suspicious of what they called 'sectarian' devotion to specific creeds or denominations, and believed that morality was cultivated through education, not dogma or diktat."[66] Said seemed to be reaching for a different kind of ecumenism, one that maintained the distinctive nature of Latter-day Saint belief while folding in other religious people whose traditions overlapped in key ways.

As Said's letter pointed out, the scale of the epidemic was overwhelming, striking more people each day than could be accommodated in existing hospital facilities. Many municipalities in Utah (as elsewhere in the United States) therefore had to create emergency hospitals. These were often housed in buildings owned by religious congregations, both Latter-day Saint and otherwise. Ogden, Utah, is a good example: The emergency hospital headed by Nurse Myrtle Swainston was started in the amusement hall of one of Ogden's

Latter-day Saint congregations. A few days after opening, it moved from these temporary quarters to the basement of the First Congregational Church, where more beds could be added, expanding the hospital's capacity. The hospital moved again less than two months later, this time to a building offered by the local chapter of the Elks Club.[67] Housed in locations provided by religious and fraternal organizations over the course of its existence, the hospital itself was funded by the city of Ogden and the American Red Cross.[68] The epidemic led to a rough ecumenism, where sectarian differences were set aside in favor of working together for a common cause. This was also true in the case of the ARC: Local chapters were often headed by ecclesiastical leaders of groups other than the LDS Church. These efforts, though often housed in buildings provided by religious institutions, eschewed healing methods identified as religious (fasting, prayer, anointing with oil) and focused on biomedical healing methods and public health efforts instead. In this arena, then, Latter-day Saints joined the liberal Protestant consensus, acceding to the humanistic ecumenism that linked Christianity to American democracy and situated religion so far in the background that denominational differences were indiscernible. In private, though, Latter-day Saints leaned into their religious difference, explaining the epidemic in terms offered by distinctively Latter-day Saint scriptures and using Latter-day Saint ritual practices to counteract the lethal disease.

Conclusion

In their response to the 1918 flu epidemic, Latter-day Saints drew together multiple threads of their ongoing secularization project. The epidemic thus became a moment for Latter-day Saints to theorize religion, determining its appropriate location and extent in their lives and deciding how closely they would conform to the prevailing Protestant models of American religion. In their response to the epidemic, Latter-day Saints seemed to submit quite thoroughly to the demands of the US state. But if we look closer, we see that Latter-day Saints carved out pockets of resistance to those demands: The *Deseret News* editorial asking for consistency pointed out the mismatch in official guidelines; the practices of ordinary Latter-day Saints illustrated an inclusive approach to healing; the official day of fasting and prayer demonstrated skepticism about the adequacy of science; and Ballard's conference talk showed the resilience of Latter-day Saint identity and Latter-day Saints' resistance to fitting in with other white Protestant denominations.

In some ways, the secularization strategy of the Latter-day Saints here resembled the politics of assimilation pursued by Rev. John Misao Yamazaki, as Chrissy Yee Lau discusses in her essay in this volume: Yamazaki's politics of assimilation aimed to secure the position of Japanese and Japanese Americans vis-à-vis their white American neighbors in Los Angeles by conforming to those neighbors' expectations regarding how Japanese bodies should be visible, how Japanese homes should be kept, and how youth should be raised with American civic values. At the same time, Yamazaki continued to include a "bicultural Americanization" program for Japanese immigrants and their children, ensuring that Japanese language and culture would be maintained in the community. Similarly, Latter-day Saints pursued a strategy of outward secularization, publicly enacting their assent to the American Protestant secular regime while privately shoring up Latter-day Saint distinctiveness in ways that belied that public acquiescence.

This story about the secularization of the Latter-day Saints, then, shows us again how complicated the terrain of US empire was and how fraught were the stakes of inclusion therein. The LDS Church's General Conference in June 1919 began with memorial tributes to Joseph F. Smith, for whom the church was not able to mount a traditional funeral the previous fall because of public health restrictions then in place to combat the spread of influenza. But it also included tributes to Brigham Young, over whose birthday the conference was scheduled. Young was the prophet who led the Latter-day Saints out of the United States to the Salt Lake Valley (which was claimed by Mexico at the time). He formed the Mormon Battalion, a body of men who joined the US armed forces for the US–Mexican War, and a decade later he directed Latter-day Saints to resist US troops in the conflict known as the Utah War. Finally, the June 1919 General Conference included the LDS Church's most overt public theologizing on the influenza epidemic. Apostle Melvin J. Ballard's talk despaired of scientific understanding of the epidemic and turned instead to Latter-day Saint theology to make sense of the tragic loss of life the world had experienced. For Latter-day Saints, the influenza epidemic offered opportunities both to maintain—and possibly enhance—their place in the modern secular United States; and to resist modern secularity and the demands it made on the hearts and minds of the people it touched.

Notes

This essay relies heavily on the stellar research assistance of Spencer M. Goldberg. I thank Goldberg for his invaluable work, and Hamilton College for funding it. I am also grateful to Jennifer Barkdull for her assistance in plumbing the depths of the Church of Jesus Christ of Latter-day Saints Church History Library; Jennifer Ambrose, Celeste Day Moore, Benjamin Widiss, James B. Bennett, Max Greenberg, Nicole Kirk, and Kristine Wright for reading and commenting on various drafts of this essay; and Brandi Denison and Brett Hendrickson, along with all of the other contributors to this volume, for their invaluable feedback on this essay as it developed.

1. With regard to Smith's death, it is possible that influenza was involved, but the cause of death given on the death certificate was pneumonia. Influenza was not listed as a contributing factor. State of Utah, Department of Health, Office of Vital Records and Statistics, *Death Certificates*, Series 81448, entry 0066685, Utah State Archives, accessed May 25, 2023, via "Utah State Archives Indexes," database and images, https://archives.utah.gov/research/indexes; image at https://axaemarchives.utah.gov/cgi-bin/indexesresults.cgi?RUNWHAT=IDXFILES&KEYPATH=IDX208420066685.

2. The Church of Jesus Christ of Latter-day Saints requested in 2018 that the terms "Mormon" and "Mormonism" not be used to refer to the institution, its members, or the religion it teaches. It further requested that the abbreviation "LDS" also not be used. Instead, it suggested that the church's name be shortened to "the Church" or "the Church of Jesus Christ." Although I comply with the first part of this request, eschewing the terms "Mormon" and "Mormonism," and I describe people, practices, ideas, and so on as "Latter-day Saint" rather than "LDS," per the church's request, I retain the abbreviation "LDS Church" for ease of reading and because the shortened names suggested by the church imply theological convictions that I do not share. The institution's articulation of its preferences may be found at "Style Guide—The Name of the Church," *Newsroom*, The Church of Jesus Christ of Latter-day Saints, accessed May 25, 2023, https://newsroom.churchofjesuschrist.org/style-guide.

3. In 1978, Official Declaration 2 was added to the LDS Church's D&C. Here, I am distinguishing between sections and Official Declarations. It is worth noting as well that, though the section added in 1918 (D&C 138) is written as a narrative of Smith's visions, Official Declaration 2 is framed in a way much more analogous to a press release.

4. For comparison, see the descriptions of Wilford Woodruff's funeral in the *Deseret News*, September 8, 1898; Lorenzo Snow's funeral in the *Deseret News*, October 14, 1901; and Heber J. Grant's funeral in the *Deseret News*, May 18, 1945.

5. "No Public Funeral," *Deseret News*, November 19, 1918.

6. "Salt Lake Goes Mad and Rejoices over Peace," *Ogden Standard* (Ogden City, UT), November 12, 1918. I found this source via Leonard J. Arrington, "The Influenza Epidemic of 1918–19 in Utah," *Utah Historical Quarterly* 58, no. 2 (1990): 165–82. The article from the *Ogden Standard* is quoted on page 170.

7. Arrington, "The Influenza Epidemic," 171–72.

8. Centers for Disease Control and Prevention, "History of 1918 Flu Pandemic," accessed March 31, 2023, www.cdc.gov/flu/pandemic-resources/1918-commemoration/1918-pandemic-history.htm.

9. Arrington, "The Influenza Epidemic," 167; John M. Barry, *The Great Influenza: The Story of the Deadliest Pandemic in History* (Penguin Books, 2009), 4–5.

10. Gustavo Benavides, "Modernity," in *Critical Terms for Religious Studies*, ed. Mark C. Taylor (University of Chicago Press, 1998), 196.

11. Benavides, "Modernity," 197.

12. David Walker, *Railroading Religion: Mormons, Tourists, and the Corporate Spirit of the West* (University of North Carolina Press, 2019), 47, 73.

13. W. Paul Reeve, *Religion of a Different Color: Race and the Mormon Struggle for Whiteness* (Oxford University Press, 2015), especially 193–210.

14. Hendrix-Komoto, *Imperial Zions: Religion, Race, and Family in the American West and the Pacific* (University of Nebraska Press, 2022), 192–93; Reeve, *Religion of a Different Color*, 187, 246.

15. Kathleen Flake, *The Politics of American Religious Identity: The Seating of Senator Reed Smoot, Mormon Apostle* (University of North Carolina Press, 2004), 147–58; Peter Coviello, *Make Yourselves Gods: Mormons and the Unfinished Business of American Secularism* (University of Chicago Press, 2019), 175.

16. See, for example, Reeve, *Religion of a Different Color*; George Lipsitz, *The Possessive Investment in Whiteness: How White People Profit from Identity Politics*, 20th anniversary ed. (Temple University Press, 2018).

17. See, for example, Jonathon S. Kahn and Vincent W. Lloyd, eds., *Race and Secularism in America* (Columbia University Press, 2016).

18. Joan Wallach Scott, *Sex and Secularism* (Princeton University Press, 2018), 30–34, 43–49.

19. Amy Hoyt and Sara M. Patterson, "Mormon Masculinity: Changing Gender Expectations in the Era of Transition from Polygamy to Monogamy, 1890–1920," *Gender and History* 23, no. 1 (April 2011): 78–80; Natalie Kaye Rose, "Courtship, Marriage, and Romantic Monogamy: Young Mormon Women's Diaries at the Turn of the Twentieth Century," *Journal of Mormon History* 42, no. 1 (January 2016): 180–96.

20. For other examples of this phenomenon in American history, see Peter J. Thuesen, *Tornado God: American Religion and Violent Weather* (Oxford University Press, 2020), and Philippa Koch, *The Course of God's Providence: Religion, Health, and the Body in Early America* (New York University Press, 2021).

21. I thank Carleigh Beriont for articulating this insight.

22. Christine Talbot, "The Church Family in Nineteenth-Century America: Mormonism and the Public/Private Divide," *Journal of Mormon History* 37, no. 4 (Fall 2011): 210–11, 219–38.

23. Margaret Parry Kirkpatrick, "Joseph and Maggie Parry," on FamilySearch.org, s.v. Joseph Parry (KWCR-H2C), Memories. Contributed by Laurie Ward Call, February 24, 2016. I thank Jonathan Stapley for pointing me to this story.

24. I am indebted to Laurie Maffly-Kipp for the insight that World War I was a "men's war" whereas the flu epidemic was a "women's war." Laurie Maffly-Kipp, personal communication, June 3, 2022.

25. Arrington, "The Influenza Epidemic of 1918–19 in Utah," 167–68 and 175–77.

26. Benjamin Michael Cater, "Health, Medicine, and Power in the Salt Lake Valley, Utah, 1869–1945" (PhD diss., University of Utah, 2012), 157. I thank W. Paul Reeve for pointing me to this invaluable source.

27. Cater, "Health, Medicine, and Power," 155–56.

28. Jonathan A. Stapley and Kristine Wright, "Female Ritual Healing in Mormonism," *Journal of Mormon History* 37, no. 1 (2011): 45–47, at 47.

29. Stapley and Wright, "Female Ritual Healing," 72.

30. The basics of the Relief Society's history are well known. I pulled these facts from *Daughters in My Kingdom: The History and Work of Relief Society* (Church of Jesus Christ of Latter-day Saints, 2011).

31. Marian Moser Jones, "The American Red Cross and Local Response to the 1918 Influenza Pandemic: A Four-City Case Study," *Public Health Reports* 125, suppl. 3 (2010): 93–95.

32. For a full explanation of Thomsonianism, see James C. Whorton, *Nature Cures: The History of Alternative Medicine in America* (Oxford University Press, 2002), 25–48.

33. Thomas J. Wolfe, "Steaming Saints: Mormons and the Thomsonian Movement in Nineteenth-Century America," in *Disease and Medical Care in the Mountain West: Essays on Region, History, and Practice*, ed. Martha L. Hildreth and Bruce T. Moran (University of Nevada Press, 1998), 25–26.

34. Wolfe, "Steaming Saints," 27.

35. Wolfe, "Steaming Saints," 26.

36. Stapley and Wright, "Female Ritual Healing," 12.

37. "Let's Be Consistent," *Deseret Evening News*, January 21, 1919.

38. "Formal Parade for Utah Artillery Abandoned," *Deseret Evening News*, January 23, 1919.

39. Dean L. May, "A Demographic Portrait of the Mormons, 1830–1980," in *The New Mormon History: Revisionist Essays on the Past*, ed. D. Michael Quinn (Signature Books, 1992), 125. I am grateful to W. Paul Reeve for pointing me to this source.

40. Talbot, "The Church Family in Nineteenth-Century America," 220.

41. Nyan Shah, *Contagious Divides: Epidemics and Race in San Francisco's Chinatown* (University of California Press, 2001), 14.

42. Hoyt and Patterson, "Mormon Masculinity," 79.

43. On patriotism and Latter-day Saint masculinity, see Hoyt and Patterson, "Mormon Masculinity," 78–79.

44. "'Welcome Home' Posters Greet Soldiers; Salt Lake War Mothers Place Displays," *Salt Lake Tribune*, January 24, 1919.

45. "Thousands Greet Utah Artillerymen," *Salt Lake Tribune*, January 25, 1919.

46. *Eighty-Ninth Annual Conference of the Church of Jesus Christ of Latter-day Saints* (Deseret News, 1919), 86–89.

47. *Eighty-Ninth Annual Conference*, 87.

48. *Eighty-Ninth Annual Conference*, 87.

49. Alastair Bonnett, "The Metropolis and White Modernity," *Ethnicities* 2, no. 3 (September 2002): 350–51.

50. "Men Are Arrested for Gathering in Greek Coffee House," *Deseret News*, October 31, 1918. By emphasizing that the location was a *coffee* house, the Latter-day Saint–owned *Deseret News* may also have been trying to draw a distinction between the lawbreakers and Latter-day Saints, whose dietary code prohibited coffee.

51. "Runaway Patient May Spread Influenza in City," *Deseret News*, November 5, 1918.

52. "Arrested on Charge of Failing to Wear Mask," *Deseret News*, November 27, 1918.

53. "Several Cases of Influenza Are Reported," *Deseret News*, October 4, 1918.

54. "Italian Succumbs to Spanish Influenza," *Deseret News*, October 5, 1918.

55. Shah, *Contagious Divides*, 12.

56. See, for example, Cater, "Health, Medicine, and Power," 1–3, 12–14, 54–58, 72–76.

57. Church News Archives, "United States Information: Oregon," *Church News*, www.thechurchnews.com/2010/2/2/23228898/united-states-information-oregon, last updated February 2, 2010.

58. Christopher McKnight Nichols, "What We Can Learn from the Influenza Pandemic of 1918–1919," Oregon Historical Society in partnership with WorldOregon, April 23, 2020, accessed June 1, 2023, video recording at www.ohs.org/events/what-we-can-learn-from-the-influenza-pandemic.cfm.

59. *Eighty-Ninth Annual Conference*, 88.

60. *Eighty-Ninth Annual Conference*, 89.

61. *Eighty-Ninth Annual Conference*, 89.

62. Heber J. Grant, Anthon H. Lund, and Charles W. Penrose, "Day of Fasting and Prayer," *Deseret Evening News*, December 20, 1918. This notice was also printed the following day in the same location in the paper.

63. John M. Knight, Frank Y. Taylor, Hugh J. Cannon, Sylvester Q. Cannon, and Nephi L. Morris, "Notice," *Deseret Evening News*, December 20, 1918.

64. "Thousands Pray That Scourge Be Banished," *Deseret Evening News*, December 23, 1918.

65. John Said, "Urges Observance of Solemn Family Prayer," *Deseret News*, December 7, 1918.

66. Matthew Bowman, *Christian: The Politics of a Word in America* (Harvard University Press, 2018), 33.

67. Arrington, "The Influenza Epidemic," 167–68, 175.

68. Arrington, "The Influenza Epidemic," 167.

PART III

Religious Responses to Insecurity

The reality of life in the West in the late nineteenth and early twentieth centuries was one of religious, racial, and ethnic heterogeneity. Still, white Protestant hegemony created difficult living conditions for those who did not conform, requiring them to forge internal support networks to make life bearable. One historiographical tension in the study of religion in the American West is how to capture the region's religious diversity without overstating the creativity and freeness of religious life in the West. The essays in this section note that, although there are moments of religious diversity and pluralism, the history of religion in the American West is also a story of exclusion and religious communities' self-care in light of oppression, hardship, isolation, and insecurity.

Brennan Keegan reframes the stories of Catholics and American Indians by detailing alternative economies of care that arose alongside and in resistance to the atomized market economies of American capitalism. Rather than accepting exploitation, Keegan notes how Montana Catholic miners and Arapaho wage laborers responded to the attempts of governmental and mining authorities to stymie their communal efforts to strengthen and care for the members of these religious communities. Her comparison of these two ethnic and religious communities shows that strategies of economic and religious resistance were not equally available to all.

Similarly, Nicole Kirk's essay on religious practices in traveling circuses highlights two essential components of religion in the American West. Circuses became an agent of empire and a place for developing alternative modes of community care. Kirk shows that the myth of the American West became packaged through circuses as early versions of Wild West shows and became self-referential for those living in the West. Second, the life of circus performers demonstrates how religious people supported each other through treacherous travel, in which children were born, couples married, and people died, and the role of ritual invention in celebrating and coping with these life transitions.

Finally, Chrissy Yee Lau's essay demonstrates that, despite numerous claims to the contrary, California was not a happy haven of pluralism but rather the site of soft-infrastructure building to promote whiteness, which communities of color had to negotiate. Lau's examination of St. Mary's Japanese Episcopal Mission in Los Angeles shows the lengths community leaders went to ease white concerns about the Japanese church. While Keegan and Kirk show how Western religious communities drew together to resist the logic of economies of empire, Lau shows the exhausting labor necessary to keep non-white communities intact and safe from the anxieties of their white Christian neighbors. Ultimately, these three essays push against the narrative of the American West as a unique laboratory for religious diversity and tolerance; instead, they depict the West as a site of communal religious care under the shadow of white Protestant norms.

Chapter 8

The Working West

Religion, Labor, and the Making of Western Spaces

BRENNAN KEEGAN

Keywords: labor, Northern Arapaho, Irish immigrants, miners, Ghost Dance, Catholicism

The nineteenth-century American West was a crucial battleground in the national struggle to define what it meant to be American. As influential Congregational minister (and staunch anti-Catholic) Lyman Beecher famously claimed in 1835, "The religious and political destiny of our nation is to be decided in the West." While Atlantic commerce and manufacturing might provide some advantages to the East, "the West is destined to be the great central power of the nation, and under heaven, must affect powerfully the cause of free institutions and the liberty of the world."[1] Presbyterian theologian Albert Barnes noted in an address to a home mission society in 1846, "Everything, too, in the natural scenery is on a scale so vast and grand . . . the very immensity almost of the rich domain which is spread out there as to make man vast in his schemes, gigantic in his purposes, large in his aspirations, boundless in his ambitions."[2] Eastern leaders and settlers imagined the region as a space of unscripted potential, empty and ready for the taking—an American Eden that would bring forth an exceptional future.

Yet the West was and remains a site of enormous religious, racial, and national diversity, never empty or available for the taking.[3] Despite a multivalent effort to claim the region as a piece of the burgeoning US empire, communities living on the margins of American nationhood strategically subverted national markets, reinforced communal dependency, and created alternative spatial relations to the expanding US state. Indeed, it was through encounters with this diversity that Protestant officials, journalists, scientists, missionaries, and federal agents were forced to confront and negotiate the boundaries of who counted as American.[4] As the introduction to this volume argues, the American West functioned as a laboratory for working out who deserved care as part of the body politic. Through two case studies, this chapter explores the myriad ways communities responded to the crisis of care produced by the conditions of empire—notably, a lack of institutional support and broken kinship networks. Northern Arapaho wage laborers in central Wyoming and Irish Catholic miners in Butte, Montana, did not simply integrate into the fabric of American society but held distinct identities that challenged US empire and the political, religious, and economic techniques for homogenizing the nation. By telling these stories together, this chapter unearths the stories of western communities not as isolated or passive but as firmly emplaced within the negotiation of American nation-making.

The case studies presented offer a glimpse at the complexity of national debates about what it meant to be American in a region imagined as the repository of American ideals. As W. Paul Reeve argues, whiteness was constructed as an ideal of American identity that excluded not only Native Americans and African Americans but also all non-Protestant groups.[5] Irish Catholics were both white settlers *and* racialized for their religious commitments, while the Northern Arapaho were a racialized and dispossessed sovereign nation. Irish Catholics were connected to a transnational religious world, whereas American Indians traced their history and religious life to North America. Power relations between these communities were uneven, a fact Catholics exploited as they often joined in national sentiments against those whom they considered the most uncivilized: American Indians. In a single region over the span of a few decades, diverse communities grappled with the questions of who wanted to be American and who counted as such. Irish Catholics and the Northern Arapaho approached these questions in distinct yet overlapping ways, giving voice to a wide range of responses that defined the region and the era. The West was made through myth, violence, and the practices of everyday life, and within this struggle, religion and labor were key markers of belonging.

An American Eden?

In December 1830, the same year his Indian Removal Act passed Congress, President Andrew Jackson asked in his annual address: "What good man would prefer a country covered with forests and ranged by a few thousand savages to our extensive Republic, studded with cities, towns, and prosperous farms, embellished with all the improvements which art can devise or industry execute, occupied by more than 12,000,000 happy people, and filled with all the blessings of liberty, civilization, and religion?"[6] The transformation of the region required a new map, one occupied and remade by a colonial logic that only settlers possessed the ability to make proper use of the land. Resultant grids of labor and networks of exchange naturalized inequalities and the violence that maintained them, erasing those who did not conform and naming the unequal social relations as natural, obvious, destined. In 1845, newspaperman John L. O'Sullivan coined the term "Manifest Destiny," giving name to the sentiment pro-expansionists had voiced for decades. Referring to the annexation of Texas, O'Sullivan wrote it was the nation's "manifest destiny to overspread the continent allotted by Providence for the free development of our yearly multiplying millions."[7] Naturalizing expansion under the banner of morality and republican virtue, Manifest Destiny reconciled American imperialism with a highly favorable and united national image. It was not simply a question of land hunger or the quest to secure ports on the Pacific; it was also a racist doctrine of white supremacy that granted no American Indian or non-white claims to belonging. As Thomas Bremer argues in this book, race, religion, and capitalism are inextricably intertwined with colonialism. Many prominent Americans viewed the United States as a "civilizing" force, which included bringing the perceived benefits of Protestant society west.[8] The West was understood as God's gift for his chosen people; in turn, they believed it was their responsibility to bring forth an American Eden.

Although many nineteenth-century scholars, political leaders, missionaries, and artists may have regarded western settlement as preordained, in practice it was an act of manifest design, not destiny.[9] In a sense, the West had to be *made* empty, both rhetorically and physically for an American moral universe to be mapped onto the landscape. Many eastern elites mobilized the West as a Protestant possession,[10] forging a political and economic philosophy that embraced democracy via a path that American Indians, African Americans, Chinese immigrants, Catholics and Latter-day Saints, confined to their primitive, theocratic, and precapitalist worlds, could not follow.[11] In 1875, President Ulysses S. Grant spoke before a reunion of Union soldiers, referencing Catholicism as a geopolitical threat: "If we are to have another contest in the near future of our national existence, I predict that the dividing line will not be Mason and Dixon's but between patriotism and intelligence on the one side, and superstition, ambition and ignorance on the other." The democratic experiment of the United States called for citizens fit for self-governance, which excluded American Indian "domestic dependent nations" and religious communities that looked to international leaders such as the pope of the Roman Catholic Church.[12] The transformation of the region into an *American* West was neither simple nor guaranteed but, rather, a point of constant struggle. It is within that struggle that minoritized western communities found the possibility of self-determination and colonial resistance, however incomplete.

Religion, Labor, and the Making of Western Spaces

At its core, expansion west was a capitalist project. Capitalism is not merely an economic system, but a mode of relationship, a particular understanding of the world that attaches significance to the transformation of land, forests, water, and human labor into commodities for purposes of acquiring wealth. Historian Frederick Jackson Turner cited western "free lands" as democratizing, but they did so only as they were transformed into commodities—raw material into resource and man into liberal citizen subject.[13] As Cedric J. Robinson argues, however, capitalism serves "not to homogenize but to differentiate—to exaggerate regional, subcultural, and dialectical differences into 'racial' ones."[14] Capitalism requires distinct spatial and cultural organization—networks of exchange, compartmentalized social relations, systems of infrastructure, territorial boundaries, production chains, and trade routes—designed to ensure economic growth. But within these social relations exists an inherent hierarchy, which Robinson calls "racial" but extends well beyond phenotype to include racialized subjects such as the Irish, Jews, Chinese, and other non-Protestant immigrants. Examples of legislation and spatial organization that drew lines (at times literally) around belonging and exclusion in the growing capitalist state included the Dawes Allotment Act, the Homestead and Mining Acts,[15] the construction of the transcontinental railroad,[16] telegraph wires, and land-grant school systems and hospitals. In this way, US empire was enacted not just through violent conquest but through infrastructure building and congressional policies that "legally" denoted who deserved care while simultaneously limiting the freedoms of American Indians,[17] as well as through western boosterism, popular imaginings of the West in art and philosophy, and the physical presence of white settlers who sought to make the myth real.

However, it is by everyday practices that people subvert dominant power. The Northern Arapaho adapted a system of wage labor in order to endure the transition to reservation life while maintaining collectivism, and Irish Roman Catholic immigrants concentrated in western mining towns combined Catholic social teachings with labor politics to establish the first American unions. Although American Indian and Catholic communities often clashed, they also shared commitments to principles of economic cooperation and communal solidarity that stood adjacent to capitalism. Religious institutions, leaders, and norms encouraged and mandated contribution to the collective good, guiding everyday actions and creating alternative networks of exchange and caretaking that undermined American expansion and economic exceptionalism. Michel de Certeau argues that minority populations often transformed the rituals, representations, and laws imposed on them into "something quite different from what their conquerors had in mind; they subverted them not by rejecting or altering them, but by using them with respect to ends and references foreign to the system they had no choice to accept."[18] Western communities may not have completely overturned the growing US empire, but they did subvert a singular national identity by creating alternative ways of being American, religious, and Western.

Wind River Wage Laborers

In the fragments of the Northern Arapaho creation story available to a non-Arapaho audience, creation starts with water. At first there was nothing but water and the peak of a tall mountain, on which sat an Arapaho, crying in his loneliness. Looking up, he saw the Creator, or *Je-van-e-au-thau*, walking on the water toward him. The Creator called the waterfowl by name and commanded the birds to dive under the water and find a country for the Arapaho, but they failed. Next, a turtle was sent beneath the water and succeeded in finding clay, from which the Creator made the world and every living creature.[19] Later, tribal member William C'Hair notes the Arapahos were given a turtle's shell and told it was the map to their homeland.[20] Tribal history places the Arapaho in the Great Lakes region, occupying northern Minnesota sometime prior to 1700, where they were semisedentary horticulturists.[21] They eventually arrived in the Rocky Mountains, where, looking at the turtle shell, they "realized that the bulge on top was the mountains, the line along the ridge of the back was the continental divide and the other lines on the back were the rivers flowing down from the mountains. They knew that they had found their home."[22] For the next century, the Arapaho lived as nomadic hunter-gatherers in the High Plains bordering the Rocky Mountains.[23]

Communalism and cooperation were central to Northern Arapaho life. The Northern Arapaho age-grade lodges, or *bäyaā'wu*, structured the tribe and directed all individual actions to the overall welfare of the community. Named for the enclosures in which they were held, the age-grade lodges delegated responsibility for the tribe's religious, economic, and social welfare to distinct ceremonial groups, divided by gender and stage of life. As the Arapahos progressed through the age-grade lodges, "they became the hunters, warriors, the police, the councilors, conductors of ceremonies and chiefs of the tribe. Each society had several primary functions, and its own ceremonies."[24] The lower lodges were responsible for the actions that interacted with the world beyond the tribe, such as hunting, participation in war parties, and material maintenance of the camp circle. As one progressed through the lodges, responsibilities turned increasingly inward, to the protection and maintenance of tribal governance, stories, ceremonies, and sacred objects.[25]

The age-grade lodges set ceremonial life and governance together, as interdependent cogs, in a bundled network of tribal unity, religiosity, and care.

According to Tall Bull, a Southern Arapaho, the origin of the age-grade lodges came from a vision of an Arapaho man hunting. The man was about to shoot a buffalo cow when the buffalo spoke, telling the Arapaho that she had a message for the benefit of his people: "I have taken pity on you, although you tried to kill me . . . there shall be lodges for different societies among your people; in these my whole body can be used for various purposes."[26] The man then went to the people and related to them what the buffalo had said, thereafter passing the message from generation to generation by secret rites contained within each lodge. In this way, the age-grade lodges represented the entire community as pieces of the whole, directing patterns of care within the tribe.

The California gold rush and the migration of Latter-day Saints west in the 1840s, followed by the 1862 Homestead Act, greatly increased white settlement in the Rocky Mountains. In 1868, a treaty with the Eastern Shoshone promised exclusive occupancy rights to a three-million-acre reservation in what would one day become central Wyoming. In 1878, however, after an unsuccessful negotiation for a separate reservation, the Northern Arapaho were moved from southeastern Wyoming and Colorado to the Wind River Indian Reservation. Immediately, the age-grade lodges were regarded as communist structures by reservation agents and were derided as barriers to achieving American citizenship: "I am firmly of the opinion that the policy of recognizing and perpetuating any tribal tribal [*sic*] organization of these Indians is a mistake, and that the development of the individual is hindered and handicapped continually by such policy."[27] Federal Indian Law reflected a growing fear of the socialist and communist movements in Europe.[28] Government officials believed participation in a cooperative economy would only hinder Arapaho acculturation to Americanism.

In 1867, President Ulysses S. Grant and the Department of Interior assigned religious denominations to oversee the moral and educational needs of new reservations. Under what would be called Grant's "Peace Policy," the Episcopal Church was assigned to the Wind River Indian Reservation in the 1870s. By 1878, at the time of arrival of the Northern Arapaho, most Shoshone had been baptized into the Episcopal Church and regularly participated in mission ceremonies and events.[29] When the Arapaho settled in the Southeast corner of the reservation, the Catholic Church saw an opportunity to expand into the large reservation. Bishop James O'Connor, the Catholic Bishop of Omaha, Nebraska, contacted the government and offered to pay for a new school and mission headed by Father Jutz. By 1884, two schools had been erected to serve the separate needs of the Arapaho and Shoshone: the

Episcopal-run Shoshone Government School in Fort Washakie and the Arapaho School at the Catholic St. Stephen's Mission. The schools kept Arapaho and Shoshone children six days a week, fearing that contact with their uncivilized relatives would result in dangerous backsliding.[30] As in many corners of the American West, religious groups performed acts of governance in the absence of federal or territorial oversight.

The growing relationship between St. Stephen's Indian Mission and the Northern Arapahos added another layer of prejudice against the tribe. The majority-Protestant communities of Lander and Riverton, the two largest towns near the reservation, participated in a national distrust of Catholicism. By the 1890s, the Arapaho were accused of "being under Catholic influence and, therefore, a distinctly undesirable group."[31] Already considered hostile for their unwillingness to adhere to the reservation system until 1878, the Northern Arapahos' involvement at St. Stephen's Mission furthered Euro-American settler distrust. In a 1900 controversy, Agent Herman G. Nickerson, a leader of Lander's American Protective Agency, a national anti-Catholic league, ruled that a Shoshone or Arapaho child had to attend the Episcopal Government School for his or her family to receive rations. This forced people to remove their children from the Catholic St. Stephen's Mission School until the Commissioner of Indian Affairs rebuked the agent.[32]

In 1887, the Bureau of Indian Affairs adopted the Dawes Allotment Act. Implemented from 1887 to 1934, the act was part of a larger belief system asserting that if an American Indian were forced to wear white clothing, practice a white religion, and take responsibility for a private 160-acre farm, his "Indian-ness" would be eliminated as he assimilated into the American population. Allotment was perceived as a step toward removing federal oversight in order to "hasten the arrival of civilization and Christianity at the tribal doorstep."[33] The act also allowed for "surplus" land, tracts of reservation land left over after allotment, to be sold to white migrants, further shrinking reservations and opening more western land to Euro-American settlers. Despite the efforts of missionaries and government policies and practices, however, central Wyoming was not well suited for farming. And in the late 1880s, a severe drought took a serious toll on settlers and Northern Arapaho alike.

Prior to the reservation era, the federal government exerted power through brute force: the killing and rounding up of American Indians. By the end of the nineteenth century, however, the United States largely exerted power not through outright violence but by disciplining the body into specific roles as pieces or cogs in the machine of American society. It was only through the control of the landscape and social relations that American ideological hegemony could be maintained. As Sherman Coolidge, a Northern Arapaho tribal member noted at a "Friends of the Indians" conference in 1913: "The white man has a way of putting his European morals, religion and mental machinery inside of the Indian body and then mapping out the probable process of development accordingly. The inevitable result is that the Indian must spend much of his time and ingenuity in disentangling himself from mistaken policies and abuses."[34] Yet the Northern Arapaho were not passively victimized in the onslaught of American acculturation policies and ideologies. Rather, they relied on the age-grade lodges to disentangle themselves and repurpose the top-down structures of American hegemony to form new modes of caretaking, survival, and self-determination.

The reservation system and Euro-American settlement sought to destroy the political economy of the Northern Arapaho, which was based on the carefully delineated responsibilities of the age-grade lodges. For the elder lodges, responsible for ceremonial life and Arapaho traditions, access to sacred places off reservation was nearly impossible, and religious practices were increasingly banned under the 1883 Indian Crimes Code. For the lower lodges, responsible for the material maintenance of the tribe, hunting was restricted within the borders of the reservation and agriculture remained unproductive. As Northern Arapaho Eaglehead noted in 1890, "We never got what was then promised to us, and we were driven out by the Whites: that is why we are so poor now."[35] The age-grade lodges, however, which encouraged flexibility and innovation among the lower lodges, provided the Arapaho with the tools to create new ways to maintain the tribe. Thus, while the elder lodges attempted to uphold older rituals such as the Sun Dance and Flat Pipe ceremonies, as well as the overall structure of the lodges and tribe, the lower lodges began to experiment with new religious movements and modes of survival.

In 1889, members of the lower lodges became practitioners of the Ghost Dance, a new religious tradition that privileged both tribal unity and strategic assimilation to Euro-American labor systems. The Ghost Dance originated among the Paiute in the 1870s but gained national notoriety in its second iteration when a Northern Paiute ranch hand, Wovoka, had a vision in 1889 of a catastrophic earthquake that would destroy the Euro-Americans and restore the land to the American Indians. The Ghost Dance offered a bridge between a pre-reservation community of care to one situated within the boundaries of the Wind River Indian Reservation. As Arapaho leader Left-Hand said, "When I heard of this new religion I felt the same as I used to when I went with the war parties . . . I continued to urge my people in this religion, because God made all things, and I was anxious to help my people."[36] As a 1905 *Report to the Commissioner of Indian Affairs* claimed, the Northern Arapaho "were the 'great apostles' of the Ghost Dance among the prairie tribes."[37] And the Wind River Indian Reservation "was really the Mecca of the Craze."[38] Although millennial excitement defined the Ghost Dance, Wovoka's message included a call to adopt a key to American capitalism: wage labor. In a widely shared letter, Wovoka reportedly commanded: "Do not refuse to work for the whites and do not make any trouble with them until you leave them."[39] As Louis Warren argues in *God's Red Son*, the support of wage labor was a common tenet of Ghost Dance movements.[40]

Ghost Dance commandments to not lie or steal agreed with older ideals of the Northern Arapaho, but the emphasis on work was a considerable innovation. By way of the Ghost Dance, work became a commandment from God and legitimatized the transition from prior regimes of labor, such as hunting and gathering, to the accrual of wages. In a major turn from previous agency reports, 1890 government reports began to praise the Arapaho for their acceptance and commitment to wage work: "Those who have employed them say they are good workers; they have done all the manual labor in the construction of a large irrigating ditch, about 4 miles in length."[41] Later that year, another report claimed, "The Arapahoes show quite a disposition to work, whenever it is offered to them, they have furnished the extra supply of wood needed for the school, besides furnishing myself and many of the employes [*sic*] with the larger part of our firewood."[42] The same forms of labor that disrupted their traditional modes of life, namely, agriculture and ranching, also increased demand for their labor. As Chief Black Coal requested in a meeting at St. Stephen's Mission in 1890, "We pray the Government to give us means to work."[43] They cut wood and hay, drove cattle, hauled coal, and dug irrigation ditches for government offices and settlers.

Although the traditional standards for movement through the lodges, such as acts of bravery in war and giveaways from hunting, were no longer possible, a new form of community caretaking and achievement emerged to take its place: the sharing of wages. Tribal elder Ernst SunRhodes noted, "Our Indian people, they shared with their neighbors, friends, families . . . regardless of what little we had our old people used to tell us to share . . . it's always been the traditional saying of the Indian people—share and love one another."[44] As life on the reservation increasingly became proscribed from the top down, the age-grade lodges, as an open and responsive social technology, enabled the Northern Arapaho to experiment, vet, and recode the doctrines of the Ghost Dance to ensure the tribe's survival within new socioeconomic circumstances.

Wovoka's call to work for whites in anticipation of the coming Kingdom did not stand alone in the Arapaho's adoption of wage labor, but rather, was placed within a network of actants. Industrial education, the efforts of Catholic missionaries, the poor farming prospects of central Wyoming, and Arapaho prophecies and ancestral beliefs, all influenced the acceptance of the Ghost Dance and the command to work. For example, by the 1890s, education at the reservation schools had taught a generation of Northern Arapaho students industrial training in farming, stock raising, and mechanics, as well as housework and cooking.[45] This ensured that by the time the Ghost Dance emerged on the Wind River Indian Reservation, religiously sanctioning the change in labor, the Northern Arapahos in their twenties and thirties had already gained the practical skills necessary for participation in wage labor.

Furthermore, a central tenet of Catholic teaching was an ideology of redemptive suffering. Catholic missionaries at St. Stephen's Mission taught the Arapaho that the suffering of this world would be blessed in the next; that the odious conditions of the reservation would be redeemed in the coming paradise. Wovoka's call to make peace with white settlers and to work whenever asked likewise commanded the acceptance of the hardships of reservation life in order to herald the coming of a millennial future. As Tribal Historic Preservation Officer Yufna Soldier Wolf noted, the Ghost Dance made "Catholic and Native religion make more sense to each other."[46] The Ghost Dance did not promise immediate transformation by supernatural means but instead offered a way to cope with the immediate present through eschatological hopefulness. Visions experienced by the dancers revealed a world of green hills and roaming buffalo, of joyous reunions with lost tribe members.[47] As Warren argues, "Ghost Dance teachings reached backward and forward in time, hearkening back to an all-Indian world with abundant land and autonomy and urging followers to take up modern means of survival while awaiting the millennium."[48] Despite rising national fears of Ghost Dance practitioners and both local and national anti-Catholic sentiment, wage labor enabled the Northern Arapaho to move within the reservation along networks of their own design. The Northern Arapaho transitioned to reservation life not by rejecting traditional beliefs and practices but by accepting Euro-American ways and standards and molding them to tribal ones.[49] It was a matter of survival through adaptation and subversion, not outright rejection or revolution. Despite the devastating crises of authority precipitated by federal policies and local acculturation initiatives, the Northern Arapaho of central Wyoming strategically adopted new religious traditions, specifically the Ghost Dance, in order to adapt to and survive within reservation life.

Catholic Miners

Nestled in the Rocky Mountains, astride the Continental Divide, stands Butte, Montana. Extractive industries shaped and defined this "black heart" of Montana, a gritty industrial center gouged out of the state's pastoral ranchlands. Butte emerged as a gold camp in 1864—a loose gathering of individual miners and temporary housing. With the discovery of a major copper lode in

1878, however, Butte began a transformation of colossal proportions. It was the beginning of the electrical age, and Thomas Edison's new electric lighting transmitted currents through copper cable, increasing international demand for the metal. As the copper market grew, so too did demand for laborers in Butte, and immigrants streamed into the city to find work. At the end of the nineteenth century, Butte was producing 25 percent of the world's supply of copper, and one corporate giant controlled its extraction: the Anaconda Copper Mining Company.[50]

Mining operations drove thousands of immigrants from all over the world to the more than seven thousand miles of underground tunnels, fiercely defended ethnic neighborhoods, and a burgeoning industrial city known for gambling, prostitution, and drink. The company, however, provided little beyond employment for the residents of Butte. As one trade unionist noted, "The average wage slave's home is a miserable, dingy, dirty board shack . . . there are no sewers anywhere and everyone throws their slops, garbage, or waste of any kind out of the front of, or behind the house."[51] Framed by the stunning Rocky Mountains and rich in red metal, Butte gained the slogan "The Richest Hill on Earth"—although it was rarely the miners who benefited.

Jesuit priests were among the first Euro-American settlers to the Territory of Montana, sent as missionaries to Montanan tribes: the Flathead Indians in 1840, the Kalispell and Pend De Oreille in 1844, and the Blackfeet and Piegan in 1858.[52] Jesuit missionaries, however, only sporadically served the growing mining camps. Appointed the first acting governor of the Territory in August 1865, Thomas Francis Meagher saw Montana as an opportunity for Irish Catholics. An Irish nationalist, Meagher was tried for high treason after an aborted Irish revolution in 1848, was sentenced and transported to Tasmania, and escaped four years later to the United States, where he fought in the Civil War as a Union general for the Irish Brigade.[53] On his journey to Montana, he met with the Archbishop of St. Paul John Ireland, and claimed he wished to "colonize Montana with Catholics, drawing settlers, principally from Irishmen in Ireland and Irishmen in America," secure Irish priests, and establish a bishop in Montana.[54]

Although Meagher drowned in the Missouri River only two years after his appointment, the gold mines of Montana had turned to silver, drawing a wave of miners from mining operations further west, including Chinese immigrants, as well as "tenderfoot" (untested) miners from the East. In 1876, Irish Catholic immigrant Marcus Daly bought the Anaconda Silver Mine.[55] Although geologists believed the mine to be near exhaustion, at one-hundred-feet deep Daly struck lucky with the discovery of copper. At three hundred feet, the copper vein was five feet wide; at four hundred feet, it was fifty. Less than five years later, the Anaconda's payroll was $100,000 more than any other mine in the region.[56] Word of a poor Irish immigrant's success traveled quickly and attracted more Irish to the growing industrial center. One such Irishman was Patrick Daly, who read about the copper boon and "having knowledge of a distant relationship between the [County] Caven [*sic*] Dalys and [his] own clan decided to go direct to Anaconda where he landed in February 1888"; from there he quickly sent his brother a prepaid passage ticket from Ireland to Butte.[57] As Father Patrick Brosnan, parish priest of St. Mary's Rectory, noted forty years later: "Marcus Daly was the man that made Butte an Irish town. He was a poor Irish man that became a millionaire here. He did not care for any man but an Irishman and consequently did not give a job to anyone else."[58] Regardless of his true commitments, Daly commanded loyalty from his employees and was regarded as a protector of Irish jobs and culture. In a form of paternal care, he donated to Irish fraternal organizations and the Catholic Church, gave his employees St. Patrick's Day off from work, and even gave each family a Christmas turkey.[59]

From 1890 to 1900, the city's population increased by 184 percent, and nearly all new arrivals were foreign-born.[60] Butte was an "overwhelmingly Catholic" city, and the Irish-Catholic immigrants comprised a majority of the underground labor.[61] To support the growing working-class population, Butte residents built ten parishes, nine parochial schools, two Catholic high schools, and eight convents.[62] Catholic steeples were as much a part of the Butte landscape as the iron gallus frames that lowered miners to their stations below the surface.

The city was an urban industrial center populated by those whom nativists and the anti-Catholic Know-Nothings labeled anti-modern, clannish, and not quite white. Beecher's *Plea for the West* lamented that "poor Catholics could vote and hold office just like the white man," reinforcing a racial hierarchy tied to religion.[63] The influence of the American Protective Association, a branch of the same anti-Catholic organization located in Lander, Wyoming, was at its height in the 1880s and 1890s and fought fiercely to exclude Roman Catholics from holding public office. Rival mine owner William Clark, an Irish-born Protestant and British loyalist, successfully petitioned for the Montana state capital to be in Protestant Helena rather than in his hometown of Butte, a decidedly Catholic city. And in an 1895 election, the Montana American Protective Association sent a circular to all members of the Montana House of Representatives threatening political death if they cast their vote for any "avowed representative of a foreign power that has the miserable audacity to dictate to free American citizens what they shall do and what they shall not do."[64] As on the Wind River Indian Reservation, individualism was touted as a marker of Americanism, and Catholicism was regarded as anathema—a religious system regarded as uncivilized, pagan, and irrational by many Protestants. For the Irish, the acceptance of particular forms of labor and participation in a transnational Church were fraught with racial signification. Satirical cartoons, political speeches, plays, and novels often depicted Irish Catholics as apelike or reptilian, standing outside of American society.[65] Yet, although Irish immigrants may have shared an experience of racial inferiority with American Indian peoples in social practice and public stereotypes, at the level of political, civil, and legal rights, the Irish formally faced few restrictions and likewise repudiated the notion of similarity, self-situating on the other side of the American color line from Black and Native Americans.[66]

Marcus Daly stands as one such example. Although Daly "wore his Irish Catholicism like a badge" and was just as likely to be found alongside his miners at a saloon as in a pew at Mass, he was also an avowed capitalist and found great economic success in Butte.[67] As the Anaconda Copper Mining Company grew, Daly sought outside investors, including the Rothschilds and Rockefellers, who helped solidify the company's robber-baron identity. Company mangers bought off city officials and territorial representatives as they pursued the bottom line above all else, leaving Butte residents without basic services or even funds to support public schools.[68] In Montana, capital controlled the territory. Human labor was commodified, and wage laborers became cogs in an organism of production, a human machine extracting ore from deep beneath the city's surface. All of this combined with poor working conditions, no insurance or accident benefits, long hours, and low wages. It fell to the community and the Church to establish systems of caretaking to protect one another and their collective interests.

As the company and its investors became richer, the working class of Butte grew poorer. And yet, as one laborer noted, "The class that grows poorer each year produces the very wealth upon which the other class grows richer every year."[69] In response, Butte's first union was formed on June 13, 1878, as the Butte Working Men's Union (BMU)—one of the first local unions in the world. The Butte miners did not seek to overturn the American system of industrial capitalism entirely, as they participated in the economic system by seeking economic security through wages. But they also recognized the power of unity to end exploitative practices, create safer working conditions, and secure a living wage. And as the city grew, Catholicism offered tools for creating alternative networks of care and institutional support.[70]

In lieu of municipal or territorial oversight, Catholic parishes, clergy, and social teachings offered a systematic framework for the social order of Butte, one in which gender relations, education, social justice, and economic welfare were strictly regulated, with the institutional church standing at the center.[71] The Sisters of Charity of Leavenworth, Kansas, sent for by Butte's first permanent priest, Father John Dols, organized hospitals, schools, and orphanages long before local and federal government offices could do so.[72] Irish Catholic fraternal organizations held a particularly important place in the social worlds of Butte's residents. Women participated in the Young Ladies' Sodality of Our Lady and Ladies Aid and organized church socials and dances.[73] Men joined one of three divisions of the Ancient Order of Hibernians (AOH), the Knights of Columbus, and other Irish-Catholic organizations.[74] The Church provided an alternative map—in both physical infrastructure and social relations—to the one created by industrial capitalism.

As with the Northern Arapaho, Butte's Catholic Churches stepped in for absent governance but with distinct outcomes. For the Irish miners, the Church offered stability and a sense of belonging through infrastructure building and educational systems. For the Northern Arapaho, these same offerings were a source of cultural genocide, meant to assimilate the American Indians to "civilized" ways of being. In both cases, Protestant onlookers regarded Catholicism as an inferior and suspect path to Americanization.

In the 1880s, increasing numbers of North American Catholics were joining the largest and most preeminent labor organization in the United States: The Noble and Holy Order of the Knights of Labor. And on May 15, 1891, Pope Leo XIII published the encyclical *Rerum Novarum*, or "Of New Things." Composed of seven sections, *Rerum Novarum* was the culmination of five decades of Catholic reflection on the Industrial Revolution and one of the few encyclicals responding primarily to English-speaking Catholics—namely, working-class Irish, English, and Americans.[75] In the last pages of the encyclical, the pope made a last-minute addition: support for workers' efforts to organize trade unions and collective bargaining in resistance to unrestricted capitalism.[76] As with the age-grade lodges of the Northern Arapaho, labor unions were often regarded as socialist threats to national hegemony. The pope's encyclical sought to offer an alternative route, arguing social justice must mediate between the clashing systems of the day: free-market liberalism and socialism.

The Butte Miners Union came to prominence in this climate—ethnic and religious bonds united the miners together in a shared desire for steady, safe work and in their disavowal of participation in more radical labor organizations founded in socialism. By the end of the 1880s, Butte boasted more than eighteen thousand union members, with thirty-four different unions representing local trades: one for every form of construction, brewers, beer wagon drivers, blacksmiths, musicians, and even theatrical ushers.[77] In an 1897 history, Guy Piatt wrote, "Butte is the head center of the labor organizations of the west, and exercises a vast and telling influence upon the interests of the workingmen of the state."[78] Known as the "Gibraltar of Unionism" to labor historians, Butte contained the largest local unions in the world. Through walkouts and strikes, Butte citizens physically—and regularly—disrupted the flow of capital.

In the wake of *Rerum Novarum*, Butte's labor organizers cited Catholicism as a source of union power and legitimacy. Priests gave homilies on community unity, wrote editorials in local publications, and managed bond drives for strike sufferers.[79] On Labor Day in 1892, a leader of the Silver Bow Trades and Labor Assembly gave a speech in front of the largest crowd ever gathered together in Montana, proclaiming, "The Knights of Labor are new crusaders with a noble work to perform, but the weapons are the pick and shovel and the trowel and saw, the emblems of religion and deliverance, and of the Christianity taught by Christ, the first Knight of Labor."[80] In Butte, mass was scheduled around the shift change of the underground laborers, and Labor Day was celebrated as a Catholic holiday.[81] As unionist and lay member William Sylvis noted, he found no conflict in his support for trade unions and his belief that the worker's "task" was to "found the universal family—to build up the City of God" through trade unions, which Sylvis called an "association of souls" formed by "the Sons of God."[82]

Butte miners hoped by banding together they could maintain community stability in an occupation tied to an uncertain industry. Unionization, as a piece of Christian life, was the remedy to the wrongs of industrial capitalism. Given Pope Leo XIII's global blessing in *Rerum Novarum*, Butte miners engaged their Irish and Catholic identities on the local stage to negotiate between company politics and community economic stability. The working bodies of the miners, their struggles for success, and their anxieties about the future produced social spaces entangled with the physical world of the mines. Butte was a community that responded to the environmental and social conditions of its world using the tools provided by ethnic and religious identities. Like other communities predominately dedicated to a single occupation, the spaces and social structures of the community reflected the work and labor that sustained it.[83] Indeed, they were produced in tandem. The history of Butte's miners is not a story of acculturation to free-market capitalism, nor of outright resistance, but rather the subversion of economic domination in the struggle to maintain a community of care. Labor was the element that gave meaning to their world, and steady work was required.

Conclusion

In the everyday lives, homes, and streets of nineteenth-century Western communities, there was not a strict binary between material acts of labor and transcendent acts of belief. Indeed, participation in the community's economic system was a performance of religious belief, denoting varying degrees of insider and outsider status. As Richard Callahan argues, "religion was itself a form of *work*—an ongoing work of interpretation and orientation, in thought and imagination as well as in behavior and interaction with the world."[84] Despite the intrusion of American markets, the placement on federal reservations, and the plight of working deep underground for absentee owners, westerners renegotiated the tools of the expanding nation-state to their advantage in the ways they were able. These two case studies offer examples of communal caretaking under the conditions produced by US empire. The changing circumstances inspired cultural innovation and response: new networks of commerce and exchange, forms of labor, and means of banding together.

The westerners studied here did not outright reject an ideology of American exceptionalism—indeed, many saw themselves as participating in and upholding the virtues of Americanism—but they also did not wholly assimilate to free-market capitalism and ideals of self-sufficient individualism. Instead, they chose a middle ground, drawing on the communal commitments of their religious identities, which challenged what it meant to be American and Western. These communities provide powerful illustrations of the multiplicities of American experience and the invented nature of the mythic West. In light of the presence of American Indian nations and others regarded as beyond the American pale—namely, Catholics, African Americans, Asian immigrants, and Latter-day Saints—an American hegemony had to be developed, legitimized, and maintained. Yet despite the concealing mechanisms of a single, idealized trajectory of American nationhood, the narration of nationalism was haunted and disrupted by the persistence of alternate but interconnected religious stories and networks of care. Northern Arapaho wage laborers and Catholic miners did not disappear into the fabric of American pluralism but continued to actively set themselves apart by subverting American markets and ideologies in order to build a world of their own making.

These are only two of many thousands of possible stories. In a single region over the span of a few decades, diverse communities grappled with the questions of who wanted to be American and who counted as such. Although their relationships to settler colonialism were not equivalent, Northern Arapaho and Irish mining communities created linked but distinct responses to the isolating circumstances of empire. Both created communities of care that facilitated survival, grounded in principles of economic cooperation born of religious commitments, which were formed in counterpoint to the extractive economy of empire. Telling these stories as part of a larger regional history reveals the generative role of religion and labor in the production of power and identity. Western communities were not isolated from each other or the larger drama of American life, but were deeply enmeshed in the transformations of the late nineteenth and early twentieth centuries.

Notes

1. Lyman Beecher, *Plea for the West* (Truman and Smith, 1835), 17.

2. *The Home Missionary* 19, no. 1 (May 1846), quoted in Laurie Maffly-Kipp, *Religion and Society in Frontier California* (Yale University Press, 1994).

3. Laurie Maffly-Kipp, "Eastward Ho!," in *Retelling US Religious History*, ed. Thomas Tweed (University of California Press, 1997), 130; Quincey Newell, "Religion in the American West," *Religion Compass* 6, no. 11 (2012): 490.

4. See Joshua Paddison, *American Heathens: Religion, Race, and Reconstruction in California* (University of California Press, 2012).

5. See W. Paul Reeve, *Religion of a Different Color: Race and the Mormon Struggle for Whiteness* (Oxford University Press, 2015); Matthew Frye Jacobson, *Whiteness of a Different Color: European Immigrants and the Alchemy of Race* (Harvard University Press, 1999); and Nell Irvin Painter, *The History of White People* (W. W. Norton, 2010).

6. Jackson, State of the Union Address (December 6, 1830).

7. John O'Sullivan, "Annexation," quoted in Thomas Hietala, *Manifest Design: American Exceptionalism and Empire* (Cornell University Press, 2003), x.

8. See Josiah Strong, *Our Country: Its Possible Future and Present Circumstances* (Baker & Taylor, 1885), 152–53, 161.

9. Andrew C. Isenberg and Thomas Richards, Jr, "Alternative Wests: Rethinking Manifest Destiny," *Pacific Historical Review*, 86, no. 1 (February 2017): 4–17.

10. Aileen Moreton Robinson, *The White Possessive: Property, Power and Indigenous Sovereignty* (University of Minnesota Press, 2015), xii.

11. In some cases, these communities were literally brought in to be laborers on behalf of empire, but only as the foot soldiers, never the beneficiaries.

12. Ulysses S. Grant, quoted in William B. Kurtz, *Excommunicated from the Union: How the Civil War Created a Separate Catholic America* (Fordham University Press, 2016), 138; see also Frederick Cooper and Ann Laura Stoler, "Between Metropole and Colony: Rethinking a Research Agenda," in *Tensions of Empire: Colonial Cultures in a Bourgeois World* (University of California Press, 1997), 12; Jacobson, *Whiteness of a Different Color*, 29; and Adam Dahl, *Empire of the People: Settler Colonialism and the Foundations of Modern Democratic Thought* (University of Kansas Press, 2018), 148.

13. Frederick Jackson Turner, "The Significance of the Frontier in American History" (1893), 9, 259, 293, http://nationalhumanitiescenter.org/pds/gilded/empire/text1/turner.pdf.

14. Cedric J. *Black Marxism, Revised and Updated Third Edition: The Making of the Black Radical Tradition* (University of North Carolina Press, 2020), 26.

15. Melinda H. Benson, "Mining Sacred Space: Law's Enactment of Competing Ontologies in the American West," *Environment and Planning A: Economy and Space* 44, no. 6 (2012):1443–58, doi:10.1068/a44579.

16. Manu Karuka, *Empire's Tracks: Indigenous Nations, Chinese Workers, and the Transcontinental Railroad* (University of California Press, 2019); David Walker, *Railroading*

Religion: Mormons, Tourists, and the Corporate Spirit of the West (University of North Carolina Press, 2020).

17. Patrick Wolfe, Settler Colonialism Then and Now: A Conversation Between J. Kehaulani Kauanui and Patrick Wolfe," *Politica & Societa* 2 (2012): 235–85.

18. Michel de Certeau, *The Practices of Everyday Life* (University of California Press, 1984), xiii.

19. George A. Dorsey and Alfred L. Kroeber, *Traditions of the Arapaho* (Smithsonian, 1903), 1–7.

20. William C'Hair, Andrew Cowell, and Alonzo Moss Jr., *Arapaho Stories, Songs, and Prayers: A Bilingual Anthology* (University of Oklahoma Press, 2005), 41–42.

21. Judith A. Hollinger, "A Comparison of the Differential Rates of Change of the Religious and Family Structures of the Northern and Southern Arapaho," advised by Dr. Bruner, Loretta Fowler Papers, Box 12. American Heritage Center, University of Wyoming (hereafter, AHC).

22. C'Hair, Cowell, and Moss, 41–42.

23. *The Wind River Reservation Yesterday and Today: The Legends-The Land-The People.* Workshop directed by Larry Murray, with tribal consultants, 7, Loretta Fowler Papers, Box 12, AHC.

24. Bureau of Indian Affairs, "History and Economy of the Indians of the Wind River Reservation, Wyoming," Missouri River Basin Investigations, Report no. 106, Department of the Interior, Bureau of Indian Affairs, 1950, 4.

25. Alfred Kroeber, *The Arapaho* (American Museum of Natural History, 1902–1907), 153–54.

26. Victoria Cole Trenholm, *The Arapahoes, Our People* (University of Oklahoma Press, 1970), 70.

27. "Election of Tribal Council," Superintendent to Commissioner of Indian Affairs (February 2 1910), 2; Records of the Wind River Agency of the Bureau of Indian Affairs, Record Group 75, Entry 8, Box 6, National Archives, Denver.

28. The Socialist Labor Party of America was founded in 1871.

29. Ethelbert Talbot, *My People of the Plains* (Harper & Brothers, 1906), 14.

30. B. Feusi to Very Rev. Monsignore J. A. Stephan, Director Catholic Bureau, November 20, 1898, Loretta Fowler Papers, Box 6, AHC.

31. Joseph Henry, "Catholic Missionaries on the Wind River: The Saint Stephen's Mission to the Arapahoes, 1884–1911" (master's thesis, University of Wisconsin, 1984), 55.

32. Director of Catholic Missions to Rev. Wm. McMillan, S. J. at St. Stephen's Mission, March 21, 1908, Loretta Fowler Papers, Box 6, AHC. See also Robert Hutt, "St. Michael's Mission Project at Ethete, Wyoming," [s.n.], 1924, 11; Zdeněk Salzmann Papers, Box 5, AHC.

33. *United States v. Kagama*, 118 US 375 (1886).

34. Sherman Coolidge, "Indian American—His Duty to His Race and to His Country, the United States of America," *Quarterly Journal of the Society of American Indians* 1, no. 1 (1913), 20–22.

35. Eaglehead, September 29, 1890, A meeting at St. Stephen's Mission, Loretta Fowler Papers, Box 9, AHC.

36. Left-Hand, March 2, 1907, American Baptist Home Mission Society, Virginia Grace Trenholm Papers, Box 2, Folder 1. AHC.

37. *Report of the Commissioner of Indian Affairs*, 1905, 56; Zedněk Salzmann Papers, Box 3, AHC.

38. Beatrice Crofts and Elinor Markley, *Walk Softly, This is God's Country: 1883–1949 Among Shoshone and Arapaho Indians, Wind River Reservation* (Mortimore Publishing, 1997), 48.

39. James Mooney, *The Ghost Dance Religion and the Sioux Outbreak of 1890* (University of Chicago Press, 1972), 781; 1890 Commissioner Report on all of Indian Affairs for the Country from J. T. Gregory, 260; Zedněk Salzmann Papers, Box 15, AHC.

40. Louis Warren, *God's Red Son: The Ghost Dance Religion and the Making of Modern America* (Basic Books, 2018), 205.

41. Report of Special Agent Peter Moran, July and August 1890, 633.

42. 1890 Commissioner Report on All of Indian Affairs for the country from J. T. Gregory, 260. Zedněk Salzmann Papers, Box 15, AHC.

43. Chief Black Coal, "Resolutions Taken by the Arapahoe Indians at a Meeting at St. Stephen's Mission," September 29, 1890. Loretta Fowler Papers, Folder 7, Box 9, AHC.

44. Ernst SunRhodes, *Valley of Three Cultures Oral History Project*, File 84, recorded February, 19, 1987, AHC.

45. "The industrial training of both boys and girls is such as to fit them for practical results upon leaving schools. Irrigation farming in all its phases is taught the boys, including care and handling of horses and cattle. Carpentry and blacksmithing, as is necessary upon a farm, is also taught. The girls are taught cooking, sewing, general housework, etc." Agency Report, 1909, Wadsworth, page 6, National Archives, Group 75, Box 1.

46. Yufna Soldier Wolf, interview with author, July 2016.

47. Elaine Wanstall interview, August 1978, Loretta Fowler Papers, Box 7, AHC.

48. Louis Warren, "Wage Work in the Sacred Circle: The Ghost Dance as Modern Religion." *Western Historical Quarterly* 46, no. 2 (May 2015): 143.

49. "History and Economy of the Indians of the Wind River Reservation, Wyoming." Missouri River Basin Investigations, Report no. 106. Billings, MT: Department of the Interior, Bureau of Indian Affairs., 1950, 8. Zedněk Salzmann, Box 7, AHC.

50. Pat Kearney, *Butte Voices: Mining, Neighborhoods, People* (Skyhigh Communications, 1998), 37.

51. Letter from J. A. Stromquist (Chicago) *Industrial Union Bulletin*, March 24, 1908.

52. Rev. C. Pauwelyn, "The Beginning and Growth of the Catholic Church in the State of Montana," (Butte, MT: The Montana State Council Knights of Columbus, 1918), 2. Bishop Brondel Papers, Folder 4, Box 1), The Diocese of Helena Archives, Helena, Montana (hereafter, HDA).

53. Paul Wylie, *The Irish General: Thomas Francis Meagher* (University of Oklahoma Press, 2007), 3.

54. John Ireland to LB Palladino, "Origin of the Diocese of Helena, Montana," January 30, 1912. Bishop Brondel Papers, Folder 4, Box 1, HDA.

55. George Everett, "From the Emerald Isle to the Copper Mines: An Historical Look at the Irish of Butte, Montana," *Irish America* 26, no. 4. (2000): 126.

56. "Early Day Butte; Some Statistics," *Redstone Review*, July 11, 1921. Butte, MT-History, Vertical File, Montana Historical Society, Helena, Montana (hereafter, MHS).

57. Hugh Daly, "Life History of Hugh Daly," 7. David Emmons Collection, Butte Silver-Bow Archives, Butte, Montana (hereafter, BSB).

58. Patrick Brosnan to his father (February 18, 1917), 2. Father Patrick Brosnan Papers, BSB.

59. David Emmons, *Beyond the American Pale: The Irish in the West, 1845–1910* (University of Oklahoma Press, 2010), 277.

60. Emmons, *The Butte Irish*, 13.

61. Emmons, 95.

62. John Mihelich, "An Ethnographic Account of Industrial Capitalism, Religion, and Community," (PhD diss., Washington State University, 1999), 201.

63. Painter, *The History of White People*, 136.

64. J. D. Caldwell, "The A.P.A. Protest" (Butte, MT, January 18, 1895). Scrapbook II, HDA.

65. Kevin Kenny, *The American Irish: A History* (Pearson Education Limited, 2000), 67.

66. Painter, *The History of White People*, 143.

67. David Emmons, "The Orange and the Green in Montana: A Reconsideration of the Origins of the Clark-Daly Feud," *Arizona and the West* 28, no. 3 (1986), 234.

68. Jerry Calvert, *The Gibraltar: Socialism and Labor in Butte, Montana, 1895–1920* (Montana Historical Society Press, 1988), 4–5.

69. "Asking Too Much," *Butte Bystander*, December 17, 1892: 1. BSB.

70. Butte Miners' Union No. 1, "Constitution and By-Laws, Wage Scale and Agreement," 4. Vertical File, Labor History/Miners' Union, BSB.

71. *Montana Catholic* 1, no. 23, September 23, 1899: 2.

72. "St. James' Hospital, Butte," *Souvenir Centenary Edition, The Register: A Century of Catholicity in Montana, 1841–1941*, Aug. 27, 1941: 16. BSB.

73. Michael J. Hannan, *Father English and St. Mary's Parish, Butte, Montana: The Miners Catholic Church and Parish* (Butte, 1917), 35. Vertical File: St. Mary's Parish, BSB.

74. "The Ancient Order of Hibernians," *Montana Catholic*, 1 (no. 8, June 10, 1899: 5. MHS.

75. George Pell, *Rerum Novarum: One Hundred Years Later* (Boston University Press, 1992), 6.

76. Joe Holland, *Modern Catholic Social Teaching: The Popes Confront the Industrial Age, 1740–1958* (Paulist Press, 2003), 144. American industrial elites at the end of the nineteenth century were overwhelming Protestant and participated in a religious tradition that supported and sustained the values, beliefs and worldview of capitalism. See E. Digby Baltzell, *The Protestant Establishment: Aristocracy and Caste in America* (Yale University Press, 1987); Tyler B. Flynn, "Calvinism and Public Life: A Case Study of Western Pennsylvania 1900–1955" (PhD diss., Pennsylvania State University, 2007); Timothy E. W. Gloege, *Guaranteed Pure: Fundamentalism, Business, and the Making of Modern Evangelicalism* (University of North Carolina Press, 2015); Frederick Jaher, *The Urban Establishment: Upper Strata in Boston, New York, Charleston, Chicago, and Los Angeles* (University of Illinois Press, 1982); and Thomas F. Rzeznik, *Church and Estate: Religion and Wealth in Industrial-Era Philadelphia* (Pennsylvania State University Press, 2013).

77. Calvert, 4.

78. Guy X. Piatt, *The Story of Butte* (The Standard Manufacturing & Printing Co., 1897), 77–78.

79. *Butte Daily Miner, Butte Miner, Butte Weekly Miner, Labor World, Labor Weekly*, and *New Age*. Significantly, an anonymous column in *Montana Catholic* implored Catholics in the Rocky Mountain West to heed the call of impoverished workers and to support organized labor. "Publications Relating To Labor." *Monthly Labor Review* 8, no. 6 (1919): 354–75.

80. "The Largest Crowd Ever Gathered Together in Montana," *Butte Bystander*, 28 Sept. 10, 1892: 1. BSB.

81. Michael J. Hannan, *Father English and St. Mary's Parish, Butte, Montana: The Miners Catholic Church and Parish* (Butte, 1917), 18. Vertical File: St. Mary's Parish, BSB.

82. Sylvis, 96–117, 443–46, quoted in Gutman, *Work, Culture, and Society in Industrializing America*, 98.

83. A number of excellent place-based studies on the intersection of religion and work have been produced. See Murphy, *Ten Hours Labor*; Callahan, *Work and Faith in the Kentucky Coal Fields*; Wallace, *Rockdale*.

84. Richard Callahan, "Allegories of Progress: Industrial Religion in the United States." *Journal of American Academy of Religion* 78, no. 1 (March 2010): 50.

Chapter 9

Religion on Tour

Circuses and the American West

NICOLE C. KIRK

Keywords: circus, railroad, performance, chaplain, commodification

On May 21, 1905, at two o'clock in the morning, the John Robinson Ten Big Shows circus train rolled to a stop at the bottom of a steep set of tracks near the small town of Tyrone, Pennsylvania. It was a planned stop. Circus workers and performers were roused from their boxcar beds and climbed down to hold trackside "memorial services . . . for the dead" under a "starlight" sky.[1] In 1893, on the same stretch of track, the Walter L. Main Circus and Menagerie train took the sharp curve on the mountain too quickly. Fifteen train cars derailed, smashed into the mountainside, and "piled in a confused mass," killing six circus workers and crushing hundreds of animals, including over fifty trained horses.[2] Dozens of workers and performers were injured. Adding to the distress, many animals, some of them dangerous tigers and lions, escaped their broken cages and roamed the chaotic scene of the wreck and the surrounding woods.[3]

The 1905 Robinson Circus route book, a diary and yearbook of the circus's travels for that season, described the elements of the early morning trackside memorial service.[4] The lecturer for the menagerie, a United Brethren minister, the Rev. William Sheak, "feelingly spoke" of those who had tragically died and "warned" the circus company that they must "be ready for the call to the Great Beyond."[5] The circus's bands provided "appropriate music" for the service while members of the circus unloaded "two car loads of flowers—one from the show people, and the other from the Pennsylvania Railway" and "wreathed the Mountain Side" crash site with them.[6] After the minister's sermon, the music, and the placement of flowers, the route book and local newspapers reported one final element in the memorial service: an unnamed group of Native circus performers contributed to the memorial service; "the Indians executed a death dance."[7] The route book did not disclose whether all the American Indians traveling with the show participated in the dance or only a few, and, like other publications in the era, the book did not disclose tribal affiliations or specifics of the dance. Additionally, the route book's description of the event rendered the Native dance religious by including it as a part of an account of the eclectic circus memorial service.[8] Newspaper articles on the memorial, likely circulated by the circus's publicity team, titled the event "Weird Memorial Services at Circus."[9]

The late-night memorial service, along with the religiously diverse ceremony, gives us a glimpse into the self-referential mythologies of the American circus and the role of the myth of the American West in shaping both the circus entertainment and American ideas about the West. Railroad circuses, like immigrants to the American West, were no strangers to disaster. The widely reported original circus wreck, as well as the publicized memorial service, intersected with the risk and ambition associated with early American settlers, helping to shape the mythology of the American West.

Notions about Native Americans are central to this mythology. Since the 1840s, Native performers have been a part of American circuses and other traveling entertainments. Before the advent of independent Wild West shows in 1883, Native Americans performed dances, feats of horsemanship, and choreographed skirmishes between white settlers and Native Americans. They also participated in ethnographic congresses and reenactments of village life.[10] Recent scholars have argued that these performances were complicated instances of exploitation and agency. Native performers sought out these performance opportunities as a means to leave the reservation, make money, and preserve dance traditions, even as the endeavors amplified stereotypes about Native life and culture.[11]

Beginning this story in Pennsylvania is seemingly incongruent with a volume on the American West. However, this essay centers the American circus as a central driver of the mythmaking of the American West. Using (and promoting) railroads, circuses circulated, created, and amplified stock stereotypes of life on the frontier, long after the frontier had closed. The stop in Pennsylvania highlights the reach of the circus's mythmaking. Although the memorial service purportedly occurred on a Pennsylvania mountainside, the John Robinson Circus's trackside ritual for the dead is a story about the American West, religion, and empire.

From 1872 to 1920, the circus was one of North America's most popular forms of entertainment and "reached virtually all Americans," including scattered audiences stretching from west of the Mississippi to the Pacific Ocean.[12] While the World's Fairs in Philadelphia in 1876, Chicago in 1893, and St. Louis in 1904 drew millions of visitors from across the United States and around the world, circuses and itinerant entertainment eclipsed the Great Expositions by reaching more people. Circuses entertained audiences of diverse economic and racial backgrounds across the nascent United States and its territories.[13]

Even Gold Rush encampments and boomtowns in Indian Territory received visits from multiple circuses.

Circuses and circus performances are central to understanding the cultural landscape of American life, and historians have traced some of the impact of the circus on American culture. Scholar Janet Davis argues that "the turn-of-the-century railroad circus was a powerful cultural icon of a new, modern nation-state" and a "complex case of cultural and ideological production" that formed "contradictory meanings."[14] Davis and other scholars claim that railroad circuses nurtured and performed cultural, ideological, and national myths through performances, menageries, sideshows, and large-scale publicity, bending societal norms and expectations while simultaneously reinforcing them. The powerful ways American railroad circuses intersected with American religion(s) and helped shape American West myths reveal how popular culture framed the United States as an empire.

The popularity of railroad circuses rose in tandem with the growth of the United States and its assertion of control over land and peoples across the continent and the Pacific Ocean.[15] Circuses followed US expansion on the railroads, first trailing settlers and their capital along roads, rivers, and canals. Soldiers and settlers claimed the land, but circuses told the conquest story. The adoption of railroads by large circuses expanded their reach and helped solidify the mythology of the American West. Riding the rails, circuses served as instruments of US colonization through their performances, exhibitions, and logistical expertise. The expansion of railroad networks and the completion of the transcontinental lines enabled circuses to tour the American West and, in turn, export ideas and myths of the West to audiences across the continent and the world.

This chapter serves as a case study examining how railroad circuses capitalized on ideas of empire by mythologizing, commodifying, and exoticizing the American West and how religious practices intersected with the circus. Drawing on railroad circus route books and newspapers, it briefly explores how American railroad circuses developed a national (and global) circuit of ideas and representations of the American West and religion before the advent of Wild West shows and after their popularity faded. Circuses acted as mirrors and mythmakers of the West long before Buffalo Bill and dozens of other Wild West shows helped give rise to the phenomenon.[16] The intersection of the American circus and religion highlights the continued complexity of empire and religion on both the imagined and real American frontiers. Much like the circus, and the trains that carried it, the relationship among the circus, the American West, and religion follows many pathways. This essay traces a few of those nodal points to map out these intersections.

Empire Builder: Circuses on the Rails

The rapid development of railroad infrastructure allowed for the movement of people and objects over a broad geographic area in a relatively short time. Trains eased the flow of people, material goods, and ideas across the country. Railroads reframed North American rural and urban life by disrupting time and space, claiming audiences could explore the globe by attending the circus. Railroad circuses linked far-flung communities by drawing audiences from nearby towns, bustling cities, isolated farms, small settlements, and Indian reservations. Circuses traveled relentlessly, crisscrossing North America, with the larger circuses giving up to two hundred performances in a single season.[17] The radical mobility of circuses echoed the mobility of settlers moving across land and water to settle across the continent.

Historian Pamela Klassen has called the railroad "the spinal cord of colonialism."[18] Construction of rail lines ushered in an expansion of territory, the occupation of Native American lands, and the expanded presence of US military.[19] As such, railroads loomed large in the Manifest Destiny imaginary—the belief that the United States was designated to expand its territory across North America—and accelerated the exploitation of Native peoples and the continent, contributing to the creation and sustaining of the American settler colonial empire.[20] If the railroad was the spinal cord of colonialism, the circus circulated colonialism through its mobile performances of colonialist ideology. The relationship between the circus and the railroad was symbiotic; both created and sustained the technologies of US settler colonialism.

While circuses experimented with railroads prior to the Civil War, the completion of the transcontinental railroad in 1869 represented an expanded business opportunity and another source of entertainment for audiences, since the circuses themselves were modern wonders.[21] Circuses embraced the railroad as a lucrative yet risky mode of transportation. In doing so, managers developed customized railroad cars for equipment, tents, and animals, enabling shows to move between towns and providing performers with living space for life on the rails. They also designed railroad cars that accelerated the process of loading and unloading equipment and animals so a show could arrive in the morning and depart after the day and evening performances. A reordering of workers further fueled railroad circuses' efficiency; labor was systematized to set up and break down the show.[22] Railroads granted the largest circuses access to more areas of the country, and through discounted fares on feeder lines, circuses offered rural audiences the opportunity to see bigger shows.

The brightly colored, custom-made circus trains, where animals and people lived together, were as much a fascination as the show itself for townspeople.

The logistics of setting up and tearing down a canvas city in one day became part of the circus's spectacle and drew curiosity and wonder. Eager onlookers gathered at train yards to watch the circus trains unload and reload after the performances.[23]

The circus logistics were not merely entertainment; they also became proving grounds for colonializing governments. As a case in point, the Prussian and US armies studied circus trains as models for the rapid deployment of troops and supplies during their colonial campaigns.[24] A 1895 McClure article declared, "No army knows such severe discipline as the troop of the circus trains." The same article noted that Army generals spent a week with the circus at Fort Leavenworth to learn how to move people and equipment swiftly.[25]

In addition to serving as a model of technical efficiency for the military, the American railroad circus also contributed to empire-building by transporting and circulating visual representations of people, places, and religion through circus posters, route books, and newspaper advertisements, as well as embodied representations through the bodies of performers. Circuses, like railroads, promised to make faraway places and other cultures knowable to a wider public long before the advent of radio and cinema.[26] Circuses commodified colonialism through their displays and performances, repackaging it as entertainment and education.[27] One of the ways they did this was through their construction and performance of "the West."

The Myth of the American West Circulates

Thousands gathered to watch a herd of buffalo stampede down a street in Hoboken, New Jersey, on August 31, 1843—or at least newspaper advertisements promised a stampede at a "Grand Buffalo Hunt" that was "free for all," except for the price of a special ferry ticket. More than twenty-four thousand people crossed the Hudson River, with more spectators arriving from New Jersey and surrounding areas. The "hunt" featured fifteen buffalo calves and their captor, Mr. C. D. French, a white man "painted and dressed as an Indian," armed with a sharp stick to prod the frightened animals and a lasso to make a show of "capturing" them.[28] But the event did not go as expected. When the shed doors opened, the calves froze, prompting the crowd to explode into laughter; the noise startled the animals, who ran wildly into the crowd, frightening the spectators. The stampede that ensued consisted of men, women, and children trying to escape the spooked bison. The showman P. T. Barnum profited handsomely from the stunt and, in the process, helped introduce one of the staples of nineteenth-century circus entertainment: exhibitions of animals and people, outfitted in costumes, performing vignettes ostensibly from the American West.

The East Coast Buffalo Stampede drew on popular images of the American West. Throughout the nineteenth century, Americans consumed a steady diet of stories, paintings, living dioramas, drawings, displays of people and animals, newspaper reports, dime novels, and live performances depicting a variety of American Wests. The wave of mythmaking started in the 1830s, when newspapers published exciting stories from explorers such as cartographer John Charles Frémont, drawn from his five extensive tours of the region. Frémont's wife Jessie, an avid expansionist, rewrote his richly detailed reports, turning them into immensely popular "patriotic adventure" stories. His reports included elaborate depictions of the terrain, people, and animals of the land, tailored to entice interest in the West.[29] One scholar has called Frémont the "ad man for Manifest Destiny."[30] His father-in-law, a powerful senator from Missouri and also an enthusiastic advocate of Westward expansion, promoted Frémont's reports aggressively in Congress and arranged for the publication of his reports in newspapers throughout the United States and its territories.

Artists also contributed to the West's mythic world-building, as illustrated in Thomas Bremer's chapter in this volume. A generation before Moran, artists like John Mix Stanley, Alfred Jacob Miller, Karl Bodmer, and George Catlin produced hundreds of paintings portraying Indians, fur trappers, violent encounters between white settlers and Indians, and magnificent Western landscapes. All four created Indian portrait galleries that toured and exhibited across the eastern United States. Painted for elite Eastern audiences, their work promoted a romanticized vision of westward expansion, the people who dwelled in the region, and its terrain.[31] Popular writers like Washington Irving and James Fenimore Cooper added to these depictions by penning some of the first novels and travelogues set in the American West.[32]

Even as circuses constructed entertainment around the myth of the American West, the settlement and romance of western lands also enticed circuses. Without an efficient transcontinental route, the first circus to visit the West Coast arrived by steamer in 1849, when Joseph Andrew Rowe's circus heard that gold had been discovered in the mountains of California.[33] The circus proprietor and performer Joseph Andrew Rowe had toured his small circus that season through Cuba and several cities in South and Central America. He was in Lima, Peru, with his troupe when he heard that gold had been discovered in California in the Sierra Nevada. Rowe secured passage on a ship to San Francisco and loaded his animals and performers for the long and arduous three-month trip.[34] The construction of the first transcontinental railroad, nearing completion in May 1869, persuaded Costello Circus and Menagerie to take a cross-country tour that included stops in Colorado, Wyoming, and Utah until they reached their destination of California. By the turn of the century, there were five transcontinental railroads and hundreds of new rail lines that circuses used to traverse the country and beyond.[35]

Constructing a West

Like the writers, artists, and showmen like Barnum, circuses tapped into the mythic power of a multiplicity of American Wests decades before the 1883 launch of Buffalo Bill's Wild West Show.[36] Circus owners incorporated people, animals, and reenactments of the West into performances. The Wild West shows did not create the myths of the American West; they were tapping into a larger American West zeitgeist that circuses helped create. Among the versions of Wests circuses constructed in their shows included a West of the Indian Wars and violent attacks between settlers and "savage, wild" Indians; a romanticized West where the last of the Indians wandered; and a West no longer populated by bison but by cowboys and herds of cattle. P. T. Barnum blazed the trail for other entrepreneurs when he experimented with incorporating elements from the West at his museum and in the shows he invested in before he started his traveling show. In addition to the buffalo run in Hoboken (an event copied by other showmen), Barnum displayed Native Americans in ethnographic displays and live dioramas at his American Museum.

Through his partnership with Cooke's Royal Circus, Barnum recruited a former shoemaker from Massachusetts—turned fur trader and later a showman—who went by the names Grizzly Adams and Old Grizzly Adams. Through his travels, Adams captured and trained several large bears, including a grizzly he called Ben, and soon began touring his collection of over seventy animals from the American West under the name "The California Menagerie." He also trapped and shipped western animals for eastern circuses and menageries. Adams developed national fame when a writer, Thomas Hitter, published a serialized dime novel about his adventures. P. T. Barnum and Cooke's Royal Circus employed Adams, along with his bears and menagerie, until his death, popularizing the image of the American West's animals and mountain men.

Central to circuses' construction of the "West" was their incorporation of Native American performers. As Buffalo Bill would later discover, "audiences were willing to pay for depictions that emphasized wildness, savagery, and the suggestion that the activities were religious in nature. Barnum's inclusion of Native performers, both Indigenous people and impostors, in his pop-up entertainments, displays at his American Museum, and circus shows helped initiate a trend that grew following the Civil War and the forced movement of Native Americans onto reservations. When he launched his full circus in 1871, he included performances of "Indian life" in his shows, with performers recruited from the Omaha tribe.[37] Barnum's circus helped solidify the presence of Native Americans in popular entertainments, but other circuses had featured Indigenous performers decades earlier. For example, in 1855, the Washburn Circus and Menagerie advertised an "Indian amphitheater" as a major attraction, claiming they featured "a large Troupe of genuine Wild Indians, from the vast Planet, from beyond the Rocky Mountains, consisting of Chiefs, Braves, Warriors, and Squaws, dressed in all the paraphernalia of their respective nations."[38] Historian Kathryn Gin Lum, in her study of the term "heathen," argues that classifications like "wild" racialize the people to whom they are applied and reinforce the idea that "real" religion belongs to white American Protestants. Additionally, though, in the context of the circus, the phrase "wild Indian" acted as a shorthand for the American West and as a central symbol of both the wildness of the United States and the grit of its people.

The exoticization of non-Christian religions was a key piece of circus entertainment. Many circus advertisements promised not only Indians riding and shooting but also dancing and performing "ceremonies." After the Civil War, circuses hired Native performers at a growing pace.[39] In 1871–1872, the Great Central Park Menagerie, International Circus, and Iroquois Indian Troupe boasted twenty-five members of the Iroquois in a "Life in the Wilderness" pantomime that served as the show's finale, showcasing their "characteristic Songs and Dances" in addition to a reenactment of the story of Pocahontas.[40] By 1889, Adam Forepaugh's immense railroad circus hired twenty-five Lakota to tour with his show, and it featured programs with Native performers throughout the 1890s. During the 1891 season, following a grand display of "Red Hussars" in elaborate costumes and a circus spectacle presenting "historical pictures" of the *Arabian Nights*, the entertainment shifted to another exotic and mythic locale: the American West. They offered a series of presentations promising "realistic illustrations" of "life in the West, vividly presenting the progress of civilization, its dangers, war, frontiers sports, and peaceful pleasures."[41] These performances and displays exoticized Native American life and the West, helping to circulate ideas about both the "progress" of civilization and the religious lives of American Indians.

The concept of "progress" in these performances and other exhibitions functioned as code for white Protestant Christianity. The code associating whiteness with civilization became increasingly explicit. Indians were portrayed as animals by locating them in menageries and displaying them in "scientific" exhibitions of people and cultures. Although most Wild West shows had closed by 1913, circuses continued to incorporate Indian performances into their programs. Through the circus routes, the myth of the American West as a landscape conquered by a white Protestant people became an unquestioned element of the American story.

Care and Itinerancy Rituals: Chaplains and Circus Religion

Traveling with a circus was a dangerous enterprise. Performers, workers, and animals faced numerous challenges, from devastating railroad wrecks like the one memorialized at the opening of this chapter to accidents during performances. Workers were routinely injured by falling tent poles or frightened animals. Unpredictable weather meant circus crews regularly faced hazards from lightning, heavy rain, and tornadic winds. Violent encounters between circus workers and townspeople were also common. The arrival of a circus drew not only eager audiences but also pickpockets, con artists, and thrill seekers hoping to profit from the crowds. The festive atmosphere around a circus's arrival provided an opportunity for heavy drinking. In other words, circuses produced a steady stream of situations that called out for pastoral care—both ministry to the sick and grieving and paternalistic care. When accidents occurred, circuses frequently invited local clergy to attend to their needs although sometimes they refused. Local ministers buried circus workers and performed weddings. Circuses also participated in, adapted, and extended many Protestant Christian rituals, such as the christening a newborn elephant by Forepaugh's circus in 1900. In some cases, circuses hired chaplains to provide spiritual counsel in the midst of danger and violence, to oversee the religious education of the troupe's children, and tend to the rituals of everyday life.

Ministers joining the circus titillated newspaper readers because American church leaders often opposed circuses. Protestant ministers and cultural elites criticized circuses as sites of moral corruption, vice (heavy drinking and gambling), and sexual impropriety. Circuses had a reputation for showcasing scantily clad women, crude entertainment, and bodies that transgressed societal norms. Many regarded the circus as an entertainment "wallowing in fraud [and] graft," with performers "who violated boundaries of all kinds," and they envisioned the circus grounds as places where con artists and pickpockets abounded.[42] The Methodist Church's General Conference went as far as to explicitly ban attending circuses in 1872, along with drinking "intoxicating liqueurs," dancing, gambling, "attending theatre," "horse races," and other activities deemed to have a "misleading or questionable moral tendency."[43] Some states and towns, under pressure from the clergy, banned circuses from performing altogether. Protestant ministers preached sermons and wrote articles for local newspapers and denominational periodicals warning of the dangers of attending the circus.[44] Even the American Sunday School Union published pamphlets advising parents against taking their children to the circus.[45]

Circus owners assuaged criticism with a variety of techniques. Most circuses gave free tickets to orphanages so that children could attend, and the

Robinson Circus even performed in a Pennsylvania penitentiary yard to entertain prisoners. Not only did they perform these charitable acts every year, but they also advertised their good works, often including images of the children, orphanages, or prison yards in an attempt to improve their reputation.

Within this context, Reverend William Sheak decided to join the circus as a zoologist. However, as noted at the beginning of this essay, he also lent his expertise in leading memorial services, funerals, and other religious events. During his time with the circus, Sheak offered his moral authority as an ordained minister to the Robinson menagerie and circus. Sheak translated and adapted religious practice for his new, ever-changing context. The circus—its animals, props, tents, and the railroad—remade ritual, dictating the schedule and locations of circus religious life. While Sheak found a connection with the circus community as a Protestant minister among a people who were not entirely Protestant or even Christian, it is evident he did not bring religion to the circus. It was already there.

Circuses were sites of active religious practice. Despite some newspaper headlines, when Sheak joined the circus, he did not leave the ministry behind. He attended to the spiritual needs of Robinson Circus's nearly one thousand traveling performers and workers. Sheak held worship services, offered pastoral care, performed weddings, and delivered eulogies and prayers for fallen circus workers. His employment there extended well beyond the cages and the canvas flaps of the menagerie tent. Like most circus employees, Sheak's position as lecturer in the menagerie entailed more than giving talks on the animals. He was also charged with kicking out rowdy and drunk patrons, running errands, and driving tent poles into the ground. Sheak's new role also involved chaplaincy work, or, as a newspaper described it, "look[ing] after the spiritual welfare of the people who travel with the show."[46] He ministered to the circus workers, and the show's publicity department publicized his pastoral activities to further evidence the circus's moral standing.

Not only did Sheak minister to the circus's workers, but to its audiences too. On Sundays, he arranged with circus management to hold worship services on the circus grounds for the public. The time for the service was dictated by the circus's arrival in town and by the conclusion of the circus parade through the town center. Circus time preceded worship time. Sometimes the Sunday crowds that came to hear the circus preacher swelled to more than two thousand.[47] Praised for his "magnetic power" as a preacher, Sheak's sermons touched on many Bible stories about animals and topics connected to the local area. During his 1906 tour, he preached sermons titled "The Coal Miner and His Relationship Man and God," "The Flood Story," and "The Story of Balaam."

Sheak's services brought potential audience members to the circus grounds before the evening show for undoubtedly Christian reasons, blurring the lines between church and entertainment. The circus advertised Sheak's ministerial activities by recording his sermon titles, the size of the Sunday crowds for his preaching, his circus worker chapel services, and his trackside memorial services. For Sheak, these acts were a part of his ministry; for the circus, they were a part of their sensational publicity machine. His audiences were likely a mix of both spectators seeking entertainment and worshippers.

Sheak also worked for the Barnum and Bailey Circus for one season. There, his role as circus chaplain developed into an official position for the show. While maintaining his duties as lecturer in the menagerie, Sheak continued to lead worship on Sunday and was on call as a minister. Early in the 1904 season, during a performance at Madison Square Garden, an aerialist fell mid-act. A workman who witnessed the accident ran to retrieve the minister, believing the performer had died. Sheak arrived in the ring at the side of the fallen performer, only to discover, to everyone's relief, that the aerialist had survived. Although circuses mostly sustained and reflected the cultural hierarchies of their time, new ideas of community and religious practice emerged from living in motion and in close quarters.[48] The story of the mountainside memorial service at two a.m. that opened this chapter provides an example of the adaptations circus workers made for life on the rails—what historian Stuart Thayer called "rituals of itineracy."[49] Workers and performers mourned and celebrated together through invented and spontaneous acts of care.

Circus workers liked incorporating their livelihood into their sacred rites. In 1905, in the village of Shawneetown, Illinois, Sheak preached a Sunday sermon entitled "I am the Light and the Way" and then performed the wedding of the circus's ballet queen, Irene Schroder, to US Cavalryman James French. The ceremony was held inside a revolving sphere, the Aerial Circle Whirl, that was a part of a circus act and moved at twenty-five miles an hour. The nuptials went smoothly until Sheak "lost his balance and fell overboard, breaking his right arm."[50] When another circus member, Louise Ambrose, one of the horse riders, eloped with performer Grant Humphries, Sheak tracked down the couple and officiated their wedding on the back of an elephant under the Big Top.[51] The circus used Sheak's actions to advertise the circus as moral.

The demands of the show did not allow performers to take a leave of absence when there was a death in the family back home. One journalist captured this challenge of circus life. He reflected after learning the story of one performer: "There is often a sad touch to circus life that the outside public is not aware of." In the dressing room, before a performance, a message arrived for equestrian Gertrude Davis that her mother had died. Despite the devastating news, "Miss Davis put her trained horse 'Sultan' through his act. The audience applauded, not knowing the sorrow the appreciated performer was carrying in her breast."[52] Life on the move prevented circus members from participating in the rituals of mourning and celebration in the same ways that those who were not constantly traveling. They crafted new rituals for life on tour and their circus community when members of the troupe died or married, and within these contexts, circus chaplains like Sheak fulfilled needs similar to those met by military chaplains.

Sheak's chaplaincy with the circus served as an inspiration for other circus chaplains. One of the publicity men from the Robinson Circus followed Sheak into circus ministry and became a popular revival minister known as the circus evangelist. Starting in the late 1920s, at the invitation of John Ringling North, the local Catholic priest in Sarasota, Florida, started blessing the Ringling circus train at the beginning of each season, and later, priests and nuns joined circuses as a part of the Vatican's Traveling Ministries. Just as the US military saw an opportunity to learn from circus logistics, American Christians also found ways to integrate themselves into the circus and to use it well-worn circus pathways for ministry.

Conclusion

The birth of the railroad circus corresponded with the expansion of the American empire westward and across the globe. Through their performances, advertisements, and route books, American railroad circuses produced, circulated, and reinforced ideas about religion in the American West and staged an imagined American colonial empire. Through their displays, menageries, performances, and advertisements, American railroad circuses portrayed a revised history of the American West, circulating images, sounds, and ideas that were simultaneously hegemonic and transgressive. Circuses formed a part of several overlapping global circuits that moved people, animals, and cultures throughout the United States. They commodified animals, bodies, religions, and culture in new ways. Big railroad shows became places of negotiation where Native performers left home, earned a living, saw the world, and critiqued the white world. Religious practices were incorporated into circus life and performances, even as they were transformed to meet the demands of unrelenting travel. By adopting the railroad, showmen propelled the circus into a symbol of the US empire—its prowess, its dazzle, its violence, its logistics, its reach, its precision and timing, and its invention of mass media. The circus was a modernizing project, mobilizing the same impulses that shaped world's fairs, department stores, and art museums. At the center of all these nodal points—animals, Native performers, Christian chaplains, railroads—is the myth of the American West.

Notes

I am grateful for the rich conversations and support for this essay from the Religion in the American West Symposium. I want to thank Jim Bennett, Quincy Newell, Max Greenberg, Jennifer Graber, Lynne Gerber, Rachel Gross, Rachel Lindsay, and especially Brandi Denison, and Brett Hendrickson along with members of the North American Religion Workshop (NARW) at Northwestern University for their extraordinary support and encouragement.

1. Doc Waddel, *Looking Backward Thirty-Three Weeks with a Circus: A Complete History of the John Robinson's Ten Big Shows for the Season of 1905*, 1906, CWB_158, Circus Route Books Digital Collection, Circus World Museum, https://digital.library.illinoisstate.edu/digital/collection/p15990coll5/id/4750, and "Weird Circus Ceremony," *The Plain Speaker* (Hazelton, Pennsylvania), 5.

2. "No Verdict Yet," *Tyrone Daily Herald*, June 2, 1893.

3. To remain financially solvent, circuses usually continued their tours and stayed on schedule even after accidents and the death of troupe members. Cecil B. DeMille's 1952 movie, *The Greatest Show on Earth*, depicts a version of the train wreck near Tyrone and its aftermath.

4. "Circus Memorial Services," *Pittson Gazette* (Pittson, PA), May 22, 1905, 2; *The Sentinel* (Carlisle, PA), June 2, 1905; *The Press Herald* (Pine Grove, PA) June 2, 1905, 3.

5. *Looking Backward Thirty-Three Weeks with a Circus*. There is a question about which branch of the Brethren Rev. Sheak belonged to. The circus publicity listed him as United Brethren, while North Manchester College (now Manchester University) was a Church of the Brethren institution. North Manchester College was founded in 1889 by the United Brethen but then sold to the Church of the Brethen in 1895.

6. *Looking Backward Thirty-Three Weeks with a Circus*.

7. *Looking Backward Thirty-Three Weeks with a Circus*.

8. Kathryn Gin Lum, *Heathen: Religion and Race in American History* (Harvard University Press, 2023), 13. Another description provided by several Pennsylvania local newspapers declared that the "death dance" honored the Lakota Chief Lone Bear, who reportedly died in Dakota. These articles appeared to be press releases from the Robinson Circus's publicity department.

9. *The Virginian-Pilot* (Norfolk, VA), May 23, 1905.

10. L. G. Moses, *Wild West Shows and the Images of American Indians, 1883–1933* (University of New Mexico Press, 1996), 19.

11. See, for example, Patricia Curtin, "Discourses of American Indian Racial Identity in the Public Relations Materials of the Fred Harvey Company: 1902–1936," *Journal of Public Relations Research* 23, no. 4 (October 2011): 368–96; Leah Dilworth, *Imagining Indians in the Southwest: Persistent Visions of a Primitive Past* (Smithsonian Institution Press, 1996), 21–75; and Carey Snyder, "'When the Indian Was in Vogue': D. H. Lawrence, Aldous Huxley, and Ethnological Tourism in the Southwest," *Modern Fiction Studies* 53, no. 4 (Winter 2007): 662. There is additional literature on tourism and Native American use of cultural

tourism for self-determination and representation. See Michelle M. Jacob, "'We Wanted Those People to See That Indians Aren't Stupid': Identity, Representation, and Resistance in the Cultural Tourism of the Wapato Indian Club," *American Indian Quarterly* 36, no. 4 (2012): 465–78; and Doreen E. Martinez, "Wrong Directions and New Maps of Voice, Representation, and Engagement: Theorizing Cultural Tourism, Indigenous Commodities, and the Intelligence of Participation," *American Indian Quarterly* 36, no. 4 (2012): 545.

12. Janet Davis, *The Circus Age: Culture and Society under the American Big Top* (University of North Carolina Press, 2002), 11. The reach of the circus exceeded the borders of North America. Even the earliest circuses traveled widely, taking ships to South America, islands in the Caribbean and Pacific, and Europe.

13. See Robert W. Rydell, *All the World's a Fair: Visions of Empire at American International Expositions, 1876–1916* (University of Chicago Press, 1984), passim.

14. Davis, *Circus Age*, 41.

15. I define "empire" following the work of Tisa Wenger and Sylvester Johnson in their edited volume, *Religion and US Empire: Critical New Histories* (New York University Press, 2023). They describe empire as "a geopolitical system in which one powerful polity controls a large landscape of differentiated and subordinate others." See also Matthew Wittmann, "The Transnational History of the Early American Circus," in *The American Circus*, eds. Susan Weber, Kenneth L. Ames, and Matthew Wittman (Yale University Press, 2012), 54–81; and Davis, *Circus Age*, 47.

16. Davis, *Circus Age*, 11.

17. Linda Simon, *The Greatest Shows on Earth: A History of the Circus* (Reaktion Books, 2014), 101.

18. Pamela E. Klassen, *The Story of Radio Mind: A Missionary's Journey on Indigenous Land* (University of Chicago Press, 2018), 9; Manu Karuka, *Empire's Tracks: Indigenous Nations, Chinese Workers, and the Transcontinental Railroad* (University of California Press, 2019). See also Julia H. Lee, *The Racial Railroad* (New York University Press, 2022).

19. Manu Karuka, *Empire's Tracks: Indigenous Nations, Chinese Workers, and the Transcontinental Railroad* (University of California Press, 2019), 42.

20. See Wenger and Johnson, *Religion and US Empire.*

21. Janet Davis, "The Circus Americanized," in *The American Circus*, eds. Susan Weber, Kenneth L. Ames, and Matthew Wittman (Yale University Press, 2012), 31.

22. Davis, *Circus Age*, 95.

23. Davis, *Circus Age*, 94.

24. Joel R. Parkinson, "The Circus Went to War: Show Business among the Troops in World War I," *Bandwagon* 62, no. 2 (2018): 58–59; Peta Tait, "Animals, Circus, and War Reenactment: Military Action to Colonial Wars, Cambridge Companion to the Circus, ed. Gillian Arrighi and Jim Davis (Cambridge University Press, 2021), 127–40, 33; Pascal Blanchard, Nicolas Bancel, Gilles Boëtsch, Eric Deroo, Sandrine Lemaire, and Charles Forsdick, eds., *Human Zoos: Science and Spectacle in the Age of Colonial Empires*, trans. Teresa Bridgeman (Liverpool University Press, 2004).

25. Cleveland Moffett, "How the Circus Is Put Up and Taken Down," *McClure's* 5, no. 1 (June 1895): 3–14.

26. Timothy Cresswell, *On the Move: Mobility in the Modern Western World* (Routledge, 2006).

27. See Adria L. Imada, *Aloha America: Hula Circuits through the U.S. Empire* (Duke University Press, 2012), 10.

28. P. T. Barnum, *The Life of P. T. Barnum* (Redfield, 1855). Baltimore hosted a similar event the following year with "a party of Indians." See *The Buffalo Commercial*, May 10, 1844, 3. Entrepreneur Sydney Barnett recruited "Wild Bill" Hickok for a Grand Buffalo Hunt at Niagara Falls in 1872.

29. Steve Inskeep, "The Remarkable Life of Jessie Benton Frémont," *The Atlantic*, January 12, 2020, www.theatlantic.com/ideas/archive/2020/01/first-celebrity-first-lady/604003.

30. Fremont later served as the military governor of California and supported the US–Mexico war. See "John Charles Frémont: Ad Man for Manifest Destiny," Utah Stories from the Beehive Archive, October 24, 2014, www.utahhumanities.org/stories/items/show/281.

31. Elizabeth Broun, "Forward," *The West as America: Reinterpreting Images of the Frontier, 1820–1920*, ed. William H. Truettner (Smithsonian Institution Press, 1991), viii.

32. Howard R. Lamar, "An Overview of Westward Expansion," in *The West as America: Reinterpreting Images of the Frontier, 1820–1920*, ed. William H. Truettner (Smithsonian Institution Press, 1991), 7.

33. Chang Reynolds, *Pioneer Circuses of the West* (Westernlore Press, 1966), 19.

34. Chang Reynolds, *Pioneer Circuses of the West*, 18.

35. Davis, *Circus Age*, 8.

36. L. G. Moses, *Wild West Shows*, 19.

37. P. T. Barnum, *The Life of PT Barnum: Written by Himself, Including His Golden Rules for Money-Making, Brought up to 1888* (Courier Company Printers, 1888), 67–68. Barnum first recruited members of the Sac and Fox tribes to perform traditional dances in small traveling shows and at his famous New York City Museum.

38. "Washburn's Colossal American Circus and Indian Amphitheatre," *Charleston Daily Courier* (Charleston, SC), December 24, 1855, 5.

39. L. G. Moses, *Wild West Shows*; and Linda Scarangella McNenly, "Foe, Friend, or Critic: Native Performers with Buffalo Bill's Wild West Show and Discourses of Conquest and Friendship in Newspaper Reports," *American Indian Quarterly* 38, no. 2 (Spring 2014): 143–76, at 160.

40. "The Great Central Park Menagerie, International Circus an Iroquois Indian Troupe, *New York Clipper*, April 13, 1872.

41. Frank S. Redmond, *Season of 1891 Official Route Book of the Adam Forepaugh Shows: Presenting a Condensed Resume of the Principal Events, Interesting Items and Valuable Records of the Movements of the Organization* (1891), SPC_005, Circus Route Books Digital Collection, Special Collections, Milner Library, Illinois State University, 30.

42. Louis S. Warren, *Buffalo Bill's America: William Cody and the Wild West Show* (Vintage Books, 2005), 229.

43. "Move to Change Methodist Ban on Dancing and Amusements," *New York Times*, September 2, 1923. Reporters delighted in the contradiction of a minister—a Methodist minister, no less—leaving the ministry for the forbidden circus. The circus's publicity team capitalized on the novelty, planting stories across the United States to highlight the chaplain's presence.

44. Janet Davis, *The Circus Age*, 17; Linda Simon, *The Greatest Shows on Earth: A History of the Circus* (Reaktion Books, 2014), 23.

45. Simon, *The Greatest Shows on Earth*, 23.

46. "Reverend: W. H. Sheak Becomes Circus Chaplain," *Daily Republican-Register* (Mount Carmel, IL), July 27, 1903, 1.

47. The 1906 John Robinson Route Book records crowd numbers for many of the Sundays Sheak preached. Many of the services attracted thousands.

48. Scott C. Zeman, ed., *Scatter the Believers: Chasing the Ghosts of the American West* (University of Nebraska Press, 2014), 10.

49. Stuart Thayer, *Traveling Showmen: The Circus before the Civil War* (Astley & Ricketts, 1997).

50. *Looking Backward Thirty-Three Weeks with a Circus*, 67.

51. *Looking Backward Thirty-Three Weeks with a Circus*, 27–28.

52. "Circus Was a Good One," *Burlington Free Press*, June 28, 1905, 9.

Chapter 10

To Always Be Better Neighbors

How the Japanese Episcopal Mission Leveraged Americanization in Exclusion-Era California

CHRISSY YEE LAU

Keywords: Japanese American, Episcopal or Protestant Christianity, Americanization, Alien Land Law, California

In the midst of the Great Depression, Reverend John Misao Yamazaki held two celebrations for the opening of the newly built hall of St. Mary's Japanese Episcopal Mission in Pico Heights, California. The first ceremony was an informal celebration for the Japanese American community in February of 1932. The church and the community were overjoyed to finally see a large hall—a project that cost over $100,000 and had taken several years to complete—dedicated to the spiritual and cultural nourishment of the second-generation youth. Members of the church, who for years had been eager to build larger facilities to accommodate their new Americanization programs for youth attendees, were glad to be working in a glorious new building instead of squeezing their class into the church bus or teaching outside on a small lawn. At the ceremony, program leaders—including teachers from the well-attended kindergarten and Sunday school, organizers of the Girl Scouts and Boy Scouts, and a representative of the Gakuen board of trustees for the Japanese language school—gave addresses. Community organizations that had long invested in the uplift of second-generation youth also offered their congratulations, including the local Japanese immigrant newspaper, the Japanese Chamber of Commerce, and Southern California Education Society. That night, as an example of their bicultural approach to Americanization, attendees enjoyed an entertainment program that included arts and music ranging from Japanese dances to a short reel of the American cartoon *Felix*.[1]

A second, more formal dedication followed in October, a ceremony for the dignitaries and white friends of the Episcopal church. They were glad to see a new building dedicated to the Japanese Episcopal Mission, which had done so much to work toward resolving "the Japanese Question." For years, they had been impressed with the large number of attendees at their little mission and stressed that the Christianization of Japanese immigrants had done much to ease the animosities stirred by the anti-Japanese movement. Members of the building committee included white Episcopalian friends who gave donations to the church, as well as significant representatives of the Japanese American communities across Los Angeles who had a vested interest in the new building for their youth. On the day of the ceremony, among the dignitaries of the Episcopal denomination who gave addresses were the bishop of Los Angeles, the Standing Committee of the Diocese, and the Dean of St. Paul's Cathedral. Members of the vestry, all Japanese American Christian leaders, were present.[2]

The new building of St. Mary's Japanese Episcopal Mission and the various community interests at stake change our understanding of the religious history of California in the interwar period. Although scholars have framed this period as one of continual migration and religious diversity, the story of St. Mary's Japanese Episcopal Mission renarrates it as a period of migration restriction and religious homogeneity. Eldon Ernst has noted that twentieth-century California was a place of religious pluralism and diversity, particularly in the Progressive Era, when new migrants brought new religions. By the 1920s and 1930s, however, restrictive immigration policies stifled the addition of foreign-born peoples and shifted new migration patterns.[3] Darren Dochuk, for instance, has examined the Sunbelt migration from the South to California during the Great Depression, which he argues reflected the broader essence of faith in California: a sojourning spirit, a predilection for politics, and the ability to adapt to new technology.[4]

The story of the Japanese Episcopal Mission, however, highlights the racial tensions and conflicts that arose within US empire-building, between new white migrants from the East Coast and the Japanese immigrants who were disenfranchised from the body politic. This research builds on Kathryn Gin Lum's history of religious othering through the paradigm of the heathen by showing how anti-Japanese groups applied the term to Japanese immigrant neighbors.[5] As previous scholars like Brian Hayashi have also shown, Japanese American Christians approached Americanization not simply as assimilation but as a means to achieve their political ends.[6] The politics of assimilation played out in neighborhood squabbles and church-building disputes, serving as a precursor to what Becky Nicolaides and James Zarsadiaz coin "design assimilation," when, in the 1970s, ethnic settlers moved into predominantly white neighborhoods and consented to existing design mores, making their presence scarcely visible.[7] I show that by the 1920s, Yamazaki developed a politics of Americanization that intertwined the religious and racial uplift of Japanese immigrants. He urged Japanese immigrants to be "better neighbors":

a religious uplift project whereby Japanese immigrant residents should carefully abide by aspirational white middle-class aesthetics and homeownership practices to maintain an amiable yet unequal relationship. Their stories show that, as much as California is celebrated for its religious pluralism and racial diversity, in actuality it was not as celebratory of difference as presumed. In line with other authors in this volume—Joshua Paddison and James Bennett, who both highlight how California was not a paradise of racial harmony and religious freedom—my essay argues that whiteness and Protestant Christianity continued to unequally define and shape the contours of Japanese American Protestant life and religious freedom.

This chapter explores how the Japanese Episcopal Mission navigated anti-Japanese sentiment to build a church to serve the Japanese American Christian community in Los Angeles during the first three decades of the twentieth century. The mission faced both a liberal administration that consistently underfunded its evangelical efforts and anti-Japanese housing movements that limited its constituency. The story of the Japanese Episcopal Mission reveals three shifts in organized immigrant religion under the US empire in the interwar period: investing in the next generation, turning toward the secular, and developing an uplift politics as a means to an end. First, despite the 1924 immigration act and alien land laws, Japanese immigrant Protestant churches grew. Although no new migrants entered the neighborhood, the church focused its attention toward the next generation of youth. Second, the church turned toward Americanization as the primary means for expanding Christian principles. This shift points to an important way of understanding California religious history as a story of secularism: Dimensions of what had been considered Christian were recast as racial and socioeconomic tenets during the period of anti-Asian exclusion.[8] Finally, Yamazaki developed a politics and language of uplift of immigrants and Americanization that incentivized white allies to view Japanese American interests as aligned with their own.

A Fledgling Mission

In 1913, missionary and founder Mary Louise Paterson chose to relocate the Japanese Episcopal Mission to 961 South Mariposa Avenue, a house in Pico Heights in a largely wealthy white suburb west of downtown Los Angeles, because she wanted to work with the small population of Japanese immigrant families who resided there. Incorporated into the city of Los Angeles seventeen years earlier, Pico Heights envisioned and proudly promoted itself as an all-white neighborhood. Newspaper advertisements touted Pico Heights as the "finest location for a home around Los Angeles" and attracted what they called the "best class of citizens."[9] Not only did state laws like the California Alien

Land Law of 1913 ensure that no Japanese immigrants would be able to purchase land, but the city also successfully blocked Black property owners' attempts to create an elder home for Black residents. However, white landowners began to outsource the gardening labor for their craftsman homes. John Modell argues that many white homeowners preferred to hire Japanese immigrant laborers because, like European immigrant laborers, they were nonunionized and willing to work long hours. As a result, by 1919, about one hundred Japanese families lived in Pico Heights.[10]

The 1920 census shows a range of Japanese immigrants residing on South Mariposa Avenue, including gardeners. Zempachi John Murasaki, a gardener, lived there with his wife Mitsu and their two children as renters. Saburow Karashima, also a gardener rented a home on the same street with his wife and two children. The Kawata family also lived on Mariposa Ave, where the father worked as a gardener, and after his death the mother worked in a laundry to support their two daughters.

Not all residents were families. Another house was rented by a farmer from the Imperial Valley, Kurata Kavanami, who lived with a number of boarders, including gardeners—some single and others were married but living apart from their wives.[11] A single man, Sengaro Kehara, also rented on Mariposa Avenue and worked as a gardener. Another single man, Kei Nakadegawa, had worked as a gardener on South Mariposa Avenue before moving to Long Beach to work in produce.

Nor were all residents gardeners. Seitaro Ishihara, a fisherman, rented a home on Mariposa Avenue with his wife Shinako and their three children. Chester Kaichiro Nagao, a dentist, lived there with his wife Yoshiko. Daisuke Iwataki, an insurance agent, resided on South Mariposa Avenue with his wife and two children.[12]

The Board of Missions had discussions about self-support and the hiring of Japanese clergy to lead their congregations, and Paterson knew just the right candidate. A majority of her pupils were young Japanese schoolboys, students who had come to the United States intending to pursue a western education.[13] One of them, John Misao Yamazaki, who hailed from a wealthy and highly educated family and had his first encounters with Christ Church in Japan, immigrated to the United States in 1904 in hopes of studying medicine at an American university.[14] After studying the Bible with Paterson, he was sponsored in 1909 to attend Berkeley Divinity School in Connecticut. After finishing his seminary training, Yamazaki moved to Los Angeles in 1913 to become the vicar at the Japanese Episcopal Mission.

Between 1914 and 1920, Yamazaki focused on evangelizing the local residents in and around Pico Heights. In that first year of his priesthood, he recorded that sixty souls—eight families and twenty-eight individuals—attended

Figure 10.1 Reverend John Yamazaki. Courtesy of Thomas R. Guzman.

the Japanese Episcopal Mission.[15] Because most Japanese immigrants were Buddhist, Yamazaki offered services that met immigrants' practical needs as a way of introducing them to Christianity. The mission provided educational and community services, including English classes, Bible studies, men's clubs, and women's charity and home-economics groups.[16] Bible classes were held two evenings a week and drew about twenty attendees.[17] Other ways to attract attendees, particularly women, included offering classes in cooking and dressmaking. While the women gathered to sew garments for poorer Japanese immigrants, Yamazaki preached from the Bible.

Yamazaki aimed to expand the church through opening a kindergarten in 1916.[18] The progressive movement endorsed kindergartens as key to social and educational reform among poor immigrants, but Yamazaki also believed they played a special role in evangelizing Japanese immigrant families. First, a kindergarten grew out of a local need: many working parents needed daycare but did not have extended family to care for their children. They also could not enroll their children in public schools because, as Yamazaki explained, the children did not speak English. Nor did the teachers speak Japanese. Second, while the kindergarten helped to fill this gap in the

Figure 10.2 Japanese Episcopal Mission, June 1, 1913. Courtesy of Thomas R. Guzman.

community's domestic care, it also served as a form of outreach to non-Christian families. By 1916, the kindergarten enrolled thirty-two pupils in the morning and fourteen in the afternoon each day, and the Sunday school also had forty-three pupils.[19]

In 1917, Yamazaki appealed to the Episcopal Church to hire an "American teacher"—implicitly a white teacher—for the kindergarten and Sunday school, arguing that the children were American born. "If the Church backs the work," he pleaded, "many American-born Japanese will be Christianized and Americanized through the Church."[20] The Church's researchers likewise proposed kindergartens as a way "to bridge the gap between the foreign-language family and the American public schools," believing the kindergarten to be the most effective way of spreading Christian influence.[21] However, the Episcopal Church refused to fund a salaried employee for either their kindergarten or Sunday school. Yamazaki considered shutting down the program because it had put them in debt, especially because they used an expensive automobile to pick up children and then return them to their homes.

Mary Louise Paterson, the original founder of the Japanese Episcopal Mission, had been their biggest advocate and openly criticized Episcopal leaders for their lack of support. Since spearheading the mission, she had repeatedly requested financial assistance. In 1906, for instance, at the Los Angeles Assembly, Paterson asked for assistance in servicing the five thousand Japanese immigrants in Los Angeles.[22] For years, the Woman's Auxiliary had provided funding to the mission; they purchased the property in Pico Heights and donated it to the mission. With the request for funding for the kindergarten, Paterson argued that their work was of the utmost importance because they wanted to teach these children "all that is best in American Christian civilization."[23] In 1919, the Women's Auxiliary again provided funds and hired a Japanese teacher for the Sunday school. Just a year later, the mission had a thriving Sunday school, where the church reported five teachers and eighty-six pupils in Sunday school.[24] Other constituents of the Japanese Episcopal Mission included twenty-nine families and twenty-five individuals.[25]

Paterson continued to plead for more resources for their small church and plot of land, which were quickly being outgrown by the increasing number of attendees and the needs of their leadership. She argued that there should be a national campaign for evangelizing Asian immigrants but that there had been very little interest in doing so.[26]

On paper, Los Angeles Episcopal Church leaders conveniently praised the value of the evangelical work of the Japanese Episcopal Mission as the tense political climate in California centered on Japanese immigration. As the anti-Japanese movement mobilized to renew the California alien land law and support a national immigration act that restricted Japanese immigration, church leaders pointed to the Christian work at the Japanese Episcopal Mission as a solution to anti-Japanese racism. Thomas C. Marshall, archdeacon of the Missions of Los Angeles, believed that to combat anti-Japanese propaganda, which provoked hostility between white and Japanese peoples, "The promotion of mutual understanding and sympathy between the two races by the spread of Christianity among the Japanese seems to be the only alternative to strife and possible war." By placing the burden of maintaining peace onto one underresourced mission, leaders paid lip service to their evangelical work toward Japanese immigrants, noting, "The quality of the work of Saint Mary's is of the highest, its inadequacy to the situation is of course apparent."[27] In practice, however, Yamazaki witnessed firsthand that Episcopal leaders were very wrong: The Christian conversion of Japanese peoples would not resolve white racism so long as the anti-Japanese movement could mentally map Japanese immigrants as the latest iteration of the heathen.

Anti-Japanese Eviction Crusades

The heathen, as religious studies scholar Kathryn Gin Lum argues, is a form of religious othering that shapes the American's self-identification as exceptional or civilized. Heathen implies the attendant racialization of the non-white inferior against the white Christian superior. Lum suggests that "heathen" is best understood as an elastic category that can stretch to include different groups across history—a process she calls the "replacement narrative." By the end of the nineteenth century, the concept of heathenism fundamentally shaped American racial governance: It became the rationale for why Chinese people were supposedly different, why Americans were deemed exceptional, and why Chinese immigrants should be excluded from the body politic. Although the term became outdated by the twentieth century, the mental maps through which Americans envisioned the heathen did not disappear but were reborn.[28] In the case of Japanese immigrants during the interwar period, the term "heathen" was not used as explicitly as it had been with Chinese immigrants, but its characterizations and associations were projected onto Japanese communities to justify their exclusion.

Historian Charlotte Brooks argues that by 1920, the shifting racial and class composition of Pico Heights had resulted in a particular kind of Los Angeles nativism based on housing segregation. Middle-class residents no longer desired to live in Pico Heights; the dentists, lawyers, bookkeepers, and small businessmen who originally purchased homes in the area were largely replaced by laborers, clerks, laundrymen, and chauffeurs. Fewer and fewer residents owned their homes, and more and more rented. As growing numbers of Southern and Eastern Europeans, Mexicans, and Catholic Angelenos moved in, anti-Japanese groups attracted working-class white residents by speaking to their burning resentment toward middle-class whites who "dumped" Japanese immigrants into their neighborhoods.[29] Within this socioeconomic context, new migrants rehearsed older ideas of the heathen into a secular project around race and housing. The common slur "Jap" became a religious and racial epithet that encompassed a catch-all of any and all qualities deemed excludable and unsavable.

Recent newcomers to Pico Heights allied themselves with anti-Japanese groups through an emerging narrative that Japanese immigrants were "dirty renters." For instance, Guy H. Duffey, who had recently migrated from Chicago to Pico Heights in 1920 and was a member of the Roman Catholic church, arrived to find a prevailing anti-Japanese sentiment among his neighbors.[30] Many of these residents complained that "they were so dirty in their homes," calling the health department to inspect their homes and enforce regulations. Duffey explained: "They don't take care for any of the places where they live. They are a detriment to the property because they can't buy and they have no interest and don't care for the places."[31] Reasoning that "property went all to smash" and that "when the Japs came nobody wanted to live next to them," Duffey took it upon himself to clean up the neighborhood to achieve his ideal of a white-only city. He formed the Pico Heights Protective Association, a makeshift group that utilized political avenues and intimidation tactics to kick out and keep out Japanese immigrants.

First, the Association formed a neighborhood campaign to evict Japanese immigrants currently residing on Mariposa Avenue. Association members pressured white homeowners who rented to Japanese tenants, asking them to quietly terminate those leases and rent instead to white tenants. Some white homeowners participated, but others balked at the cost of renovating their properties for white renters. To resolve this, the Association often cut a deal where they would fix up the homes themselves, evict the Japanese tenants, and manage the new white rentals until repair costs were recuperated, at which point the properties were handed back to the original owners. As a result of such organizing, between 100 and 250 Japanese immigrant families were displaced.[32] Anti-Japanese crusaders took pride in having evicted Japanese immigrants "legally" and maintained that white neighbors acted "civilly" during the commotion. Its success, however, was often temporary. Other property owners remembered that the white families who moved in ended up unhappy with the rental conditions and demanded more improvements. When their demands were not met by the landlord, they moved out, and Japanese immigrant families moved back in.[33]

Second, the Pico Heights Protective Association spearheaded direct opposition to a proposed Japanese church, arguing that Christianity was an avenue for Japanese immigrants to circumvent the Alien Land Law. Between 1922 and 1923, the Japanese Methodist Episcopal Church, sought to build their sanctuary in Pico Heights. They decided on a primary location at 13th and New Hampshire streets, a central hub where all the car lines met, four churches stood next to small businesses and stores, and about 150 Japanese families lived nearby. Shortly after the property was purchased, anti-Japanese residents campaigned against the project, claiming that it would attract undesirable Japanese immigrants. In response, Methodist Episcopal leader Dr. Herbert Johnson categorized the congregation as the "superior type of Japanese." To reassure those who feared the church would attract a "lower class" of residents, he asserted, "We don't intend to cater to that class; our members belong to the better class, such as clerks, bank tellers, lawyers, and doctors, etc."[34]

Echoing similar arguments made against the "heathen Chinese" decades earlier, Duffey argued that Japanese immigrants converted to Christianity only as a method for "takeover." Duffey claimed, "Their religion is the religion of the Mikado; the Mikado isn't just a human being to them, he is Christ on earth. They are born with that religion and that is always their religion at heart." Doubting the sincerity of Japanese immigrants' conversion to Christianity, Duffey reasoned, "If they ever adopt any other religion, they do it for some ulterior motive, not because they really believe any other way. A Jap is always a Jap at heart."[35] At a neighborhood meeting, Duffey protested to Dr. Johnson, "I don't believe you can ever Christianize those people anyway—they are too ignorant." The Pico Heights Protective Association warned that Japanese immigrants were only using the Methodist Episcopal church to evade the Alien Land Law and that if the church was successful, "Pico Heights will, in a short time, become a Jap stronghold."[36] Locally, the group began to circulate a petition and intimidated other white neighbors into signing—or, as one reverend put it when he refused, they would see to it that "life was made very miserable in that community."[37] The association also convinced the Los Angeles City Council to deny the permit, forcing the Methodist Episcopalians to abandon their plans to build a Japanese church.

The Pico Heights Protective Association mirrored widespread anti-Japanese campaigns across Los Angeles. The Los Angeles Anti-Asiatic Association issued a citywide statement that claimed Japanese churches were intended to serve as an "opening wedge to Oriental invasion of white men's homes."[38] Many did not believe their stance against the Japanese church was un-Christian. Rather, the directors argued that Japanese immigrants used Christianity as "a door to force themselves forward in material and social ways." They still maintained Japanese immigrants should become Christians but not use their faith as a tool to demand civil rights, such as neighborhood integration. Comparatively, they argued, no other group—including Chinese, Koreans, Blacks, Mexicans, and Europeans—asked for "social recognition because of their faith." As a result, they doubted the "sincerity" of Japanese immigrants' conversion to Christianity. Members of the Los Angeles Anti-Asiatic Association not only sought to prevent the construction of churches for Japanese immigrants but also submitted a resolution that supported the immigration bill that would prohibit entry for "aliens ineligible for citizenship."[39]

The anti-Japanese campaigns in Pico Heights and across Los Angeles exemplify how white migrants utilized the enduring tropes of the "heathen" to disenfranchise a group based on religion through neighborhood segregation and national exclusion. It is part of the larger history of twentieth-century secularism, whereby the "heathen" was reborn as the slur "Jap"—an unchanging, conniving machine incapable of conversion. White migrants reapplied earlier mental maps of "heathen Chinese" as a means to mobilize and achieve Japanese exclusion. The actual impact of such religious othering not only successfully prevented the building of new Japanese churches as well as home rentals to Japanese immigrants but also made it very difficult for churches already present in the neighborhood—like Yamazaki's—to perform their religious work among the Japanese immigrants still residing in the area.

Yamazaki, too, had repeated the narrative that Japanese immigrants were "dirty," especially in formal conversation with his white Christian counterparts. In 1924, Chloe Holt, a sociologist from the *Survey of Race Relations*, reported that when Yamazaki and his wife Mary first arrived at the Japanese Episcopal Mission Church in Los Angeles 1913, "They were very disappointed in the way the Japanese were living—they were so dirty." In one example, the Yamazakis held a social gathering one evening at the church, where they served bananas, but when the Japanese guests finished, they threw the peelings on the floor. Yamazaki commented, "It was awful. I had to ask them to pick the peelings up." However, he later shared that they were "doing better now." Yamazaki may have purposefully rebuked Japanese immigrants to Holt to safely distance himself from being racialized as "dirty," but he also used such examples as a way to show the need for Christian ministering. In a noted difference from the perspective of anti-Japanese crusaders, Yamazaki believed that Japanese immigrants could be racially uplifted through the work of his church.

When he was interviewed about the anti-Japanese housing crusades in Pico Heights, Yamazaki's opinions were mixed. At the time the Japanese renters were being evicted, Yamazaki did attempt to appeal on their behalf. He called upon the property owners who planned to evict Japanese renters and asked if they had failed to meet their payments. Many admitted they were "good tenants," but Yamazaki witnessed about 20 percent of the families get evicted. Still, Yamazaki thought it was "a mistake" to build a second Japanese church in that district since his own church had been there for ten years. He may have believed a second church would have brought unnecessary agitation to an already brewing anti-Japanese landscape, or he may have considered the Japanese Episcopal Methodists as competition. Still, his church was growing. By 1924, Yamazaki recorded ninety-eight baptized members, including thirty-two families and thirty individuals.[40] But Yamazaki did not believe the anti-Japanese crusades had any foundation for their arguments that the churches might bring more Japanese residents into their neighborhoods. He argued that the Japanese immigrants could only find residences where owners would be willing to rent to them, and the churches had nothing to do with it. In fact, Yamazaki guided the residents of Mariposa Avenue, Christian or not, on how to guard against eviction and maintain a hospitable environment for his church.

Residents of South Mariposa Ave formed the Mutual Betterment Association to discuss and define how to navigate white racism in their neighborhood. During the eviction crusades, Yamazaki held a meeting for the association at his church. In line with the larger community call for "emergency uplift," Yamazaki urged the residents of Mariposa to assimilate themselves into the aesthetics of white suburban homeownership culture to placate and disarm anti-Japanese opposition. Yamazaki added a list of these practices as the eighth section of the association's bylaws, which focused on "overcoming prejudice" by becoming "better neighbors" and maintaining a "reputation for cleanness."[41] These bylaws outlined what Japanese immigrant residents should and should not do according to the social preferences of white suburbanites—often at the expense of the residents' own time and labor, lest they risk expulsion from their neighborhood. Yamazaki's approach toward suburban practices operated similarly to the case described by Quincy Newell's research in this volume on Latter-day Saints, who pursued a strategy of outward Protestant secularization while maintaining their distinctiveness.

Many of the bylaws were created in direct response to the complaints of white neighbors. For example, Myrtle Eldred, a music teacher and member of the American Methodist Church, explained that while her Japanese pupils were among her best students, the Japanese immigrants "do not as a rule do enough to make their homes attractive." She recalled that the Japanese district was among the poorest of neighborhoods, and the houses were rather "miserable little shacks." She complained, "The Japanese did very little to improve the appearance of the houses in which they live." However, Eldred believed, "If they kept their front yards up nicely, the Americans would not object to them so much."[42] As a result, to build an alliance with white Christians, the first bylaw added to the new eighth section was: "To keep the front lawn and back yard always green and clean and most beautiful."

White neighbors also complained to Yamazaki about the Japanese neighbors gathering and socializing at the mission and around the neighborhood, which they viewed as noisy disruptions. If Japanese families had guests who lingered on the front steps for a few minutes as they were leaving, or if they started their automobiles or motorcycles at night, neighbors would file a complaint with Yamazaki. Further, if a party continued after 9 p.m., the neighbors complained to Yamazaki. Consequently, Yamazaki wrote bylaw no. 3—"To take utmost care not to give any disturbance to the neighbors," which established a rule of "strict quietness after 10 p.m. and before 6 a.m." Prohibited activities included "no music, singing or phonograph or playing of any musical instruments or dancing or starting of automobiles during the afore-described hours!" Exceptions were made for American holidays such as Christmas, New Year's Eve, and Halloween. Although Yamazaki warned Japanese immigrants to limit their socializing, he recognized that white neighbors' complaints were hypocritical because they often had parties that lasted until one in the morning.[43]

Community responses to this bylaw were mixed. Many stopped attending the services because they could not perform their regular activities at the church. For instance, Yamazaki started a young men's club that met in the evenings. When they would make speeches to one another and clap, or when they played music, neighbors called the church immediately to complain. When Yamazaki told the club members to be quieter, saying, "You must not do this, you must not do that," many of them stopped attending. Yamazaki felt that anti-Japanese sentiment obstructed his work within the community.

Yamazaki did at times feel that the church played a limited role in resolving neighborhood disputes. Some residents refused to acquiesce to neighbors' complaints. One time, a maternity home complained to Yamazaki about Japanese neighbors whose dog kept barking at night while the couple worked at their café. When Yamazaki reminded the couple that the maternity home also served Japanese mothers, they argued that they had as much right as anyone to keep a dog to guard their house. Yamazaki concluded, "That doesn't look as though the church has any great influence in regulating the lives of the Japanese people."[44]

Nevertheless, Yamazaki believed that the residents needed to do all they could to maintain a public "reputation for cleanness." It was quite common to hear both white and Japanese elites complain about how Japanese farmers and gardeners appeared "so dirty" in public. Yamazaki recognized that most residents were gardeners and that their jobs required a certain amount of dirt. However, he believed that when they were not working—and instead running errands around town, such as going to the bank—they should change out of their work clothes and wear more presentable garments. Accordingly, Yamazaki also included as bylaw no. 5: "To dress decently according to American custom. Laboring apparels must be changed with decent street clothes when one go [*sic*] out except in time of actual working."[45]

Yamazaki abided by his own bylaw. In July 1924, Yamazaki tried to make a favorable impression during his interview with sociologist Chloe Holt for the *Survey of Race Relations*. When Holt arrived at the Japanese Episcopal Mission, Yamazaki suggested they conduct the interview at his home behind the church. While Holt drove over to his home, Yamazaki ran across the yard, quickly changed into dress clothes; as Holt described, he "looked immaculate" when he stepped in to welcome her. Holt further observed that Yamazaki's home was "very clean and the living room attractively furnished," noting that "it looked much the same as the home of the average middle-class American family." She even caught a glimpse into Yamazaki's kitchen, and described that "it looked clean and in perfect order."[46] Holt's confirmation of Yamazaki's cleanliness—or as she put it, "he certainly practices what he preaches"—served to show how Yamazaki's efforts built an alliance with the sociologist during a particularly egregious period of local anti-Japanese housing evictions.

Just as he maintained the community's public reputation through an immaculate personal appearance, Yamazaki ensured that the larger narrative of the Japanese Episcopal Mission was one of exceptionality. When Episcopal church leaders came to visit, they were also impressed. In his 1924 report to the Board of Missions, Bishop Joseph Johnson proudly praised the mission: "When the bishops visit the congregation for parish festivals and confirmations, they are always impressed with the large congregations, including some of the most influential Japanese citizens of Los Angeles. The number of young Japanese men identified with the mission is exceptionally large."[47] Buoyed by the pastoral care of Yamazaki and the residents of South Mariposa Avenue, the Board of Missions could boast of the church's success to the larger Episcopal community. Yamazaki would soon leverage this perception of the mission as "a solution to the Japanese Question" to ensure that leadership moved beyond simply paying lip service to their cause.

Toward Americanization of the Next Generation, 1924–1931

In the post-1924 period, as anti-Japanese eviction crusades waned, Yamazaki refocused his efforts on Americanizing the youth. Yamazaki turned toward the younger generation for several reasons. First, mirroring other Japanese immigrant businesses and organizations that had largely appealed to and serviced the first generation, he wondered how he could draw in the youth as new consumers or constituents in order to expand their franchises or institutions. Second, Yamazaki found shared values with other Japanese American parents who believed Christianity was the best vehicle for Americanization. Many worried about their children adopting what they viewed as "bad" forms of Americanization, like truancy, gambling, or excessive dancing. Finally, Yamazaki found institutional support in other youth programs like the Boy Scouts and the Girl Reserves, which also attracted youth invested in racial uplift. These new programs by Christian organizations also mirrored a general societal turn toward Americanizing the youth, which many viewed as a solution to widespread racism. For these reasons, Yamazaki was able to attract a larger congregation made up mostly of young people.

Yamazaki embraced American institutionalization by adopting youth clubs to obtain resources for his church and community. This acceptance stands in contrast to John Garcia's research in this volume, which discusses how nineteenth-century Penitentes fiercely resisted American institutionalization by maintaining performative Hispano Catholic rituals during the transition between Mexican and US control. The difference can be explained by the expansion of US and Japanese empires by the early twentieth century, the impact of US exclusion, and Yamazaki's approach to Americanization as a strategic religious endeavor to grow his church during a period of immigration exclusion. While the mission continued to run children's programs that serviced the needs of the immigrant community, it also added new ones that began to shape the next generation's values. As before, Yamazaki continued established services, including a daily kindergarten of fifty children and a Sunday school with an enrollment of 250 children. Yamazaki also created new services such as a daily afternoon parish school with seventy pupils, a young citizens' club of sixty, a troop of Boy Scouts, and candidates' classes of the Girls' Friendly Society and Girls' Reserve.[48] However, Yamazaki practiced a bicultural approach to Americanization. For example, the mission offered a Japanese language school where children could learn their parents' native tongue. Publicly, Yamazaki argued that if he did not provide these lessons, the children would seek them elsewhere, perhaps at a Buddhist temple, and not be Americanized as well.

The Americanization efforts impressed local neighbors. By 1924, the mission had about twelve teachers and served 135 pupils in its kindergarten.[49] The church gathered children between the ages of two and a half years old to five, picking them up in an automobile and bringing them to the church. One neighbor, McLellan, who lived across the street from the church and had business dealings with many of the Japanese gardeners, found their kindergarten favorable. He observed that they had hung many American flags and never closed their services until they sang "America."[50] He further recalled that the mission took great care to teach the children to respect others' properties: "The lady next door spoke to the minister one day about the children getting into her lawn . . . He spoke to the children right away and told them they must stay right in their own place, and I have never heard any other objection. They are very careful to keep them on their property."[51] From then on, Yamazaki made every effort to ensure the children stayed on their own grounds.

By the late 1920s, several Americanization clubs and troops had formed at the Japanese Episcopal Mission. The St. Mary's Boys and Girls Club expanded into different clubs, including Boy Scouts, Knights of Chi Beta, Girl Reserves, the Cherry Club, and the Chrysanthemum Club.[52] They planned camping and beach trips, had dinners, performed plays and sang choir, viewed moving pictures, celebrated American holidays, listened to speakers visiting from Japan, and gave benefit programs for their camping trips.[53] The Girls' Friendly Society, an Episcopal organization for young girls, worked with the Girl Reserves, a movement to empower girls through the YWCA, to create a space for young girls.[54]

Figure 10.3 Daily kindergarten at Japanese Episcopal Mission, March 1, 1930. Courtesy of Thomas R. Guzman.

While these services drew a large youth crowd, the mission outgrew its space, using every room at their disposal. Yamazaki explained, "Four classes are taught in the Mission House, three large classes in the Parish Hall, one in the bus, a large kindergarten class out in the yard and one in Miss Morehouse's apartment. Sometimes a class is held in the rector's parlor or dining room, and even in the garage."[55] Because of the increasing number of youth clubs, the parish hall could only accommodate a limited range of games, including football, ping-pong, and boxing.[56] Members looked forward to the day when they could meet in their own club rooms or a gymnasium suited for their games.[57]

By 1927, Yamazaki spearheaded a fundraising campaign calling on the Episcopal Church to financially support the mission's work of Americanizing second-generation youth. He reasoned with the larger Diocese of Los Angeles that the community, "instead of resenting the passage of the anti-Japanese laws, which certainly make it rather hard on them, [is] rather inclined to accept them as a challenge." He stated that Japanese immigrants "are sincerely trying to have their second generation brought up in the Church, in order that they may be good American citizens, and to prove by them what they will be in the future, that they are not such undesirable and unassimilating people."[58] Highlighting the church as the main site in which the youth could learn how to become good citizens, Yamazaki urgently asked the Episcopal Church to grant the mission's request for $10,000. He also created and mailed pamphlets to illustrate the Japanese Episcopal Mission's Americanization efforts. Their pages were adorned with pictures of the kindergarten, the Sunday school, the Boy Scouts, the Girl Scouts, and the Knights of Christ Kingdom, and readers were invited to submit donations.[59]

By 1931, the appeal based on Americanization succeeded, and Yamazaki was able to raise long-overdue funds for a new church. He first secured $15,000 from his own congregation; moreover, even members of the immigrant generation who did not attend services saw the mission's value for their children and pledged one month's salary.[60] Matching the generosity of these pledges made by Japanese immigrants, white Episcopalians across the diocese gave as well.[61] Bishop Joseph H. Johnson contributed $15,000 to build a new parish hall.[62] Other donors included Mr. and Mrs. Thomas Fleming, who gave $15,000 in cash and parish furniture. Additionally, Mrs. Fleming personally donated a new rectory with a cash value of $40,000. The National Council also promised $15,000, supplemented by $5,000 from the Trew Memorial Fund.[63] This was a victory for Yamazaki, who had finally secured the Episcopal funds needed to build a larger church; however, another daunting task lay ahead: obtaining a building permit from the city.

An Exigent Politics, 1930s

When Yamazaki submitted his building permit to the city, neighborhood associations once again decried a "Japanese takeover" and attempted to block the application. This time, however, circumstances were different. Yamazaki had spent the previous decade building a reputation as "better neighbors" with the Episcopal leadership, local residents, and city officials. As the associations reverted to their old political tactics, Yamazaki developed an exigent politics that mobilized Christian leaders, the political power of the police, and supportive neighbors to get his permit passed.

Yamazaki faced a familiar opposition: the Electric Railway Homestead Association. Although the 1920s anti-Japanese crusades had been led by an organization operating under a different name—the Pico Heights Protective Association—Yamazaki believed that the two groups comprised the same people who had tried to oust Japanese immigrant residents ten years prior. On April 28, 1931, the Electric Railway Homestead Association requested the City Council to deny a building permit to the Japanese Episcopal Mission.[64]

Additionally, A. J. Spencer, a new political candidate for chief of City Council, ran his campaign on renewed waves of anti-Japanese sentiment. To get voters to the polls for the May 5th elections, he posted inflammatory posters to spread misinformation that would support his candidacy. First, he disseminated the lie that a new Japanese church was being proposed for Pico Heights. Second, he embellished on potential economic impact, claiming the church would drive down property values and decrease city tax revenue by nearly a million dollars a year. Finally, Spencer campaigned on the promise to propose an ordinance that prohibited "Asiatic Aliens from acquiring property for any purpose in Los Angeles, either by purchase or by lease."[65] Spencer appealed to long-standing white supremacist anxieties that Pico Heights must "remain American."

While neighborhood associations and anti-Japanese campaigns continued to use old tactics, Yamazaki pivoted, for the first time utilizing white allies to mobilize their political power in favor of the mission. He appealed to Bishop W. B. Stevens to write a letter of support to the City Council and coached him on the major talking points. Yamazaki clarified a number of issues the opposition had fabricated. First, a new church was not moving in; the Japanese Episcopal Mission had already resided there for twenty years. Second, there was no threat of "colonization," as Japanese American population in Pico Heights had remained stable between 1920 and 1930, with about two hundred Japanese American residents, both renters and owners, (with about thirty houses owned by Japanese residents).

Moreover, Yamazaki argued, the 1924 Immigration Act had resolved the "Japanese Question," so there should be no reason for further agitation. Finally, current residents were majority second-generation American citizens and trained in Americanization through the church. Of the 200 residents, about 150 were US-born children who attended local schools, were baptized in the mission and went to Sunday school, and participated in programs like the Boy Scouts and the Girl Reserves. Bishop Stevens responded swiftly. On May 4, 1931, he wrote a letter of support to the Public Welfare Committee for building the Japanese Episcopal Mission, adopting the very reasoning Yamazaki had laid out for him: that the new church would serve as an ornament and valuable asset to the community.[66]

Yamazaki also tapped into the racial hierarchies of California's white and Black color line as well as the city's governance structure to undermine the opposition of one particular neighbor. Morgan and Georgia Robinson lived in the lot next to the church.[67] Robinson often called the police during the mission's Friday night for the Boy Scout or Girl Reserves. When Yamazaki canvassed neighbors to assess local opinion on the permit (and perhaps advocate for their support), he found that all the neighbors directly bordering the lot supported the building permit—except for the Robinsons.

Yamazaki relied on the city's history of racial segregation to qualify the objection of the Robinsons. He mocked up his own census–a list of the neighbors, their race, and their position on the permit. He identified that most white neighbors did not oppose the church, but that the Robinsons, who he labeled as "colored," happened to be the only ones who did. Interestingly, the 1930 US census had labeled Morgan and Jordan Robinson as "white."[68] Either the Robinsons themselves identified as white, or the census taker identified them as such. In his own mock-up, Yamazaki highlighted the fact that his neighbors were "colored" in order to use the anti-Black sentiments of the city to devalue the Robinsons' dissent. Moreover, since the Robinsons had called the police to complain about the church on occasion, Yamazaki asked the chief of police to support his case to rebut any concerns linked with those reports. The chief of police wrote letters in favor of Yamazaki and his Americanization work, claiming that the Robinsons were "prejudiced people" who made "unnecessary agitation."[69]

Finally, Yamazaki canvassed to clarify misinformation among neighbors. Pico Heights residents, including members of the Electric Railway Homestead Association, had submitted a petition to request a change of zone in order to prevent the building expansions of the Japanese Episcopal Mission. In August, the City Council ordered a proposed change of zone from R-4 (unlimited income residential), where churches were permitted, to R-2 (no more than four families per lot), which prohibited such buildings.[70] Yamazaki spoke with white property owners on Mariposa Ave and Normandie avenues, the site of the proposed zone change, and clarified how the zone change might immediately impact their own property values. Ahead of the August meeting, the property owners located in the proposed zone change wrote and signed a petition against the change of zone, arguing that the proposed change would "materially reduce [the] value" of their land and "prevent a reasonable return on investments in property already made in the particular district." At least one person who had signed the original petition for the zone change, and who identified as a member of the Electric Railway Homestead Association, admitted they had been misinformed and therefore signed this new petition to protest the change of zone.[71]

Conclusion

The new rectory of St. Mary's Japanese Episcopal Mission was the culmination of twenty years of maneuvering racial politics within the Episcopal Church and the city of Pico Heights. Reverend John Yamazaki had to face two issues: an ecclesiastical administration that underfunded their mission and local neighborhood associations that sought to make Pico Heights white-only. Along the way, Yamazaki developed an uplift politics aimed to placate anti-Japanese eviction campaigns while appealing to white Christian liberals on the grounds that Americanization would resolve anti-Japanese racism. The Japanese Episcopal Mission used Americanization as both a template of protection and a source of leverage for expanding the resources of the community during an era of exclusion.[72]

The story of the St. Mary's Japanese Episcopal Mission changes our understanding of religion in California in the interwar period. First, although scholarship on the interwar period has focused on the new white migrants and how they reshaped religion in California, the building of a new rectory reveals that Japanese immigrant communities also continued to expand in religious ways despite no new immigration. Although the 1924 Immigration Act halted Japanese immigration, the church continued to build its constituency by focusing on the next generation. It laid the foundation for growth on a generational politics that placed youth and youth programs front and center. Second, older forms of religious othering took shape in new secular ways, which in turn required secular tools to claim religious inclusion. While anti-Japanese neighborhood associations drew on familiar narratives of the heathen to exclude Japanese immigrants, Yamazaki used Americanization to navigate the terms of religious inclusion. Third, Americanization reveals the church's method of appealing both to white liberal Christians as well as Japanese elites in order to realize the expansion of its religious institution. By portraying themselves as far away from the heathen and as close as possible to the white Christian American, church leaders were able to obtain religious resources for their community. Ultimately, for non-white migrants, the interwar period was not the era of new migrants and religious diversity scholars have previously depicted, but one marked by migration restriction and religious homogeneity.

Notes

My gratitude extends to the many colleagues who partook in the workshopping of this chapter, including faculty in the Asian American Studies program at Cornell University, participants in the Asian Pacific American Religions Research Initiative (APARRI), and attendees of the Clements Center symposium. Funding for archival travel was made possible through an Episcopal Church Archives Grant. I am grateful to the archivists whose assistance proved invaluable, including Jamie Hendricks at the Japanese American National Museum (JANM) and Christopher Ann Paton at the Archives of the Episcopal Church in Austin, Texas. Finally, thank you to those who assisted me in the beginning stages of research, including Tom Guzman at St. Mary's, the dean and librarians at the Berkeley Divinity School at Yale University, and Dr. James Yamazaki.

1. "Episcopal Church to Hold Ceremony for Opening Day," *Rafu Shimpo*, February 14, 1932.

2. "St. Mary's Mission Opening Set Today," *Rafu Shimpo*, October 16, 1932.

3. Eldon G. Ernst, "The Emergence of California in American Religious Historiography," *Religion and American Culture* 11, no. 1 (2001): 31–52.

4. Darren Dochuk, "Chapter Fifteen: Religion in the Early Twentieth Century," in *A Companion to California History*, eds. William Deverell and David Igler (John Wiley & Sons, 2014), 331–49.

5. Kathryn Gin Lum, *Heathen: Race and Religion in American History* (Harvard University Press, 2022).

6. Brian Hayashi, *For the Sake of Our Brethren: Assimilation, Nationalism, and Protestantism Among the Japanese of Los Angeles, 1895–1942* (Stanford University Press, 1995).

7. Becky M. Nicolaides and James Zarsadiaz, "Design Assimilation in Suburbia: Asian Americans, Built Landscapes, and Suburban Advantage in Los Angeles's San Gabriel Valley since 1970," *Journal of Urban History* 43, no. 2 (2016): 332–71.

8. I apply Kathryn Gin Lum's concept of heathen to the story of the Japanese Episcopal Mission/St. Mary's Church in the interwar period, when Japanese immigrants became religiously "othered" in the replacement narrative. I draw upon Lum's understanding of the replacement narrative as a story of secularism: the management of what counts as acceptable and unacceptable expressions of religion. Lum's definition of secularism builds on Terrence Keel's idea that the "secular acts as a mask for the religious" and "a new story can be told . . . if we think of secularization not in terms of a rupture from the past but instead as a transference of religious forms into nonreligious spaces of thought and practice." See Lum, *Heathen*.

9. Robert Peterson, "How a Neighborhood Disappears: The Life and Death of Pico Heights," KCET, January 10, 2017, www.kcet.org/shows/lost-la/how-a-neighborhood-disappears-the-life-and-death-of-pico-heights.

10. John Modell, *The Economics and Politics of Racial Accommodation: The Japanese of Los Angeles, 1900–1942* (University of Illinois Press, 1977).

11. 1920 US Census, Los Angeles, California, population schedule, www.ancestry.com. Images reproduced by FamilySearch. Original Data: *Fourteenth Census of the United States, 1920* (NARA microfilm publication T625, 2076 rolls), Records of the Bureau of the Census, Record Group 29, National Archives, Washington, DC. Enumeration Districts 819–839 are on roll 323 (Chicago City). For details on the contents of the film numbers, visit www.archives.gov/research/census/publications-microfilm-catalogs-census/1920/part-07.html.

12. Ancestry.com, *California, Alien Land Ownership Records, 1921–1952* (database online), Ancestry.com Operations, Inc., 2014. This collection was indexed by Ancestry World Archives Project contributors, www.ancestrylibrary.com/handler/domainrd.ashx?Domain=CommunityDomain&url=/wap/dashboard.aspx.

13. "Survey of Oriental Communities and Oriental Students," *Survey of Race Relations*, Box 20, Hoover Institution Library & Archives, Stanford University. Many of those surveyed would later become reverends themselves, including L. S. Mayekawa and P. H. Murakami, who served in Japan, as well as others who remained in the United States, including Uchida, Paul Ito, and John Misao Yamazaki.

14. In Reverend John Misao Yamazaki's Life Story, n.d., he writes that his earliest encounters with Western Christianity included his baptism in the Christ Church in his hometown of Matsumoto, Japan. James Yamazaki graciously sent a copy of this to me.

15. *Journal of the Nineteenth Annual Convention of the Church in the Diocese of Los Angeles: Held in St. Paul's Pro-Cathedral, Los Angeles, May 13 and 14, 1914* (1914), 215, Archives of the Episcopal Church, Austin, TX (hereafter AEC).

16. "Survey of Oriental Communities and Oriental Students," Box 20.

17. While the "Survey of Oriental Communities and Oriental Students" records twenty attendees, the journal of the Diocese recorded in 1920 that they had twenty-three attendees and two teachers. *Journal of the Twenty-Sixth Annual Convention of the Church in the Diocese of Los Angeles: Held in St. Paul's Pro-Cathedral, Los Angeles, January 26 and 27, A.D. 1921* (1921), 147, HathiTrust Digital Library.

18. Personal interview with Dr. James Yamazaki, May 13, 2017.

19. Domestic and Foreign Missionary Society, *Annual Report of the Board of Missions for the Fiscal Year 1916–1917* (1917), AEC.

20. *Annual Report of the Board of Missions, 1916–1917.*

21. "Survey of Oriental Communities and Oriental Students," Box 20.

22. *The Churchman* (New York), December 1, 1906, 865.

23. "Survey of Oriental Communities and Oriental Students," Box 20.

24. *Journal of the Twenty-Sixth Annual Convention*, 147.

25. *Journal of the Twenty-Sixth Annual Convention*, 146.

26. "Survey of Oriental Communities and Oriental Students," Box 20.

27. Domestic and Foreign Missionary Society, *Annual Report of the Board of Missions for the Fiscal Year 1919* (New York, 1919), 103–4, AEC.

28. Kathryn Gin Lum, *Heathen: Race and Religion in American History* (Harvard University Press, 2022).

29. Charlotte Brooks, *Alien Neighbors, Foreign Friends: Asian Americans, Housing, and the Transformation of Urban California* (University of Chicago Press, 2009).

30. 1920 United States Federal Census. Sources match Guy H. Duffey to the "Mr. Duffy" interviewed in the *Survey of Race Relations*. Duffey lived in Flower Street, District 64, right next to District 63, the location of the Japanese Episcopal Mission. Dr. Johnson suspected the leader of the anti-Japanese movement to have the backing of the Roman Catholic Church.

31. "Names of People Seen in Connection with Pico Heights, Los Angeles, Conflict," *Survey of Race Relations*, Box 26, Hoover Institution Library & Archives, Stanford University.

32. G. E. Delevan cites 250 families as having been evicted, but Duffey cites 100. "Names of People Seen in Connection with Pico Heights, Box 26."

33. "Names of People Seen in Connection with Pico Heights," Box 26.

34. "Names of People Seen in Connection with Pico Heights," Box 26.

35. "Names of People Seen in Connection with Pico Heights," Box 26.

36. "Methodist Church Helping Japs," *The Grizzly Bear*, February 1922.

37. "Names of People Seen in Connection with Pico Heights," Box 26.

38. "Los Angeles County Anti-Asiatic Association on the Building of the Japanese Churches," *Survey of Race Relations*, Box 29, Hoover Institution Library & Archives, Stanford University.

39. US House Committee on Immigration and Naturalization, *Hearings*, 67th Cong., 4th Sess., Serial C (Government Printing Office, 1923), HathiTrust Digital Library.

40. *Journal of the Twenty-Ninth Annual Convention of the Church in the Diocese of Los Angeles: Held in Saint John's Church, Los Angeles, January 30 and 31, 1924* (1924), 158–59, AEC.

41. "Interview with Reverend John M. Yamazaki," *Survey of Race Relations*, Box 25, Hoover Institution Library & Archives, Stanford University.

42. "Interview with Miss Myrtle Eldred," *Survey of Race Relations*, Box 26, Hoover Institution Library & Archives, Stanford University.

43. "Interview with Reverend John M. Yamazaki."

44. "Interview with Reverend John M. Yamazaki."

45. "Interview with Reverend John M. Yamazaki."

46. "Interview with Reverend John M. Yamazaki."

47. Domestic and Foreign Missionary Society, *Annual Report of the National Council for the Year 1924* (1924), 171, Records of the National Council UP232, AEC.

48. John Misao Yamazaki, "Shall Our Future Citizens Be Christians?," *The Spirit of Missions* 92 (1927): 493–95, Archives of the Episcopal Church, Austin, Texas.

49. *Journal of the Twenty-Ninth Annual Convention*, 158–159.

50. "Names of People Seen in Connection with Pico Heights."

51. "Names of People Seen in Connection with Pico Heights."

52. "St. Mary's Club Organizes Scout Group," *Rafu Shimpo*, November 22, 1926; "St. Mary's Boys and Girls Club," *Rafu Shimpo*, February 27, 1928.

53. "St. Mary's Boys and Girls Club," *Rafu Shimpo*, July 11, 1926; August 30, 1926; February 21, 1927; May 16, 1927; June 6, 1927.

54. "St. Mary's Boys and Girls Club," *Rafu Shimpo*, April 4, 1927. "St. Mary's Girl Reserves Club Gets New Advisor," *Rafu Shimpo*, April 27, 1928.

55. "Pamphlet," St. Mary's Episcopal Church Records, 99.106, Japanese American National Museum, Los Angeles, CA (hereafter St. Mary's Records).

56. "St. Mary's Boys and Girls Club," *Rafu Shimpo*, December 13, 1926.

57. "Episcopal Church Clubs," *Rafu Shimpo*, December 5, 1927.

58. Yamazaki, "Shall Our Future Citizens Be Christians?," 494.

59. "Pamphlet," St. Mary's Records.

60. John Misao Yamazaki, "The Rev. John Misao Yamazaki, S.T.D., D.D.," n.d.

61. *Journal of the Thirty-Sixth Annual Convention of the Church in the Diocese of Los Angeles:* Held in St. Paul's Cathedral, Los Angeles, January 28 and 29, 1931 (1931), 118.

62. *The Spirit of Missions* 96, no. 1 (January 1931).

63. *Journal of the Thirty-Seventh Annual Convention of the Church in the Diocese of Los Angeles: Held in St. Paul's Cathedral, Los Angeles, January 27 and 28, 1932* (1932), 88.

64. "Notes for St. Mary's Japanese Mission, Diocese of Los Angeles," St. Mary's Records.

65. "Pico Heights Must Not Be Colonized by the Japanese," St. Mary's Records.

66. Bishop W. B. Stevens to Mr. E. Snapper Ingram, May 4, 1931, "Notes for St. Mary's Japanese Mission," St. Mary's Records.

67. "Notes for St. Mary's Japanese Mission, Diocese of Los Angeles," St. Mary's Records.

68. 1930 US Census, Los Angeles, California, population schedule, enumeration district (ED) 19-482, sheet 13A, household 312, Morgan and Georgia Robinson, accessed August 28, 2022, ancestry.com.

69. "Notes for St. Mary's Japanese Mission, Diocese of Los Angeles."

70. "Notice of Proposed Change of Zone," St. Mary's Records.

71. "Protest Against Change of Zone," St. Mary's Records.

72. By World War II, members of St. Mary's Japanese Episcopal Mission were forcibly removed and relocated to incarceration camps. For a history on St. Mary's Japanese

Episcopal Mission during the war, see Joanna B. Gillespie, "Japanese-American Episcopalians During World War II: The Congregation of St. Mary's Los Angeles, 1941–1945," *Anglican and Episcopal History* 69, no. 2 (June 2000): 135–69. Gillespie argues that while the Episcopal Church acquiesced to plans for incarcerating Japanese Americans, specific individuals and denominations offered assistance within the camps. Furthermore, she notes that churches helped to organize the resettling of incarcerees outside the camps after the war.

PART IV

Caring for Bodies on the Imperial Margins

The making of the US West was a modern endeavor that we have recognized in this volume as an imperial project of making subjects, imposing norms, racializing bodies, and consolidating territory through settlement, theft, and violence. A dire human cost is paid—typically by racialized and minoritized communities—when modern imperial regimes rely on enforced difference and exclusion to create and impose the metropole's racial, religious, and economic norms. The many deleterious results of exclusion and aggressive prejudice include anomie, physical and social isolation, and physical and mental illness. Modern, secular caregiving systems—including hospitals, social policies and benefits, and efforts to maintain healthful environments—tend to be inclusive primarily of acceptable subjects and to exclude others. The chapters in this section focus precisely on groups on the margins, often excluded from standard forms of care. Religious (and religio-ethnic) caretaking arises and responds in complex ways to suffering, exclusion, and stigma.

Partnerships often arose among racial and ethnic groups marked as "unacceptable" or "unworthy" of care in the US West. Such partnerships, though instrumental in creating spaces of care and comfort, sometimes created new frictions—new sites where the processes of inclusion and exclusion could play out. Jennifer Graber's contribution to the volume examines the microhistory of a Chinese man married to a Paiute woman in and around the Walker River Paiute Reservation in Nevada. Paiute–Chinese alliances pooled the protections of both the reservation and Chinese *huiguan*, benevolent fraternal organizations that worked to meet the needs of Chinese laborers. Graber demonstrates, however, that despite these strategies of mutual care, the forces of the surrounding empire, which Graber memorably characterizes as a "cannibal giant," often worked with devastating effect.

Lynne Gerber's chapter focuses on San Francisco in the late twentieth century during the hardest years of the AIDS epidemic. The gay community in San Francisco had long maintained multiple registers of care for LGBTQ people; in this period, caring for those dying of AIDS became paramount and, as Gerber contends, "a taut religious crisis." Gerber shows that various spiritual and religious organizations and networks cared for the sick in their final days. Her research demonstrates how the internal dialogues and debates of these organizations reflect broader concerns about religion, spirituality, race, and sexuality in the US West and beyond.

The final chapter, by Max Greenberg, draws on historical methods and ethnic studies analysis to ask how memory functions (and is permitted to function) for different religious and ethnic groups in the US West. Greenberg explores Jewish cemeteries on ancestral Tohono O'odham land in southern Arizona. In part, his findings contribute to the history of Jewish settlement in the Southwest, but his chapter also highlights how public memorialization in the region is a precision instrument for remembering some while obliterating others. Greenberg invites us to wonder with him: What is to be gained—and by whom—for southern Arizonans to maintain cemeteries and monuments dedicated to nineteenth-century Jewish pioneers?

Chapter 11

Religion Among the Cannibals

Chinese–Paiute Rites of Care and Feeding

JENNIFER GRABER

Keywords: cannibals, Native Americans, Chinese Americans, kinship, care

In 1877, a Central Pacific Railroad executive complained of his difficulty securing Chinese laborers in Nevada Territory. Northern Paiutes, whose traditional lands the railroad bisected, had scared them away with fantastic stories of giant cannibals and snakes that ate men. According to the executive, more than one thousand potential workers fled the Nevada desert for fear of being eaten alive.[1]

Scholars have considered this story for what it reveals about US domestic colonialism and the inter-ethnic strife it produced. These readings are particularly useful in highlighting the ways Chinese and Native people challenged US colonial expansion, or what Manu Karuka has called "countersovereignty." There are, however, additional ways to think about how Paiute cannibal stories functioned as the United States invaded and colonized Paiute homelands.

Stories about giants and cannibals (or giant cannibals) are foundational to Paiute peoplehood.[2] More broadly, narratives of human flesh-eaters can be found across Native North America. Some connect to origin accounts or times deep in tribal histories; others speak to more recent episodes of conflict with neighboring Native nations. In both cases, cannibal stories demonstrate how protocols for eating food and interacting with dead bodies are central to maintaining social order and assessing external threats.[3]

Consider, for instance, one contemporary Paiute account of a mythic race of giant cannibals. Wilson Wewa (Confederated Tribes of Warm Springs) tells of a giant called Nuwuzo'ho, who hunted down the original Animal People, speared them, ground them up with a mortar and pestle, and ate their crushed bones out of an oversized soup bowl.[4] Wewa's story details a threatening outsider who broke all the rules about eating food and interacting with the dead. It also contains a survival strategy. According to Wewa, the Animal People defeated the cannibal giant by teaming up with Coyote, often an unreliable and somewhat marginal figure. To secure his cooperation, the people's leader promised Coyote his daughter's hand in marriage. Surviving Nuwuzo'ho's invasion, then, entailed unconventional forms of kinship and long-term alliance.[5]

Wewa's cannibal story differs markedly from those penned by European and Euro-American colonizers, who frequently remarked on human flesh-eaters in their accounts of global exploration. Scholars have analyzed the function of cannibalism in this so-called discovery literature. While debate persists, there is some consensus about how accusations of cannibalism functioned: They contributed to a broader vocabulary of Indigenous savagery in which cannibalism signaled the gulf between the civilized and savage, elevated that difference to a crisis level, and thereby justified suppression, if not genocide.[6]

In an ironic turn, colonizers' occupation of Native homelands—which they justified by their status as civilized—frequently involved acts that, if not of literal flesh-eating, nonetheless echoed the kind of fantastic destruction attributed to Nuwuzo'ho. Conquest often meant upsetting norms around food: harming the lands and animals that provided it, as well as disrupting traditional practices of food gathering, distribution, and blessing. It entailed violations of human bodies, both living and dead. And it included acts of captivity, taking and sequestering the land's inhabitants against their will. Measured against Paiute stories, American occupation of Paiute homelands—justified by narratives of Indigenous savagery fueled by cannibal musings—operated as its own form of cannibal attack.[7]

Wewa's Nuwuzo'ho story draws our attention to how Paiute ancestors responded to an outsider's acts of terror. In this cannibal story, they made an unlikely alliance: The leader married his daughter to Coyote, who ultimately defeated Nuwuzo'ho. The story presents alliance as a way to survive enemies that invade homelands, upset foodways, harm bodies, and take captives. In light of Wewa's story, this chapter considers Paiute–Chinese alliances. Although a number of these associations occurred in this period, I focus on one family's story.[8] Sam Leon (born ca. 1879) and Daisy Benton (born ca. 1888) met while working on a ranch outside Yerington, Nevada. Sam, of Chinese descent if not birth, worked as the ranch cook. Daisy, affiliated with Paiutes at the Walker River reservation, labored as a ranch hand. They married in 1906 and had a daughter, Laura, in 1912. My discussion of this family history draws on documents, oral traditions, and material culture found in the colonial archive as well as Indigenous history-keeping traditions.[9]

The Leons moved through spaces that allowed a degree of freedom, such as Chinese boarding houses and Native gatherings of extended kin. They also experienced the surveillance and coercion that characterized mining towns, reservations, boarding schools, and jail cells. As they navigated this challenging landscape, the Leons practiced both mundane and ritualized acts of feeding and bodily care. They participated in mutual aid, offered medicine, and signaled their respect for food-gathering traditions and duty to ancestors.[10] In the face of a colonial cannibalism that destroyed food, harmed bodies, and took captives, their lives frequently exhibited what Hobart and Kneese have called "radical care" for "enduring precarious worlds."[11] Like other families across the American West, they bore scars of cannibal attack even as their survival testified to the power of alliance-making. Tracing these surprising relationships allows us, as Jodie Byrd suggests, "to decenter the vertical interactions of colonizer and colonized" and focus instead on what Paul Lai and Lindsey Claire Smith call "alternative contact."[12]

Food for Cannibals

> . . . bones and everything, mixing everything together. Then [Nuwuzo'ho] would eat that mixture. Just like soup. He would eat them all . . .[13]

According to Wilson Wewa, Nuwuzo'ho violated the most basic food taboo: he ate people. He flouted all established food protocols. As a form of cannibal attack, American colonizers' occupation of Paiute country disrupted foodways on many levels. At the same time, food was a medium for strategizing survival and securing alliances.

For Sam, this experience began before he met Daisy. It started in the kitchens and boarding houses he shared with fellow Chinese workers. Like many Chinese immigrants who remained after earlier mining booms, Sam moved beyond California and found work in one of the only jobs available: food service.[14] He also participated in the eating practices of the mostly single men who made up small Chinese communities throughout the region. Archaeological evidence from boarding houses and adjacent restaurants reveals them to be centers of Chinese social life. Artifacts attest to common meals, shared domestic spaces, and leisure activities.[15]

These practices of food sharing contrasted with those practiced at the multiethnic worksite where Sam and Daisy met. As on many Nevada ranches, white owners and workers refused to eat with Chinese and Native laborers.[16] They also sometimes barred those same Native workers from eating in local restaurants.[17] Work-related pressures on foodways also manifested in lower wages paid to Chinese and Native workers, making sustenance more difficult to secure.

Immigrants from China needed to feed not only themselves but also those who had died. Their deathways included burial rites with food offerings. Despite the difficulty of procuring food, Chinese mourners found ways to observe death traditions. Contemporary accounts attest to meals served at

Chinese funerals. Archeologists working at the large Chinese cemetery at Laporte, California (just west of Reno), found broken rice bowls beside graves, physical evidence attesting to practices of food offering.[18]

At times, white settlers feasted on these materials of filial duty. One settler's account recalled Chinese mourners leaving "elaborate feasts" at gravesites in Bodie, California, just across the border from Nevada. The practice "amused" white residents, and teenage boys were known to "consume the funeral feast."[19] Sue Fawn Chung, who has written extensively on Chinese American deathways, found evidence that some communities posted guards to ensure that food and wine left as offerings would not be eaten.[20]

Daisy's experience of segregated tables at the ranch where she worked with Sam only magnified the food instability she had experienced at Walker River. The hunger brought about by American invasion contrasted sharply with the time-tested cycle of food collection that gave Paiute groups their names. Paiutes living at Walker River, for instance, are called the *Agai Dicutta* after the trout that once filled nearby waterways. The 1840s Euro-American entry into Paiute lands disrupted the seasonal food-gathering round; settlers frightened game animals and trampled plants and seeds. In the process of settlement, they diverted water and impeded seed and plant growth.[21]

The 1874 establishment of the reservation restricted Paiute movement, making traditional food gathering even more difficult. Reservation agents promoted farming as a substitute, but these efforts often failed when settlers diverted the water necessary for growing crops.[22] Rations promised by treaties hardly made up the difference, and a series of late nineteenth-century policy changes further stressed the situation. The 1883 Code of Indian Offenses discouraged the very dances Paiutes performed to ensure good harvests and hunts. Daisy was born just as these new restrictions came into effect. Simultaneously, rules to mandate American-style education allowed agents to withhold food rations from parents who refused to send their children to day and residential schools.[23]

Hunger continued in the new century as Daisy grew up. Reservation agents reported on food insecurity to authorities in Washington, DC, even as they restricted rations to only the elderly.[24] This precarity helps explain the ongoing interest in the Ghost Dance movement, with its promise of the landscape's restoration, which would in turn transform Paiute diets. A 1911 letter from Daisy Bell to Jack Wilson (Wovoka) mentioned hunger during the winter and the overall difficult conditions of her life.[25] Daisy Leon's search for work off the reservation was likely prompted by the need to earn money in order to feed her parents and younger siblings.[26]

Daisy's experience of labor migration mirrored that of many Paiutes. As noted above, worksites facilitated intercultural exchange that often centered on food. Paiute elder Edna Jones recalled Chinese laborers introducing her family to cabbage.[27] Other interviewees remembered episodes of hunger in which Chinese acquaintances provided relief; in one instance, a cook fed cheap cuts of meat to the white American miners who employed him while saving the good cuts for residents of his Chinese boardinghouse and "Indian friends."[28] Gifting moved in the other direction as well. An Umatilla elder recalled his family's stories about railroad expansion into their homelands: "They had to feed the Chinese laborers. . . . And they would get something in return and I don't remember what that was. But it was always they just had to."[29]

Sam and Daisy met at the Yerington ranch and married in the "Indian custom" in 1906.[30] While not legally recognized by the state, the union was acknowledged by relatives and recorded in Walker River's tribal rolls, which featured a handful of Chinese–Paiute partnerships.[31] Food became an important medium connecting Sam to his new Paiute relations. According to descendants, Sam visited frequently and brought food for his wife's parents, thereby fulfilling a traditional expectation for Paiute husbands.[32] They recalled that "he was good to the People. He brought them rice and vegetables."[33] The cannibalizing attack on Paiute country, then, involved breaking food protocols, even as food also remained at the heart of people's care for one another and a medium for forging alliances.

Cannibal Violation

> When [Nuwuzo'ho] found a village, or a lone traveler or a hunter or some woman out gathering roots and berries, he would spear them . . .[34]

According to Wewa, Nuwuzo'ho inflicted bodily harm on his victims before capturing and eating them. Cannibal attack in the American West similarly involved the violation of Native and Chinese bodies. In response, care for bodies—both living and dead—provided one line of defense against cannibal destruction. Sam's experiences prior to meeting Daisy encompassed forms of bodily care practiced within communities of Chinese workers, specifically, traditional Chinese medical practices for which there is extensive archaeological and documentary evidence.[35]

Chinese laborers also joined benevolent associations to care for bodily needs. Modeled on fraternal organizations or district associations called *huiguan*, these groups connected immigrants in the American West and Hawaii to Chinese communities across the Pacific. As Chinese workers spread across the West, they established *huiguan* in new places and eventually merged them into a national organization. Along with establishing schools and temples, *huiguan* leaders cared for the sick and poor, collecting fees from workers to maintain pools of money that functioned as social insurance.[36]

Huiguan played a particularly important role in caring for the dead. They purchased land for cemeteries, provided free coffins, facilitated burials, and organized the necessary rites of passage. Membership fees also paid for spring festivals that honored the dead and involved organizing large processions and preparing food for crowds.[37] Since most immigrants lacked close family in the United States, *huiguan* made arrangements for members who wanted their remains to be exhumed later and repatriated to China. Immigrants chose disinterment and transport so they could permanently rest near family in their ancestral homelands.[38]

Based on the historical context, we can hypothesize about Sam's own experiences of bodily care in Nevada. Several of the small mining towns he lived in had Chinese neighborhoods and *huiguan* chapters. Given the widespread participation of immigrant workers, Sam was very likely involved in these networks of mutual aid. Several of these towns also had Chinese cemeteries.[39] Specific accounts of Chinese deathways are available for Bodie, where Sam lived in the 1920s and 1930s. Observers recalled Bodie's Chinese residents hosting elaborate funerals with hired mourners. Cemetery burials in Bodie were sometimes temporary, as some Chinese arranged to have their bones returned to China for permanent interment.[40]

At the same time, Sam lived with the ever-present possibility of bodily vulnerability and violation. Again, Bodie serves as an example. Residents remember it as a sundown town, requiring Chinese (and Native) visitors and residents to retreat to the outskirts by nightfall. Chinese workers could not join Bodie's labor union, which sought safe conditions for miners. Neither could Chinese in Bodie find redress or protection from the police or courts, despite the number of attacks on Chinese neighborhoods that involved property loss as well as bodily injury.[41] Settlers periodically engaged in such violent assaults on people and property in towns throughout western Nevada.[42]

Chinese cemeteries were sites of another form of bodily violation: the desecration of the dead. Across the West, settlers defaced Chinese gravestones and looted graves in search of gold and silver coins rumored to be buried with the deceased. They stole human remains, sometimes selling them to curio collectors or medical schools.[43] In Elko, Nevada, for instance, settlers disturbed remains that had been disinterred and prepared for repatriation to China. "Teenage pranksters" opened bone containers and scattered the remains, making transport and reburial impossible.[44]

Daisy experienced a different form of bodily violation: the disruption of traditional care practices related to childbirth and illness. According to her descendants, Daisy returned to Walker River in 1912 to give birth because she wanted her daughter, Laura, to be born "on Indian land."[45] While we know little about this particular birth, scholars of Native midwifery and ethnographic materials from the period offer insight into Paiute childbirth and child-rearing. Typically, female relatives guided women throughout pregnancy, and midwives attended labor and delivery. Afterward, they cared for mother and child, including ritualized forms of feeding and bathing. Fathers, too, were expected to follow food and social taboos, which required relatives' support for proper observation.[46]

Daisy gave birth at Walker River, where colonizers had disrupted Native care and medicine practices for decades. Broadly speaking, reservation agents enforced policies that criminalized Native healing practitioners and sought to replace them with American-trained doctors. Federal officials also directed agents to monitor Native childbirth closely. As early as the 1880s, so-called reformers advanced racist arguments about Native women's bodies and blamed Native people for conditions of malnutrition and disease that threatened mothers and children.[47] By the time of Laura's birth, these officials campaigned for hospitalized births attended by Euro-American physicians rather than Native midwives.

US efforts to control reproduction extended into Native forms of child-rearing and household management. A close study of federal policy enacted on the Crow reservation, for example, found several interventions: officials discouraged practices of "flexible child-rearing," in which relatives took responsibility to teach children their primary obligations to others, and instead they promoted nuclear families and the singular importance of biological parents. They also disapproved of the adoption and sharing practices that allowed Native communities to support children when their primary caregivers were compromised.[48]

During this period of drastic change, Paiutes maintained certain care traditions for mothers and children, while adapting others. Ethnographers working among nearby Paiute communities in the 1920s found the continued use of traditional healing practices for an array of ailments, while the Walker River agent observed a hybrid of Indigenous practices and the allopathic medicine available from American doctors.[49] Even so, disease proved devastating. Despite the sustained healing efforts by the community, Walker River recorded more deaths than births in the early decades of the twentieth century.[50]

Despite these obstacles, the care of bodies through healing practices served as another opportunity for intercultural connection. Paiutes at Walker River welcomed Sam into their medicine traditions. According to his granddaughter, he participated in ritual sweats.[51] In interviews, Paiute elder Corbett Mack recalled Sam being doctored by a traditional healer named Tom Mitchell.[52]

Conversely, Chinese doctors in western Nevada sometimes exchanged herbal and botanical remedies with Native practitioners. And when laws made it difficult for Chinese doctors to immigrate, workers near Tuscarora and Island Mountain often sought treatment in Native villages and on reservations.[53]

The intercultural experience of bodily care extended even to the dead, as evidenced by oral histories collected among the Umatilla. These accounts tell of Chinese laborers being "work[ed] to death" as they built railroad lines in the Pacific Northwest. When fellow workers buried them on a hill where the Umatilla people harvested plants for food, the Umatilla shifted their gathering practices. As one man recalled, "We could only dig on one side because they said that Chinese were buried on the other side."[54]

Sam and Daisy came from communities with long traditions of bodily care. Both systems of medicine were under strain: Chinese practitioners faced the challenges that come with diaspora, and Paiute medicine was actively suppressed by US officials. Their shared history reveals elements of sustained tradition, systemic obstacles, and profound moments where bodily care served to bring people together across cultural divides.

For the Leon family, the challenge of bodily care in a cannibal environment became all too real when Daisy became ill with tuberculosis not long after Laura's birth.[55] Tuberculosis raged through Indian Country at the turn of the century: its spread quickened during the transition to permanent housing and boarding school enrollment, as both environments typically involved cramped spaces lacking good ventilation. Native people in Nevada, including Paiutes, were hit especially hard. In 1912, nearly 15 percent of the Native population was known to be infected.[56] While few details of Daisy's specific care survive, she likely relied on Paiute healing traditions as well as the reservation physician. These efforts failed, and Daisy died in August 1914.[57]

Cannibal Captivity

> [Nuwuzo'ho] would take the pestle out and grind the people he had captured all up.[58]

According to Wewa, the cannibal giant Nuwuzo'ho walked the land in search of prey. Some people tried to evade him by hiding or running. Some succeeded, but the cannibal caught others, gathering them up and keeping them close until he was ready to eat. American occupation of Paiute and other Native homelands displayed a similar pattern of surveillance, custody, and captivity, even as Native people struggled to evade the state's grasp and escape.

As a Chinese laborer, Sam's experience of surveillance began with his arrival at port. According to family tradition, he was born in Guangdong, the

Chinese province that produced the largest number of economic migrants in this period.[59] Census and archival records, however, list his birthplace as Hawaii or California.[60] This discrepancy reflects survival strategies Chinese migrants employed because of strict immigration policies. The 1882 Chinese Exclusion Act barred legal entry for most laborers, and subsequent legislation made emigration for Chinese women and other family members especially difficult.[61] In response, migrating workers entered by way of Canada and Mexico or altered documents to facilitate entry at American ports. Sam's paper record likely reflects such an effort to enter the United States and avoid immigration detention.[62]

Daisy's experience of surveillance and custody began on the reservation, an institution established to separate Paiutes from Nevada's growing population of silver miners and to restrict their movement over vast lands. Technically, Paiutes required permission from the reservation agent to leave. By the time Daisy was born in 1888, federal Indian policy had shifted. Officials and reformers were frustrated that reservations had not achieved their assimilation goals and moved to dismantle them. The 1887 Dawes Allotment Act initiated the breakup of communally held Native lands in favor of individual ownership of parcels.[63] While this process ostensibly offered the freedoms associated with landholding, American reservation agents continued to monitor Native movement into non-Native spaces. Allotment procedures began at Walker River in 1906, around the time Daisy left her family home in search of work.

Sam and Daisy also endured the threat of racially targeted detention. The 1883 Code of Indian Offenses called for the establishment of tribal police and courts to adjudicate offenders. As mentioned previously, the code forbade Native forms of dancing, healing, grieving, and marriage. Native people deemed guilty of these "offenses" paid fines or served time in reservation jails. Soon after the code's implementation, Walker River's agent established a police force and built a log cabin jail to punish offenders, especially those who broke marriage laws.[64] The police unit eventually disbanded, but as Daisy came of age after 1900, a reservation official still tried to enforce the code's dictates concerning marriage.[65]

While there is no evidence that Daisy was subject to court proceedings, sources detail Sam's numerous interactions with law enforcement. Authorities in western Nevada towns arrested him at least once for alcohol- and opium-related offenses prior to his meeting Daisy.[66] In the years after Laura's birth, Sam was arrested on several occasions for the distribution of opium and alcohol.[67] Prohibition prompted further run-ins.[68] Sam's most serious encounter with the law came in 1924, when he was arrested after a gathering with Paiute friends turned violent.[69]

Even as Sam engaged in illegal activities, he was also subject to heightened scrutiny as law enforcement focused inordinately on Chinese and Native lawbreakers.[70] The same system also refused to hear their voices when they were victims of racially motivated crime. For instance, witnesses to the 1903 attack on Tonopah, Nevada's Chinatown could not testify at trial as Nevada law barred Chinese from testifying against whites.[71]

The extent of cannibal surveillance, custody, and captivity is most clearly seen in Laura's childhood experiences. After Daisy's death, Laura stayed with her Paiute grandparents, but they passed away just a year later.[72] Sam, who worked outside the reservation, faced a decision regarding his daughter's care. According to descendants, he picked her up and headed for San Francisco's Chinatown. Around 1918, he enrolled her in the Tooker Memorial Home, Oakland's recently founded institution for Chinese girls.[73] Descendants explain that Sam wanted Laura to "learn about her Chinese heritage."[74]

Whatever his motive, missionaries operated the Tooker Home to address their long-standing concern for Chinese women and girls. Since the 1870s, mission workers had scanned their surroundings to identify and extract Chinese women from sex work or other arrangements they considered as enslavement.[75] They saw a related need for Chinese girls, some of whom endured abusive situations and others they deemed to be orphans.[76]

To be sure, some girls at Tooker came from awful situations. Even so, Tooker administrators justified their custody by focusing on the most extreme cases and well-worn stereotypes about the Chinese. Publicity materials featured girls "rescued from domestic slavery" and decried Chinese families who withheld food from their children.[77] Other materials omitted references to the girls' families altogether, referring to residents as orphans, half-orphans, or homeless.[78]

Residential staff differentiated between life in Chinese American families and the "proper" domestic experience offered at Tooker. The mission "home" included school lessons, domestic training, and religious instruction,[79] but it also reinforced the children's second-class racial status. Through Tooker's outing program, children were temporarily sent to Euro-American households and institutions. Older girls worked as farmhands during summers, while some were sent to Euro-American families to work as servants.[80] Other girls were sent to worship at Presbyterian churches and attend classes at the recently formed Bible Institute of Los Angeles (BIOLA).[81] In these cases, Tooker residents entered majority white spaces in the submissive position of communicant, student, or laborer.

While enrollment at Tooker involved lengthy separations, it did not keep father and daughter totally apart. Descendants report that Sam regularly traveled to Oakland to see Laura.[82] And Tooker families often visited them during summers. Even so, Laura lacked day-to-day interactions with her father. She also did not grow up at Walker River, where children typically helped with household chores and cared for younger siblings. Ultimately, she missed the chance for female relatives to guide her through childhood and puberty.

Eventually, Laura pushed for more contact with her family and administrators responded with custody that looked more like captivity. Around 1924, Laura went to Tooker's director, Donaldina Cameron, and "expressed a desire to know more of her mother's people."[83] A Presbyterian missionary and reformer, Cameron was well-known for her work with Chinese women and children in California and lauded for "rescuing" them. But Cameron's record also included guardianship disputes in which she leveraged police and judicial power to maintain custody over children seeking emancipation.[84]

Cameron responded to Laura's request in a similar way. Instead of helping her enroll in a school close to Walker River, Cameron arranged for her to attend a mission school within the Navajo Nation run by fellow Presbyterian missionaries. Isolated from her Chinese or Paiute relations, Laura returned to Oakland within the year. Cameron noted she was "very homesick." Only then did Cameron seek a school closer to Walker River and Sam's home. In fall 1929, Laura enrolled at Stewart Indian School in Carson City.[85]

A residential boarding school for Native children, Stewart was established after Paiute parents refused to send their children to schools farther away.[86] Parents made efforts to visit, sometimes camping near the school grounds. Administrators, however, discouraged contact and offered a variety of justifications for taking custody of Native children. Officials and boosters criticized Native parents as uncaring and unfit; some even claimed to be saving children from the "dangers" of reservation life. One supporter claimed Paiute parents sold their daughters to "chinamen" [*sic*] for sex, concluding, "It is only a mercy to take them away."[87]

School records reveal Donaldina Cameron's ongoing efforts to control Laura's interactions with family even after she matriculated at Stewart. Cameron counseled the principal to keep Laura away from Sam, asserting that he was "not the proper guardian for her." She wrote to Stewart repeatedly to ask for Laura's transport back to Oakland. Throughout the correspondence, Cameron either disparaged Laura's family or erased them altogether, describing her as "neither Indian nor Chinese," a "lonely hearted, truly homeless girl."[88]

While many Stewart students ran away to be reunited with family, Laura responded to captivity by making her dual priorities clear.[89] She wrote letters to administrators stating her goals to acquire an education *and* see her family. Sometimes she achieved both. Her Stewart record notes several visits from Paiute relatives, and as school ended in spring of 1930, Laura managed to secure a spot at a new high school and arrange for a summer visit with Sam.[90] At other times, however, school administrators derailed Laura's efforts. In 1931, Laura once again made plans to see Sam, and he sent money to support her trip. In response, Stewart's principal tried to make alternate arrangements for Laura and argued for Sam's "unsuitability" as a parent. Under pressure and worried about her future schooling, Laura canceled her visit. Both Donaldina Cameron and the Stewart principal "highly commended" Laura for her decision.[91]

School officials continued for years in their efforts to contain Laura, including meddling with her landholdings and denying her salaried work. For instance, Cameron wrote to the Walker River's administrator to inquire about Laura's land allotment, expressing concern that property might draw Laura back to her Walker River relations, an outcome Cameron wished to avoid.[92] The Stewart principal also remained involved even after Laura graduated from high school. While training to be a nurse at a mission hospital in Arizona, Laura applied for a position at Stewart so she could live closer to family. The principal refused her, writing, "I believe you will be better off where you are than to be near your own people."[93]

Cameron's questions about Laura's allotment signaled another way colonizers captured what was not theirs: They took control of both people *and* elements of the landscape. Settlers had long ago appropriated Paiute lands, and they continued to divert water resources from Walker River, leaving reservation residents with barely enough to survive.[94] At the turn of the century, reservation administrators eager to "detribalize" Native nations pushed for an allotment agreement to make three-quarters of Walker River Paiute tribal lands available for sale to settlers.[95] They made allotment inheritance procedures especially complex for children of mixed descent like Laura.[96]

Legal and extralegal processes also allowed white settlers to appropriate Chinese American holdings. As noted in Chrissie Lau's chapter, California passed a series of policies barring Chinese and other Asian immigrants from owning land. Sam spent most of his adult life in Nevada, where Chinese were allowed to buy property. But those holdings were threatened by racially motivated violence that sometimes led to land theft. For instance, in 1908, white residents burned down Reno's Chinatown and claimed its valuable land for themselves.[97]

Surveillance and captivity—enacted through immigration laws and drug codes, boarding schools and allotment procedures—placed devastating burdens on Sam, Daisy, and Laura. Even so, they sometimes managed to evade these institutional traps and survive. Although Sam was arrested numerous times, he somehow avoided long-term incarceration. Laura, who suffered loneliness at school, used the experience as a stepping stone to a nursing career.

And Daisy, even with her life cut short, had land in her name to pass on to her daughter. Laura eventually returned to Walker River, married, and claimed her allotment.[98]

Descendants attest to Sam and Laura's ongoing relationship, realized through acts of feeding and bodily care. Laura and her husband had seven children, one of whom recounted Sam's visits when new babies arrived. "While visiting, he would constantly be cooking," she recalled. She also remembered accompanying Laura on visits to Sam's restaurants.[99] Laura also attended to Sam as his life came to an end. He died in Reno in 1955, just four weeks after learning he had colon cancer.[100] He left no instructions for his remains to be shipped to China, a practice that had certainly declined by the 1950s, though it persisted among some Chinese immigrants. Money was likely tight, as Sam was buried in a charity plot in Reno's Odd Fellows Cemetery.[101] Laura and her children attended both the funeral and the burial.[102]

Laura continued Sam's food practices as she established her life at Walker River. Her daughter, Juanita, says Laura taught her to speak Chinese and cook Chinese food.[103] Laura also dedicated her education to the care of others, working as a nurse for many years. She died in 1987 and is buried in the Walker River Paiute cemetery. An obituary in the local newspaper described her as a "lifelong resident," a remarkable testimony to Laura's ability to make a home in cannibal country.[104]

Conclusion

> They say that the Nuwuzo'ho's body is still lying there in those
> red dirt hills—called the Connolly Hills . . .[105]

Coyote defeated Nuwuzo'ho. According to Wilson Wewa, the cannibal giant's dead body became part of the Paiute landscape: His blood can be seen in the red cinder near Newberry Crater, and three nearby salt lakes are said to have been formed by his tears.[106] The story prompts a question: If we start with a cannibal's dead body at the center of the American West, what ways of thinking about religion in the region become possible?

When a Nevada railroad executive complained about cannibal stories in 1877, he was concerned that fanciful Native tales would scare away Chinese workers, thereby jeopardizing his capital. More broadly, though, his comment figures into a long history of projecting cannibalism onto colonial subjects. As David Chidester has noted, such accounts influenced emerging discourses about religion, especially as eating human flesh was sometimes associated with the absence of religion and at other times as the predictable outcome of "primitive" religious systems.[107] And as noted above, European and American dedication to identifying cannibalism among colonized cultures obscured the devastating violence of the settlers' own invasion.

Native cannibal stories, and specifically the Paiute stories considered here, share in this potential to flip the script, calling out colonizers as catastrophically destructive *outsiders* and *invaders*. But they also invite something more, an option in which cannibal stories serve as lessons in proper sociality. In this context, they reinforce cultures of care and recommend surprising alliances as a strategy for survival. While cannibals transgress boundaries by stealing people, taking life, and eating flesh, Paiutes and others responded by upholding established protocols for eating and by caring for the dead. Some of these acts were mundane while others, such as harvest dances and burial rites, were highly ritualized. Together, these practices invited others to join in observing these protocols, thereby strengthening survival chances for both parties.

The Leon family faced a particular instantiation of the cannibal: the United States and its settler-colonial regime. They survived it—or at least two of them did—through acts of care and alliance. They did so in a landscape that reminded them that cannibals could be defeated. Their experiences, then, invite us to consider religion in the American West in a new way. The stories of Paiutes defeating Nuwuzo'ho, coupled with the Leons' survival of invasion, untether us from cannibal stories that prop up colonial theories of religion or even reversals that call out Europeans and Euro-Americans as the true cannibals. These experiences represent, instead, the beating heart of religious practice, a lesson in proper social relations built on both mundane and ritualized acts of care and feeding.

Notes

1. Manu Karuka, *Empire's Tracks: Indigenous Nations, Chinese Workers, and the Transcontinental Railroad* (University of California Press, 2019), 1. The Central Pacific Railroad was built between 1863 and 1869 and ultimately brought many Chinese workers to Nevada. See Sue Fawn Chung, *In Pursuit of Gold: Chinese American Miners and Merchants in the American West* (University of Illinois Press, 2011), 84. I thank Aixin Aydin for her suggestions to improve this chapter.

2. Ean T. Barnett, "Cultural Mapping of a Folkloric People" (master's thesis, University of Nevada, Reno, 2011).

3. Gregory D. Smithers, "Rituals of Consumption: Cannibalism and Native American Oral Traditions in Southeastern North America," in *To Feast on Us as Their Prey: Cannibalism and the Early Modern Atlantic*, ed. Rachel B. Herrmann (University of Arkansas, 2019), 19–35.

4. The Animal People predated human beings. According to Paiute stories, animals and humans are related peoples, making it inappropriate for Nuwuzo'ho to eat them.

5. Wilson Wewa, *Legends of the Northern Paiute*, as told to James A. Gardner (Oregon State University Press, 2017), 33–42. Wewa's is one of many recorded Paiute stories with cannibal characters. Smithers notes other traditions in which cannibals are vanquished. See Smithers, "Rituals of Consumption," 32.

6. Watson provides a helpful introduction to this extensive literature. See Kelly L. Watson, *Insatiable Appetites: Imperial Encounters with Cannibalism in the North Atlantic World* (New York University Press, 2015), 1–15.

7. I'm hardly the first scholar to make this observation. The tradition goes back to Montaigne's 1580 essay "Of Cannibals." My hope here, though, is not simply to unmask hypocrisy but to ask what can be learned by attending to Native voices speaking about cannibals. Here, too, I'm not the first. See Eduardo Viveiros de Castro, *Cannibal Metaphysics* (University of Minnesota Press, 2014), 193–96.

8. On the possibilities of studying marginalized, interethnic family and social formations among Asian migrants to North America, see Nayan Shah, *Stranger Intimacy: Contesting Race, Sexuality, and the Law in the North American West* (University of California Press, 2011), 1–4.

9. Sources from the colonial archive, such as census and boarding school records, demand critical reading and understanding of their production in context. I also use sources produced by or directly tied to Chinese and Native communities. This strategy allows focusing on individual Native and Chinese actors without losing sight of the context's constraints. On issues with the census, including the ways people of mixed descent appear in it, see Benedict Anderson, *Imagined Communities: Reflections on the Origin and Spread of Nationalism*, rev. ed. (Verso, 2016), 163–66; and Fawn Chung, *In Pursuit of Gold*, xviii–xx. On issues with Chinese names in American sources, see Fawn Chung, *In Pursuit of Gold*, xxix–xxxii. Some sources likely related to Sam Leon use the name Ah Sam. I correlate with other sources when possible and also note instances that lack corroboration. On oral traditions, see Hsinya Huang, "Tracking Memory: Encounters between Chinese Railroad Workers and Native Americans," in *The Chinese and the Iron Road: Building the Transcontinental Railroad*, ed. Gordon H. Chang and Shelley Fisher Fishkin (Stanford University Press, 2019), 184–85.

10. Huang refers to "specific, life-preserving practices" within these intimate relations in "Tracking Memory," 184. Pierce draws on Indigenous scholars' notions of good relations, namely, ethical decision-making that considers human and non-human kin within the context of colonialism; see Joseph M. Pierce, "In Good Relations: Native Adoption, Kinstillations, and the Grounding of Memory," in *Queer Kinship: Race, Sex, Belonging, Form*, ed. Tyler Bradway and Elizabeth Freeman (Duke University Press, 2022), 95–96. On the role of intimate relations within empire, see Ann Laura Stoler, *Haunted by Empire: Geographies of Intimacy in North American History* (Duke University Press, 2006).

11. Hiʻilei Julia Kawehipuaakahaopulani Hobart and Tamara Kneese, "Radical Care: Survival Strategies for Uncertain Times," *Social Text* 38, no. 1 (2020): 2.

12. Jodi A. Byrd, *The Transit of Empire: Indigenous Critiques of Colonialism* (University of Minnesota Press, 2011), xxxiv; Paul Lai and Lindsey Claire Smith, "Introduction," *American Quarterly* 62, no. 3 (September 2010): 407.

13. Wewa, *Legends of the Northern Paiute*, 112.

14. Heather R. Lee, "A Life Cooking for Others: The Work and Migration Experiences of a Chinese Restaurant Worker in New York City, 1920–1946," in *Eating Asian*

America: A Food Studies Reader, ed. Robert Ji-Song Ku, Martin F. Manalansan and Anita Mannur (New York University Press, 2013), 53–77; Madeline Yuan-yin Hsu, *Dreaming of Gold, Dreaming of Home: Transnationalism and Migration between the United States and South China, 1882–1943* (Stanford University Press, 2000), 30. Chinese cooks worked on a number of farms and ranches in western Nevada and eastern California. See Loren B. Chan, "Chinese in Nevada: An Historical Survey, 1856–1970," *Nevada Historical Quarterly* 25, no. 4 (1982): 293; Sue Fawn Chung, *Chinese in Nevada* (Arcadia Publishing, 2011), 20; "An Interview with Frank Yparraguirre," 1984, University of Nevada Oral History Collection, 49; Sue Fawn Chung, "Beyond Railroad Work: Chinese Contributions to the Development of Winnemucca and Elko, Nevada," in *The Chinese and the Iron Road: Building the Transcontinental Railroad*, ed. Gordon H. Chang and Shelley Fisher Fishkin (Stanford University Press, 2019), 318–29; Emil W. Billeb, *Mining Camp Days* (Howell-North Books, 1968), 126.

15. Adrian Praetzellis and Mary Praetzellis, "'Let My Body Be Buried Here': A Long View of Chinese Immigrants in the American West," in *Chinese Diaspora Archaeology in North America*, ed. Chelsea Rose and J. Ryan Kennedy (University Press of Florida, 2020), 202–3; Lani Ah Tye Farkas, *Bury My Bones in America: The Saga of a Chinese Family in California, 1852–1996* (Carl Mautz Publishing, 1998), 203; Emily Dale, "Households of the Overseas Chinese in Aurora, Nevada," in *Beyond the Walls: New Perspectives on the Archaeology of Historical Households*, ed. Kevin R. Fogle, James A. Nyman, and Mary C. Beaudry (University Press of Florida, 2015), 150–56.

16. "An Interview with Frank Yparraguirre," 48.

17. Samantha M. Williams, *Assimilation, Resilience, and Survival: A History of the Stewart Indian School, 1890–2020* (University of Nebraska Press, 2022), 38–39.

18. Farkas, *Bury My Bones in America*, 135.

19. Marguerite Sprague, *Bodie's Gold: Tall Tales and True History from a California Mining Town* (University of Nevada Press, 2011), 96.

20. Sue Fawn Chung, "An Ocean Apart: Chinese-American Segregated Burials," in *Till Death Do Us Part: American Ethnic Cemeteries as Borders Uncrossed*, ed. Allan Amanik and Kami Fletcher (University Press of Mississippi, 2020), 96.

21. Edward C. Johnson, *Walker River Paiutes: A Tribal History* (Walker River Paiute Tribe, 1975), 58–61. Fewer food plants particularly affected Paiute women's routines. See William J. Bauer, "The Giant and the Waterbaby," *Boom* 2, no. 4 (December 2012): 114.

22. Johnson, *Walker River Paiutes*, 61–64.

23. Johnson, *Walker River Paiutes*, 88; Williams, *Assimilation, Resilience, and Survival*, 25. The broader context also mattered as the economic depression of 1890 led to corporate takeover of lands surrounding Walker River. New owners cleared and flooded even more land, creating a water crisis for Paiutes. Johnson, *Walker River Paiutes*, 64–65.

24. *Annual Report of the Department of the Interior: Indian Affairs, Report of the Commissioner* (hereafter *ARDI*) (Washington, DC: Government Printing Office, 1900), 493; *ARDI*, 1903, 210; *ARDI*, 1904, 243.

25. Grace M. Dangberg, "Letters to Jack Wilson, the Paiute Prophet, Written between 1908 and 1911," in *Bureau of American Ethnology, Bulletin* 164, *Anthropological Papers*, no. 55 (Smithsonian Institution, 1957), 296.

26. On seeking work, see Ruth Kretzler Billhimer, "Pawns of Fate: Chinese/Paiute Intercultural Marriages, 1860–1920" (master's thesis, University of Nevada, 1995), 98; Bauer, "The

Giant and the Waterbaby," 114; Charlotte K. Sunseri, "Capitalism as Nineteenth-Century Colonialism and Its Impacts on Native Californians," *Ethnohistory* 64, no. 4 (October 2017): 471–95.

27. Huang, "Tracking Memory," 189–92. For evidence of Chinese immigrants eating foods Paiutes gathered, including pine nuts, see Charlotte K. Sunseri, "Alliance Strategies in the Racialized Railroad Economies of the American West," *Historical Archaeology* 49, no. 1 (2015): 91–94. Some Chinese Americans learned to speak Paiute and exchanged food with them. Billhimer, "Pawns of Fate," 44–45.

28. Billeb, *Mining Camp Days*, 127.

29. Huang, "Tracking Memory," 191.

30. Billhimer, "Pawns of Fate," 99. Had Sam and Daisy also sought legal marriage, they would have been free to do so. As both husband and wife were classified as non-white, they were free to marry each other. On Nevada statute, see Huang, "Tracking Memory," 189–90. Although Walker River's administrators did not create a formal Court of Indian Offenses, they did try to enforce its marriage provisions. See *ARDI*, 1906, 270.

31. Walker River Paiute Rolls, 1911, in *Walker River Valley Paiute Rolls*, ed. Doreen Robinson (Quintin Publications, 2000), 10. The same census documents attest to other marriages between Paiute women and men with Chinese names, including a man listed as "Ah Son." As Paiute descendants later remarked, "Lots of tribal people had Chinese relatives." See Billhimer, "Pawns of Fate," 97, 102. Sam and Daisy's relationship aligns with research on Chinese men who married across racial lines: These couples tended to be working-class and often met at work sites. See Huping Ling, "Negotiating Transnational Migration: Marriage and Changing Gender Roles Among the Chinese Diaspora," in *Routledge Handbook of the Chinese Diaspora*, ed. Chee-Beng Tan (Routledge, 2012), 239.

32. Steward's fieldwork speaks to family involvement and gift giving in the 1920s. See Julian Haynes Steward, "Ethnography of the Owens Valley Paiute," in *American Archaeology and Ethnology* 33, no. 3 (1933): 295.

33. Billhimer, "Pawns of Fate," 97. These items likely came from the dining room he opened in Yerington in 1909. "Little Locals," *Yerington Times*, October 2, 1909, 1. The article references "Ah Sam & Co."

34. Wewa, Legends of the Northern Paiute, 111.

35. Farkas, *Bury My Bones in America*, 70; Sue Fawn Chung, "Their Changing World: Chinese Women on the Comstock, 1860–1910," in *Comstock Women: The Making of a Mining Community*, ed. Ronald M. James and Elizabeth Raymond (University of Nevada Press, 1998), 205; Barbara L. Voss, "Interethnic Relationships in Nineteenth-Century Chinatowns: New Perspectives from Archaeological Research and Missionary Women's Writings," in *Chinese Diaspora Archaeology in North America*, ed. Chelsea Rose and J. Ryan Kennedy (University Press of Florida, 2011), 129–33.

36. *Huiguan* practices came to the United States with Chinese immigrants (9–11) and played an important role domestically as well as in transnational Chinese politics. See Yucheng Qin, *The Diplomacy of Nationalism: The Six Companies and China's Policy toward Exclusion* (University of Hawaii Press, 2009), 1–2, 9–11. On mutual aid functions, see Elizabeth Sinn, "Practicing Charity Across the Chinese Diaspora, 1850–1949," in *Chinese Diaspora Charity and the Cantonese Pacific*, 1850–1949, ed. John Fitzgerald and Hon-ming Yip (Hong Kong University Press, 2020), 19–31. *Huiguan* were not the only Chinese organizations.

Some Western cities also had chapters of so-called secret societies, including the Chinese Masons.

37. Farkas, *Bury My Bones in America*, 17–19.

38. The *huiguan* met a need prompted by transnational migrants, creating a new kind of mutual aid association. See Hon-ming Yip, "*Huiguan* as an Overseas Charitable Institution: Homebound Burials and the Global Chinese Diaspora, 1850–1949," in *Chinese Diaspora Charity*, ed. John Fitzgerald and Hon-ming Yip (Hong Kong University Press, 2020), 72–95; John Molenda, "Moral Discourse and Personhood in Overseas Chinese Context," *Historical Archaeology* 49, no. 1 (2015): 56. On the details of burial for later repatriation, see Fawn Chung, "An Ocean Apart," 100–1; Fawn Chung, *Chinese in Nevada*, 50. The CCBA still coordinated shipments of remains and Laporte's cemetery has evidence of exhumations into the 1920s. See Nicholas J. Smits, "Roots Entwined: Archaeology of an Urban Chinese American Cemetery," *Historical Archaeology* 42, no. 3 (2008): 115; Farkas, *Bury My Bones in America*, 135. Studies of Portland's Chinese cemetery attest to disinterment and transport into the late 1940s. See Smits, "Roots Entwined," 111; Molenda, "Moral Discourse and Personhood in Overseas Chinese Contexts," 56.

39. Including Tuscarora, Carson City, Virginia City, Elko, Carlin, and Hawthorne. See Fawn Chung, "An Ocean Apart," 90, 97, 99, 102, 107, 110–11.

40. Sprague, *Bodie's Gold*, 94–96.

41. "An Interview with Frank Yparraguirre," 48; Sprague, *Bodie's Gold*, 95, 90. Threats against Native people also marked Bodie's history, including horrifying newspaper editorials about bodily desecration. See Sprague, *Bodie's Gold*, 93.

42. In 1903, a white mob in Tonopah killed Chong Bing Long, who owned a laundry. His killers went unpunished. See Fawn Chung, *Chinese in Nevada*, 66.

43. Fawn Chung, "An Ocean Apart," 95–96; "The Second Exhumation and Return of the Remains," in *From the Gold Rush to the Present*, ed. Judy Yung, Him Mark Lai, and Philip P. Choy (University of California Press, 2006), 28; Yip, "*Huiguan* as an Overseas Charitable Institution," 80; Teresa Bergen and Heide Davis, *Historic Cemeteries of Portland, Oregon* (Arcadia Publishing, 2021), 83.

44. Fawn Chung, "An Ocean Apart," 102.

45. "Walker River Paiute Rolls, 1912," in *Walker River Valley Paiute Rolls*, 10. According to Billhimer, Daisy was not the only Paiute woman returning to the reservation to give birth on Indian land. See Billhimer, "Pawns of Fate," 93, 102.

46. For more general trends, see Brianna Theobald, *Reproduction on the Reservation: Pregnancy, Childbirth, and Colonialism in the Long Twentieth Century* (University of North Carolina Press, 2019), 29–33. For Paiute specifics, see Steward, "Ethnography of the Owens Valley Paiute," 289–90; Theobald, *Reproduction on the Reservation*, 63.

47. Theobald, *Reproduction on the Reservation*, 34–36. To be sure, morbidity and mortality were issues across Native North America, including among Paiutes. See Steward, "Ethnography of the Owens Valley Paiute," 290.

48. Theobald, *Reproduction on the Reservation*, 20, 25, 27–28, 38–40. Paiutes maintained traditions of extensive support from female relatives; see Steward, "Ethnography of the Owens Valley Paiute," 291. These would have been discouraged by the field matron, a position appointed in 1901.

49. Steward, "Ethnography of the Owens Valley Paiute," 238. For evidence of ongoing consultation with traditional healers at Walker River, see *ARDI*, 1903, 210.

50. The year 1904 was particularly bad as twenty-three deaths outnumbered the ten births. See *ARDI*, 1904, 602.

51. Billhimer, "Pawns of Fate," 97, 99.

52. Michael Hittman, *Corbett Mack: The Life of a Northern Paiute* (University of Nevada Press, 2013), 199–200.

53. Fawn Chung, *In Pursuit of Gold*, 110–11.

54. Huang, "Tracking Memory," 191. On the death toll of Chinese railroad workers, see Fawn Chung, "An Ocean Apart," 90–91.

55. Several sources reference Daisy's illness without noting specifics. For the record citing tuberculosis, see "Case Record," Student Case Files 1902–1981, Sherman Indian High School, Box 206, Folder "Leon, Laura," Record Group (RG) 75, Records of the Bureau of Indian Affairs, National Archives and Records Administration (NARA).

56. David N. DeJong, *"If You Knew the Conditions": A Chronicle of the Indian Medical Service and American Indian Health Care, 1908–1955* (Lexington Books, 1955), chap. 2, between note 30 and note 31, and table 5; Elizabeth James, "'Hardly a Family Is Free from the Disease': Tuberculosis, Health Care, and Assimilation Policy on the Nez Perce Reservation, 1908–1942," *Oregon Historical Quarterly* 112, no. 2 (2011): 146–48.

57. "Walker River Paiute Rolls, 1915," in *Walker River Valley Paiute Rolls*, 1. Daisy is noted in the remarks column as having died on August 2, 1914. Her burial site in Yerington was confirmed during a September 2022 author visit.

58. Wewa, *Legends of the Northern Paiute*, 112.

59. Billhimer, "Pawns of Fate," 97. Between 1840 and 1900, 2.3 million Chinese migrated. See Hsu, *Dreaming of Home*, 10.

60. References to birth in Hawaii appear in the 1920 US Census, East Fork, Douglas, Nevada, ED 5, sheet 7B, NARA microfilm publication T625, roll 1004. Records indicating birth in California (specifically San Francisco) appear in the 1930 US Census, Bodie, Mono, California, ED0003, sheet 1A, NARA microfilm T626, FHL 2339913; and 1940 US Census, Bodie, Mono, California, ED 26-3, sheet 1B, NARA microfilm T627, roll 266. All census data accessed July and August 2022 via Ancestry.com.

61. Colleen Fong, "Establishing and Maintaining a Family in the Shadow of Chinese Exclusion: A Case Study of the Fong Family of Santa Barbara County, California," *Chinese America: History and Perspectives* (2013), 39. Fawn Chung confirms the ratios in her analysis of Nevada census data, finding nineteen Chinese men for every Chinese woman in 1900, seventeen to one in 1910, and eleven to one in 1920. See Fawn Chung, *In Pursuit of Gold*, 87.

62. Hsu, *Dreaming of Gold*, 55–57, 69–87; Erika Lee, *At America's Gates: Chinese Immigration during the Exclusion Era, 1882–1943* (University of North Carolina Press, 2003), 183–208.

63. C. Joseph Genetin-Pilawa, *Crooked Paths to Allotment: The Fight Over Federal Indian Policy After the Civil War* (University of North Carolina Press, 2012).

64. Johnson, *Walker River Paiutes*, 88–89.

65. *ARDI, 1902*, 636; *ARDI, 1905*, 255; *ARDI, 1906*, 269.

66. "Sold Opium," *Lyon County Times* (Yerington, NV), April 1, 1899, 3. Unlike the smaller town newspapers, references to "Ah Sam" in the Carson City paper are more likely to refer to individuals other than Sam Leon. See "US Court," *Daily Appeal* (Carson City, NV), March 22, 1898, 3.

67. "Sold Opium," *Yerington Times*, December 19, 1914, 3; "Opium Peddler Held to Appear," *Yerington Times*, January 9, 1915, 1. Accounts of both arrests (of Ah Sam) mention sales to Native people. For Paiute recollections of Sam's involvement with opium and state scrutiny of users, see Hittman, *Corbett Mack*, 245, 319–20.

68. "Notice," *Gardnerville Record-Courier*, April 6, 1923, 4.

69. "Federal Men Will Invade Yerington," *Nevada State Journal*, March 29, 1924. See also Hittman, *Corbett Mack*, 248, 310, 350–51.

70. Reformers and Indian Office officials called for a crackdown on Chinese who sold opium to Native people. See *ARDI, 1900*, 493; *ARDI, 1905*, 255. For statistics on Chinese imprisoned for selling alcohol and opium to Native people between 1865 and 1904, see Billhimer, "Pawns of Fate," 54. On opium background, see Fawn Chung, *In Pursuit of Gold*, 111–14.

71. "Gang of Thugs Attack Chinese Quarter," *Tonopah Bonanza*, September 26, 1903, 3. On the murder and trial testimony, see Fawn Chung, *Chinese in Nevada*, 66. Chinese residents had no redress when Tonopah residents attacked Chinatown *again* a few years later. "The Fire Fiend," *Tonopah Bonanza*, January 21, 1905, 8.

72. Billhimer, "Pawns of Fate," 98–99.

73. Billhimer, "Pawns of Fate," 99. According to Fawn Chung, many Chinese women in Nevada died during their children's early years, leaving Chinese fathers and other family members to raise them. See "Their Changing World," 215. Sam might have had prior experience caring for the child of a Native friend after the mother's death. See "Did Not Buy Child," *Lyon County News*, October 6, 1906.

74. Billhimer, "Pawns of Fate," 94, 99.

75. Kirsten Twelbeck, "The Donaldina Cameron Myth and the Rescue of America, 1910–2002," in *Chinatowns in a Transnational World: Myths and Realities of an Urban Phenomenon*, ed. Vanessa Kunneman and Ruth Mayer (Routledge, 2011), 135–41; Michelle A. Lettieri, "Maximize Our Missions: Mui Tsai, Missionaries and Material Representation" (master's thesis, University of Las Vegas–Nevada, 2006), 167.

76. On Tooker House (later renamed the Ming Quong Home), see Eva Armentrout Ma, *Hometown Chinatown: A History of Oakland's Chinese Community, 1852–1995* (Routledge, 2014), 72, 77.

77. Laura was not alone in having a family. See *Eighty-third Annual Report of the Board of Foreign Missions of the Presbyterian Church of the United States of America* (1920), 187–88. Lettieri found references to withholding food as far back as 1837. See "Maximize Our Missions," 27. Even though some residents, like Laura, were not orphans and did not come from abusive situations, pamphlets lumped all the girls together in their descriptions of their residents' former lives. See Peggy Pascoe, *Relations of Rescue: The Search for Female Moral Authority in the American West, 1874–1939* (Oxford University Press, 1990), 52–56.

78. Gerrye Wong, "Ming Quong Home," in *Chinese Argonauts* (Foothills Community College, 1971), 178. *Eighty-third Annual Report*, 187–88. Laura was certainly not alone in having living family members who were unable to care for her. In 1917, for example, mission reports indicate that three children were brought to the home by relatives. See *Eightieth Annual Report of the Board of Foreign Missions of the Presbyterian Church in the United States of America* (Presbyterian Board of Publication, 1917), 192.

79. *Eightieth Annual Report*, 191–92. See also Wendy Rouse Jorae, *The Children of Chinatown: Growing up Chinese American in San Francisco, 1850–1920* (University of North Carolina Press, 2009), 157–59.

80. *Eighty-third Annual Report*, 188.

81. *Eighty-third Annual Report*, 188. According to school records and her daughter, Juanita, Laura affiliated with the Presbyterian Church while living at Tooker. Billhimer, "Pawns of Fate," 99.

82. Fawn Chung, *Chinese in Nevada*, 75. For references to Sam's visits, see application and Frederic Snyder to Donaldina Cameron, August 16, 1931, both in Box 21, Folder "Laura Leon," Student Case Files, 1919–1980, Carson/Stewart Indian School, RG 75, NARA.

83. Donaldina Cameron to Frederic Snyder, August 3,1929, Box 21, Folder "Laura Leon," Student Case Files, 1919–1980, Carson/Stewart Indian School, RG 75, NARA. Williams notes that negotiating for family visits was common for Native students enrolled in boarding schools. See *Assimilation, Resilience, and Survival*, 16–17. She also notes that school officials required parents to pay for their children's travel expenses and scrutinized parents to see if their records justified a visit. See *Assimilation, Resilience, and Survival*, 41–42.

84. Jorae, *Children of Chinatown*, 150–54. As historian Peggy Pascoe has observed, missionaries increasingly partnered with social welfare groups, such as the Society for the Prevention of Cruelty to Children, and eventually with the emerging criminal justice system for juveniles, to identify and absorb Chinese children. See Peggy Pascoe, *Relations of Rescue: The Search for Female Moral Authority in the American West, 1874–1939* (Oxford University Press, 1990), 186.

85. Donaldina Cameron to Frederic Snyder, August 3,1929, Box 21, Folder "Laura Leon," Student Case Files, 1919–1980, Carson/Stewart Indian School, RG 75, NARA.

86. Williams, *Assimilation, Resilience, and Survival*, 27–31. The field matron expressed frustration at parents' reluctance to send children to school, especially in the wake of disease outbreaks. See *ARDI, 1903*, 210.

87. Williams, *Assimilation, Resilience, and Survival*, 4–5, 33–34.

88. Donaldina Cameron to Frederic Snyder, February 25, 1930; Donaldina Cameron to Frederic Snyder, July 30, 1931; Frederic Snyder to Donaldina Cameron, August 16, 1931, all in Box 21, Folder "Laura Leon," Student Case Files, 1919–1980, Carson/Stewart Indian School, RG 75, NARA.

89. On runaways and techniques (including a jail on school grounds) used to punish them, see Williams, *Assimilation, Resilience, and Survival*, 32–35, 54–55. In an application, Laura wrote that she wanted to enroll because she "want[s] to be among Indian students." Application for Admission, Box 55, Folder "Leon, Laura," Student Case Files, 1902–1989, Phoenix Indian High School, NARA Riverside, California.

90. On visits from relatives, see Frederic Snyder to Donaldina Cameron, January 4, 1930; on Laura's efforts to enroll in school, see Laura Leon to Frederic Snyder, June 7, 1930, and June 10, 1930; on her desire to visit Sam, see Laura Leon to Frederic Snyder, June 19, 1930; Frederic Snyder to Donaldina Cameron, February 10, 1930, all in Box 21, Folder "Laura Leon," Student Case Files, 1919–1980, Carson/Stewart Indian School, RG 75, NARA.

91. On Sam's support for Laura's plans, see Sam Leon to Laura Leon, July 10, 1931, Box 206, Folder "Leon, Laura," Student Case Files, 1902–1981, Sherman Indian High School, RG 75, NARA. On the administrators' efforts, see Frederic Snyder to Donaldina Cameron, August 5, 1931, and August 16, 1931, Box 21, Folder "Laura Leon," Student Case Files, 1919–1980, Carson/Stewart Indian School, RG 75, NARA. Snyder, the Stewart principal, derailed other students' efforts to see family as well. See Williams, *Assimilation, Resilience, and Survival*, 43–45.

92. Donaldina Cameron to Frederic Snyder, January 2, 1930; Frederic Snyder to Donaldina Cameron, January 4, 1930; Ray Parrell [*sic*] to Frederic Snyder, January 4, 1930, all in Box 21, Folder "Laura Leon," Student Case Files, 1919–1980, Carson/Stewart Indian School, RG 75, NARA. The land question is crucial as Fong's work shows how property ownership was a strong predictor for avoiding family separation among Chinese Americans. See Fong, "Establishing and Maintaining a Family."

93. Laura Leon to Frederic Snyder, November 5, 1932, Box 21, Folder "Laura Leon," Student Case Files, 1919–1980, Carson/Stewart Indian School, RG 75, NARA. Frederic Snyder to Laura Leon, November 15, 1932, Box 21, Folder "Laura Leon," Student Case Files, 1919–1980, Carson/Stewart Indian School, RG 75, NARA.

94. *ARDI, 1900*, 493; *ARDI, 1904*, 243; *ARDI, 1905*, 255.

95. *ARDI, 1901*, 546; *ARDI, 1906*, 270.

96. On allotment, Native people of mixed descent, and blood quantum, see Anne F. Hyde, *Born of Lakes and Plains: Mixed-Descent Peoples and the Making of the American West* (W. W. Norton, 2022), 309–15.

97. Fawn Chung, *The Chinese in Nevada*, 79; Debbie Hinman, "Reno and the Chinese Experience," *Footprints* 13, no. 4 (Fall 2010): 3.

98. Billhimer, "Pawns of Fate," 95, 99. In her application to Phoenix Indian High School, Laura claimed to have a home among her "mother's relations" and attested to having four allotment shares at Walker River. Application for Admission, Box 55, Folder "Leon, Laura," Student Case Files, 1902–1989, Phoenix Indian High School, RG 75, Records of the Bureau of Indian Affairs, NARA.

99. Billhimer, "Pawns of Fate," 97.

100. Sam Leon, Certificate of Death, Nevada Department of Health, Carson City, NV; *Nevada Death Records*; "Sam Leon Succumbs in Local Hospital," *Nevada State Journal*, February 22, 1955, 19.

101. Kaylee Byle (Records Office of Mountain View Cemetery), email message to author, September 19, 2022.

102. Billhimer, "Pawns of Fate," 100.

103. Billhimer, "Pawns of Fate," 99.

104. "Laura Thom," *Mason Valley News*, June 5,1987, 6.

105. Wewa, *Legends of the Northern Paiute*, 113.

106. Wewa, *Legends of the Northern Paiute*, 40–41.

107. David Chidester, *Savage Systems: Colonialism and Comparative Religion in Southern Africa* (University of Virginia Press, 1996), 35–36; David Chidester, *Empire of Religion: Imperialism and Comparative Religion* (University of Chicago Press, 2014), 199–200.

Chapter 12

Religious Labor at the Edge

AIDS, Religion, and Spirituality in San Francisco's Ward 5B

LYNNE GERBER

Keywords: HIV/AIDS, San Francisco, LGBTQ, chaplaincy, counterculture

In June of 1983, East Coast AIDS activists met their West Coast counterparts for the first time. Two years after the first public reports of the new disease, activists gathered in Denver at a national gay and lesbian health conference that included a forum on AIDS. Over two hundred people attended, including Michael Callen and Bobbi Campbell, authors of the first two pamphlets about safe sex directed at gay men. Callen, a New Yorker, coauthored "How to Have Sex in an Epidemic." Campbell, San Francisco's self-declared "KS Poster Boy," wrote "Play Fair!" with his fellow Sisters of Perpetual Indulgence under his spiritual name, Sister Florence Nightmare.[1] The meeting was foundational. The Federation of AIDS Organizations (FARO) was started, marking the first formal collaboration between AIDS groups, and fourteen people with AIDS (PWAs) drafted the Denver Principles, a statement outlining how they expected to be treated by health-care professionals and others. Callen was impressed by the San Francisco contingent's political vision and its level of on-the-ground organization. New Yorkers, he thought, had a lot to learn. But he was also annoyed by his left coast comrades—especially when "the San Francisco men needed time out for spiritual reflection."[2]

The emergence of HIV/AIDS in the early 1980s brought the United States to its epistemic, moral, and social limits. A mysterious, devastating disease of unknown cause and almost universally lethal outcome, AIDS marked the edge of medical knowledge at a time when American medicine was at the height of its powers. People facing it dwelled for years, sick and scared, at the ever-receding horizon of what was known about the disease and how it might be treated. It took three years from the first reports of the disease to identify the human immunodeficiency virus (HIV), the virus that causes AIDS, and fifteen years for effective treatment. Those most vulnerable, gay men and IV drug users, lived at the edge of moral recognition, making sociopolitical responses slow, piecemeal, and terribly inadequate.[3]

AIDS was also a taut religious crisis. On one side, it raised, magnified, and proliferated the kinds of problems addressed by religion. The new disease evoked the mystery of the unknown and the existential terror of living in that unknown. The physical agony and often painful death that were the hallmarks of AIDS raised profound questions about what meaning, if any, could be made from suffering and what possibilities there were in death and what lies after. On the other side, the people most vulnerable to the disease were alienated from and suspicious of the institutions that historically addressed those questions. Gay men and IV drug users were vulnerable to a virus transmitted by bodily fluids. They were also vulnerable to moral condemnation by religious institutions. Religious moralization of homosexuality and drug use left many people with AIDS ambivalent, at best, about turning to religion. In some cases, religion became an actual threat as religious leaders with prominent public voices interpreted the disease as God's rightful punishment for sin, generating greater stigma, fear, and isolation from those who might provide support. The tension between extreme religious need and extreme religious mistrust generated personal and organizational experiments straddling the spiritual and the religious.

The ways Americans draw distinctions between the spiritual and the religious have been of great interest to students of American religion. Surveys of American religious life document the steady rise of so-called "religious nones"—people who do not identify as religious or with any specific religious tradition—and the subset of these people who consider themselves "spiritual but not religious," or SBNR.[4] The study of SBNR is most often framed as a problem of personal religious identification in a society where seeming secularization is less about the waning of religious sensibilities than a decreased identification with religious institutions.[5] But the distinction can also be institutionally useful for organizations navigating specific religious binds in American society.

Distinctions between religion and spirituality also have significance for the study of religion in the American West. Quincy Newell, Max Greenberg, and James Bennett, all contributors to this volume, note the particular urgency of the need to theorize religion in the West. They trace the source of that urgency to the incompleteness of Protestant hegemony and the relative weakness of religious institutions in the West, in contrast to other regions and especially the socially and economically dominant eastern seaboard.[6] Those traits make the American West seem less religious as conventionally measured, but this volume, along with the wider literature of the region, documents how vast and varied spiritual practices and communities are in the region.

San Francisco's religious history is emblematic of this regional tendency. The land that became the city was initially inhabited by the Ohlone and

Costanoan peoples and then colonized by the twin Spanish imperial powers of the military and the Catholic Church. Devastating as it was, the church's religious conquest of Native peoples was incomplete, and Spain's colonial power lost sway. When gold was discovered in the Sacramento Valley in 1848, the San Francisco peninsula became the site of competing efforts to gain control of the land for the developing American state. This meant an influx of Anglo people and institutions that sought the kind of cultural and institutional hegemony they had achieved in other places on the continent. But in the case of religion, that hegemony was never realized. Protestant religious institutions had difficulty gaining an institutional foothold in San Francisco, a city whose growth was fueled, in part, by activities and people deemed outside Protestant moral approval.[7] Spiritual beliefs and practices emerged that reflected different social locations, economic practices, and moral concerns.[8] From the second half of the nineteenth century through the twentieth century, San Francisco saw cyclical efforts to institute the moral and civic constraints of institutional religion—and ongoing, often stronger, resistance to such efforts, resistance that generated religious and spiritual innovations that reflected the ethos of this "wide-open town."[9] San Francisco has long navigated the spiritual and the religious within this context of unsuccessful bids for religious hegemony and the influence of moral outsiders to American Protestantism. Such boundaries became strategic tools to be used carefully when faced with an existential public health crisis and the needs for care it wrought.

This chapter looks at how the boundaries between religion and spirituality were negotiated and renegotiated in three interrelated but distinct San Francisco organizations that engaged people with AIDS, their friends, lovers, and families in the first four years of the epidemic, 1981 through 1985. The history of AIDS is one of microhistories shaped by stages in scientific knowledge, the populations impacted, and the relentless power of stigma diffused through different communities and institutions. Focusing on these years allows us to examine an early discursive template of sorts about religion and AIDS, one that shifted and changed as AIDS grew and spread but remained influential.

The Shanti Project (Shanti), a service organization focused on death and dying, turned its attention exclusively to AIDS in the 1980s. The AIDS Interfaith Network (AIN) was founded to provide theological support to people with AIDS and counter claims about AIDS made by the religious right. Sojourn, a hospital chaplaincy program, started in the Episcopal chaplain's office at San Francisco General Hospital and in the 1980s adapted a long-standing religious role to a novel medical setting. The three groups overlapped in personnel, purpose, and history. All three came together in Ward 5B at San Francisco General, the first hospital ward dedicated exclusively to AIDS.[10] They all engaged in work that could be deemed spiritual, and all had functions that traditionally fall under the rubric of religion. But in an emergent organizational field, they differentiated themselves by how they divided their religious and spiritual labors and how they parsed their self-representation.

In the discussion that follows, I look at how each group claimed and/or disavowed "religion" and "spirituality" in what it did and how it described itself. In doing so, I attend to what those different signifiers meant in the context of AIDS. I also suggest that San Francisco's spiritual and religious grappling with AIDS in its earliest years had an outsized effect on American culture through efforts to institutionalize the San Francisco Model of AIDS care.[11] I show that grappling with "spiritual" versus "religious" is not only a matter of individual identification but also an organizational negotiation of particular tensions within a field—tensions that encourage groups to embrace and/or disavow religion and spirituality both internally and in relation to other organizations.

Psychology and the Spirituality of Death and Dying

The Shanti Project attended to death and dying by combining psychology and spirituality, an intersection of great interest to San Francisco's countercultural spiritual explorers. In the mid-twentieth century, a generation of seekers migrated to San Francisco to escape the constraints of institutions like religion and to find freedom in spiritual experimentation. Largely young, white, and middle-class, these people were attracted to the city for a range of spiritual reasons. Some came in search of the Beats and to explore Eastern spirituality as an alternative to the Christianity and Judaism in which they had been raised. Others sought enlightenment through psychedelics and pursued the religious experiences drugs could facilitate. Many turned to alternatives in health and healing, exploring Chinese medicine, visualization, macrobiotics, bodywork, and other holistic practices. Yet others were drawn by experiments at the intersection of spirituality and psychology that animated the human potential movement centered in California. Together, these diverse spiritual experiments, communities, leaders, and practitioners contributed to a culture of spiritual vividness and religious skepticism in the city.

Shanti was founded in 1975 by Dr. Charles Garfield, a psychiatrist working with cancer patients at the University of California, San Francisco. Garfield was inspired by the work of Dr. Elisabeth Kübler-Ross, a Swiss-American psychiatrist and countercultural spiritual figure. Kübler-Ross's 1959 book *On Death and Dying* revolutionized how American medicine approached the end of life by focusing on the experience of the dying and introducing her notion of the five stages of grief.[12] In the ensuing decades, Kübler-Ross's work with the dying became increasingly spiritually oriented, and she spoke publicly about her communication with the dead and experimentation with out-of-body experiences.[13] Garfield took a lighter touch to spirituality at Shanti in order to broaden the group's appeal, but the project's foundations at the intersection of psychology and spirituality continued to shape it.

In the early 1980s, Shanti underwent a transformation in mission to focus exclusively on AIDS. In 1978, Jim Geary, a gay man, activist, and massage therapist, became a Shanti volunteer. Geary was involved with the Vedanta society, the Loving Brotherhood—a social group for gay men interested in spirituality—and the spirituality-psychology interface that was integral to bodywork training.[14] His interest in working with the dying reflected his general spiritual commitments rather than any single practice or community.[15] In 1981, Paul Dague, a gay psychologist at the University of California Medical School, suggested to Geary that Shanti start a support group for what was then called GRID (gay-related immune deficiency).[16] Dague had been conducting intake interviews for the first studies of people with Kaposi sarcoma (KS) and was alarmed by the lack of psychological support available to them.[17] The first Shanti AIDS group started in November 1981, with "KS poster boy" Bobbi Campbell, one of its members.[18]

In 1982, the Shanti board dissolved and reconstituted itself with Geary as executive director. In 1983, it moved to a former convent in San Francisco and began working on AIDS full-time, becoming the most prominent AIDS social service group in the city. It ran multiple support groups, hosted public meetings and planning sessions about AIDS, and trained volunteers to meet the emotional and practical needs of PWAs (People with AIDS). By 1984, AIDS was enshrined in Shanti's mission statement, and the organization began developing housing and other services for PWAs. Shanti was also integral to the planning, opening, and operation of Ward 5B, which was designed and directed by Clifford Morrison, a psychiatric nurse and Shanti volunteer.[19] The unit was staffed with three full-time Shanti counselors who worked with AIDS patients and hospital staff to alleviate fears about the disease at a moment when little was known about it.[20]

Spirituality was integral to Shanti's culture. Its founding was rooted in countercultural spirituality and the intersection of spirituality and psychology, one of the organization's hallmarks. Its techniques reflected those spiritual influences. Shanti relied heavily on visualization and guided imagery to help people engage with the psychological dimensions of AIDS. Visualization, common in countercultural circles reached a wider public through Shakti Gawain's 1978 book *Creative Visualization*; Gawain was a self-proclaimed teacher of consciousness based in Marin, just north of San Francisco.[21] Visualizing AIDS, healing, and even death were tools Shanti used in almost every context in which it worked. Staff and volunteers led visualization exercises in support groups, trainings with hospital staff, conferences (including the 1983 Denver conference), and even meetings with San Francisco's Department of Public Health.

This infusion of spirituality in Shanti's culture was also evident in its earliest newsletter, which contained the Shanti Resource network. This list did not include a doctor, nurse, or other medical professional, but it did feature three visualization guides, a psychic, a transpersonal psychologist, two massage therapists, a Rosen bodyworker, a shiatsu practitioner, a tarot reader, and an art therapist, along with an accountant/bookkeeper, and a notary public.[22] The former chapel in Shanti's building was the site of early volunteer trainings and numerous AIDS funerals.[23]

Shanti's spiritual roots were also evident among its volunteers. The organization recruited two kinds of volunteers to work with people with AIDS: Practical support volunteers helped PWAs with tasks such as grocery shopping and laundry, transported them to doctors, and assisted with other daily needs. Emotional support volunteers provided a listening ear to help clients process their feelings and strategize ways to navigate the psycho-social dimensions of AIDS. Many were drawn to Shanti as an expression of their personal spiritual commitments.

All volunteers underwent the Shanti training, which prepared them to work with PWAs. The training gave up-to-date information about the medical aspects of AIDS, including transmission and treatment. New volunteers met more seasoned ones and learned about living with AIDS from PWAs themselves. They also participated in sessions focused on death and dying and fears about AIDS that incorporated visualizations and guided imagery. Volunteers were trained to attend to people with AIDS through listening rather than doing, an orientation Shanti volunteers shared with the chaplains discussed below. An early Shanti volunteer manual explained, "Shanti believes that only by first listening and sensitively hearing one another can we help in a truly meaningful way."[24] Many who went through the early Shanti training described it in spiritual, if not exactly religious, terms. Longtime Shanti volunteer Ed Wolfe told researcher Brendan McHugh, "I had seen the ad [for the training] and I felt called; as kind of woo-woo as that sounds. I was called to go to this thing."[25] Dave Lawson was almost evangelical about the training, saying, "I was so moved by the experience I wanted to share it with others."[26] But despite Shanti's evident spiritual influences, the organization was ambivalent about being explicit about them.

Spirituality was much more ambiguous in relation to Shanti clients. Despite its unmistakable influences, Shanti did not see itself as a spiritual organization and maintained a policy of minimizing talk of spirituality with clients.[27] According to Jack Pantaleo, who worked closely with Shanti as part of the AIDS Interfaith Network, "As Shanti you're not allowed to bring up spirituality. And if the client brings it up, you could listen, but you're not supposed to say anything."[28] Like the volunteers, many Shanti clients engaged in countercultural and metaphysical spirituality, but volunteers were instructed to maintain a certain neutrality regarding spirituality. Geary wrote of the tension in this position as well as the benefits he saw in maintaining it:

> One thing that both attracted and frustrated me about Shanti Project was the project's lack of spiritual focus. My work with people with a life-threatening illness has always been immensely spiritual and has paralleled my own spiritual journey and unfolding. . . . Many of Shanti Project's early volunteers were drawn to the project because of their attraction to the work of Dr. Kübler-Ross, Stephen Levine, and Ram Dass—individuals known for their spiritual and metaphysical leanings. . . . I wondered occasionally if I lacked special guidance of some sort. Yet part of me was grateful that Shanti Project didn't expound any set beliefs about life after death. It enabled us to work with a diverse clientele. Even as I became increasingly fascinated with metaphysical and life-after-death issues, I continued to believe that by putting aside our own agendas and being open to the diverse beliefs our clients had regarding afterlife, we were providing an immensely valuable service.[29]

Geary's frustration was not with the lack of spirituality in Shanti, but with the absence of a specific spiritual understanding, one that might deepen staff and volunteers' spiritual understanding but also ran the risk of alienating a diverse clientele. This interest in spirituality in general but lack of commitment to a particular path is emblematic of today's spiritual-but-not-religious claimants. It is akin to what Cadge and Sigalow call "spiritual secularism" in their work on interfaith chaplains and also parallels the approach Sojourn chaplaincy takes in its contemporary work.[30] But, as with secularism more generally, this doesn't signal a lack of spiritual perspective so much as its unmarking, a concealment that can make it more powerful.[31]

This dissociation from religion and agnosticism about spirituality made Shanti well-suited for white gay men, but was one of many factors that made it inadequate for people of color. Shanti's internal demographics and responsiveness to communities of color shifted over time, but in these early years its pervasive whiteness spurred the founding of groups that offered similar support in communities with different strategies for navigating the social tensions of AIDS. Some Latinx groups, for example, objected to Shanti's wariness toward biological family and insisted on including parents and siblings in their trainings.[32] And African American groups found they couldn't ignore religion in the ways Shanti did.

The Rafiki project, founded in 1988 by the Black Coalition on AIDS (BCA), found it impossible to bracket religion and spirituality. They, too, confronted the religious dilemmas of AIDS, but rather than trying to diffuse them by careful demarcations and strategic silences, Rafiki engaged both religion and spirituality more directly. Like Shanti, Rafiki was shaped by countercultural spirituality, but in an Afrocentric key. Former director Randall Miller remembers that "it was surrounded by people who came in who were practitioners of African religious practices. We did libations and acknowledged the ancestors."[33] But Rafiki also engaged the Black church and its theology directly. "Unlike Shanti and the AIDS Foundation," Miller said, "we explicitly talked about Christian religion . . . And the religious piece was particularly difficult because of this belief that . . . good things happen to you if you're a believer, and bad things happen to you if you're not. That's what many people articulated was the core of what they were hearing in Black churches in San Francisco at the time, and that [it] kind of left them—either as parents or sisters or as gay men living with HIV/AIDS—kind of left them cold."[34] Black clergy, as we will see below, were not necessarily more receptive to supporting people with AIDS, nor were they theologically less problematic. But for Black people with AIDS, and those who supported them, the church and their spiritual lives were too integral to step around or parse out to others.

Mobilizing Religion

Shanti may not have been explicit about its own spiritual foundations, and it did not address religion directly. But it recognized that religion was important in the context of AIDS and that supporters of PWAs would need to address it in some way. In the epidemic's early years, Shanti served as an organizational launching pad for other AIDS-related projects. One of them would, with Shanti's support, take on the religious dimensions of AIDS directly.

Shanti's first public workshop on AIDS included a session on religion featuring gay Catholic public theologian Kevin Gordon. Gordon used the occasion to address questions of religious meaning raised by AIDS and the theological problem of blame and responsibility. He urged listeners to move past theologies of blame—whether directed at God or oneself—and toward a more complex faith that recognizes the role of randomness in life. According to a newspaper account, "Gordon feels strongly that this 'tit for tat' theology is the *opposite* of the message of Judeo-Christian philosophy. 'That blaming is just what Judeo-Christianity is *not* about,' declares Gordon. What is the wisdom of our religious tradition on these questions? As Gordon perceives it, the wisdom is 'how to properly raise these questions, or how not to.'"[35]

At this early moment, it was becoming alarmingly clear that certain segments of American religion were not raising these questions in a fair or responsible way. Jerry Falwell represented many on the Christian right who saw AIDS as God's punishment and were willing to use that view to delegitimize gay and lesbian people and the gay rights movement.[36] In 1982, PWAs associated with Shanti identified the religious right as a particular threat. In an open letter to the gay community, members of the Shanti KS support group wrote, "Lately, we have been attacked by the moral majority [*sic*], who distributed literature stating that our illness is God's punishment for our perverse lifestyle. . . . We deplore these accusations which attribute our disease to a vengeful God. They have absolutely no idea of us as persons or of our unique and individual relationship with the Universe."[37] In criticizing the religious condemnation of people with AIDS, the signers also reaffirmed their own spiritual significance. This helped identify the work supportive religious people could do in response to AIDS—condemn AIDS-phobic theology and affirm PWAs' spiritual worth.

In order to develop that work, Shanti hosted a gathering for clergy. Organizers were concerned about the needs of gay and lesbian religionists in the era of AIDS and about the role of religious institutions as interpreters of AIDS to the American public.[38] A month later, at the Denver conference, FARO called for religious leaders to respond to AIDS and conservative theological messages about its meaning, asking gay religionists to take on religious issues. Gay non-religionists, they knew, had little use for, familiarity with, or skill in engaging the harmful religious discourse emerging about AIDS.[39]

The San Francisco AIDS Interfaith Network (AIN) was formed in response to these two events. It was initially organized by Jeremy Landau (a Methodist minister and Shanti staff person), Coni Staff (a lay leader in the gay- and lesbian-identified Metropolitan Community Church), and Jack Pantaleo (a leader in Evangelicals Concerned, a caucus group for gay evangelicals).[40] Although it wasn't a Shanti program, AIN was fiscally sponsored by Shanti for many years and accountable to its board. Its purpose was twofold: to meet the religious needs of PWAs and "to provide information, education and training to the religious community at large regarding the AIDS crisis."[41] But the implicit purpose of AIN was to engage and counter the religious right. "Why was there a need to form an interfaith network specifically for those with AIDS?" asked Jack Pantaleo in a history of AIN. "Because no religious group had ever proclaimed cancer was God's wrath."[42]

AIN's initial members and leaders were drawn from gay-identified religious groups, including gay and lesbian Jewish and Christian congregations, gay and lesbian caucuses of mainline Protestant denominations, and gay and lesbian interest groups emerging from but not affiliated with more conservative traditions.[43] It also included lay and clerical leaders from progressive congregations and religious groups across the city. Its early leadership included a representative from the San Francisco Council of Churches and a retired San Francisco police sergeant known for his pioneering work with the city's transgender community, who was an active Presbyterian layperson.[44]

As it developed, AIN recruited a wider range of participants; at its height, it crossed significant theological divides. San Francisco's first Foursquare Gospel congregation became a member after being recruited by AIN leader and PWA David Hummel. Its pastor, Rev. Greg Romine, had been involved in ecumenical work in an earlier ministry and was more open to engaging diverse religious groups than many other conservative clergy. Inspired by Foursquare founder Aimee Semple McPherson, Romine was interested in sharing the church's healing practices with PWAs. The congregation remained theologically conservative but started attracting PWAs who were drawn to the possibility of healing in a context that, while not gay-positive, was not condemnatory. Romine became personal pastor to Hummel, who was known for confronting conservative church leaders while carrying a sign that read "Thank God I'm Gay."

AIN also included the self-proclaimed "left wing," namely, the city's Unitarian Universalist Association.[45] It attracted metaphysical practitioners as well, people who identified more as spiritual than religious but valued participating in an organized religious response to AIDS. Michael Zonta, founder of the AIDS Metaphysical Network, organized a daily, worldwide meditation and prayer session for healing AIDS under AIN's banner.[46] And Louis Nassaney, a PWA who attributed his relative health to the teachings of New Thought leader Louise Hay, spoke at numerous AIN events.[47]

The inclusion of such spiritual groups did not detract from the group's explicitly religious purpose. AIN focused on work that engaged religiously marked ideas, people, and places. Its first project was a theological response to the Christian right and its interpretation of AIDS. "Is AIDS God's Wrath on Homosexuals?" was a pamphlet aimed directly at the right's most harmful theological claims. It began by establishing what AIN saw as the most foundational theological counter those claims: "Whether or not God approves or disapproves of homosexuality does not change the fact that God does *not* punish through disease."[48] Rather than treating AIDS as evidence of alienation from God, the pamphlet depicted it as an opportunity to experience God's love and personal spirituality more fully than before. "Gay and Lesbian People," it said, "are being called to break further out of their spiritual closets and to claim their place as God's children who are as lovable and precious as any other."[49] The first version of the pamphlet was written in direct response to claims made by Christians and relied heavily on Christian ideas and scriptural examples. This shifted as the group diversified and Jewish and other non-Christian groups refused to distribute AIN materials in their communities.

AIN worked directly with clergy to develop their understanding of AIDS and also served as a gatekeeping body to shield people with AIDS from AIDS-phobic clergy. A 1983 Shanti volunteer memo announced the availability of "Shanti-trained religious leaders" for PWAs who wanted spiritual counseling or support, a practice that predated AIN's fully distinguishing itself from Shanti. Over time, AIN developed and maintained a list of "AIDS-sensitive spiritual and religious counseling and referrals."[50] It included clergy who had either trained with AIN or were known by AIN members to be supportive of people with AIDS and not condemnatory of homosexuality. The list was used in hospitals across the city to refer PWAs and their families to clergy available for visitation.

It was also used to screen clergy and refuse their admission to the rooms of AIDS patients, especially in Ward 5B. In its first years Ward 5B attracted visitors from conservative religious groups who tried to enter hospital rooms in order to proselytize to PWA and encourage deathbed repentance from homosexuality. The *Bay Area Reporter*, the city's largest gay newspaper, reported on one such effort in the spring of 1984, when a group of conservative Christians entered Ward 5B by claiming they were delivering toiletries. "Hospital officials ejected them from the ward within minutes," the story said, "but for some of the patients, it was too late; they had been bombarded with a message that only further worsened their own self-doubts, and heightened their spiritual anguish."[51] As stories like these proliferated, AIN became the source hospital staff turned to in order to evaluate clergy and keep track of those who should be refused admission. AIN cofounder Jack Pantaleo recalled, "As the Interfaith Network grew and our list of clergy grew, hospitals who had AIDS patients—which happened to be all the hospitals eventually . . . they would call us and say, 'Is this person okay?' And it was very painful being a judge in that sense. Saying, 'I'm sorry, you—you're not allowed in there.'"[52] Judgment was necessary, though, and was delegated to the religiously marked AIDS Interfaith Network.

AIN was able to bridge many religious differences, but some proved too vast. Pantaleo remembered AIN's most significant failure: its inability to work with the city's Black churches. "That was the hardest," he recalled. "We never broke through. We tried and we tried."[53] Some Black and Black-led churches were deeply engaged in AIDS from early on. Glide Memorial Church hosted many groups for people with AIDS. Double Rock Baptist Church partnered with the largely white, largely gay Metropolitan Community Church of San Francisco to produce gospel fundraisers for AIDS. Its children's choir sang for patients at Ward 5B. But efforts at bringing Black churches together to work on AIDS collaboratively, such as the 1988 Black clergy conference on AIDS sponsored by Glide, were largely unsuccessful.

The lack of an organized response by Black clergy was a source of great frustration for Black AIDS activists.[54] While this wasn't unique to San Francisco, there were factors related to the city that made engagement difficult.[55] One was the particular confinements of the closet in Black San Francisco, where the historic African American community was politically pitted against the large, well-organized gay community that was overwhelmingly white and composed largely of migrants to the city.[56] Another was the still-vivid history of the Peoples Temple, the horrifying outcome of that interracial religious experiment, and the ways in which Bay Area African American religious leaders were reckoning with their participation in it.[57] San Francisco's AIDS organizations would have to wait for Black-led religious groups, such as Bishop Yvette Flunder's Ark of Refuge, to emerge and build their own organizations before trust with Black churches around AIDS could be built.[58]

Religion and Spirituality in the AIDS Ward

The third group that attended to the spiritual needs of AIDS is the most recognizably religious, but AIDS was a catalyst for moving the chaplaincy at San Francisco General Hospital in a less tradition-specific and more broadly spiritual direction.[59] Sojourn Chaplaincy began as the hospital's Episcopal chaplaincy. In the late 1970s and through the first years of Ward 5B, the hospital's Episcopal chaplain was August O'Connor, a laywoman who combined curiosity and compassion in her hospital work. Her interest in connecting with patients gave her an affinity for wards such as the prison ward and the psychiatric ward, which were often neglected by others in the chaplain's office.[60] When she began working at SF General, there were three chaplains—a Catholic priest, a Baptist minister, and O'Connor herself—working under the supervision of the head nurse.[61] Her time was largely spent sitting with patients, talking with them, and praying with them. As part of that work, she started developing a list of clergy from different traditions who were available for visitation for people from a range of religious backgrounds. "There were people who were from a variety of different backgrounds, because San Francisco attracts a lot of people. And I would find someone for them if they needed somebody, or if they already had somebody I would contact their priest or clergy person and invite them to come."[62] Her matching of patient with clergy included both those with religious commitments and those who wanted spiritual care but recognized no religious authority as their own.

O'Connor was chaplain in a moment where the role itself was in transition; the Episcopal church was grappling with the religious authority of women as well as the professional requirements for chaplaincy. And she was chaplain when the hospital started seeing AIDS patients. As staff, she was part of hospital-wide briefings about the new disease. "They invited me because I was so intricately involved with it," she told me. "We were learning every bit on the fly, so none of us knew anything anybody else didn't. None of us knew much of anything. I just knew what I could do with my prayers."[63] She also gave input on the design and opening of Ward 5B. One of the biggest changes in the ward was the presence of Shanti and its work with AIDS patients and hospital workers. Shanti brought a new division of labor to the work of chaplaincy. "Shanti would deal with the sacred," she explained, "and the chaplaincy would deal with the sacred and religious."

> Because religion means you've got an association with a group who have a specific way of being spiritual together. And Shanti was trying to make it all inclusive, and that was great because there were a lot of people who were spiritually involved with maybe just their own prayer life. And didn't have a bigger community. And Shanti gave them that possibility. Whereas the chaplaincy—if somebody wanted someone, a Catholic chaplain; if somebody wanted a Buddhist priest; if somebody wanted, you know, whatever they wanted—I would make sure they got what they wanted in a religious, specifically religious context. As well as what they wanted spiritually.[64]

Shanti and the chaplaincy overlapped in some significant ways and came to be similar in their approaches to working with PWAs. But the chaplaincy office had specifically religious functions that overlapped with AIN as well.

These included work with clergy. AIDS brought a wider range of religious groups into the hospital, giving O'Connor the opportunity to expand the network of clergy she was developing to serve the range of patients' religious needs. Dignity, the gay Catholic affinity group, started a hospital ministry under the rubric of the chaplaincy office, and other gay-identified clergy were welcome to minister in Ward 5B under O'Connor's leadership.[65] Her work developing lists of clergy from diverse traditions was a step toward the interfaith chaplaincy that manages spiritual care at San Francisco General today.

It also overlapped with AIN on policing the borders of AIDS chaplaincy. The chaplain's office likewise shielded AIDS patients from those trying to enter Ward 5B to proselytize to PWAs. The Nursing Record Book from Ward 5B noted efforts by rogue clergy to enter the ward by presenting themselves as chaplains or Shanti volunteers. A September 1983 entry by 5B director Cliff Morrison, for example, warned, "We need to watch for the proselytizing ministers and others. Carl Garcia is an SOS follower. David Putnam passes himself off as a Shanti counselor. Please keep a watchful eye out for these types."[66] O'Connor was a source for the newspaper account of such activity quoted above.[67] Although both AIN and the chaplaincy office developed the list of "AIDS sensitive clergy," it was the chaplaincy office that was tasked with on-the-ground engagement and removal of rogue clerics.

O'Connor left San Francisco General just over a year after Ward 5B opened. The Episcopal church had a new bishop, and church leaders wanted a chaplain with more formal credentials. Connie Hartquist was hired for the position at O'Connor's suggestion. Hartquist was an ordained Episcopal deacon who had spent two years as a Franciscan sister.[68] Her ordination training included Clinical Pastoral Education (CPE), aimed at giving chaplains and other religious counselors clinical knowledge and experience.[69] When she was hired, she had a vision for the chaplaincy, now named Sojourn: "I wanted to develop a CPE-like program at San Francisco General, particularly focused on providing services to the AIDS unit."[70] Under her leadership, Sojourn grew into the foremost trainer of chaplains in AIDS ministry.

Sojourn's chaplaincy training worked to increase AIDS sensitivity in religious leaders, a task it shared with AIN. It developed a model of AIDS ministry rooted in the values of listening, presence, and nonjudgment that would become increasingly influential in American chaplaincy.[71] Hartquist recalled that when she began working on AIDS, she received calls from clergy around the country who were struggling to develop the pastoral skills needed to address AIDS. In her words, it was "not only about AIDS but also about nonjudgmental, really effective pastoral care."[72] The program aimed to use AIDS as an opportunity to broaden the theological perspective of those who wanted to work with this disease, "forc[ing them] to look at [it in] a more real way, at this illness and how it impacts human beings."[73]

Sojourn chaplains were, in many ways, trained to do the same work as Shanti volunteers: to be listening, supportive presences in the lives of people with AIDS. One participant, Hartquist, recalled, "just nicknamed the training the 'Shut the Fuck Up' training."[74] But rather than deflecting questions of spirituality, Sojourn chaplains thought of their work as explicitly religious—even when they weren't saying so. By being a loving presence, Hartquist explained, "under the name of chaplaincy, without having to preach, we would embody the loving and supportive presence of God. And that's what I wanted to see more than anything else—that these folks learned you are the presence of God in that moment. You don't have to say anything religious, you don't have to quote the Bible. You have to be loving and open."[75] Sojourn chaplains may have articulated the source of their religious and spiritual foundations more explicitly than Shanti volunteers, and they may have used more religiously explicit language in understanding what they were doing and why. But in practice, the similarities between the two approaches were evident.

One way they differed, however, was in their work with the biological families of PWAs. Hospital chaplains served as cultural interpreters to parents and other family members visiting from places that were geographically and culturally distant from San Francisco, the gay subculture of many AIDS patients, and the spiritual subculture of Shanti. Family members visiting patients at Ward 5B found themselves in socially challenging circumstances. Some did not know their loved ones were gay and learned only when learning their loved one had AIDS. Some were suspicious of, or in open conflict with, a patient's lover or community of support. Some struggled with whether they should even visit at all and turned to the chaplaincy office to grapple with that decision. At the 1987 Interfaith Conference on AIDS, Hartquist told the audience:

> Every time we walk into a patient's room and say, "Hi, I'm Connie; I'm the chaplain on this unit," and I'm wearing this big old badge that says "chaplain," without saying another word, I have evoked from that patient or family member materials[76] that not even the best Shanti counselor or social worker could evoke. The label "chaplain" evokes from people all the rage and all of the disappointment and all of the hope and all of the love that people have ever felt in their lives toward God and the church. There is nobody else to catalyze that material. So, we are an evocative presence for patients and family and everyone else. We are also a normative presence, particularly in San Francisco, for families who are arriving from Iowa, Indianapolis, and Indiana. The chaplains become the ones on the unit who represent middle-class, normal, stable, recognizable America. Families who come to San Francisco to discover that their child is dying and is gay are in a state of chaos. The chaplains, who represent the church, a mainstream institution, become the tent pegs in the middle of the chaos.[77]

Chaplains modeled for family members the possibility of a church and a theology that did not condemn gay people or see AIDS as a reflection of sin. "I think that that was a really important service that we did," Hartquist said, "to be able to say the church is with you in this. And you and your son, or daughter, are not being cast into the outer darkness."[78] For some people with AIDS, the spiritual ambiguity of Shanti was a useful way to resolve the contradiction between the religious needs and the religious alienation of people with

AIDS. But for others, ambiguity could not reach the core of their theological concerns. For those who needed to address religion directly, the organizations with explicitly religious purposes were the ones to turn to.

Conclusion

In April 1985, the *Bay Area Reporter* published "The Church and Us," a three-part op-ed arguing that gay people must sever themselves from religion in the name of spirituality. The series was not about AIDS, but the epidemic made the tensions between gay and lesbian people and organized religion exquisitely painful. "The church," author Brian Jones asserted, "wants to kill gay people."[79] Yet while religion was an ever-present danger, he argued, spirituality was necessary for gay people to survive and thrive. "We need our spirituality," Jones said. "We need our Higher Power—however we define that power. But along this path to spiritual growth, the church in America is an enemy, not a friend. We are alone: alone with each other, and alone with God. That is enough."[80] This sundering was understandable for people facing profound spiritual need alongside great religious alienation. But for organizations negotiating that tension, the distinction between the two was neither simple nor clear.

In studying the lived religious lives of people who identify as "spiritual," "religious," or both, sociologist Nancy Ammerman argues that the choice laid out in the "spiritual but not religious" framework is a false binary. While some of her research subjects made much of this distinction discursively, empirically there is no clear divide. "Spiritual-but-not-religious, then, is more a moral and political category than an empirical one," she writes. "Researchers should not take the rhetoric as a guide for understanding either spirituality or religion per se."[81] But seeing the way organizations parse this distinction—and the underlying similarities between those groups—offers a useful guide to analyzing tensions and contradictions within the religious field and the strategies different groups use to manage them.

For Shanti, the AIDS Interfaith Network, and Sojourn chaplaincy, religion and spirituality were overlapping spheres that they tried to differentiate in terms of mission and labor, but they were always extending into spaces where they were uninvited, or at least unspoken. Shanti, with its strong but unarticulated roots in countercultural spirituality, met many of the needs of PWAs that earlier generations and different populations met in church—personal support volunteers were like modern church mothers showing up with casseroles. Emotional support volunteers embodied the kind of supportive presence people of faith have aimed for, and at times achieved, in other times and places. But to carry out this spiritual work, Shanti trained its volunteers away from explicitly spiritual or religious language.

Religion, in the context of AIDS in San Francisco, became the domain of the AIDS Interfaith Network and Sojourn chaplaincy. Together, they worked with clergy to understand and meet the spiritual needs of people with AIDS, in part by countering the toxic theologies circulating among their coreligionists. They spoke to the context of specific traditions, specific communities, and specific histories of alienation as well as acceptance. Both also overlapped significantly with Shanti—AIN in form and Sojourn in substance. For all three, the conundrum of spirituality, religion, and their relation was a pragmatic one they wrestled with throughout the crisis, especially in its first five years.

These three cases, and the ways they navigated the spiritual and religious contradictions of AIDS, would have an impact on the rest of the country. As a cornerstone of the San Francisco model, Shanti became the basis for countless similar projects around the country. Political leaders, social service providers, and AIDS activists regularly toured the organizations that made up the San Francisco model, including Shanti, seeking training, guidance, and inspiration. The San Francisco model also informed federal AIDS funding guidelines, notably the 1990 Ryan White Care Act. For years, the Sojourn chaplaincy was the most visible program training chaplains specifically for AIDS care. When the epidemic started to wane, the chaplaincy program took over when Shanti's services were cut. Sojourn not only outlasted Shanti in the hospital setting, but it applied what it had learned from AIDS ministry to hospital chaplaincy more broadly, both in the wider San Francisco General community and in hospitals across the city and the country. The AIDS Interfaith Network became part of a national network of religious groups working on AIDS. The AIDS National Interfaith Network (ANIN) partnered with local AIDS religious networks and also with AIDS interest groups in national and global denominations to shape the response to AIDS in more liberal religious groups.

AIDS was not only a medical catastrophe but also a religious and spiritual one. It had a significant, still understudied impact on American religion, the distinction between religion and spirituality, and the increased moral and political salience of that distinction in American culture. California—and San Francisco in particular—played an important role in shaping that impact. Early AIDS activists in San Francisco drew on spirituality in their work and understood that the religious tension at the heart of AIDS would have to be addressed if the epidemic was to be engaged holistically. They attempted to do so, in part, through organizations that shared spiritual outlooks but could claim or disavow religion in distinct, strategic ways. The San Francisco model was an exemplary model of community-based health care provision, but it was also an exemplar of what would come to be known as "San Francisco values." The two converged in Ward 5B, where Shanti, AIN, and Sojourn worked together to meet the spiritual needs of people with AIDS and their loved ones while defending them from the religious threats they faced. "San Francisco values" is a term often used today with the kind of eye roll Michael Callen directed at San Francisco's AIDS activists and their seemingly incessant spiritual processing during the Denver meeting. But both the processing and the values were significant and influential, both in the history of AIDS and in the history of American religion.

Notes

1. Kaposi sarcoma, or KS, was one of the first opportunist infections many people with AIDS contracted. Its emblematic purple lesions were a dreaded sign of the disease.

2. David French, *How to Survive a Plague: The Inside Story of How Citizens and Science Tamed* AIDS (Alfred A. Knopf, 2016), 106–10.

3. Randy Shilts, *And the Band Played On: Politics, People and the AIDS Epidemic* (St. Martins, 1987); Steven Epstein, *Impure Science: AIDS, Activism and the Politics of Knowledge* (University of California Press, 1988).

4. Pew Research Center, *"Nones" on the Rise* (Pew Forum on Religion and Public Life, 2012), www.pewresearch.org/religion/2012/10/09/nones-on-the-rise/.

5. William B. Parsons, ed., *Being Spiritual But Not Religious: Past, Present and Futures* (Routledge, 2018).

6. Quincy D. Newell, Max Greenberg, and James Bennett, "Pondering Western-ness" (email to participants in the Religion and the American West Symposium, February 15, 2023). See also Quincy D. Newell, "Religion and the American West," *Religion Compass* 6, no. 11 (2012): 488–99.

7. Sandra Sizer Frankiel, *California's Spiritual Frontiers: Religious Alternatives in Anglo-Protestantism, 1850–1910* (University of California Press, 1988); Laurie Maffly-Kipp, *Religion and Society in Frontier California* (Yale University Press, 1994).

8. Maffly-Kipp, *Religion and Society in Frontier California.*

9. San Francisco Council of Churches, *Heritage and Hope: A History of the Protestant, Anglican and Orthodox Church Movement in San Francisco on the Occasion of the 75th Anniversary Year (1978–1979) of the San Francisco Council of Churches* (San Francisco Council of Churches, 1979); Nan Amilla Boyd, *Wide-Open Town: A History of Queer San Francisco to 1965* (University of California Press, 2005); Fred Rosenbaum, *Cosmopolitans: A Social and Cultural History of the Jews in the San Francisco Bay Area* (University of California Press, 2009); Nayan Shah, *Contagious Divides: Epidemics and Race in San Francisco's Chinatown* (University of California Press, 2001).

10. This paper uses Ward 5B as a shared space where all three of these groups worked, but it is not a religious history of 5B. That project begs doing but is beyond the scope of this piece. For more on Ward 5B, see the documentary *5B*, directed by Dan Kraus and Paul Haggis (Hwy 61: Sayville Productions, 2018); on the exclusion of Shanti from the film, see Brendan McHugh, "Just Being There: The AIDS Crisis and the Shanti Project's Hospital Counselor Program," *Nursing Clio*, January 27, 2020, https://nursingclio.org/2020/01/27/just-being-there-the-aids-crisis-and-the-shanti-projects-hospital-counselor-program/.

11. "The San Francisco Model of AIDS Care" was a term used in the 1980s and 1990s to refer to the interconnected network of medical, research, and advocacy organizations in the city focused on minimizing the hospitalization of people with AIDS and maximizing their quality of life.

12. Elisabeth Kübler-Ross, *On Death and Dying*, 40th anniversary edition (Routledge, 2009).

13. Sandy Rovner, "The Dying and the Light: Kübler-Ross's Comforting Convictions," *Washington Post*, March 22, 1980, C1.

14. Jeffrey Kripal, *Esalen: America and the Religion of No Religion* (University of Chicago Press, 2008).

15. Jim Geary, *Delicate Courage: An Exquisite Journey of Love, Death, and Eternal Communication* (iUniverse 2010), 23–53.

16. Geary, *Delicate Courage*, 82–83.

17. Geary, *Delicate Courage*, 82.

18. Bobbi Campbell, "KS Support Group," *San Francisco Sentinel*, April 15, 1982, 6.

19. Clifford Morrison, interview by Sally Smith Hughes, *The AIDS Epidemic in San Francisco: The Response of the Nursing Profession, 1981–1984*, vol. 3, Regional Oral History Project, 82, https://oac.cdlib.org/ark:/13030/kt2t1nb1sc/.

20. "AIDS Unit at SFGH," *Eclipse: The Shanti Project Newsletter*, Fall 1983. Shanti Project Records, University of California at San Francisco Special Collections, Box 1, Folder 27.

21. Shakti Gawain, *Creative Visualization: Use the Power of Your Imagination to Create What You Want in Your Life* (Whatever Publishing, 1978).

22. "Shanti Resource Network," *Shanti Project Volunteer Memo*, December 1983, Shanti Project Records, University of California San Francisco Special Collections, Box 1, Folder 27.

23. Shilts, *And the Band Played On*, 427.

24. "What is the Shanti Project?" *Shanti Project Training Manual*, n.d., Shanti Project Records, University of California San Francisco Special Collections, Box 1, Folder 27.

25. Ed Wolfe, quoted in Brendan McHugh, "Shanti Trainings," in *Shanti Projects—Intimate Histories of the AIDS Epidemic* (online exhibit), https://shantiprojects.com/shanti-training-pride-center/.

26. Lawson, quoted in McHugh, "Shanti Trainings."

27. Despite documenting this in numerous sources, I can't say with great confidence why this was the policy. In a public lecture on this material, Hugh Urban asked me whether Shanti's reluctance to identify spiritually was a reflection of the ways in which many countercultural spiritualities were dismissed or stigmatized as "bad religion." It's an intriguing possibility that merits further research.

28. Jack Pantaleo, author interview, October 2, 2018.

29. Geary, *Delicate Courage*, 59–60.

30. Wendy Cadge and Emily Sigalow, "Negotiating Religious Differences: The Strategies of Interfaith Chaplains in Healthcare," *Journal of the Scientific Study of Religion* 52, no. 1 (2013): 146–58.

31. Tracy Fessenden, *Culture and Redemption: Religion, the Secular and American Religion* (Princeton University Press), 5.

32. The Report of the 1988 Presidential Commission on AIDS noted the willingness of family members in minority communities to support people with AIDS and the need to

provide culturally appropriate training for them. See *Report of the Presidential Commission on the Human Immunodeficiency Virus*, June 24, 1988, https://archive.org/details/reportofpresidenoopres/page/6/mode/2up.

33. Randall Miller, author interview, August 22, 2018.

34. Miller, interview.

35. Gordon, quoted in Michael Helquist, "AIDS Workshop: Exploring 'Safe Sex,'" *San Francisco Sentinel*, April 14, 1983, 12.

36. He said this on several occasions, including during a 1983 debate on CBC's *The Journal* with gay-identified Rev. Troy Perry. In that exchange, he attempted to soften his stance by claiming that God also judges heterosexual promiscuity—though, in his framing, with markedly lower penalties. "Jerry Falwell and Troy Perry Debate the Morality of AIDS in 1983," *The Journal*, CBC, July 6, 1983, video, 11:24, www.cbc.ca/player/play/1622155489.

37. "Bringing Cancer Out of the Closet (letter to the gay/lesbian community from men with Kaposi sarcoma)," *San Francisco Sentinel*, April 29, 1982, 6.

38. "AIDS: A Workshop for Religious Outreach," *Bay Area Reporter*, May 26, 1983, 4.

39. Bobbi Campbell, "Second National AIDS Forum," *San Francisco Sentinel*, June 23, 1983, 4.

40. Staff was also engaged with the human potential movement and began her spiritual journey—and ultimately found MCC San Francisco—through her participation in the Advocate Experience, a seminar for gays and lesbians modeled on Werner Erhard's est. Coni Staff, author interview, June 17, 2015. On the Advocate Experience, see Frances FitzGerald, *Cities on a Hill: A Journey Through Contemporary American Cultures* (Simon and Schuster, 1986), 61–62.

41. AIDS Interfaith Network, *AIDS Interfaith Network Resource Manual*, Draft, September 12, 1985, 1, Jack Pantaleo Personal Collection.

42. Jack Pantaleo, "The Gift of AIDS: The Origin and Evolution of the AIDS Interfaith Network," unpublished manuscript, n.d., 3, Jack Pantaleo Personal Collection.

43. The original members of the AIDS Interfaith Network were The Parsonage (Episcopal), Dignity (Catholic), Affirmation (Methodist), Affirmations (Latter Day Saints), Lutherans Concerned, SF Friends Meeting, Kinship (Seventh Day Adventist), Ministry of Light (Presbyterian), Metropolitan Community Church, SF Network Ministries (Presbyterian), Evangelicals Concerned, UCC Gay/Lesbian Caucus, Presbyterians for Lesbian/Gay Concerns, the Orthodox Office of Peace and Justice, The Healing Community of the San Francisco Council of Churches (ecumenical Protestant), Sha'ar Zahav (Jewish—reform). AIDS Interfaith Network, "AIDS Interfaith Network Organizational Style," August 26, 1983, 3. Jack Pantaleo Personal Collection.

44. Elliott Blackstone was also a member of San Francisco Network Ministries, a nondenominational ministry led by Rev. Glenda Hope that worked with intravenous drug users with AIDS in the Tenderloin. For more on Blackstone, see Susan Stryker, "MTF Transgender Activism in the Tenderloin and Beyond, 1966–1975," interview with Elliott Blackstone, transcript, n.d., Elliott Blackstone Papers, http://docs.glbthistory.org/oh/Blackstone_Elliot11-6-1996_web.pdf.

45. Rev. Orloff Miller, "Recording of David Hummel memorial service," August 14, 1987, Coni Staff Personal Collection.

46. Pantaleo, author interview, October 2, 2018.

47. Louise Hay, author of the best-selling book *You Can Heal Your Life!* (Hay House, 1984), got her start in part by recording *AIDS: A Positive Approach*, a cassette of her teachings and meditations on AIDS (1983). The tapes were sold widely in New Age bookstores and health food stores. As AIDS spread and her popularity grew, she sponsored revival-like events called "Hayrides" for people with AIDS and gay men afraid of contracting the disease to practice developing self-love, the lack of which, she believed, was the spiritual cause of the disease.

48. AIDS Interfaith Network, "Is AIDS God's Wrath on Homosexuals?," pamphlet, Jack Pantaleo Personal Collection.

49. AIDS Interfaith Network, "Is AIDS God's Wrath on Homosexuals?"

50. "AIDS Interfaith Network," *Bay Area Reporter*, July 9, 1987, 38.

51. Dion Sanders, "AIDS Interfaith Network Counters Fundamentalists," *Bay Area Reporter*, April 28, 1984, 10.

52. Jack Pantaleo, author interview, October 12, 2018. He also recalled that a group of conservative clergy threatened to sue AIN for denying them access to Ward 5B.

53. Pantaleo, interview, October 2, 2018.

54. On the frustration of Black AIDS activists re: the Black church, see Naomi Gray, comments at the 1987 AIDS Interfaith Conference in "The Asian, Black and Native American Communities," *Interfaith Conference on AIDS/ARC*, AIDS History Project Audio/Video Collection, 1983–1992, University of California Special Collections, Carton 10, Item 10/22, Tape 28; and Dr. Amanda Houston-Hamilton, testimony before the Presidential Commission on the Human Immunodeficiency Virus, *Hearing on the Western Response*, March 24–25, 1988, transcript 3–11). The most successful and enduring effort to organize Black churches came from New York in 1989, when Pernessa Seele organized the first Harlem Week of Prayer for HIV/AIDS, which developed into the organization Balm in Gilead.

55. On the failures of Black churches to respond to AIDS, see Cathy Cohen, *The Boundaries of Blackness: AIDS and Breakdown of Black Politics* (University of Chicago Press, 1999), 256–86.

56. Miller, author interviews, August 22, 2018, and December 13, 2018.

57. See, for example, Alfred J. Smith, "Breaking the Silence: Reflections of a Black Pastor," in Rebecca Moore, Anthony Pinn, and Mary R. Sawyer, eds., *Peoples Temple and Black Religion in America* (Indiana University Press, 2004), 139–57.

58. Ellen Lewin, *Filled with the Spirit: Sexuality, Gender, and Radical Inclusivity in a Black Pentecostal Church Coalition* (University of Chicago Press, 2018).

59. Wendy Cadge's work on chaplaincy discusses this tension between tradition-based and tradition-neutral orientations to contemporary chaplaincy work. See Wendy Cadge, *Paging God: Religion in the Halls of Medicine* (University of Chicago Press 2012); Wendy Cadge, *Spiritual Care: The Everyday Work of Chaplains* (Oxford University Press, 2023).

60. August O'Connor, author interview, January 27, 2020.

61. O'Connor, interview.

62. O'Connor, interview.

63. O'Connor, interview.

64. O'Connor, interview.

65. Allen White, "Fundamentalists Make Hay Out of AIDS Dead and Dying," *Bay Area Reporter*, March 29, 1984, 5.

66. Entry in Nursing Communication Book, September 6, 1983, San Francisco General Hospital AIDS Ward 5B/5A Archives, 1983–2003, San Francisco History Center, San Francisco Public Library, Box 2, Vol. 1. SOS is an evangelical street ministry, still active in the Bay Area, that targeted the Castro in the years before AIDS. During the AIDS crisis, its leader, Larry Rosenbaum, tried to circulate a letter about a friend who supposedly repented of his homosexuality before dying of AIDS. White, "Fundamentalists Make Hay Out of AIDS Dead and Dying."

67. Allen White, "Fundamentalists Make Hay Out of AIDS Dead and Dying,"

68. Connie Hartquist Jacobs, author interview, August 9, 2018.

69. On the history of Clinical Pastoral Education, see Cadge, et al., "Training Chaplains and Spiritual Caregivers: The Emergence and Growth of Chaplaincy Programs in Theological Education," *Pastoral Psychology* 69, no. 2 (2020): 187–208.

70. Jacobs, interview.

71. See, for example, Winnifred Fallers Sullivan, *A Ministry of Presence: Chaplaincy, Spiritual Care and the Law* (University of Chicago Press, 2014); Cadge, *Paging God*; Cadge, *Spiritual Care.*

72. Jacobs, interview.

73. Jacobs, interview.

74. Jacobs, interview.

75. Jacobs, interview.

76. I believe that her use of the term "materials" here refers to emotional or psychological materials (feelings, conflicts, tensions) that would be evoked in a way that made them available to be felt, processed, and hopefully healed.

77. Connie Hartquist. "Specialized Ministries: Hospitals, Prisons and Military," *Proceedings from the AIDS Interfaith Conference*, 1987, Special Collections, University of California at San Francisco, AIDS History Project Audio/Video Collection, 1983–1992. Series 3, Box 10, Item10/10.

78. Jacobs, interview.

79. Brian Jones, "The Church and Us: First of Three Parts," *Bay Area Reporter*, April 25, 1985, 6. This first installment was published three weeks after AIN sponsored their first AIDS Healing Service at Grace Cathedral, presided over by Episcopal Bishop William Swing.

80. Brian Jones, "The Church and Us: Last of Three Parts." *Bay Area Reporter*, May 9, 1985, 6.

81. Nancy T. Ammerman, "Spiritual but Not Religious? Beyond Binary Choices in the Study of Religion," *Journal for the Scientific Study of Religion* 52, no. 2 (2013): 258–78.

Chapter 13

Jewish Pioneer Cemeteries

Implicated Sacred Spaces in the Arizona–Sonora Borderlands

MAX GREENBERG

Keywords: US–Mexico Border, Jewish cemeteries, cultural memory, settler colonialism, Palestine

> A two-tier pedestal made of rock from nearby mountains has been built at the center of the 50-foot-by-50-foot cemetery. Ceremonial items were sealed into a burnished safe adorned with Jewish and Indian symbols atop the pedestal. The contents include a yarmulke, a menorah, a Kaddish cup, prayer and hymn books, and an Israeli bowl filled with dirt from Jerusalem.
>
> The reason for the bowl, Mr. Sirota said, was "so we can bring Israel closer to Tombstone, Ariz."
>
> —"An Old West Cemetery For Jews is Rededicated in Tombstone," *New York Times*, February 29, 1984

In November 2018, I drove to the US–Mexico border wall in search of the real history of Jews in Arizona. I was looking for the Bisbee-Douglas Jewish Cemetery, or what I'd been told was an abandoned, historic Jewish burial site next to the border wall separating Arizona and Sonora, Mexico. I left Tucson, Arizona, drove south on state route AZ-80, and crossed through the town of Tombstone. I was not planning on stopping there. Tombstone was a place for those seeking a nostalgic and immersive experience in the self-proclaimed "most authentic western town left in the United States." Tombstone was a performance of the American West, redesigned as a tourist attraction in the mid-twentieth century, like so many other mining-turned-ghost towns. I was here to research *authentic* Jewish history.[1]

Approaching the city limits, I saw billboards for saloons, curio shops, museums, and gunfight reenactments at the O.K. Corral.[2] Nothing caught my eye until I drove past a massive roadside sign for the "Boothill Graveyard and Jewish Memorial." The faded, self-important designation, "This Property is on the National Register of Historic Places," could be seen at the bottom of the entrance sign. *Had I accidentally discovered some real Jewish history?* I made a quick decision to pull over and explore.

Walking through Boothill's parking lot, I looked around at the other visitors, eager to identify some fellow public historians. Who else was here to learn about the "many violent deaths of the early days" of the Old West?[3] I noticed a car whose back windshield was decorated with Punisher stickers, and wondered if its passengers were members of the vigilante border-patrol group common in Southern Arizona.[4] The Jewish memorial lies on the outer periphery of the Boothill Graveyard. A carefully arranged rock formation and golden sculptures sit atop a platform with a bronze dedication plaque that reads, *To the Jewish Pioneers and Their Indian Friends.* At first, the burial site felt spatially and aesthetically disjointed from the rest of Boothill and the town more broadly. But the commemorative plaque's claim that Jews were Pioneers, and *Jewish Pioneers* and *Indians* were *friends*, transformed the otherwise distinct sacred space into part of Tombstone's settler-fantasy landscape.

I left Tombstone with many questions and wondered whether the next cemetery would finally offer the authentic Jewish history I was seeking. I drove fifty miles southeast until I arrived at the US port of entry that divided Douglas from Agua Prieta. I did not know where the cemetery was located, nor did Google Maps. With few expectations, I stopped at the Douglas Historical Society and was met with great enthusiasm. Among the modest exhibitions dedicated to the history of copper mining and US military bases, an entire room was dedicated to an exhibition on the "Jewish Families in Douglas." Cindy Hayosek, the Historical Society secretary and exhibit curator, who knew her hometown in the sharpest detail, told me exactly which unmarked roads to follow to reach the cemetery. I was to drive to the edge of the town's commercial and residential centers, heading east with the border wall to my right. Hayosek offered to take me into Agua Prieta, the town on the other side of the wall, in Sonora, Mexico, to meet Mr. Nayul, an Agua Prieta resident and business owner who is both Jewish and Mexican. I declined the invitation as I did not have my passport with me, though Hayosek assured me I would have no problem crossing through customs without identification.

When I arrived at the Bisbee-Douglas Cemetery, it felt like the ghost town that Tombstone refused to become. I walked along the barbed wire surrounding the headstones, many of them toppled over or unmarked. Another commemorative plaque, affixed to a cement pedestal, bore a familiar dedication: *To the Memory of the Jewish Pioneers of Cochise County.* I looked south, beyond the barbed wire fence encircling the cemetery, until my gaze landed on the wall that separates Douglas from Agua Prieta. Leaving the interior of the cemetery boundaries, I walked three hundred yards toward the border wall. The entire US-facing portion of the wall was covered in barbed wire, a federal

Figure 13.1 Welcome sign at the Boothill Graveyard in Tombstone, Arizona, November 10, 2018. Courtesy of the author.

response to the surge of political refugees and asylum seekers arriving in the transborder urban centers of Ciudad Juárez/El Paso and Tijuana/San Diego the month before. I was within a hundred yards of the wall when I was approached by the familiar white and green Chevrolet Tahoe of the US Border Patrol. The Customs and Border Protection (CBP) officer rolled down his window and asked what I was doing walking so close to the wall.

I recalled the advice that long-time border commuters had shared with me in the past: Make yourself as non-threatening as possible by talking about your family and religion. I told him I was Jewish and was here to visit the Jewish cemetery, pointing behind me. Intrigued and almost apologetic, the officer replied, "You didn't look illegal," explaining my image had come up on the cameras, and he was required to check me out. Eager to keep the encounter as peaceful as possible, I engaged the officer in polite conversation as he told me about a Jewish colleague "named David" and advised me to head back toward the cemetery for my own safety. He raised his hand in a salutary gesture, signaling his departure, and shouted, "Shalom!"—the Hebrew greeting for "hello," "goodbye," and "peace"—before driving away.

The "Jewish Pioneer" memorials discussed in the autoethnography above exist within a broader constellation of western Jewish heritage sites, including synagogues and burial grounds, produced through two successive European Jewish migrations to the American West between the mid-nineteenth and early twentieth centuries. Like many other European-origin groups, German and Eastern European Jewish immigrants arrived in Arizona's southern border region during an unprecedented period of US nation-building marked by militarized border fortification and extractive industrialization. Liberal promises of land ownership, economic mobility, and religious freedom incentivized the migration of many Euro-American settlers to the new border zone. These promises were made possible through, and dependent upon, racialized violence against Native peoples, as well as Mexican, Chinese, and other groups deemed to be undesirable and unassimilable foreigners.[5] The establishment of Jewish sacred places along the border at the turn of the twentieth century cannot be separated from these histories of land theft and militarized surveillance. They should be read as part and parcel of the underlying *religio-racial* imperatives underlying US settler colonialism in the border region during this period.[6]

A century later, the Jewish Pioneer archetype emerged as a frequent and central protagonist in the western Jewish commemorative landscape. By the mid-twentieth century, Jewish residents had largely migrated away from small border towns and into bigger cities, but burial grounds like the Bisbee-Douglas

Cemetery offered material evidence of a Jewish past. The Jewish Pioneer monuments that accompanied many preservation projects offer a celebratory framework through which to interpret Euro-American Jewish participation in US settler colonization in the nineteenth and early twentieth centuries in the American West.[7] It was through the protection of Jewish sacred sites, in the absence of a local Jewish community, that Jewish Americans who lived elsewhere could maintain a place-based connection. In sum, efforts to protect and maintain these spaces reveal the complex ways in which Jewish and non-Jewish stakeholders remember and memorialize Western religio-racial history through place.

Alongside US Confederate memorials, protected religious sites have also been fertile ground for challenging and reimagining practices of memorialization and preservation in public space. In California and Oregon, for example, activists have used direct action to force the removal of monuments and heritage sites that celebrate the histories of religious colonization, including the Spanish Catholic mission system, and Protestant Manifest Destiny.[8] Though not synonymous with monuments to Catholic and Christian colonial legacies in the West, sacred places of Jewish public memory are nonetheless implicated sites in the history of settler violence in North America, and therefore should be included in ongoing debates about public memory and the politics and potential of representing histories of racial violence in the present.

Michael Rothberg's language of implication is a useful framework for exploring how religious places can protect settler colonial memory through material form while also propping up ongoing dynamics of colonial violence in the present. Rothberg deploys implication as a lens to capture the subjectivity of those persons and places that enable, perpetuate, benefit from, or inherit histories of violence and structures of inequality.[9] The establishment of the Tombstone and Bisbee-Douglas Jewish cemeteries in the late nineteenth and early twentieth centuries was made possible only after multiple colonial occupations of the land, which culminated in the forced removal and resettlement of the Chiricahua Apache. The money used to purchase the land on which the cemetery was built was a product of the commodification of stolen land, also known as real estate, and of commercial activities bound up with border militarization and copper-mining industries. The history of Jewish settlement in the border region fits within Rothberg's model of implication, as Jewish socioeconomic livelihoods were interdependent with the marginalization of the region's Native and otherwise racialized residents. Furthermore, the framework of implication helps us approach the politics of memory within our protected religious sites, or how the maintenance of religious places can "propagate the legacies of historical violence and prop up the structures of inequality that mar the present."[10]

The following chapter applies the framework of implication to explore how people remember the American West through Jewish places, and how maintenance of Jewish place is a process implicated by US settler memory and the foregrounding of the West as a religious refuge rather than a site of religio-racial violence and inequality, historically and presently. Alongside my autoethnographic account, I draw from secondary and primary sources of the Tombstone and Bisbee-Douglas cemetery restoration projects to trace how Jewish and non-Jewish community stakeholders remember the American West as a triumph of American liberalism and democracy, as a genocidal project to be mourned through the restoration of Jewish space, and as a spiritual throughline to occupied Jerusalem, as it exists under a Jewish nation-state. Through the prism of Jewish place, the multiple and contradictory memories of the American West reinforce a singular myth of the region as a religious sanctuary and refuge in an otherwise inhospitable landscape.

In the discussion that follows, I look at how maintenance of Jewish heritage sites in the American Southwest is a process implicated by the religio-racial requirements of US settler colonialism at the US–Mexico border, and how it is inextricable from the religio-racial objectives under Israeli settler colonialism in Palestine. Furthermore, I attend to how the American West remains a mobile and unfinished project of empire, translated and transmuted through a Judeo-Christian imaginary across disparate but linked settler geographies.[11] The memory-making that unfolds in the cemeteries reveals a Jewish Pioneer subject who helped settle the American frontier as a stepping stone toward settling a Jewish frontier through Israeli nation-building in Palestine. As such, the "Jewish Pioneer" cemeteries demonstrate how Jewish place-memory mythologizes the West as a necessary process that advances capitalism and produces religious refuge, from the American Southwest to Jerusalem.

Remembering "Jewish Pioneers and Their Indian Friends" in Tombstone

The earliest documented cultural memories of the Tombstone Jewish cemetery are found in a written letter from Rabbi Floyd Fierman to Jeanne Devere (1914–1977), a resident of Tombstone and descendant of Anglo-American settlers who had worked in mining and hospitality industries since the boom and bust of the silver industry in the 1880s.[12] Rabbi Fierman served as the lead rabbi at Temple Mount Sinai of El Paso, Texas, for thirty years and was a voracious collector of historical sources related to nineteenth- and early twentieth-century Jewish histories in the US–Mexico border region. Fierman and Devere exchanged several letters regarding the history of the cemetery, including Devere's memories of its original location, number of burials, and abandonment, as well as several anecdotes about Tombstone's Jewish economic history in the 1880s.

Drawing on her own mother's recollections, Devere describes the Jewish cemetery as a space once distinctively marked by seventy-five-foot-long walls, a gate, and wooden headstones with about three interned bodies. The majority of the Jewish community left Tombstone during the 1880s with the decline of the mining industry. Within the next several decades, the cemetery space became indistinguishable from "the brush of the countryside."[13] Devere suggests that the disappearance of the cemetery spaces was not an inevitable consequence of Jewish absence but rather a byproduct of how a new generation of merchants in Tombstone transformed a religious space into a commercial one. Around 1910, "a Chinese merchant gave a Mexican adobe maker the contract to build him a store. The Mexican tore down the wall around the Jewish cemetery and used the adobes in the walls of the Chinese store."[14] Devere locates her commitment to remembering the Jewish cemetery as part of her inheritance from her mother, a woman with "a deep interest in Tombstone and the history of the West." Though not Jewish herself, Devere writes to Rabbi Fierman about the Jewish cemetery and the city of Tombstone as intimate and integrated spaces, referring to the past Jewish residents of Tombstone as part of "our Jewish family."

Devere's investment in remembering and protecting Tombstone's Jewish material past is part of a longer tradition in Tombstone that interweaves history, cultural memory, and heritage tourism. In the 1920s, with the profitability of the mining boom long gone, residents capitalized on the mythology of the Wild Western frontier town by creating a "living testament to the Old West."[15] Sporadic reenactments of the town's violent frontier days evolved from a local heritage celebration in the 1920s into an elaborate historic landmark district by the 1950s. Historical cemeteries specifically have served as important spaces of preservation-turned-commodification, helping tourists visualize the "many violent deaths of the early days" in the Old West.[16] The Boothill Graveyard, an authentic nineteenth-century cemetery, was historically preserved in the 1920s, with the specific intent of bringing tourists to Tombstone.[17] According to Devere, the Jewish cemetery was just "over the crest of the hill from Boothill," and yet, despite this proximity, the Jewish cemetery existed as a nearly forgotten memory rather than a place to visit.

The restoration and integration of the historic Jewish cemetery into Tombstone's historic landmark district began in the 1980s, catalyzed by a different kind of reenactment: the reciting of the *kaddish*, the Hebrew prayer for mourning the dead. According to archival records, the restoration was a collaborative effort between two colleagues: Israel Rubin, a Jewish American and economist based between Washington, DC, and Tucson, Arizona, and Judge C.

Lawrence Huerta, a member of the Pascua Yaqui tribe and the first American Indian to graduate from University of Arizona Law School and practice law in Arizona. Over lunch in Tombstone in 1982, Rubin and Huerta were taken on an impromptu tour of the abandoned cemetery by a "local historian," Al Turner.[18] The three men walked through the Boothill Graveyard, and just beyond the boundaries of the tourist-filled burial grounds were the remains of an adobe wall that Devere had recalled in her letter to Rabbi Fierman two decades prior; this time, however, no headstones remained. The two "mused about the possibility of restoring the site for the public," and over the next eighteen months, those musings evolved into a comprehensive restoration project that brought together the Tombstone Chamber of Commerce, the Jewish Friendship Club of Green Valley, and individual community stakeholders, both Jewish and non-Jewish.

In February 1984, the Tombstone Jewish Memorial at the Boothill Cemetery in Tombstone, Arizona, was formally restored with a public unveiling of a "simple monument to commemorate all Jewish pioneers who helped to settle the west before the turn of the century."[19] A bronze plaque was affixed atop a pedestal that read, "To the Jewish Pioneers and Their Indian Friends."[20] The rededication of the Jewish cemetery site was significant not only because it gave material form to the memory of Tombstone's Jewish population, but also because it marked the inclusion of a definitively religious space in Tombstone's seemingly secular, lawless Western landscape. Community stakeholders and political proponents within and beyond the Jewish community spoke publicly about their motivations for participating in the restoration effort. Together, the proponents use the Jewish burial ground as a spatial container through which to remember the contradictions of religious history in the American West, including both the grief of religio-racial violence and the fulfillment of Western democratic freedoms.

The rededication ceremony was attended by Jewish leaders and community members in Southern Arizona, including two Jewish families who had relocated to Tombstone from New York City in the 1970s, State Representative James McNaulty of Cochise County, and the two central collaborators, retired professor of real estate finance and president of the Jewish Friendship Club, David Sirota, and the aforementioned Judge C. Lawrence Huerta. "The unanswered question of the hour [is] why a full-blooded Indian would want to associate with a bunch of Jews," Sirota said to those in attendance.[21]

In a public fundraising letter preceding the unveiling ceremony, Huerta had explained that he felt a spiritual similarity between Yaqui religious practices and Judaism, specifically a shared emphasis on land and place as necessary for maintaining connection with ancestors. "The state of the Jewish cemetery at Boothill moved me deeply," Huerta wrote. "A burial place is sacred

Figure 13.2 Dedication plaque and Jewish Pioneer monument, Tombstone, Arizona, November 10, 2018. Courtesy of the author.

to my people and I want this place to be treated with the respect it once had. In honoring my Jewish brothers I feel I am also honoring the lost and forgotten bones of my own people where they fell when the west was being settled."[22] Through the Jewish cemetery, Huerta compared his "own people," his ancestors, members of the Yaqui nation who were victims of the violence of westward expansion, to European Jewish victims of genocide. Huerta's use of the Jewish burial ground to mourn the violence of Yaqui Indian removal by both the United States and Mexico underscores the transnational dimensions of empire-building in the border region.

Like the rest of Tombstone, the Jewish cemetery occupies the ancestral homeland of the Chiricahua Apache, whose forced removal from the region was carried out incrementally under Anglo-American invasion between the 1850s and 1890s. Huerta's act of remembering and mourning "the lost and forgotten bones of my own people" in a Jewish cemetery on Chiricahua Apache land draws a wide circle around the history of anti-Indigenous genocide that homogenizes disparate experiences across tribal nations. Nevertheless, his memories also underscore the transnational dynamics of empire in the American West. Settler colonial violence against Yaqui Indians in the Arizona–Sonora border region was carried out most forcibly between 1876 and 1907, under the dictatorship of Porfirio Díaz and Mexican modernization projects. As scholar Nicole M. Guidotti-Hernandez has argued, the cooperation between Mexican and US institutions to remove Indigenous peoples, including the Yaqui Indians, as a method of modernization has remained "relatively unmarked in Chicana/o, Mexican and U.S. national histories."[23] Huerta's grief over his Yaqui ancestors' "forgotten bones" reflects the multidirectionality of memory and grief that the burial site contains. Through Huerta's memory, the Jewish cemetery serves as a reminder that Mexico and the US are implicated actors in the violence of settling the American West.

During the unveiling ceremony, Huerta's memory work draws a spiritual analogy between Jewish and Yaqui rituals, referring to the ceremony as his "bar mitzvah." The performance of spiritual likeness is also written onto Huerta's body, the *New York Times* reporter describing him as wearing both an "Indian headband and yarmulke over his braided hair."[24] Jewish-Indigenous hybridity is also built into the memorial itself, a fifty-by-fifty-foot monument that is adorned with "Jewish and Indian symbols," and contains a "yarmulke, a menorah, a Kaddish cup, prayer and hymn books, and an Israeli bowl filled with dirt from Jerusalem."[25] Huerta had donated Yaqui bowls containing unnamed sacred items. Beginning in the nineteenth century, Jewish American writers and artists have imagined an "ancient kinship" between themselves and American Indians as a method to claim Jewish belonging to North America and Western civilization more broadly.[26] In a reversal of this rhetoric, Huerta's involvement with the cemetery's restoration project exemplifies something less explored: how people indigenous to North America have also identified with, or related to, Jewish Americans. Rather than the Jewish subject "playing Indian," to claim belonging to America, Huerta turned to Jewish space and ritual to claim a kind of belonging to the American West through public memory.[27] If Jewish Americans have invoked likeness with Native subjectivity as a discursive strategy to claim American indigeneity, Huerta's identification with Jewish identity may also be a rhetorical strategy of belonging that positions Jewishness as a form of embodied representation and rhetorical strategy of inclusion within the Judeo-Christian landscape of the American West. Within the container of the Jewish cemetery, Huerta's religio-racial code-switching, from Indigenous to Jewish, is possible, and perhaps, casts the Yaqui subject as more visible and less othered in a Judeo-Christian context.

Huerta's performance of spiritual-religious hybridity can also be read in the context of Mexican, Spanish, and Sephardic histories that shaped the shifting religio-racial boundaries of Jewish identity centuries earlier, when Southern Arizona was mapped as part of New Spain's northern territory. In the sixteenth and seventeenth centuries, a number of Spanish and Portuguese *conversos*, or converted Sephardic Jews, left the Iberian peninsula for the nations' colonial projects in the Caribbean and in South and Central America. Traversing much of the present-day American Southwest and Northern Mexico, the territorial boundaries of northern New Spain are historicized as one of the earliest sites of settlement for Jews or those with Jewish ancestry in the Americas.[28] Scholarship on Sephardic or *converso* identity in present-day New Mexico has shed light on the ethno-racial and religious mixture across Jewish, Catholic, Indigenous, and Spanish ancestry that Spanish, Mexican, and US colonialism produced in the region.[29]

To interpret Huerta's evocation of Jewish-Indigenous likeness solely as a representational strategy of visibility in a white Judeo-Christian American context does not account for the regional specificity of Jewishness racialization at the border. Huerta's identification with Jewish ritual, while likely a byproduct of code-switching, also serves as a reminder that Jewish history in the border region is implicated in a multicentury project of Spanish, Mexican, and US empire-building, and as a result, has been marked by a multiracial, multireligious context.

Huerta's memories offer an important insight into how Jewish history functions on a material level in the Sonoran Desert, as a container for multidirectional religious memory in the American West. Huerta links Yaqui and Chiricahua Apache histories under the umbrella of Western colonial history while also drawing analogies between Yaqui and Jewish subjectivities through rhetoric and ritual. His memory of Jewish–Indigenous friendship in nineteenth-century Southern Arizona suggests a strategy for representation in the context of historic and ongoing erasure of Indigenous religious history in Western popular imagination. By way of Huerta's narrative, a Jewish cemetery offers a container through which to remember the transnational scope of empire-building in the border region as well as the religio-racial hybridities such imperial projects produced over time.

Alongside Huerta and Sirota's remarks, the dedication ceremony was convened by state representative James McNaulty of Cochise County, the district's congressional representative. Representative McNaulty's comments shed light on how the State remembers and preserves the West's religious history and how Jewish sacred space is woven into a mythology about the nineteenth-century Western frontier as a place of religious diversity and coexistence. During the opening remarks, McNaulty did not attend to the Jewish specificity of the burial ground at all, and rather interpreted the cemetery as material evidence that invites the memory of religious pluralism on the American

Figure 13.3 Bisbee-Douglas Jewish Cemetery rededication plaque, 2020. Courtesy of the author.

frontier. McNaulty celebrated the "hardy men and women not only for helping settle the silver camps and ranching areas [of the] 'Old West,' but also for their cooperation, mutual respect and . . . careful webbing of . . . community," that made their existence possible.[30] The cemetery commemorates the legacy of Western pioneers not only for their utility and participation in expanding American capitalism but also for how they embodied the range of new religious possibilities that the American West offered.

McNaulty mythologized the American West by drawing an important throughline between economic settlement, mobility, and religious freedom. The hardy pioneers endured life in a rugged frontier mining town like Tombstone in part because of cooperation across different ethno-religious communities, echoing Ferenc Morton Szasz's claims that, by the turn of the century, the West "had become a model of the 'social gospel' adapted to regional needs."[31] Under this cooperative model, Protestants, Catholics, and Jews enjoyed the promises of individualism and upward mobility when religious differences receded into the background.[32] McNaulty credited the restoration as a project realized by the "spiritual successors" of the hardy men and women of the Old West. Thanks to their collaborative efforts, McNaulty explained, "this historic place is now open for all visitors to come and learn something about the pioneers who had come long before us." The spiritual successors to which McNaulty refers are not descendants of "Jewish Pioneers and Their Indian Friends," but rather a vague moniker for those Arizona citizens today who uphold the cooperative religious values of nineteenth-century pioneers of the Old West. The legacy of the cooperative model today is a specific application of "religious freedom" that maintains an unspoken religio-racial norm of the Judeo-Christian paradigm.

For McNaulty, the cemetery reflects spiritual-political cooperation between Jewish American real estate developers and Arizona state interests. Through the 1970s and 1980s, Jews in Southern Arizona amassed economic and political influence in the state through their prominent roles in real estate development and speculation (1970s–80s), paving the way for collaborations between Jewish developers and Arizona politicians who looked to real estate as a way to "fill their coffers." In the years following 1967 and 1973, the "official" beginning of Israeli occupation of Palestinian lands, Jews in Arizona, especially those with economic ties to real estate development, leveraged their contacts with politicians to advocate for pro-Israeli US foreign policy from the Arizona state legislature.[33] Tucson's Desert Caucus was organized in 1977 as a political action committee that supported political candidates who were reliably pro-Israel.[34] McNaulty was reported as among the Arizona state politicians to whom Southern Arizona's Jewish community had "easy access."[35] The collaboration between Sirota and McNaulty during the Jewish cemetery restoration ceremony is part of a broader regional landscape wherein Jewish community leaders—many of whom were personally and/or professionally linked with real estate speculation—and Arizona state legislators developed cooperative relationships based on shared economic and political interests. More specifically, McNaulty's public support of the cemetery restoration reflects an ongoing interest among many Arizona politicians at the time to maintain friendly relations with Jewish community leaders and to facilitate collaborations between real estate developers and politicians who controlled zoning and other related legislation.

An important background to the economic-political cooperation between the Desert Caucus and Arizona politicians was the rise of the Moral Majority and the emphasis on Judeo-Christianity as a religious value set. When McNaulty refers to "spiritual successors," he is doing the rhetorical work of assimilating a Jewish religious practice into a Judeo-Christian model of acceptable multireligious practice that nonetheless maintains Christian dominance.[36] The preservation of a Jewish cemetery also reflects the unspoken religio-racial implications of a Judeo-Christian paradigm by the mid-twentieth century: the alignment of Jewishness with whiteness and, thus, the colonial practices of the West.[37] The creation, disappearance, and reappearance of the cemetery is like a timeline of Jewish inclusion into the kinds of religious freedom the American West offers. "Judeo-Christian Pioneers" are those who paved the way for the embodiment of Judeo-Christian values as the center of American religion in the late twentieth century.

Remembering Jewish Pioneers Across Western Empires

The Bisbee-Douglas Cemetery is one of the oldest Jewish burial sites in the Arizona territory, established around 1904 by real estate booster and Jewish settler William Klein for congregants of the Sons of Israel as an Orthodox burial site. Like the Tombstone cemetery, the burial ground was made possible through the United States' genocidal approaches to Chiricahua Apache removal. The nineteen-plot cemetery is in the town of Douglas, a former copper mining stronghold and the easternmost port-of-entry between the states of Arizona, US, and Sonora, Mexico. The cemetery was in active use from 1912 until 1963, which corresponds to an approximate timeline of Douglas's organized religious Jewish community.[38] The land deed for the burial ground was transferred from the Sons of Israel Congregation to Anshei Israel, a Conservative Jewish congregation in Tucson, roughly one hundred miles north of Douglas. The date and reason for the transfer of the land deed to geographically distant Jewish institutions remain unknown, but the transfer was likely influenced by the departure of Douglas's Jewish community and the expansion of Tucson's Jewish community in the decades after World War II. When interviewed by a local Jewish newspaper at the onset of the second restoration project in 2016, the synagogue's leadership admitted to not knowing how or why they owned the property: "Someone must have donated it . . . the history is murky."[39]

The first official restoration of the cemetery was in 1993 through a collaboration between the Bloom Southwest Jewish Archives, part of the University of Arizona's Special Collections, and the Cochise County Historical Society. In the Spring issues of the *Southwest Jewish History* newsletter, the head of the Bloom Archives, Abe Chanin, wrote that the old cemetery "was in shambles" and in "shameful condition," and the "long and colorful pioneer history" of Cochise County was at risk of being lost to time. The restoration process brought both Jewish and non-Jewish institutions and local volunteers together to help remove weeds, correct headstones that had been toppled over, and replace the collapsed barbed-wire fence to help the space "hold its southwestern look."[40] Finally, the re-dedication project installed a memorial plaque to the *Memory of Jewish Pioneers of Cochise County*, "who before the turn of the [twentieth] century, were deputy sheriffs, mining entrepreneurs, cattlemen, lawyers, bankers, and mayors." According to Chanin's report, the cemetery, "only a couple of hundred yards from the Mexican border," had regained "a look of respectability."[41]

Between 2005 and 2020, the cemetery was owned and managed primarily by two individuals—Richard Rosen and Jorge Ilitzky—who, after a chance meeting in a temple in Scottsdale, Arizona, partnered to buy the land from Anshei Israel. In fits and starts over the next fifteen years, Rosen and Ilitzky worked with the Jewish Federation of Southern Arizona and the Jewish History Museum and Holocaust History Center to fund and launch a comprehensive cemetery restoration project in early 2020. The restoration project included the resettling of gravestones, landscaping, a new wrought-iron security fence, solar lighting, security cameras, and annual maintenance. A new, second dedication plaque was installed alongside the 1993 commemoration and acknowledges the memory of the Jewish Pioneers, as well as the various Jewish American foundations and individual philanthropists who funded the restoration.

For Ilitzky, the connection to the cemetery was personal. His family had settled in the region at the turn of the twentieth century as active participants in agriculture and mercantile economies on both sides of the border, spanning Chihuahua, Sonora, and Arizona.[42] Three of Ilitzky's ancestors were Douglas residents and were buried in the cemetery in 1940, 1944, and 1963, respectively. While Ilitzky is a founding funder of the restoration project and one of the few living descendants who remains tied to the border region, he has not publicly articulated his motivations or his attachments to the space.

Despite having no familial ties, Rosen has been an active and vocal spokesperson for the restoration project since 2016, when fundraising began. The initial catalyst for his restoration efforts was family-related, however: the tragic death of Rosen's son Landon in 2012.[43] The two had visited the Bisbee-Douglas cemetery together, and Rosen began imagining the restoration of the cemetery as "a memorial to him."[44] Beyond memorializing his son, the restoration project means multiple things to Rosen, including a commemoration of the Nazi Holocaust, his religious and political commitments to Jerusalem, and the maintenance of a Jewish state in Palestine more broadly. Rosen's rhetorical uses for the Bisbee-Douglas Cemetery reflect how he engages with long-standing myths about the American West as a region, as well as ideas about the West's role in the transnational, imperialist realm.

Rosen explained that he was initially drawn into the project based on previous experience supporting the restoration of Jewish cemeteries in Poland. "I do have family in Poland . . . and I've seen the Jewish cemeteries in the woods, with questions being asked by local Polish people, why are you giving any money to the Jews?" When talking with non-Jewish residents of towns previously inhabited by Jews across Poland and Bulgaria, he heard questions like, "'We loved our Jews. Why did they leave?'" What he observed as a collective forgetting of a Jewish past through Jewish absence and material decay of Jewish space made the preservation of Jewish cemeteries across Eastern Europe an important anecdote. Rosen became directly involved in the restoration of a cemetery near Bialystok, Poland, an experience that heightened his awareness of the power and precariousness of preserving Jewish material history on a global scale.[45] The forgetting of European Jewish history is something you "wouldn't see in America," according to Rosen.

As a contrast to a disregard of Jewish history in Europe, the commitment to *remembering* Jewish history in America reflects an important way that Rosen engages with Euro-American mythology of the West as exceptional, and for Jews specifically, a space of emancipation and permanence. In the Western Jewish cultural imaginary, the American frontier has been a space through which a nationless European Jew could shake off his history of dispossession and exile and emerge as a settled, modern citizen of empire.[46] For Rosen, the dilapidated Jewish cemeteries in Europe are a reminder of the long history of Jewish diaspora that culminated in genocide, and of an absent Jewish community to care for its material past. In contrast, the American West fulfilled its promise to Jews: to be a site of wealth, religious freedom, and continuity.

When explaining the motivations for Jewish immigration to the Southwest, Rosen noted that "the area was very rich when the copper mines were there during the time of Wyatt Earp . . . it was a place where there was capitalistic viability. Let's put it that way. You know it was different than it is today." Recycling the Jewish Pioneers trope, with its rugged, individualist entrepreneurial spirit, Rosen speaks proudly of "the Jewish people [who] came to the desert . . . to be peddlers selling clothes, and guns." He believes that the cemetery can help educate the public about the transformational uplift that Jewish immigrants experienced in the border region at the turn of the twentieth century, and can remind the public that Jews were there during a time of "capitalistic viability," which he carefully notes, is "different" from how the border region is imagined currently. Through Rosen's memories, the cemetery can restore and recycle a story about what the American West used to be: a land of opportunity, where a generation of dispossessed European immigrants could settle, work hard, make their fortune, and leave behind a past riddled with persecution. The cemetery helps the public remember that Jews were among the generation of American pioneers who settled a rugged American frontier.

Rosen's evocation of the mythology of the West as a land of opportunity and refuge is not exclusively about the transformation of Jews into American pioneers, but also how Jews act as religious or spiritual pioneers in Jerusalem, a manufactured Western frontier in the Middle East. Part of Rosen's rationale for his preservation work in Douglas is his dual US-Israeli citizenship. Rosen explained how the experience of walking into the cemetery was a "type of emotional uplift. . . . It's almost like when you land in Jerusalem. I really feel this historical connection. I don't know what it's about, but it's very spiritual. Even though it's a little spot right next to our border on the American side, it has a very rich, meaningful feeling when you enter it." During an interview with an Arizona Jewish newspaper reporting on the restoration effort, he similarly analogized the feeling of "positive spirituality" in the Bisbee-Douglas cemetery to "the emotional uplift of stepping off a plane in Israel." Importantly, the myth of the West as a refuge from persecution is operating as a multidirectional and transregional narrative that images both the American Southwest and Jerusalem as two distinct yet interconnected promised land(s) for Jews. Recalling the memory of the Nazi Holocaust, as well as popular narratives of bootstrapping Jewish border merchants in the "times of Pancho Villa," the Bisbee-Douglas Cemetery serves as a repository for Rosen to remember the Southwest, as well as Jerusalem, as spaces that have transformed the dispossessed European Jewish subject into an economic and spiritual pioneer who participated in settling Western imperial frontiers.

If Rosen's attachments to the cemetery reveal the West as a multidirectional and transregional myth about Jewish refuge and opportunity, his memories also implicate the Jewish Pioneer subject in/and between Jewish history of the Southwest and Jewish nationalism as a justification for Western occupation and settlement in Jerusalem today. Rosen and I spoke in May 2021, in the wake of mass demonstrations by Palestinian residents of East Jerusalem who were protesting forced displacements and evictions in the Sheikh Jarrah, a neighborhood just north of Jerusalem's Old City. Anti-eviction protests were preceded by a series of nightly barricades by the Israeli police that disrupted access to the Damascus Gate esplanade, an important gathering site for East Jerusalemites during Ramadan. The Palestinian-led protests triggered what was called the most significant Israeli military operation in the occupied Palestinian territories in nearly a decade; within a week, the bombings had killed more than two hundred Palestinians, including more than sixty children. Hamas, the Palestinian armed resistance movement and Islamist political party, responded with rocket fire that killed twelve Israelis, including two children and one Israeli soldier.[47]

When I asked Rosen what drives his preservation work, an admittedly slow and bureaucratic process, he quantified it as part of a long-standing commitment to Jewish life globally. Rosen spoke vaguely of the omnipresent violence in Israel and concern for his youngest son, a dual US-Israeli citizen currently residing in Jerusalem. "He has been hanging out in bunkers, you know, even as a high school student." By linking Western Jewish history to contemporary Jewish settlement in Jerusalem, Rosen deploys the cultural memory of nineteenth-century Jewish Pioneers as a prologue to a new Jewish pioneer (his son), who is engaged in the work of settling and maintaining a Western frontier in Jerusalem.[48]

Though Jewish nationalism is not explicitly invoked by Rosen as the ideological core of his commitment to Jewish life, nor as the justification for his son's Israeli citizenship, his commitment to remembering Jewish Pioneers in Douglas is bound up with the image of his Jewish American son in a bunker in Jerusalem in 2021—an embodied signifier of the spiritual Jewish pioneer seeking religious refuge on a new Western frontier. Inside this Jewish sacred space, "a little spot right next to our border on the American side," the Jewish Pioneer is imagined not only as a historical subject fixed in place but as a mobile spiritual frontiersman in a bunker in West Jerusalem, one who has moved East on behalf of the Western empire. In sum, the Bisbee-Douglas Cemetery becomes a container through which Rosen remembers a history of Jewish victimization and diaspora in Europe, the power of the American West to transform the disposed Jewish subject into an American Pioneer; and the capacity of that figure to be re-embodied in Jerusalem—a Western frontier geographically beyond the American West as a place, yet discursively implicated in the American West as a process.

Conclusion

Between January and March of 2020, and with the support of the Jewish History Museum and Holocaust History Center in Tucson, I taught a ten-week course that covered over five centuries of Jewish history in the US–Mexico border region. As part of our final class, I worked with the Jewish Federation of Southern Arizona to sponsor a "Mobile Day of Learning" that included a chartered bus visit to the recently restored Bisbee-Douglas cemetery. Somewhere between Tombstone and Douglas, we crossed through the Customs and Border Patrol (CBP), the policing infrastructure that seeks to dictate all forms of human mobility in the Sonoran Desert, including the act of traveling to and protecting sacred sites. Our white sprinter van full of Jewish Federation donors was waved through the CBP checkpoint, and we went on to enjoy a peaceful and reflective afternoon at the cemetery.[49]

In my role as the "public historian," I emphasized how remembering the history of Jews in Douglas was also an act of remembering the history of the Chiricahua Apaches, whose forced removal from their ancestral homelands between the 1850s and 1890s was the precondition for the creation of Jewish burial sites in Southern Arizona. I emphasized that remembering the Jewish merchants of Douglas also meant remembering the intimacies between merchants, extractive and exploitative mining corporations, and an expanding US military presence that brought terror and violence to those considered racially and socially unfit for American society.

And yet, I couldn't shake the memory of being in the cemetery and being told by Border Patrol that I did not *look illegal*, nor how casually CBP waved our bus through the checkpoint, because in all likelihood, our bus was full of people who also *did not look illegal*. Just seventy miles west of Douglas, the same military apparatus has terrorized and criminalized the religious practices of Indigenous nations like the Tohono O'odham, whose land and water defenders were arrested and detained for protecting their sacred sites.[50] The year prior, the Trump administration had authorized the expansion of the border wall at Organ Pipe National Monument, a construction process that caused irreparable damage to lands and waters sacred to O'odham peoples. For migrants forced to pass through the dry desert terrain, the springs are also a precious, lifesaving resource.[51] To the US government, the area is a vulnerable space along the international border that opens up the nation to foreign, *illegal* invaders, just the latest iteration of how Western empires treat Indigenous places as spaces to be occupied, commodified, and militarized. The US occupies Indigenous sacred sites to reaffirm settler permanence through land use.

Jewish Pioneer cemeteries reflect the intimacies between public memory, religion, and the myth of the American West as a promised land of economic opportunity and religious freedom. Through my academic and public scholarship, I have sought to complicate the stories that the cemeteries ask us to remember, highlighting the intimacies between Jewish settlement and contemporary Jewish spaces and the ongoing Indigenous genocides, from the US border to Palestine. However, the experience of researching these sacred sites shed light on something new: Being a researcher writing about an implicated space does not absolve me of implication. Even as I historicize these cemeteries, meditate on memory, and refuse to recycle the myth of the American West through Jewish history, my body is marked by the legacy of the structural inequities I am writing about. My personal experiences visiting the cemetery and my encounters with Border Patrol reflect the ways that race, gender, and socioeconomic class are constitutive of—and constituted by—the cemeteries themselves. My body reflects the inherited powers and privileges that are embedded in the Jewish cemetery.

Changing which stories we remember through Jewish sites of memory is an important, but limited step in a broader process of resisting the ongoing ways that Jewishness is used to justify the racialized violence that settler colonialism produces. The juxtaposition between Jewish and O'odham sacred spaces along the border is one example of how the preservation of sacred spaces in the American West is a process that operates in relation to spacemaking under the US empire. Historical preservation, so often a process of caretaking for myths that prop up the empire, might be reimagined as a practice of accountability that takes up material space. Understanding our own implication is a first step towards changing how and why we care for and repair our sacred sites on stolen land.

Notes

1. Kara McCormack, *Imagining Tombstone: The Town Too Tough to Die* (University of Kansas Press, 2016).

2. Several properties in the town's commercial district have been protected by the Department of the Interior under the National Register of Historic Places for their capacity to convey "historical integrity." *National Register of Historic Places Inventory-Nomination Form* (1958; rev. 1974), United States Department of the Interior, National Parks Service, Form No. 10-300.

3. Tombstone Chamber of Commerce, "Tombstone Boothill Graveyard Visitors Guide," Tombstone, Arizona, 2005.

4. Valeria Luiselli's profile of Tombstone in the *New Yorker* explores the throughline between the town's history and contemporary status as a refuge for vigilantism and anti-immigrant militia organizing. See Valeria Luiselli, "The Wild West Meets the Southern Border," *The New Yorker*, June 3, 2019, 32–39, www.newyorker.com/magazine/2019/06/10/the-wild-west-meets-the-southern-border.

5. In their quest for territorial and racial domination throughout the nineteenth century, the United States and Mexico launched countless genocidal projects against different In-

digenous nations across what is now the US–Mexico border region. The land occupied by southern Arizona's Jewish cemeteries and Jewish Pioneer monuments is the ancestral homeland of the Chiricahua Apache, who, after decades of anti-colonial resistance, were forcibly relocated to three different reservations across northeastern Arizona, New Mexico, and Oklahoma. See Paul Conrad, *The Apache Diaspora: Four Centuries of Displacement and Survival* (University of Pennsylvania Press, 2021). State-sanctioned border vigilantism across Texas, New Mexico, and Arizona in the mid- to late nineteenth century offered a blueprint for the creation of the US Border Patrol in 1924, which helped create a landscape of surveillance and racial terror among Mexican and Chinese-origin residents who worked and lived on both sides of the borderline. See the history of *la Matanza* in Kelly Lytle Hernández, *Bad Mexicans: Race, Empire, and Revolution in the Borderlands* (W. W. Norton, 2022), 299–300; and US and Mexican anti-Chinese racism in Robert Chao Romero, *The Chinese in Mexico, 1882–1940* (University of Arizona Press, 2011), 145.

6. I use Judith Weisenfeld's term "religio-racial," to underscore the ways race and religion are mutually constitutive categories in an American context. Although Weisenfeld primarily used the term to describe how groups racialized as non-white have reclaimed their racial identities on religious and spiritual grounds, I use "religio-racial" as an analytic framework to capture how whiteness has been constructed and maintained on religious grounds in the American West. More specifically, I draw on Weisenfeld's term to capture how a Judeo-Christian imaginary shapes the border region's racial geography in order to mark some individuals as protected and worthy of belonging (read: white) to the nation while racializing others as subversive threats in need of surveillance, detainment, and even removal from the nation. See Judith Weisenfeld, "New World A-Coming: Black Religion and Racial Identity During the Great Migration" (New York University Press, 2016), 13–15.

7. Another example of Jewish burial grounds as sites of Jewish Pioneer memory culture is the "Commission for the Preservation of Pioneer Jewish Cemeteries and Landmarks in the West," established in 1962. To date, the Commission has overseen the restoration of seven Jewish cemeteries in Northern California, all originally established in the mid-nineteenth century at the onset of US occupation of the region. More information on the commission's work can be found at https://pioneerjewishcemeteries.org/about-the-cemeteries.

8. My analysis of public memory, religious colonialism, and Western commemorative landscapes has been informed by Abel Gómez and Cynthia Culver Prescott. For analysis about Spanish colonialism and monuments in California, see Abel Gómez, "Statues Topple and a Catholic Church Burns as California Reckons with Its Spanish Colonial Past," *The Conversation*, July 24, 2020, https://theconversation.com/statues-topple-and-a-catholic-church-burns-as-california-reckons-with-its-spanish-colonial-past-142809. For analysis about Manifest Destiny, and cultural memory of pioneers in the American West, see Cynthia Culver Prescott, *Pioneer Mother Monuments: Constructing Cultural Memory* (University of Oklahoma Press, 2019).

9. Michael Rothberg, *The Implicated Subject: Beyond Victims and Perpetrators* (Stanford University Press, 2019).

10. Rothberg, *The Implicated Subject*, 1.

11. As a reference to the United States as a dual-faith nation, the term "Judeo-Christian" was popularized in the mid-twentieth century by political speakers and scholars. Relatedly,

this hyphenated phrase has been used to capture the "special relationship" between the United States and Israel to identify a shared *ethos* between the two nations, or a certain moral character that underpins the values of Western civilization—regardless of geographic location. See K. Healan Gaston, *Imagining Judeo-Christian America: Religion, Secularism, and the Redefinition of Democracy* (University of Chicago Press, 2019), 175–77.

My deployment of the term throughout this chapter is similarly rooted in a mid-twentieth-century context, and I specifically understand "Judeo-Christian" as a racialized Western theological paradigm into which the Jewish subject has been assimilated in service of a larger white Christian imperial project. Thinking with the scholar J. Kameron Carter and his book-in-progress, *Whiteness: A Political Theology*, the Judeo-Christian tradition not only assimilated Jewishness into a paradigm of Western Christian humanism but also, importantly, aligned Jewishness with whiteness and thus the colonial and imperial practices of the West. In the context of my own case study, my use of the term "Judeo-Christian" refers to a post-1948 American religious imaginary in which Jewishness works rhetorically and theologically with Christianity to shape the racial boundaries of religious inclusion in the American West and, by extension, the State of Israel; when we understand Jews as part of "the West," we can also understand the maintenance of a Jewish state in Palestine as an extension of the Western frontier. For more on Jewishness and religious whiteness, see J. Kameron Carter, "Jews and the Religion of Whiteness," lecture delivered February 12, 2021, as part of the "Jews, Race, and Religion" series at the Herbert D. Katz Center for Advanced Judaic Studies, University of Pennsylvania, https://www.youtube.com/watch?v=PK-Ucq-4ZuQ.

12. "Obituary for Jeanne Macia Devere," *Douglas Dispatch*, August 25, 2077, https://www.findagrave.com/memorial/32275759/jeanne-devere.

13. "Jeanne Devere's Letter to Rabbi Floyd Fierman, October 19, 1961," Fierman Collection, Bloom Southwest Jewish Archives, University of Arizona, Tucson.

14. Devere's use of nationality to describe the contractor and merchant who "tore down the wall around the Jewish cemetery" reflects new demographic realities of the border region at the turn of the twentieth century and the transformation of national categories into racialized tropes of un-belonging within a white Anglo frontier society. The confluence of anti-Chinese US immigration restrictions, new demands for expendable labor, the influx of refugees fleeing the violence of the Mexican Revolution, and the pervasive xenophobic, nativist white-supremacist culture of the frontier worked together to transform national categories (Chinese and Mexican) into racial scripts that marked Chinese- and Mexican-identified persons as legally, socially, and otherwise un-belonging to the US. For further reading on Mexican as a twentieth-century racial category in the United States, see theories of "racial scripts" and "Mexican Brown" in Natalia Molina, *How Race is Made in America: Immigration, Citizenship, and the Historical Power of Racial Scripts* (University of California Press, 2014); and Kelly Lytle-Hernandez, *Migra: A History of the U.S. Border Patrol* (University of California Press, 2010).

15. "Welcome to the City of Tombstone," accessed January 2023, https://www.cityoftombstoneaz.gov/.

16. Boothill Graveyard pamphlet, ethnographic research, November 2018.

17. McCormack, *Imagining Tombstone*, 23–24.

18. “In Memoriam: Judge Lawrence Huerta 1924–2022,” *University of Arizona Law*, June 13, 2022, https://law.arizona.edu/news/2022/06/memoriam-judge-lawrence-huerta-1924-2022; “An Old West Cemetery for Jews is Rededicated in Tombstone,” *New York Times*, February 29, 1984, https://www.nytimes.com/1984/02/29/us/an-old-west-cemetery-for-jews-is-rededicated-in-tombstone.html.

19. “Tombstone Call to Action,” 1983, Bloom Southwest Jewish Archives, Special Collections, University of Arizona, https://swja.arizona.edu/content/tombstone-cemetery-call-action.

20. “An Old West Cemetery for Jews Is Rededicated at Tombstone,” *New York Times*, February 29, 1984.

21. “An Old West Cemetery for Jews Is Rededicated in Tombstone.”

22. “Tombstone Cemetery Call to Action,” *The Historical Jewish Cemetery at Boothill*, Tombstone, Arizona (date unknown, estimated 1983–4), Papers of David A. and Leona Bloom, Box 1, Bloom Southwest Jewish Archives, University of Arizona Special Collections.

23. Nicole M. Guidotti-Hernandez, *Unspeakable Violence* (Duke University Press, 2011), 173.

24. “An Old West Cemetery for Jews is Rededicated in Tombstone.”

25. “An Old West Cemetery for Jews is Rededicated in Tombstone.”

26. David S. Koffman, *The Jews' Indian: Colonialism, Pluralism, and Belonging in America* (Rutgers University Press), 2; Sarah Imhoff, *Masculinity and the Making of American Judaism* (Indiana University Press, 2017); Michael Rubenstein, *Members of the Tribe: Jewish Identify and Belonging in an Age of Multiculturism* (Stanford University Press, 2021).

27. Philip Deloria, *Playing Indian* (Yale University Press, 1998), 7.

28. For a partial bibliography on Sephardic and Converso history and its legacies in northern New Spain, see Fay Forman Blake, “The Hidden Jews of New Mexico,” *Journal of Progressive Judaism* 8 (1997): 5–26; Tomás Atencio, “The Converso Legacy in New Mexico Hispano Protestantism,” *El Caminante* 2 (2003): 10–15; Tomas Atencio, “Crypto-Jewish Remnants in Manito Society and Culture,” *Jewish Folklore and Ethnology Review* 18 (1996) 15–20; David Gitlitz, *Living in Silverado: Secret Jews in the Silver Mining Towns of Colonial Mexico* (University of New Mexico Press, 2019); and Stanley M. Hordes, *To the End of the Earth: A History for the Crypto-Jews of New Mexico* (Columbia University Press, 2005).

29. Janet Leibman Jacobs, *Hidden Heritage* (University of California Press, 2002); Jonathan Freedman, “Conversos, Marranos, and Crypto-Latinos,” *Klezmer America: Jewishness, Ethnicity, Modernity* (Columbia University Press, 2009), 209–50. An updated version of this book chapter can be found under the same title in Susan A. Glenn and Naomi B. Sokoloff, eds., *Boundaries of Jewish Identity* (University of Washington Press, 2011), 188–202; Seth Kunin, *Juggling Identities: Identity and Authenticity Among the Crypto-Jews* (Columbia University Press, 2009).

30. Arizona State Representative James McNulty, Congressional Report, “Restoration of a Jewish Cemetery in Tombstone, Arizona,” Bloom Southwest Jewish Archives, Special Collections, University of Arizona, https://swja.library.arizona.edu/content/restoration-jewish-cemetery-tombstone-arizona.

31. Szasz cited by Philip Goff, “Religion and the American West,” *A Companion to the American West*, ed. William Deverell (Blackwell Publishing, 2004), 294.

32. Shari Rabin argues that Jewish mobility across America's nineteenth-century frontier spaces was imagined in the context of Democratic promises of individualism and the invisibility of religious difference. See Shari Rabin, *Jews on the Frontier: Religion and Mobility in Nineteenth-Century America* (New York University Press, 2017), 7.

33. Obituaries: David Sirota, *Arizona Jewish Post*, October 24, 2014, https://azjewishpost.com/2014/david-sirota/; "History of Green Valley," Green Valley and Sahuarita Chamber of Commerce & Visitor Center website, accessed January 2023, https://www.greenvalleysahuarita.com/history50d19b98.

34. Leonard Dinnerstein, "From Desert Oasis to the Desert Caucus," *Jews of the American West*, ed. Moses Rischin and John Livingston (Wayne State University Press, 1991), 157.

35. Dinnerstein, "From Desert Oasis," 156.

36. Shaul Magid, "The Judeo-Christian Tradition," in *Theologies of American Exceptionalism*, ed. Winifred Fallers Sullivan and Elizabeth Shakman Hurd (Indian University Press), https://publish.iupress.indiana.edu/read/theologies-of-american-exceptionalism/section/0bebab72-c6b6-4839-a58a-4c86ea2fc977; Gaston, *Imagining Judeo-Christian America*, 235.

37. Carter, "Jews and the Religion of Whiteness."

38. Claims that the Bisbee-Douglas Jewish Cemetery is the first in the Arizona Territory are a common anecdotal description told to those curious about Southern Arizona's Jewish history across a range of media, including popular accounts and scholarly sources. See Jaimie Luria, "The Bisbee-Douglas Jewish Cemetery: An Ongoing Study in Preservation," *Cochise County Historical Society* 48, no. 1 (Spring/Summer 2018), 33–40; David Del Grande, "Local Jewish Cemetery, Once Derelict, Gains National Attention," *Arizona Jewish Post*, July 7, 2016, https://azjewishpost.com/2016/local-jewish-cemetery-once-derelict-gains-national-attention/.

39. Comment from Rabbi Emeritus Arthur R. Oleisky, cited in Del Grande, "Local Jewish Cemetery."

40. Abe Chanin, "An Old Jewish Cemetery Restored," *Southwest Jewish History*, Spring 1993, Bloom Southwest Jewish Archives, University of Arizona Special Collections, 3–5.

41. Chanin, "An Old Jewish Cemetery Restored, 4."

42. Phyllis Braun, "Matching Funds Sought for Historic Borderlands Jewish Cemetery Restoration," *Arizona Jewish Post*, February 7, 2020, https://azjewishpost.com/2020/matching-funds-sought-for-historic-borderlands-jewish-cemetery-restoration/.

43. According to an interview in 2020, Rosen hopes to rename the street next to the Bisbee-Douglas Jewish Cemetery for his son and see historical tours visit the site once the restoration is complete; see Braun, "Matching Funds."

44. Richard Rosen, interview with author, May 28, 2021.

45. Braun, "Matching Funds."

46. Koffman, *The Jews' Indian*, 5.

47. Mari Cohen, Joshua Leifer, and Alex Kane, "A Guide to the Current Crisis in Israel/Palestine," *Jewish Currents*, May 13, 2021, https://jewishcurrents.org/a-guide-to-the-current-crisis-in-israel-palestine#why-demonstrating.

48. Since the establishment of the State of Israel in 1948, the spiritual and political geography of Jerusalem has been imagined across a Jewish West–Palestinian East axis, despite the profound inequities that have shaped Jewish Israeli and non-Jewish Palestinian life. Among its numerous consequences, the move of the US consulate to Jerusalem from Tel

Aviv in 2017 recognized Jerusalem as the Israeli capital, affirmed Jewish nationalism as Israel's ideological core, and disrupted the thinly veiled mythology of ethno-religious pluralism between West and East Jerusalem; see Goldie Poll and Jacob Plitman, "Protesting Conservative Judaism's Support of Embassy Move," *Jewish Currents*, December 17, 2017, https://jewishcurrents.org/protesting-conservative-judaisms-support-of-embassy-move.

49. The Boothill Graveyard and the Bisbee-Douglas Cemeteries are located within the hundred-mile border zone, an area that extends hundred miles inward from the border wherein US CBP has expanded jurisdiction, including the authority to stop and search vehicles. Approximately two-thirds of people in the United States live within the hundred-mile zone. Activist and immigration scholar Harsha Walia has names this strategy of border governance "territorial diffusion," a term that highlights how border surveillance and disciplinary practices are not contained to ports of entry but can materialize anywhere within the nation-state. In short, historic sacred sites that exist in the hundred-mile zone are implicitly entangled with the present-day realities of immigration policies and the racialized surveillance on which border enforcement relies. See Harsha Walia, *Border and Rule: Global Migration, Capitalism, and the Rise of Racist Nationalism* (Haymarket Books, 2021), 30.

50. For members of the O'odham Nation, the area of Quitobaquito Springs near Monument Hill, is not only ancestral territory but a source of life—for humans and for the many non-human beings who inhabit the Sonoran Desert. Saguaros are not just sacred; they are persons in their own right, O'odham's ancestors. This understanding is articulated in Amy Goodman's interview with Nellie Jo David, "O'odham Land Defenders Lead Indigenous Resistance to Trump's Border Wall Amid Militarized Crackdown," *Democracy Now!*, October 12, 2020, https://www.democracynow.org/2020/10/12/organ_pipe_national_monument_border_wall.

51. Barbara A. Sostaita, "Water, Not Walls: Towards a Religious Study of Life That Defies Borders," *American Religion* 1, no. 2 (Spring 2020), 74–97.

Acknowledgments

Many people played a part in bringing this book into the world, and we are grateful to them. First and foremost, we thank the contributors. This really was the dream team, and we so enjoyed getting to know the authors over the course of two symposia.

Speaking of the symposia, we owe a huge debt of gratitude to the Williams P. Clements Center for Southwest Studies at Southern Methodist University in Dallas and to the Eiteljorg Museum of American Indians and Western Art in Indianapolis for sponsoring and hosting us. The Clements Center has sponsored many symposia with a variety of partners over the years, and we were fortunate to join this excellent company. Special thanks go to Andy Graybill, Ruth Ann Elmore, and Ariel Ron for shepherding us and gathering us at their beautiful Taos campus for our first meeting. We also thank our wonderful partners at the Eiteljorg, especially Jessica Nelson, Elisa Phelps, and John Vanausdall. It was such a pleasure to meet at the Eiteljorg Museum, view their impressive collections, and participate in programming related to the *Acts of Faith: Religion in the American West* exhibit that the Eiteljorg shared with the New York Historical Society Library and Museum.

At the University of North Carolina Press, we thank our editors, Mark Simpson-Vos and Cate Hodorowicz, and we have also benefited from the careful help of Tara Jordan and Jill Pellarin's copyediting. We are grateful as well to the peer reviewers identified by the press; they have made this volume stronger and more focused.

Sophie Himmel was our undergraduate project fellow at Lafayette College. We thank her for sharing her insights on the first round of drafts and for her help in organizing the first symposium.

We thank the growing community of scholars who study religion in the North American West. Many of us, including the authors in this volume, have presented their research and benefited from feedback at the American Academy of Religion and the Western Historical Association. This book exists because of the emergence of this vital and exciting subfield.

Finally, we thank all those in academia and beyond who have cared for us.

Contributors

James B. Bennett (PhD, Yale University) is associate professor of religious studies at Santa Clara University, where he teaches the history of religion in America. He is the author of publications on the intersection of religion and race in the United States, conflict within Christianity, and the anticult movement in the latter decades of the twentieth century.

Carleigh Beriont earned her PhD from Harvard University, where she studied and now teaches the history of American religions and politics. Her research focuses on the United States empire, missionaries, and militarism in the Pacific during the nineteenth and twentieth centuries. She received an MTS in religion, ethics, and politics from Harvard Divinity School and a BA from Mount Holyoke College. Previously, she lived and worked in the Republic of the Marshall Islands. She is currently running for Congress in New Hampshire's First District.

Thomas S. Bremer is professor emeritus of religious studies at Rhodes College in Memphis, Tennessee, where he taught American religious history. His scholarship explores connections between religion and tourism, with a particular interest in US national parks.

Brandi Denison is an associate professor of religious studies in the Department of Philosophy and Religious Studies at the University of North Florida. Her research focuses on religion and culture in the American West. She is the author of *Ute Land Religion in the American West, 1879–2009* (University of Nebraska Press). She has published in journals such as *Pacific Historical Review* and *Religion and American Culture.*

Jon M. Garcia is a historian of Latino religion and a visiting scholar at the University of Southern California. His work examines how religion, space, and modernity intersect in the Mexico-US borderlands. His current book project explores how Mexican Protestants shaped religious and political life in nineteenth- and twentieth-century Mexico.

Lynne Gerber is an independent scholar in San Francisco, California. She is the author of *Seeking the Straight and Narrow: Weight Loss and Sexual Reorientation in Evangelical America* (University of Chicago Press, 2012). Her current work examines religious responses to the emergence of AIDS in 1980s and 1990s San Francisco.

Jennifer Graber is professor of history and affiliate faculty in Native American and Indigenous Studies at the University of Texas at Austin. She is the author of *The Gods of Indian Country: Religion and the Struggle for the American West* (Oxford University Press, 2018).

Max Greenberg is assistant professor of Jewish and American studies at Goucher College. He researches Zionist institutions in the United States, and teaches courses on race, religion, empire, and social movements in the Americas.

Brett Hendrickson is professor of religious studies at Lafayette College in Pennsylvania, where he teaches and writes about Latinx religious history and religion and health, especially in the US Southwest. His most recent book is *Mexican American Religions: An Introduction* (Routledge, 2022).

Brennan Keegan is an associate professor of religious studies at the College of Charleston. Her teaching and research focus on Native American religious traditions, religion and geography, and the politics of recognition.

Nicole C. Kirk is the Frank and Alice Schulman Chair of Unitarian Universalist History at Meadville Lombard Theological School in Chicago, Illinois. She is the author of *Wanamaker's Temple: The Business of Religion in an Iconic Department Store* (New York University Press, 2018, 2023) and several chapters in edited volumes.

Andrew Klumpp is a public historian working at the State Historical Society of Iowa, where he oversees the society's public programs, educational initiatives, and community outreach. Since 2020, he has served as editor of the Society's award-winning academic history journal, *The Annals of Iowa*. His research and writing focus on the Dutch empire, regionalism, religion, and immigration in the nineteenth century.

Chrissy Yee Lau is an assistant professor of Asian American studies at San Francisco State University. She is the author of *New Women of Empire: Gendered Politics and Racial Uplift in Interwar Japanese America* (University of Washington Press, 2022) and coeditor of *The Auntie Sewing Squad Guide to Mask Making, Radical Care, and Racial Justice* (University of California Press, 2021).

Quincy D. Newell is professor emerit of religious studies at Hamilton College. She is an expert on religion in the nineteenth-century American West and on Mormon studies.

Joshua Paddison (PhD, UCLA) is professor of instruction in the Department of History at Texas State University. He is the author of two books: *American Heathens: Religion, Race, and Reconstruction in California* (California, 2012) and *Unholy Sensations: A Story of Sex, Scandal, and California's First Cult Scare* (Oxford University Press, 2025).

Index

Italic page numbers refer to illustrations.

www.ingramcontent.com/pod-product-compliance
Lightning Source LLC
LaVergne TN
LVHW101602151026
850117LV00028B/153

* 9 7 8 1 4 6 9 6 9 7 7 2 7 *